Jacques Pépin's
COMPLETE TECHNIQUES

More Than 1,000 Preparations and Recipes, All Demonstrated in Thousands of Step-by-Step Photographs

Photographs by Léon Perer

BLACK DOG
& LEVENTHAL
PUBLISHERS

Published by
Black Dog & Leventhal Publishers, Inc.
151 West 19th Street
New York, NY 10011
www.blackdogandleventhal.com

Distributed by
Workman Publishing Company
225 Varick Street
New York, NY 10014

Manufactured in the United States of America

Library of Congress Cataloging in Publication Data
Pepin, Jacques.
    [Complete Techniques]
    Jacques Pepin's Complete Techniques/ by Jacques Pepin.
    p. cm.
    ISBN 1-57912-165-9 (paperback) ISBN 1-57912-220-5 (hardcover)
    1. Cookery. I. Title: Complete Techniques. II. Title.

TX 651 .P397 2001
641.5<DC21
2001025066

Cover design by 27.12 Design Ltd.
Interior design by The Design Duo

ISBN–13: 978-1-57912-165-5

p o n m l k

Praise from the First Lady of Cooking!

"This is a seminal work, and like no other. Jacques Pépin is not only a renowned chef, a foremost authority on French cuisine, and a great teacher; also, as all of us know who have seen him in action, he is truly a master technician. For us to have all this information in our hands, fully illustrated and explained, is indeed a treasure."

—Julia Child

Contents

Introduction
By Jacques Pépin

Even though I wrote *La Technique* and *La Méthode* a quarter of a century ago, I am happy to say that, with some minor changes, the culinary techniques demonstrated in the books are as current and useful today as they were twenty-five years ago. A good cook still beats egg whites, bones a chicken, and makes a caramel cage in the same way. Just as in 1974, the greatest hindrance to good performance in the kitchen is an inadequate knowledge of basic technique.

For some years, *La Technique* and *La Méthode* have been unavailable, and I'm so pleased that the hundreds of techniques collected in those two volumes have been brought together here in one book, reorganized for maximum ease of use. *Jacques Pépin's Complete Techniques* is so much more than a book of recipes— although many are included in order to illustrate specific techniques. In *La Technique*, I was mostly interested in showing the techniques involved in preparing food—often without illustrating them within the context of actual recipes. Therefore, most of the recipes here come from *La Méthode*, the second volume of the two. Using step-by-step pictures (yes, those are my hands throughout!) and detailed, descriptive text, this book is meant to acquaint cooks of every level with the basic procedures that make up the core, the center, and the heart of the profession. Do you want to learn how things really work in the kitchen? It is the goal of this book to teach you, and in the process, to help you understand and hone the basic manual skills that are almost impossible to explain solely in words. This book, quite simply, will teach you *how to cook*—something a conventional cookbook could never do.

Don't be discouraged if you can't master some of these techniques instantly. Some, like the fluting of a mushroom, take practice and patience. Others, like peeling garlic, are quite simple. Remember that as your mastery grows, you will become better able to tackle even difficult recipes with ease and proficiency. In time, you will open your favorite cookbooks and experience them in a new light!

When professionals work with ease and rapidity, it is a result of long years of practice and discipline. There are no secrets or tricks, only feats of skill (*tours de main*) acquired with prolonged effort. Through endless repetition, these techniques will become so much a part of you that you'll never forget them. People often tell me that what surprises them most is watching me cook and talk at the same time. This is because my hands are trained to the point where I do not have to think about the processes I use as I make a recipe—it's automatic. Instead of fighting the mechanics of cooking, I can concentrate on thinking about the combination of ingredients, about taste, and about texture. You may be very creative and imaginative in the kitchen, but you cannot take advantage of those qualities if you don't know the basics. A solid background must precede inventiveness. An artistic mind might create a stunning decoration for a cold salmon, but the dish will be triumphant only if the salmon is first properly cleaned and poached, and the aspic rich and crystal-clear—and this requires knowledge of the proper techniques.

For many years I have dabbled in painting, and although I have occasionally come up with what I think is a great idea for a picture, my hands are rarely good enough to express what I have in my head. This is because my knowledge of painting techniques is weak; I haven't repeated them day after day after day for hours, so my hands very often are not skilled enough to realize my ideas. In cooking, however, after so many years of practice, I can eliminate a great many potential problems or obstacles along the way as I think about a recipe, and then my hands can do the rest. I can usually come pretty close to my vision on the first try.

In this book, I do not pretend to have explicated the whole spectrum of cooking skills; I haven't touched on Asian cooking, for example, concentrating more on the general cooking techniques that I have used all my life. I may have taken for granted very ordinary chores, such as peeling a potato or melting butter. And even with the help of the step-by-step photos, some of the techniques, like making a butter flower, still require a fair amount of patience and perseverance to achieve. Others, like peeling and seeding a tomato or making a rabbit out of an olive, can be mastered instantly. You will discover that there is great satisfaction in conquering dishes that may have frustrated you in the kitchen before. Knowledge of the basics is so rewarding, in that it allows you to try out new ideas, to remedy potentially catastrophic miscalculations, and to tackle any kind of recipe because you will comprehend the mechanics behind it.

Start with simple techniques and work gradually toward the more involved and complicated ones. And have fun! Remember, you are not learning new recipes, you are acquiring a whole new way of cooking, and with this book, you begin your apprenticeship.

Happy cooking!

Jacques Pépin
January 2001

Equipment

IF YEARS AGO THE VARIETY WAS SCARCE, today cooking equipment comes in all types, shapes, prices and materials. The enormous interest in food, heightened by cooking schools, cookbooks, newspapers and magazine articles, etc., has spurred the manufacturers into bringing many different types of paraphernalia onto the market, and a lot of it is good. However, it is often hard for people to differentiate. What pots should one buy? Should they be copper? Stainless steel? Heavy aluminum? No-stick? Black cast iron? Enameled cast iron? It is difficult to choose because ultimately there is no ideal pot. Every material has its good and bad points. The thick, heavy hand-hammered copper is the best to conduct, diffuse and retain heat. While attractive, it is very heavy, very expensive and needs constant polishing. Pots lined with tin become a problem when retinning is needed; it is expensive and finding someone who does it is difficult.

Heavy aluminum pans, customarily used in professional kitchens, are much lighter and easier to handle. Heavy aluminum is the best heat conductor after copper and it's tough. However it tends to discolor food, especially when acidic ingredients such as wine, vinegar, and tomatoes are used. (When using a whisk for an emulsion, such as hollandaise, you will often have a brownish dirty color mixed with your sauce.) At home the discoloration happens regularly just from boiling water. The pan is not used often enough and moisture in the air will cause darkening. The same heavy aluminum pot used in a restaurant kitchen may not discolor since it is used over and over again and is washed between each use, preventing any buildup.

The no-stick lined pans are very good for omelets but too delicate for general use. (The plain steel omelet skillet is better if used often; if not, it will stick.) They will lose their releasing quality and the coating will eventually peel off, and may even be harmful to your health. In addition, you are prevented from using a whisk or a scouring pad, since this will destroy the surface, making them unsatisfactory for normal use.

Stainless steel cleans easily, keeps shiny, does not discolor food but, unfortunately, does develop "hot spots" or patches of burn. The transfer of heat is fast but stainless steel does not retain heat well. Fortunately, stainless steel pans are now made with thick bottoms, each an aluminum or copper "sandwich" between layers of stainless steel.

The dark cast iron skillet and kettle are good, sturdy and practically indestructible. They are not expensive, easy to care for and hold the heat fairly well. However, they are heavy and if not used often will get rusty, stain and discolor food. The enameled cast iron is attractive, cleans well and will chip if dropped. Eventually, the inside will darken and discolor.

Earthenware is attractive, good for prolonged oven cooking and can be used as service pieces. Since they are very fragile, and extreme temperature may cause cracking, don't use them for stove-top cooking. For baking, flat, heavy, not too shiny, aluminum cookie sheets are the best. The iron or steel cookie sheets will warp and the heat conductivity is too rapid.

Should you have a plastic or wooden chopping block? The plastic is cleaner, not porous and can be chilled for pastry. The plain wood or laminated wood is attractive, with just enough bounce, and it does not dull the knife's blade. Both types are expensive if they are of the best quality. They should be thick, heavy and wide. Your chopping block won't perform properly if you do not have a high, sturdy table which does not bounce when you use a meat pounder or a cleaver.

What kind of electrical appliances should you get? A food processor (the stronger the better) is a must, as well as an electric mixer. Should you cook with gas, electricity or microwaves? Cooking is harder to control on electric tops; although the electric oven is excellent. Gas is our favorite. Professional stoves are a good investment. They are strong, have great capacity and never go out of style. We enjoy seeing the flames and control is there at all times. Ultimately, the best heat is wood (hard wood). For barbecuing it is a must. Never briquets. Briquets are a derivative of petroleum and they are not good for your health. A steak well charred on a dirty grill over briquets has more tar than several packages of cigarettes.

Good whisks with thick, heavy threads are a must, as well as "piano-wire" whips (very thin, flexible and tightly woven). Both are necessary—the whisk for thick sauces and the whip to whip egg whites and heavy cream. Rubber and wooden spatulas, as well as a series of bowls, wire racks, strainers, metal spoons, skimmers, vegetable peelers, etc., are all part of a necessary impedimenta. Then there are the knives, an extension of your fingers. There is always a controversy about knives. Should they be carbon or stainless? The current trend is toward high carbon steel knives. They do not discolor or oxidize when used for cutting lemons, tomatoes or onions. However, stainless steel is a very hard metal and difficult to sharpen, although it keeps a good edge once sharpened. The knives should be very sharp to perform correctly. (In addition, you are less likely to cut yourself with a smooth, well-sharpened knife than with a dull tool.) You should have a minimum of three knives. A very large (10- to 12-inch blade) chopping knife, a thinner, 8-inch slicing knife and a small paring knife. Several paring knives would be even better. Have a good sharpener. A steel or ceramic sharpener (good for stainless steel) is necessary but both sharpen only the tiny cutting edge of the knives (see technique 1). After a year or so, depending on how often you use your knives, this tiny amount of metal will be worn away. The knife must then be sent out to be sharpened professionally unless you have the know-how, and possess a large stone with which to grind the metal. Send dull knives out to a person who sharpens lawn mowers, scissors or electric saws. Then the knives can again be utilized for one year, using the steel periodically.

You will notice that expensive, good equipment is usually well designed and pleasant to look at. Visit pot and pan shops. Many specialize in gadgetry and gimmicks. Some have an enormous, confusing potpourri of paraphernalia, among which, if you have the proper lore, you will discern the good from the bad. Then, there are a few good shops that specialize in good equipment only. When you have chosen a good shop, follow the judgment of the salesperson; once you get to know a place, the people will give you good advice. Have a tag sale and get rid of your bad tools. Buy pieces one by one if you can't afford to spend a lot. Some people will spend a small fortune in a good restaurant without blinking an eye, but won't spend the same amount on a few pieces of equipment. It is worth the investment, since they will go on working for you, your children and, maybe, your grandchildren.

Have your pots, molds, strainers, etc., hung from the wall or the ceiling, as is done in a professional kitchen. They will be easy to get to and you will use them more often.

Even though you may have the best ingredients to start with, nothing is more frustrating when preparing a meal than when your oven does not keep a constant heat, your pan is discolored, your knife is dull, your pots dented, etc. It won't work! Finally, cook, cook, cook, cook and cook again! I know people who have great kitchens with all the latest and best equipment. It is only there for show. The more you cook, the easier it becomes. The more the equipment is used, the better it performs and you will get attached to certain tools.

The Basics

1. Holding the Knife *(Position du Couteau)*

AN APPRENTICE CHEF cannot "graduate to the stove" until he has mastered the basic techniques for correctly chopping, dicing, mincing and slicing vegetables, fruits or meat. Perfectly prepared vegetables not only have an attractive texture, but add a good "bite" and taste to the finished dish. Practice, obviously, is of the very essence, and good knives are just as important. Knives should be sharpened professionally at least once every year or two. In the interim, keep a good edge with either a steel or carborundum sharpener.

1. Handling your knife properly is your first concern. Hold the item to be cut with fingertips tucked under, so the blade "rests" and slides directly against the middle section of your fingers. The knife follows, in fact, "glued" to the fingers and slides up and down the fingers at the same rate all the time. The speed at which the fingers move back determines the thickness of the slices.

2. To mince an onion, peel it and cut into halves through the root. Place one of the halves flat side down and, holding your fingers and knife properly,

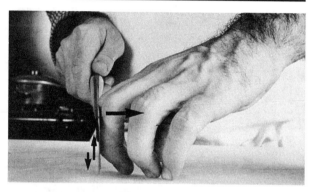

3. cut vertical slices from one end to the other, up to, but not through, the root end. The knife does not go in a straight down motion while cutting, but rather in a down and back motion at the same time.

4. Holding the knife flat, cut 3 or 4 horizontal slices from top to bottom, up to the root end.

5. Finally, cut across the onion, again up to the root end. (If the dice is not fine enough, chop some more with a large knife.)

6. To slice a potato, place it on its flattest side so that it does not roll under your fingers. If the potato is not stable, cut a slice off so the potato can sit firmly on the cut end. Slice to desired thickness by controlling the progress of the fingers that hold the potato in place.

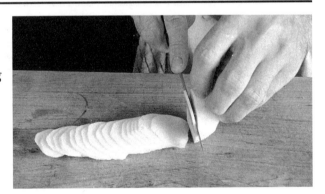

7. To chop parsley, use a bigger knife. Place the blade horizontally on the chopping block and gather the washed parsley top into a tight ball. Slice the bunch across.

8. Slice, going down and forward, or down and backward, sliding the knife along the fingers.

9. Holding the handle firmly in one hand, the other hand relaxed on top of the blade (this hand does not apply much pressure on the blade, but rather directs it), bring the front of the blade down first, then the back. Repeat in a staccato and rapid up and down motion until the parsley is finely chopped. Draw the pieces together in a heap as you go along.

10. To dice an eggplant, hold the eggplant firmly with the tips of your fingers and cut lengthwise in equal slices.

11. Stack 2 or 3 slices on top of each other. Using the same technique, cut into square sticks.

12. Cut the sticks across to form little cubes. Very small cubes or dices of vegetables are called *brunoise*.

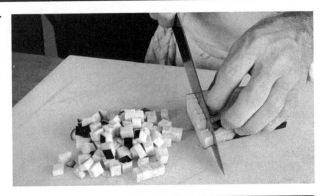

2. How to Sharpen Knives *(Aiguisage des Couteaux)*

A KNIFE IS USELESS if it is not sharp. You can tell if your knife is sharp if it can cut a soft ripe tomato into thin slices with ease. If the knife is dull, it will just crush the tomato.

If you looked at the cutting edge of a knife through a magnifying glass, you'd see that it is made up of hundreds of tiny teeth—like a saw. Through repeated use, these teeth get twisted and bent out of alignment. This is what makes a knife dull; a sharpener gets these little teeth back into alignment.

The harder the metal the knife is made of, the harder it will be to sharpen, but the longer it will hold its edge. A sharpener has to be made of a material that's a shade harder than the metal it is to abrade. (The hardness of metals is measured on the "Rockwell Scale.")

"Steels" are metal sharpeners. They have a fine grain and give a super finish to an already sharp knife. Butchers and professional cooks use a steel constantly, giving the knife a few strokes before each use. A ceramic sharpener is better than a steel for sharpening hard metals such as stainless steel. (Ceramic is harder than the hardest metal on the Rockwell Scale.)

Eventually, repeated sharpening wears away the little teeth of the cutting edge. At this point the knife needs to be ground to thin the blade into a new cutting edge. This is done with an abrasive stone.

USING A CERAMIC SHARPENER

1. Start with the heel of the blade at the tip of the sharpener and slide the knife down the length of the sharpener so the cutting edge abrades against it. Apply steady and strong pressure. Keep the knife at the same angle constantly.

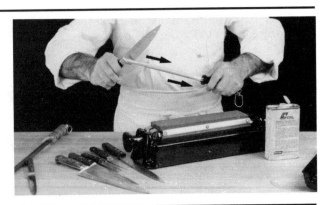

2. End with the point of the blade near the base of the sharpener. This is one steady stroke, one hand moving toward the other, every inch of the cutting edge making contact with the sharpener. Repeat on the other side of the sharpener to sharpen the other side of the knife.

USING A STEEL SHARPENER

3. This photograph is an alternative way of sharpening. In this photo, we are using a steel sharpener with a high-carbon-steel knife. Start with the heel of the blade at the base of the steel and pull the hands away from one another, finishing with the tip of the sharpener at the tip of the blade. Make sure that the whole blade gets worked against the sharpener. Keep the angle about 25 degrees and the pressure the same.

USING A GRINDING STONE

4. Once a year, twice a year, once every two years—depending on the kind of beating your knives get—you will need to grind them down to form a new cutting edge. You can send your knives out and have them ground by a professional or you can do it yourself if you have a sand wheel or a large stone like the one pictured here. This stone is held in place by suction so that you can apply a lot of pressure without having it slide around the way smaller stones do. It has three sides, each of a different coarseness. You begin with the coarsest side and finish with the finest.

5. Rub some mineral oil on the stone to keep stone grindings loose so they can be wiped off with paper and don't seal and glaze the surface of the stone, which would prevent abrasion. Start at the tip of the knife and apply strong pressure down and forward so that the whole side of the blade is in contact with the stone. Move back and forth, applying pressure. Keep the angle constant. Repeat on the other side. As the knife gets sharper and thinner at the end, go to a finer stone. When you are through clean your knife. Keep it sharp with a steel.

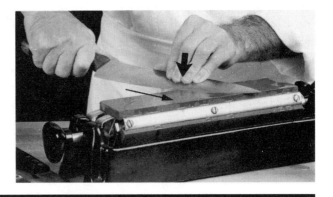

3. How to Peel an Onion *(Epluchage des Oignons)*

IT WOULD SEEM to be extremely simple to peel an onion, but it isn't always so for someone who is inexperienced. People tend not to remove enough of the root and stem, which makes it harder to peel and slice the onion properly.

1. Cut off the root and the stem end on the other side.

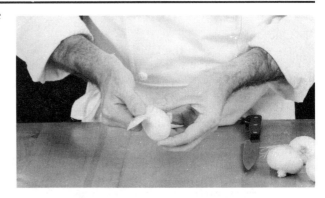

2. Some onions have extremely thin skins which are hard to remove. Some are quite thick. In either case, remove one layer of onion, or several if necessary, so there is no yellow or dry skin visible.

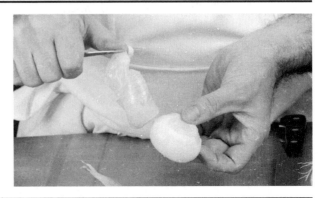

4. How to Julienne *(Julienne)*

To cut into julienne is to cut into very thin strips. A julienne is aesthetically very pleasing and very nice as a garnish for soups, fish, meat, etc.

A vegetable julienne (such as carrots, leeks and celery) is usually blanched and finished by being cooked a few minutes with fish, veal or whatever it will be served with. Being cut so thin, it cooks very fast.

JULIENNE OF CARROTS *(Julienne de Carottes)*

1. To peel: Trim both ends of the carrot to form a flat base to start from. Working toward you, peel a whole strip of carrot in one stroke, from end to end. Rotate the carrot and proceed all the way around. Use long, regular, slow strokes. Your speed will improve with practice. Short nervous strokes (or peeling one half of the carrot then turning the carrot around and peeling the other half) don't produce good results and are very tiring.

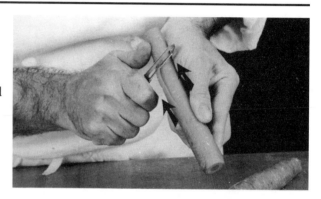

2. Slice the carrot into very thin lengthwise slices. If you do not have a *mandoline* or a similar type of vegetable slicer, and if you're not proficient enough with a knife, use a vegetable peeler. Apply as much pressure as you can so the slices are not too thin.

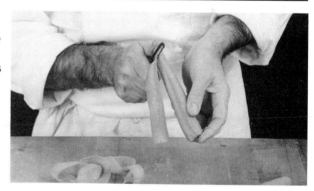

3. Stack 3 or 4 of the thin slices on top of one another, fold and then slice into a fine julienne.

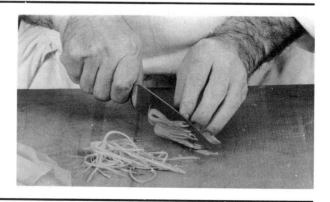

JULIENNE OF LEEKS *(Julienne de Poireaux)*

4. For the julienne of leeks, only the white and the very light green part of the leek is used. Remove the dark green part and the root, keeping the green part in the refrigerator for soups or stocks or to put in a stew. Split the trimmed leek in half.

5. Separate all of the layers of the leek. (Note that in our leek the center is woody. This happens when the leek is old and grows a tough central core. Remove and discard.)

6. Fold a few of the leaves at a time, so that the inside of the leaves shows on the outside.

7. Cut into very thin strips. Wash and then drain.

JULIENNE OF CELERY *(Julienne de Céleri)*

8. Separate the stalks. Use a vegetable peeler to remove the top layer of fiber from the large outer stalks if necessary. (By scratching the celery, you can find out if it is fibrous or not.)

9. Cut each stalk into 4- to 5-inch pieces. Flatten each piece with the palm of your hand. (It will probably crush in the center.)

10. Using the flat of your knife held horizontally to the table, cut the celery into 2 or 3 thin slices.

11. Pile all the slices on top of one another and cut into thin strips. A julienne of celery is never as thin as a julienne of leeks or carrots, but it is used in the same way.

20204783

5. Garlic (Ail)

THERE ARE MANY TYPES of garlic readily available, the best of which is the smaller "red garlic," so-called because of the reddish color of the skin. Garlic affects foods in different ways depending on how it is cut and used. You can roast a chicken with 3 full heads (about 40 unpeeled cloves) of garlic and serve them with the chicken. Guests can pick up the cloves and suck the tender insides out of the peel. Prepared this way, it is astounding how mild and sweet garlic is. The scent and taste are barely noticeable. However, the smell of one clove of garlic, peeled, crushed, chopped fine and added at the last minute to sautéed potatoes or string beans, or to a salad, can permeate a whole room and remain on your breath for hours. The same crushed chopped garlic—when cooked slowly for a long time, as in a stew—loses most of its pungency and harmonizes, quite modestly, with the other herbs and ingredients. Crushing the garlic releases more essential oil and gives more flavor than slicing it or leaving it whole. Raw garlic chopped to a purée is the most powerful. Mixed with olive oil, it becomes the garlic-loaded mayonnaise of Provence (*aioli* or *ailloli*), known as *beurre de Provence* (the butter of Provence).

One important point: When making scampi, escargots, sautéed potatoes, zucchini or any dish where the garlic is added at the end and slightly cooked, be careful not to burn it. Burned garlic hopelessly ruins a dish.

1. Holding the "head" on a bias, crush with the heel of your hand to separate the cloves.

2. First, cut off the root end of the clove. Then, using the flat side of a heavy knife, smack the clove just enough to crack the shell open.

3. Remove the clove from the shell.

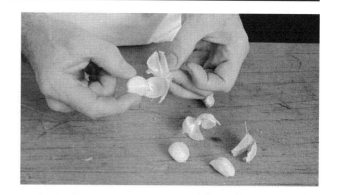

4. Place the blade flat on the clove and smack it down and forward to crush the clove to a pulp.

5. Chop to a puree.

6. Leeks *(Poireaux)*

L EEKS, CALLED THE ASPARAGUS OF THE POOR in France, are greatly underrated in the United States. This hardy winter vegetable is unbeatable for soups. It is said that Nero ate leek soup every day to clarify his voice. Leek is great cooked in water and served with a vinaigrette sauce and excellent in stews and quiches.

1. Leek has to be cleaned properly because the center is usually full of sand. Trim off the greener part of the leaves. Keep it for clarifying consommé, technique 18.

2. Remove the roots.

3. Remove the dried and yellowish skin around the leek, if any.

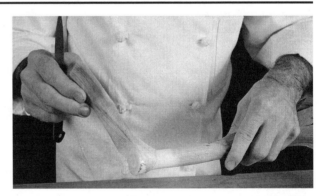

4. Holding the leek, leafy side down, insert your knife through the white part approximately 2 inches down from the root, and cut through the entire length of the leek.

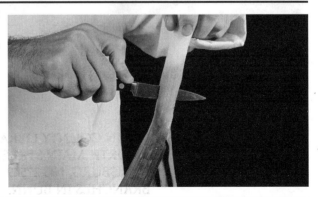

5. Repeat 2 or 3 times to split the leek open. Wash thoroughly under cold water.

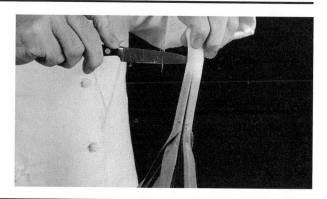

7. Duxelle of Mushrooms *(Duxelle de Champignons)*

A DUXELLE OF MUSHROOMS is a mixture of mushrooms chopped very, very fine and cooked, sometimes with shallots sometimes without, and seasoned with salt and pepper. Duxelle is one of the staples of classic French cooking and is used in many dishes—as a coating, as a stuffing, as a seasoning. With the addition of cream or milk it becomes a purée of mushrooms and is served as a vegetable.

¾ pound mushrooms, finely chopped
2 shallots, peeled and very finely chopped (½ tablespoon)
1 tablespoon sweet butter
Salt to taste
Black pepper to taste

1. One of the best ways to chop mushrooms is in a food processor. However, don't put them into the processor whole. Cut them into coarse slices or chunks first.

2. Place a large handful of mushrooms in the processor. Turn it on and then off. Then on again and off. If the machine is left on for the whole duration, half the mushrooms fly around the blade—not getting properly chopped—while the other half turns into a purée. The on-and-off technique allows the mushrooms to fall back on the blade so that they all get uniformly chopped. (Use this method whenever you chop in a food processor.) Melt the butter in a skillet, add the shallots and cook on me-

dium heat for about ½ minute. Add the chopped mushrooms, a dash of salt and a dash of pepper and cook, mixing occasionally with a wooden spoon, for about 10 minutes. The mushrooms will render some liquid, and will be ready when the liquid has evaporated and the mixture is dry and starts to sizzle. Transfer to a bowl, cover with waxed paper and set aside.

3. If you used mushrooms that were open, large and black inside, older mushrooms (which are often used for a duxelle since they are hard to use for anything else), press them in a cloth towel to extrude some of the dark juices after they have been chopped.

4. As you can see, pressing the mushrooms in a towel does get rid of the juices. From this point, proceed as explained in step 2. If the mushrooms are plump, firm and white, there is no reason to press the juices out.

8. How to Peel and Seed a Cucumber
(Evidage de Concombres)

1. To peel a cucumber properly, cut off both ends, then peel toward you, using a vegetable peeler. Remove strips of peel the full length of the cucumber with one stroke. Keep strokes straight and uniform as you work around the cucumber. If you exert uneven pressure, you will take too much flesh off in some places and too little in others and the cucumber will look multicolored.

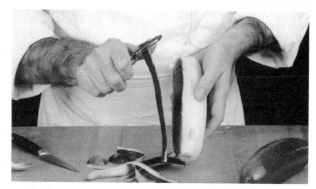

2. To seed the cucumber split it in half using a knife. Then work the edge of a dessert spoon along the seeds, close to the flesh, making a type of incision. When you are through with one side, turn the cucumber and loosen the seeds on the other side. Finally, using the bowl of the spoon, scrape out all the seeds in one stroke.

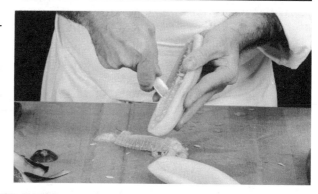

9. Cleaning Salad *(Préparation de la Salade)*

LETTUCE, PROBABLY THE BEST-KNOWN SALAD GREEN the world over, is also one of the most delicate and delectable. Bibb, oak leaf or Boston lettuce go well with a light oil and vinegar or a cream dressing because they are very tender and mild. Escarole, curly endive and the like can support a stronger, garlicky dressing.

1. Holding the lettuce upside down, cut around the center to remove the core and get the leaves loose. Remove the spoiled leaves.

2. The larger, tougher outside leaves should have the top and center rib removed. Only the tender pieces on both sides of the rib are used.

3. With the larger leaves removed, cut through the center rib to separate each leaf into halves.

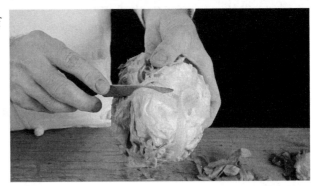

4. Separate the small leaves of the heart and leave them whole. Wash the lettuce in a lot of cold water. Lift up from the water and place on a towel.

5. Dry the leaves gently, a few at a time, to avoid bruising.

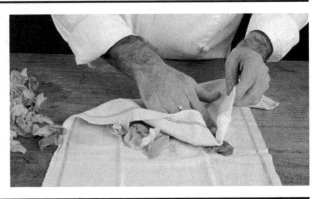

6. Or, place in a salad dryer and

7. spin a few times to extract as much water as possible from the salad.

8. It should be dry and fluffy. Remember that the best dressing will be ruined if watered down by a salad not sufficiently dried. Keep refrigerated in a towel until serving time. A tender lettuce, such as Boston, is never tossed with dressing ahead of time because it becomes wilted very fast.

10. Tomatoes *(Tomates)*

PEELED AND SEEDED TOMATOES are a requisite ingredient in many recipes. They are used to make *boules de tomates*—a perfect garnish for roasts, chicken and the like—and *fondue de tomates,* which is a fresh tomato sauce that's both easy to make and very good.

PEELING AND SEEDING TOMATOES
(Tomates Émondées)

1. Remove the stem from the tomato using the point of a knife. Dip the tomatoes in boiling water—they should be fully immersed—and let sit for approximately 20 seconds if well ripened. If the tomatoes are green, it will take a little longer for the skin to come loose.

2. Transfer the tomatoes to a basin of cold water. When cold enough to handle, remove and peel. The skin should slip off easily.

3. Cut the tomato into halves widthwise—not through the stem.

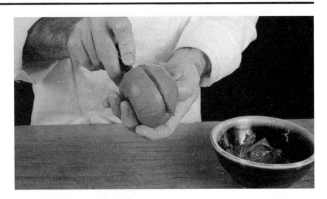

4. Press gently to extrude all the seeds. You now have pure tomato flesh or pulp. The seeds and skin can be used in a stock or long-simmered sauce. (An alternative method is to impale the tomato on a fork and, holding it by the fork handle, roll it over an open flame. "Roast" it for 15 to 20 seconds; the skin should slide off easily.)

TOMATO BALLS FOR GARNISH
(Boules de Tomates)

1. Peel and seed the tomato. Cut each half in two.

2. Place a tomato quarter in a strong kitchen towel, the outside against the towel.

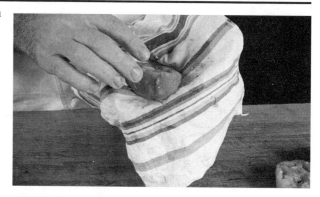

3. Squeeze the tomato pulp to form a nice small fleshy ball.

4. Sprinkle with salt and a dash of ground pepper. Moisten with melted butter and heat in a hot oven for a few minutes before serving.

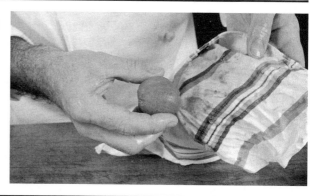

TOMATO SAUCE *(Fondue de Tomates)*

1. Peel and seed the tomatoes and cut coarsely into 1-inch cubes (*Tomates concassées* in French). Prepare 3 cups of cubed tomatoes and proceed with the recipe below.

1 *tablespoon good olive oil*
1 *tablespoon chopped onion*
3 *cups cubed tomatoes*
Salt and freshly ground black pepper
1 *clove garlic, crushed and chopped very fine*
1 *tablespoon tomato paste, optional*
½ *teaspoon chopped hot serrano pepper,*
    optional

Heat the oil in a saucepan. When it is hot, add the chopped onion and sauté for 1 minute. Add the tomatoes and the salt and pepper to taste. Cook on a high heat for 5 to 6 minutes to evaporate some of the liquid. Add the garlic, and the tomato paste if the tomatoes are too watery or too pale in color. Cook 3 to 4 minutes and taste for seasoning. Add more salt and pepper, if necessary, and some serrano pepper if you like your sauce hot.

11. Glazed Onions *(Oignons Glacés)*

G LAZED ONIONS ARE EXTENSIVELY USED as a garnish in French cooking for *coq au vin, boeuf bourguignon,* veal chop *grandmère,* chicken *Boivin* and the like.

1. Use tiny, white onions (unfortunately hard to get at certain times of the year) the size of a jumbo olive. Peel the onion by removing a small slice at the stem and one at the root end.

2. For 24 onions, you need 1 tablespoon butter, ¼ teaspoon salt and 1 teaspoon sugar. Place the onions in a saucepan in one layer. They should not overlap. Add enough water to barely cover the top of the onions. Add the butter, salt and sugar. Place on high heat and boil until all the water is evaporated (about 18 to 20 minutes). Reduce the heat to medium and shake the saucepan or turn the onions to brown them on all sides.

3. The boiling of the water is necessary because it cooks the onions. When the water has evaporated, what is left is butter and sugar. The onions will glaze in that mixture in a few minutes. If they do not glaze properly on direct heat, place for a few minutes under the broiler. Transfer the glazed onions to a plate until needed.

12. Brown Stock (Classic and Fast) Half-Glaze and Meat Glaze

(Fond Brun [Classique et Rapide] Demi-Glace et Glace de Viande)

COOKS OFTEN GET CONFUSED when they hear names such as "brown stock," *demi-glace* (half-glaze), "brown sauce," *glace de viande* (meat glaze), *sauce espagnole, fond lié* (thickened stock), *jus,* "broth," "bouillon," and so forth. In fact, it is confusing. However, it is an area that is too important to French cooking to bypass.

Let's start with the most basic—stock. (We will use the word "stock" instead of broth, bouillon or *jus.*) What is a stock? It is a liquid obtained by boiling bones with water. There are two basic stocks: one white, one brown. The white stock is bones and water boiled together with seasoning. The brown stock is a white stock made from bones that were browned in the oven or on top of the stove. The browned bones give the stock a darker color and a nuttier taste. It is as simple and as complicated as that. (The addition of meat naturally enhances and concentrates the flavor of stock, but is not really necessary, particularly at today's prices—you can get excellent results with bones only by simply reducing the liquid a bit more.)

A stock must cook a certain amount of time, which varies depending on how large the bones are and what type of bone is used. With small pieces of bones, or with thin bones like the bones of a chicken, 3 hours of cooking are sufficient, whereas larger veal or beef bones require up to 10 to 12 hours. Time is essential to extract all the nutrients and taste from the bones. Water is added to the bones, but not a fixed amount. Throughout the cooking water evaporates and more is added regularly to replenish the stock. When the stock is cooked, it is strained and reduced to proper consistency.

We make our brown stock with veal, beef and chicken bones mixed together. The chicken bones, besides being readily available and inexpensive, add a pleasant nutty and sweet taste to the stock. In fact, if we are low on other bones, we'll make up the difference with more chicken bones. It is, of course, better to use fresh bones; however, in a home kitchen you rarely have enough fresh bones on hand. So when you order a roast of beef or veal from your butcher, ask him for a few bones and then freeze them. Once or twice a year, empty the freezer, make large amounts of stock and freeze it in small containers. It should last you for a few months and be very inexpensive. Make great quantities of stock if you have pots and pans large enough, inasmuch as 3 pounds of bones take as much cooking as 20 pounds if you are making a classic brown stock.

Brown stock is a carrier—a vehicle—which permits you to make sauces. It is not a sauce in itself, but is used to "wet" (*mouiller* as we say in France) a stew or deglaze a pan, or add to other bones (game, lamb, etc.) to produce a more concentrated and differently flavored stock (see Saddle of Lamb in Crust, technique 161, for an example). Though it is gelatinous when cooked and holds together, a stock is not concentrated enough to be called a sauce. However, the 3 quarts of brown stock (made from the recipe on page 30) reduced by half will yield 1½ quarts of a slightly syrupy and darker liquid which *is* concentrated enough to become a "sauce" and which has a name of its own—*demi-glace* (half-glaze). Furthermore, if that quart and a half of *demi-glace* is reduced to its extreme, it will yield about 2 to 2½ cups of what is called *glace de viande* (meat glaze). The *glace de viande* is not a sauce any longer. It has trancended the condition of a sauce and is now a strengthening and flavoring agent. The *glace de viande* hardens enough when cooled to be unmolded and cut into cubes. Kept loosely wrapped (not in a closed jar) it will keep almost indefinitely if the reduction is correct. These cubes of *glace de viande* are added to sauces to make them stronger and richer. Thus a basic stock, taken to different stages of concentration and volume, changes its name as well as its function.

Stocks should be started in cold water and cooked, uncovered, at a slow, gentle boil. This way, the albumin in the bones and meat will harden and come to the surface of the liquid in the form of a gray foam which can be removed with a skimmer. The fat will also rise to the surface. However, if the stock is covered and boiling too fast, the albumin won't separate and the fat will emulsify back into the liquid (see the discussion of emulsion in the techniques for white butter sauce and hollandaise, techniques 19 and 20) instead of rising to the top. The stock will then be cloudy, less digestible and more caloric.

The classic brown stock is usually seasoned with carrots, onions, thyme, bay leaf, peppercorns, etc., but not salt because if salt is added at the beginning and the stock is then reduced to a glaze, the concentration of salt will be overpowering. A stock, purified by slow cooking and properly skimmed, will be high in proteins, clear, meaty and pratically tasteless. This may seem paradoxical but it's not. The stock has been too lightly seasoned to have much of an identifying taste of its own. And it shouldn't have one if it is to become a *demi-glace* transformed (as we will a little later) into a red wine sauce for beef, a chicken and mushroom sauce or sauce for a sautéed piece of veal. In each of these cases the *demi-glace* must take on the identity of that particular dish. It is the "hidden and modest" friend which enables a cook to produce a well-finished, long-simmered sauce in minutes. It is what we call in English a basic brown sauce. It doesn't have a specific name or identity of its own yet. With the addition of wine it becomes a sauce *Bordelaise,* with Madeira and truffles a sauce *Périgueux,* with vinegar and shallots a sauce *Bercy,* etc. The progression is from a stock to a *demi-glace* or basic brown sauce to a specific sauce.

What is the proper degree of reduction? The key word is "balance." Though a *demi-glace* should be concentrated, an overconcentrated *demi-glace* is just as unpalatable as a weak and bland concoction. To achieve a delicate combination of seasoning and correct concentration takes practice, knowledge and talent.

Making sauces from reduced stocks is particularly well suited for restaurant short-order cooking. It works well with diversified sauces and dishes made one portion at a time. However, it is time-consuming and expensive to make and some cooks do not feel that reductions alone produce a satisfactory result. Besides the question of time and expense, they object to the richness and concentrated taste of the reduction. A truffle sauce for a filet of beef requires a strong reduction but a small delicate quail is overpowered by too potent a sauce.

On occasion a stock will reduce and intensify in flavor but will lack the gelatinous element to thicken to the right consistency. If you feel your sauce has reached the right taste but it is too thin in texture, thicken it lightly with arrowroot. At one time a brown sauce used to be heavily thickened with flour. The classic sauce *Espagnole,* made with a stock, brown *roux* and tomato paste, though rarely made nowadays, is an example. Carême explains that the *roux,* the binding agent, separates after long, slow cooking, and the fat and the scum from the cooking of the *roux* rise to the top and should be skimmed off. The sauce clarifies and purifies through the long cooking until only the "binding elements" of the flour (the glutinous part) remain to hold the sauce together. Although this sauce works with practice and care, it is more logical and faster to use a starch such as arrowroot—which is like a purified flour (binding element only) and has no taste, cooks instantly and doesn't "dirty" the sauce.

Must one use *demi-glace* to cook well? Some types of cooking require it, some do not. Home cooking and some of the best country cooking is often done without brown stock. In our family, and at friends' where we have had some of our most memorable meals, brown stocks are practically never used. Often good cooks modify the principles behind the brown stock and use leftover juices from a roast chicken or a pot roast the way a professional uses *glace de viande*. Roasting and braising give natural strong juices, the equivalent of a strong reduction, which can be used in the same manner.

Following the Classic Brown Stock and the Fast Brown Stock are recipes using these stocks.

CLASSIC BROWN STOCK, HALF-GLAZE AND GLAZE *(Fond Brun Classique, Demi-Glace et Glace de Viande)*

YIELD: 3 quarts of stock or 1½ quarts *demi-glace* or about 2 cups of *glace de viande*

10 *pounds bones (one-third veal, one-third chicken, one-third beef), cut into 2-inch pieces*
1 *pound carrots, washed and unpeeled, cut into 1-inch chunks (about 4 to 6 carrots depending on size)*
1½ *pounds unpeeled onions, cut into 1-inch pieces (about 4 to 8 onions depending on size)*
3 *large ripe tomatoes, coarsely chopped (1½ pounds)*
1 *large leek, cut in half*
3 *celery ribs, cut in pieces*
2 *bay leaves*
½ *teaspoon thyme leaves*
½ *teaspoon black peppercorns*

1. Place the pieces of bone in a large roasting pan and brown in the oven at 425 degrees for 1½ hours, turning the bones once, halfway through the browning process. Add carrots and onions to the bones and continue cooking in the oven another ½ hour.

2. Remove the bones and vegetables from the oven and transfer to a large stock pot, using a slotted spoon so the drippings of fat are left in the roasting pan.

3. Pour out the fat accumulated in the roasting pan. (The solidified juices left in the pan are in fact a *glace de viande*.)

4. Pour water into the roasting pan, place on top of the stove, bring to a boil and, using a metal spatula, rub the bottom of the pan to melt all the solidified juices.

5. Add this liquid to the kettle and fill it with water. Bring to a boil slowly, then turn the heat down and simmer for 1 hour, removing the scum (technique 15). After 1 hour, add the remaining vegetables and seasonings. Bring to a boil again, then simmer slowly for a generous 10 hours. During the cooking process water will evaporate; replace periodically to keep the same level. The stock can simmer very gently overnight.

6. Strain the liquid through a fine strainer. (It is better to end up with more yield rather than less. When a lot of liquid is left the bones get "well washed" and the strained liquid contains all the nutrients of the stock. If the liquid is over-reduced with the bones, when you strain it, a lot of the *glace* and taste will stick to the bones and be lost.) Return to a clean pot and boil down until it reduces to 3 quarts of liquid. Let the stock cool overnight, then remove the solidified fat on the top. (The bones that have cooked for 10 hours are often recooked, instead of being discarded, to make a *glace de viande.* It is not as rich as the one made only through the reduction of stock but it's free, a bonus—you now have stock or *demi-glace* plus *glace de viande.* To make it, fill the pot containing the cooked bones with cold water, bring to a boil and simmer for another 8 to 10 hours or cook gently overnight. Strain and reduce to a *glace de viande* as described in step 9.)

7. To make *demi-glace,* reduce the stock by half (again), cool and divide into large chunks of about 1 cup each. Wrap in plastic wrap and freeze.

8. Stock, which is gelatinous but not quite as solid as the *demi-glace,* should be poured into plastic containers, covered and frozen.

9. To make a *glace de viande*, strain the *demi-glace* again and reduce to its maximum. As it reduces, transfer the liquid to a smaller, sturdy saucepan. The last hour of reduction is delicate and should be done on very low heat because the mixture has a tendency to burn as it gets thicker. The *glace* will become dark brown and form bubbles on top (like large caramel bubbles) during the last 15 to 20 minutes of cooking. As they break, no steam will escape. If there is any fat left in the mixture it will separate from the glaze and should be removed with a spoon. At that point, the reduction is completed—there is no more moisture in the mixture.

10. Note that the *glace de viande* has the thickness of a caramel. Remember also that it is unsalted.

11. Place the spoon and spatula into the saucepan, cover with water and bring to a boil. There is a lot of leftover, sticky *glace* around the pan and utensils that should be remelted to be used as a stock.

12. When the *glace de viande* is cold, un-mold and cut into cubes. They will be hard, rubbery and dark. Keep in an uncovered jar in the refrigerator or in a plastic bag with the top slightly open. It will become very hard and keep almost indefinitely. Use as a seasoning when needed.

FAST BROWN STOCK *(Fond Brun Rapide)*

YIELD: 1 quart of stock or ½ quart *demi-glace*

This is a good, classic way of making a stock and yet it is fast. However, you can only make small amounts of it at a time because the bones get browned in a saucepan on top of the stove, and a saucepan can only accommodate so many bones. The bones are cut into tiny pieces so they brown rapidly and the nutrients and flavors are extracted faster during cooking. In a classic stock, the bones are roasted in the oven, which is a slower way, yet the only way to brown a large quantity of bones.

1 *pound veal bones*
2 *pounds chicken bones (gizzards, legs, necks, wings), cut into 1-inch pieces*
2 *carrots, unpeeled, chopped coarsely (1 cup)*
2 *large onions, unpeeled, chopped coarsely (1¼ cups)*
1 *leek, chopped coarsely (⅓ cup)*
½ *cup celery stems and leaves*
1 *large tomato, cut in pieces*
½ *teaspoon thyme leaves*
1 *bay leaf*

½ *teaspoon black peppercorns*
4 *to 5 cloves garlic, unpeeled*
⅓ *cup parsley stems*

1. Cut the bones into no more than 1-inch pieces and place in a saucepan large enough to accommodate the bones in one layer. Place on the stove for 5 minutes on high heat. When they start sizzling, reduce to medium and continue cooking for 25 minutes, stirring occasionally with a wooden spoon.

2. The pieces should be well browned all around and the juices solidified in the bottom of the pan. Be careful not to burn the *glace* or solidified juices, or the stock will taste bitter.

3. After the bones have cooked for 30 minutes, use the cover to hold the bones in and invert the saucepan to pour out all the liquid fat. Add the carrots and onions to the bones and keep browning for another 10 minutes on medium to low heat. Add the rest of the ingredients and fill the saucepan with water. Bring to a boil slowly and cook uncovered on medium heat for 3 to 4 hours, replacing the water as it evaporates. Remove the scum every 10 to 15 minutes.

4. Strain through a fine *chinois*. Let cool overnight in the refrigerator and remove the fat. Reduce to 2 cups for a *demi-glace*.

STEAK "MARCHAND DE VIN" WITH MARROW (Steak Marchand de Vin à la Moëlle)

YIELD: 3 to 4 servings

1 large shell steak (about 1½ pounds, trimmed)
¼ teaspoon salt
¼ teaspoon pepper
1 tablespoon sweet butter
1 tablespoon chopped shallots
1 small clove garlic, chopped
¼ teaspoon thyme
1 cup good dry red wine
2 anchovy fillets
¾ cup demi-glace

Sprinkle steak with salt and pepper. Panfry steak in butter over medium to low heat for about 12 minutes, turning the steak every 4 to 5 minutes. Place the steak on a platter and keep warm in a 160-degree oven. Add the shallots to the pan drippings and sauté for 10 to 15 seconds. Add garlic, thyme and red wine. Reduce to ½ cup. Chop anchovy fillets or crush with the blade of a knife to a purée and add to the wine mixture with ¾ cup demi-glace. Reduce for 1 to 2 minutes. Taste for seasonings, add salt and pepper if needed and strain the sauce on top of the steak or slice the steak and serve with the sauce around. Add marrow and artichoke bottoms if desired (see technique 53).

FILET OF BEEF WITH TRUFFLE SAUCE (Filet de Boeuf Périgueux)

YIELD: 6 servings

3 tablespoons sweet butter
1 ¾-pound piece of filet of beef (completely trimmed), from the center, seasoned with
½ teaspoon salt
¼ teaspoon ground black peppercorns
1½ cups demi-glace
1 tablespoon chopped truffles
½ cup good, dry Madeira wine
Salt and pepper to taste

Brown meat on all sides in 2 tablespoons butter in a sturdy skillet or saucepan (about 5 minutes). Place the skillet in a 425-degree oven for 18 minutes. Remove, set the meat on a platter and let rest or settle in a warm place for at least 10 to 15 minutes before carving. Place the pan with the drippings on top of the stove and cook on medium heat until the fat is entirely separated from the juices, which should solidify on the bottom of the saucepan. This technique is called "pincer" (see technique 147). Set the skillet on the table for 4 to 5 minutes, inclining the

skillet so the fat comes to one corner. Pour fat out and add demi-glace. Place on stove on low heat and, with a spatula, loosen all the solidified juices as the sauce boils gently.

Place truffles in a clean saucepan with the Madeira wine. Bring to a boil and reduce by half. Strain the demi-glace from the skillet directly on top of the Madeira-truffle mixture. Reduce the sauce until it reaches

proper consistency and coats the spoon. You should have about 1½ cups of sauce left. Season with salt and pepper if needed and finally swirl in the remaining butter, cut into small pieces. Slice the meat thinly and serve 2 to 3 slices per person with the sauce around the meat and partially covering the slices. The plates should be very warm.

HUNTER CHICKEN (*Poulet Chasseur*)

YIELD: 4 servings

1 tablespoon butter
1 (2¾-pound) chicken, quartered, keep the
    carcass bones for stock
2 tablespoons chopped onion
1 clove garlic, peeled, crushed and chopped fine
½ cup dry white wine
1 large tomato, peeled, seeded and coarsely
    chopped (1 cup)
1 teaspoon tomato paste
1 bay leaf
¼ teaspoon thyme
6 to 8 mushrooms, sliced (1¼ cups, loosely
    packed)
½ cup demi-glace
1 teaspoon salt
¼ teaspoon pepper

½ tablespoon parsley, chopped
½ tablespoon tarragon

Melt the butter in a heavy saucepan and brown the chicken over medium heat for 10 to 12 minutes, starting with the skin side down and turning the chicken after 5 to 6 minutes of browning. Add the chopped onion and sauté for 15 to 20 seconds. Add the garlic, white wine, tomato, tomato paste, bay leaf and thyme. Cover and bring to a boil. Turn the heat down and simmer for 10 minutes. Add the mushrooms. Cover and simmer another 5 minutes. Using a spoon, transfer the chicken and solids to a dish. Add ½ cup *demi-glace* to the drippings, bring to a boil and reduce to 1 cup. Season, add parsley and tarragon, pour on top of the chicken and serve at once.

SAUTÉED VEAL WITH SPINACH (*Veau Sauté aux Epinards*)

YIELD: 4 servings

About 12 *veal scaloppine, 2 to 3 per person,*
    1½ *to* 2 *ounces each, completely trimmed*
    (*technique* 166)
2 10-*ounce packages leaf spinach*
⅓ *stick butter, plus* 2 *tablespoons salt and freshly*
    ground pepper to taste
¾ *cup* demi-glace

Prepare spinach (technique 119) and brown in 2 tablespoons of "brown butter." (Bring the butter to a dark stage to obtain a nutty taste.) Arrange your spinach on individual serving plates. Melt the ⅓ stick butter in one or two large saucepans and sauté the scallopini in foaming butter for approximately 40 seconds on each side. Be careful that the butter is not too hot because veal dries out very fast. Arrange the veal on top of the spinach. Deglaze the drippings in your saucepan with the *demi-glace*. Stir to melt all the juices and reduce to about ¾ of a cup. Season and pour about 2 tablespoons of the sauce on the scaloppine and around the spinach on each plate. Serve immediately.

13. White Stock *(Fond Blanc)*

The white stocks (whether they be beef, chicken, fish, etc.) are cooked in the same way as brown stock (technique 12). They are either reduced or thickened with a *roux*, although the use of flour is always a subject of controversy among cooks. The *beurre manié* is used, with excellent results, to correct and adjust sauces in some of the greatest kitchens in France as well as in private homes. When the stocks are thickened with a *roux* they are called *veloutés* (mother sauces). With the addition of cream, a *velouté* becomes a cream sauce and the cream sauce, in turn, takes on different names depending on the garnish. For example, a fish stock becomes a *velouté* of fish after it is thickened with a *roux,* then a cream sauce with the addition of cream, then a *sauce Dugléré* with the addition of sliced mushrooms and tomatoes.

In a first-class restaurant, where portions are cooked individually, the white stocks are often reduced to a *glace,* cream is added and the mixture boiled down until it reaches the proper consistency without the addition of flour. It makes a richer and more expensive sauce than a sauce made from a *velouté.* However, for economy as well as health, home cooks, except on special occasions, do not adhere to the criteria of a starred restaurant and a *velouté* is more the norm than the exception. Both methods have their own place and can be enjoyed at different times. A sauce should be light and if it looks and tastes like glue, the culprit is the cook, not the flour.

10 *pounds beef bones (knuckles, shin and marrow bones are good), or chicken bones or half beef, half chicken*
2 *large onions*
2 *to 3 cloves*
2 *stalks celery*
2 *white leeks, washed*
4 *carrots, peeled*
2 *bay leaves*
½ *teaspoon thyme*
½ *teaspoon peppercorns*
4 *to 5 cloves garlic, unpeeled*
½ *bunch parsley (1 cup loose)*

Cover the bones with cold water. Bring slowly to a boil and skim the solidified blood and albumin that rises to the surface of the water. Boil for 2 hours, skimming regularly. Most of the scum will rise to the top during these first 2 hours.

1. Stick one of the onions with the cloves. Add to the pot along with the celery, leeks, carrots, garlic, seasoning and herbs.

2. To give an amber golden color to the stock (if a *consommé* or aspic is to be made from the stock), cut an unpeeled onion in half and brown in a skillet on medium heat on top of the stove until the cut side turns quite dark. Add to the stock. Boil slowly for 6 hours, or 2 hours if you use only chicken bones. Evaporation will reduce the liquid. Add water periodically to compensate. Strain and reduce to 3 quarts. Refrigerate overnight then discard the fat, which will have solidified on top of the stock. Pack in small containers and freeze if not needed.

14. Fish Stock *(Fond de Poisson)*

YIELD: Approximately 1½ quarts of stock

IN OUR DISCUSSION OF STOCKS (techniques 12 and 13) we have explained that long cooking and reductions enrich and intensify taste. The function of a stock, moreover, is to emphasize and enhance the food it is served with, not conceal it. Paradoxically, the same dish which will improve in taste through long cooking may be destroyed in texture by that same cooking. The way to reconcile these facts is to handle each component of the dish in a different manner. Take a fish for example: The head and bones will be separated from the fillets and cooked into a stock then reduced to obtain an essence of strong reduction. On the other hand, the fillets will be barely cooked and when combined with a sauce made from the reduced stock you will have achieved the perfect balance. The same theory and technique applies to our Crayfish Tails au Gratin (technique 79) where the meat of the tail is cooked very briefly and set aside while a sauce is slowly extracted from the cooking of the carcass, and later combined and served with the tails. It works the same way with meat. Take a *salmis* of pheasant: The bird will be roasted briefly at high temperature and the meat of the breast and thighs set aside, since it is the best and most tender part of the bird. The rest of the pheasant is browned further, seasoned, deglazed with wine and stock, reduced, degreased and reduced again to intensify the taste and obtain a shiny concentrated sauce. This sauce finally gets served with the juicy, lightly cooked meat. The cycle is completed and each part of the pheasant has been utilized to the utmost and to obtain the best possible results. Contrary to other types of stocks, a fish stock cooks fast—35 to 40 minutes will be sufficient to get the nutrients and taste from the bones. A fish-court bouillon is usually done with fish bones, vegetables and water. A *fumet de poisson* consists of the bones stewed in butter, first, with the addition of vegetables, white wine, water and seasoning, and becomes the base of *veloutés* and sauces.

2½ pounds fish bones (use preferably the bones of flat fish such as sole, flounder, fluke, etc.). If fish heads are used, be sure to remove the gills and wash the bones carefully under cold water or the fish stock will be bitter.
2 tablespoons sweet butter
1 medium onion, peeled and sliced
2 to 3 stalks celery, coarsely chopped
¼ cup parsley stems
1 leek, cleaned and sliced
2 bay leaves
¼ teaspoon thyme
½ teaspoon black peppercorns, crushed (mignonnette)
1 teaspoon salt
1½ cups dry white wine
3 quarts water

1. Place the butter in a large skillet or kettle and add the fish bones. Steam on medium to high heat for 3 to 4 minutes, stirring with a wooden spatula.

2. When the bones begin to fall apart, add the onion, celery, parsley stems and leek, and mix well. Steam for another 3 to 4 minutes, stirring. Add all the other ingredients to bring to a boil. Boil on high heat for 35 to 40 minutes.

3. Strain through a fine sieve. You can freeze the fish stock and use it for soups, or thicken it with a *roux* so it becomes a *velouté*, as well as reducing it to a glaze and finishing it with cream and butter.

15. Skimming Technique *(Technique de Dégraissage)*

1. With the stock boiling gently, remove the scum with a tight, "net-like" skimmer.

2. For an alternative method, use a ladle. "Push" the fat to one side of the pot by sliding the round back of the ladle on top of the liquid. Then, using the front of the ladle, scoop the fat off. A third alternative is to let the stock cool refrigerated overnight, then remove the fat which will have solidified on top of the liquid.

16. Skimming Fat *(Dégraissage des Sauces)*

WHEN SAUCES ARE COOKING, the fat or scum comes up to the surface of the liquid and has to be skimmed off.

1. With the sauce simmering gently, push the top layer of fat or scum to one side of the pan.

2. With the spoon flat, scoop the fat from the side when it is accumulated.

3. Be sure to scoop only the fat. Repeat every 10 or 15 minutes, as needed, while the sauce is simmering.

17. How to Strain Sauces
(Passage des Sauces au Chinois)

THERE ARE TWO WAYS to strain stocks or sauces. If it is a clear stock or *demi-glace* or any of its derivatives, care should be taken to not crush the solids into liquid or it would make it cloudy.

If you are straining a thickened sauce such as a *velouté* or *béchamel* or hollandaise, you don't have to worry about "dirtying" the mixture and can rub as much through the mesh as possible. In the photographs that follow we are straining through a fine-meshed chinois (strainer) that is the equivalent of a double or triple layer of cheesecloth or kitchen towel.

To strain a stock very finely you should put it through a colander with larger holes first to remove the larger solids and then when the volume is reduced, work it through a finer-meshed chinois. It is particularly important to put *demi-glace* through a fine strainer to get the glossiness that's possible only when all the impurities have been removed.

If you are buying a chinois, be sure to get one with a guard to protect the mesh from getting dented or crushed.

Any sauce that has to do with eggs and has a tendency to curdle—from the sabayon of the hollandaise to a *crème anglaise*—can be strained through this type of fine mesh to conceal or minimize a problem.

1. To remove solids from a sauce or stock, when it's important to keep the liquid clear, bang the side of the strainer either with the palm of your hand or a wooden spatula to encourage the clear stock to strain through. If you crush the solids into the strained liquid the stock or sauce will become cloudy.

2. For thickened sauces, where clarity is not an issue, use the ladle in a plungerlike, push-lift-push motion, forcing the liquid through the mesh.

18. Strong, Clarified Stock *(Consommé)*

CONSOMMÉ IS THE BEEF OR CHICKEN concoction that, when perfectly made, is a beautifully clear and sparkling soup. It can be eaten as is or used as a base for other soups, for sauces or for aspic, technique 21. It has all the proteins of meat and none of the fat. There are two steps in making consommé. The first is to make the stock and the second is to clarify it. Clarification is the simple process that gives consommé its crystal-clear appearance.

A very strong consommé *(consommé double)* is made by adding meat to the clarification and cooking it for 1 hour, thus concentrating flavor in the liquid. A cold *consommé double* should be gelatinous without being too firm. With the addition of tomato, it becomes the celebrated *madrilène consommé*.

THE STOCK

1 *unpeeled onion, halved*
4 *pounds beef bones (or a mixture of beef and chicken bones)*
1 *bay leaf*
1 *teaspoon black peppercorns*
1 *medium-sized onion, peeled and stuck with 3 cloves*
2 *teaspoons salt*

Place the split onion, cut sides down, in an iron skillet and place on medium heat. Let cook until the onion is burned and very black. It is essential that the onion is burnt on the cut side. It will cook with the bones for hours, and will give the amber color a consommé should have.

Place all ingredients in a large kettle and cover with cold water. Bring to a boil, skimming any scum that forms at the surface. When boiling, lower the heat and simmer slowly for 6 hours. Strain.

During cooking, add water if there is too much evaporation. You should have 12 cups of liquid left. Let cool and remove fat from top.

CLARIFIED STOCK *(The Consommé)*

1 *cup cold water*
1 *pound very lean ground beef*
6 *egg whites*
½ *cup diced celery leaves*
¾ *cup diced tomato*
2 *cups sliced green of leek (or 1 cup green of scallions)*
½ *cup coarsely cut parsley and tarragon mixed*
¾ *cup sliced carrots*
½ *teaspoon black peppercorns*
2 *bay leaves*
½ *teaspoon thyme leaves*
Salt, if needed
12 *cups stock*

1. In a large kettle, combine all the ingredients except the stock.

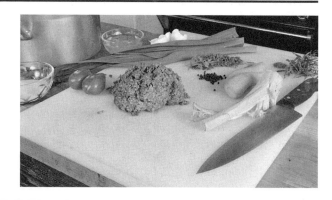

2. Add the stock and bring to a boil over high heat, stirring constantly to avoid sticking. Do not worry if the stock becomes very cloudy and a white foam forms. The albumin in the egg whites and the meat is solidifying, and this is the process that will clarify the stock. When the mixture comes to a boil, STOP STIRRING and reduce the heat to a simmer. As the mixture simmers, you will notice that the ingredients form a "crust" on the surface of the liquid with one or two holes, through which the liquid boils slightly.

3. Allow the consommé to simmer gently for 1 hour without disturbing the little "geysers" in any way. Turn off the heat and let the consommé settle for 15 minutes.

4. Strain the consommé through a sieve lined with a paper napkin, taking care not to disturb the crust.

5. Tilt the pan on one side to get all the liquid out.

6. After the consommé has rested 1 hour, check to see if there is any fat on the surface. If so, remove it by blotting the top with paper towels. The consommé can be served hot or cold. With different garnishes it takes on different names like *célestine* with shredded crêpes, or *royale* with cubes of meat-flavored custard. The crust is usually discarded, but with the addition of whole eggs, bread crumbs and seasonings, it can be turned into a satisfying meat loaf. Be careful to remove the peppercorns for this use.

19. White Butter Sauce *(Beurre Blanc)*

YIELD: About 2 cups

THE *beurre blanc* (white butter sauce) is an emulsion of butter with wine and/or vinegar which holds together because it is whipped at a proper temperature. Furthermore the whipping beats air into the mixture, which makes it light and increases its volume. In cooking, the word "emulsion" refers to a fat and liquid or other ingredient bound together into a creamy mixture. Mayonnaise is an example of a cold emulsion and hollandaise an example of a hot emulsion. Other types of emulsions appear throughout this book—in the brill recipe (technique 95), the bass with puff paste (technique 101), the mousseline of scallops (technique 85), the cauliflower with lemon butter (technique 108), as well as the asparagus stew (technique 105). In the latter recipe, butter and water are brought to a strong boil and it is the boiling that causes the mixture to bind. This is somewhat confusing as on the one hand boiling may be necessary to get some sauces into emulsion while on the other hand sauces like hollandaise or *beurre blanc* separate if they're brought near the boil. The explanation for this paradox lies in the proportions of fat to liquid.

If a small quantity of butter is mixed and boiled with a large quantity of liquid, the butter will most likely separate and rise to the surface of the liquid. If the proportion of butter and liquid are more or less equal, a strong boil will bind the ingredients together and make a creamy sauce that will hold together for some time depending on temperature (see technique 105). If there's a lot more butter than liquid (as there is in the *beurre blanc*) too much heat will make the mixture separate. This is an important point to grasp because when understood it allows you to bind liquids into fat or to separate fat from liquid at will. For example, in the roast chicken in aspic (technique 147), the natural juices are boiled down to evaporate the moisture and reduce the mixture to solidified juices and clear fat. As the moisture boils off, the proportion of fat becomes greater and this is why it breaks down and separates from the solidified juices. Once the fat is separated, it can be easily poured off and the solidified juices dissolved with water, then strained and reduced to proper consistency. To reverse the process, let's say that you don't want to remove the fat from your natural juices but the mixture has over-reduced and already separated. If you want to bind the liquid and fat back together again, you just replace some of the evaporated moisture (water), bring to a strong boil and it will bind together again. In the case of a *beurre blanc* or hollandaise which, again, is almost all fat, if the sauce starts to separate, remove from the heat, add a bit of cold water and beat with a whisk to bind together again.

The *beurre blanc* can replace a hollandaise on top of any kind of vegetable and is especially good with shellfish and fish.

1 *cup water*
⅓ *cup finely sliced shallots (3 to 5 according to size)*
½ *teaspoon freshly ground white pepper*
¾ *teaspoon salt*
½ *cup good white wine vinegar*
2 *tablespoons heavy cream*
2½ *to 3 sticks sweet butter at room temperature*

1. In a saucepan, preferably stainless steel, combine the water, shallots, pepper, salt and vinegar. Bring to a boil and simmer slowly for 25 to 30 minutes. If the mixture reduces too much during the cooking, add some water. Push the mixture into a sieve, pushing with a spoon to force the shallots through. You should have approximately ⅓ cup of mixture left. If you have too much, reduce it. If you don't have enough, adjust with a bit of water.

2. Add the cream to the mixture and place on very low heat. The mixture should be lukewarm. Add the butter piece by piece, beating rapidly and strongly with a wire whisk after each addition. Do not worry too much about temperature. Up to one stick of butter can be added to the saucepan and the whole mixture boiled without it breaking down. As the quantity of butter increases, reduce the heat to low. Keep adding the butter and beating until all of it is used.

3. You should have a warm, creamy, smooth-textured sauce. Keep lukewarm in a double boiler or on the side of your stove. As long as it doesn't cool enough to solidify, it can keep. At serving time, place back on the stove and heat while beating with the whisk until hot. Serve immediately.

20. Hollandaise Sauce *(Sauce Hollandaise)*

YIELD: About 2 cups

GENERALLY A HOLLANDAISE SAUCE IS MADE with 6 to 7 yolks per pound of butter, but the proportion of eggs to butter can be altered in either direction. If your hollandaise is high in egg yolks it will be less likely to separate but it may become too yolky in taste. If it is high in butter it will be very delicate in taste but very fragile.

Though a hollandaise sauce is usually made with clarified butter (see note), we prefer to use unclarified butter. Because unclarified butter is whole—it has not been separated into its oil and liquid components and the liquid component discarded—it is more watery, and therefore it makes a slightly thinner sauce. However, it gives the sauce a creamier taste and the extra moisture permits it to withstand higher heats than the conventional hollandaise. (The importance of the ratio of liquid to fat in emulsions such as a hollandaise is discussed in the introduction to technique 19.)

Our last modification is that we make the sauce with a base of water, not lemon juice, although lemon juice can certainly be added if desired.

A hollandaise is a base or mother sauce. With the addition of white wine vinegar, shallots and tarragon it becomes a *béarnaise* sauce. If you add tomatoes to the *béarnaise* it becomes a sauce *choron.* If you add *glace de viande* to the *béarnaise* it becomes a *sauce Foyot,* etc. Hollandaise sauce can be made with a browned butter, which gives it a very nutty taste (sauce *Noisette*), or perfumed with orange rind and orange juice to make a sauce *Maltaise,* which is excellent with broccoli, etc.

(*Note:* To clarify butter, place butter in a 180-degree oven until completely melted. Let it rest a few minutes and it will separate into two layers: a milky residue at the bottom and a transparent oily layer at the top. Clarified butter is the oily part. The milky residue is discarded.)

4 egg yolks
2 tablespoons water
2 sticks (8 ounces) sweet butter
Dash of cayenne
Dash of pepper (about ¼ teaspoon)
Salt to taste (about ½ teaspoon)

1. Place the yolks and the water in a saucepan. Beat over low heat for approximately 5 minutes.

2. The mixture should get hot, but if it comes too close to a boil the eggs will scramble. On the other hand, if the mixture is not hot enough it will get foamy, increase in volume, without acquiring much in the way of consistency, stay too thin and separate into foam and liquid. Make sure you "drive" the whisk with the palm of your hand in the corner of the saucepan, since this is where the eggs will have a tendency to scramble.

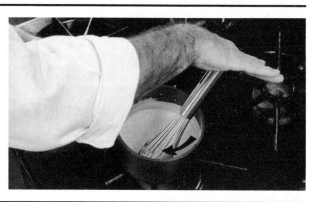

3. When the consistency of the egg yolk mixture is like a *sabayon,* you will notice that between the strokes of the whisk you can see the bottom of the saucepan. This is an indication that it is cooked enough.

4. Start adding the butter, piece by piece, beating between each addition. Keep the hollandaise on a very low heat during the addition of butter. Finally, add a dash of cayenne, a dash of pepper and the salt.

5. The sauce should be creamy, smooth and thick enough to coat eggs, fish or any other food.

6. If the sauce gets too hot, it will break down. You will recognize this sign if the sauce starts getting oily around the edges. Add 1 tablespoon of cold water or a piece of ice and beat well. The sauce will reconstitute. However, if it completely separates put it together as follows.

7. Place the sauce over heat and stir, so it separates entirely. Incline the pan to one side and let it rest 4 to 5 minutes so that all the oily part comes to the top. Scoop out the oily part and set aside.

8. Place 2 teaspoons of warm water in a clean saucepan or bowl. Take about 1 tablespoon of the thick part of the sauce and add to the water, whisking it in bit by bit. Add more, whisk until smooth, and more again, continuing the process until you have reclaimed all of the thick part.

9. When all the thick part is back together, start adding the oily part, beating as if you were making the sauce again from the start. If the sauce has gotten very hot and some parts have scrambled a bit, put through a fine strainer to eliminate (as best you can) the "scrambled" appearance.

21. Aspic (Gelée)

THE WORD ASPIC refers to any gelatinous liquid which congeals and sets when cold. With a lot of reduction, a natural stock will set. However, it will rarely become firm enough to be used for a mold unless natural aspic in the form of pig's feet, pork rind or the like is added. Also, it is not always desirable to reduce a stock to such a degree as the flavor may become too strong. For these reasons, aspic is usually made with a liquid and unflavored gelatin. The liquid is a stock which can be made from chicken, beef, game, fish, shellfish and the like.

Aspic can be used in a number of ways: it can be used to bind foods in a mold (for examples, see *oeufs en gelée*, technique 27, and *aspic de saumon*, technique 89). It can be used to glaze cold dishes, such as ham. It can be used to fill the cavity inside a pâté baked in a crust (see technique 191). It can be chopped into a dice and used as a garnish as described in the photographs below.

Because aspic should be transparent, it is important to use a stock that is crystal clear. The process of clearing a stock, clarification, is described in the preceding technique. The stock should be fat free and the equipment immaculate.

To make an aspic from a beef or chicken stock, follow the recipe for consommé on page 44, adding twelve ¼-ounce envelopes of unflavored gelatin to the kettle in step 1. Refrigerate until firm for use as a garnish.

A few words about gelatin: one ¼-ounce envelope will congeal up to 3 cups of liquid if the gelatin is stirred into the hot liquid and no further cooking takes place. In our recipe making aspic from consommé, the gelatin cooks for an hour and therefore loses much of its strength. This is the reason such a large quantity is needed.

GARNISHING WITH ASPIC

1. Unmold a solid piece of aspic. Cut it into slices. Then cut the slices into strips and,

2. finally into dice. Each piece shines like a little jewel. Using a spoon, arrange around the cold dish. You may also "twist" your knife left to right while cutting aspic. This makes "ridges" on the sides of the slices and dices, giving even more relief and glitter to the little jewels. (Though some cooks recommend chopping up the aspic and piping it with a pastry bag, it is nonsensical to have gone through the trouble of making crystal clear aspic just to chop it into a mush an smear it in the pastry bag.)

22. Butter *(Beurre)*

SWEET FRESH BUTTER, one of the main ingredients in French cooking, is widely used in the professional kitchen for everything from hors d'oeuvre to desserts. And rightly so, because there is no substitute. Buy sweet butter, rather than salted, because salt is added only to act as a preservative, and salted butter may not always be fresh. Sweet butter, on the other hand, gives away its age by turning rancid faster than salted butter.

Clarified butter is nothing more than ordinary butter that has been heated until it melts, and the milky residue (milk solids) has sunk to the bottom of the pan. The clear, yellow liquid that sits on top is clarified butter. Classically, it is used to make hollandaise, *béarnaise* and *choron* sauces, among others, and it is often called for in sautéeing because it does not burn as readily as unclarified butter. However, I personally think clarified butter loses the sweet taste of fresh butter.

Butter is so versatile it often is used for three different purposes in the same sauce: to thicken it with either a "roux" or a *beurre manié,* to enrich it by adding little "nuts" of butter and to coat the surface of the sauce to prevent a skin from forming.

A roux is a mixture of butter and flour in equal proportions which is cooked before it is combined with a liquid. A roux *blanc* (white) should be cooked slowly for 1 minute, stirring. It should not be allowed to brown. A roux *brun* (brown) is cooked until it turns a rich, nut brown. A *beurre manié* is a mixture of soft butter and flour in equal proportions that has been kneaded until smooth.

Béchamel is one of the mother sauces in French cooking. It is made with a *beurre manié.* With the addition of cream it becomes a *sauce crème.*

WHITE SAUCE *(Sauce Béchamel)*

1. Place soft butter and flour in equal proportions in a bowl.

2. Mix with a spoon until smooth. This is a *beurre manié*.

3. Bring milk to a boil. With a wire whisk, scoop the *beurre manié* and whisk into the milk *vigorously* to avoid any lumps. The kneaded butter should incorporate easily without forming any lumps.

4. Bring the sauce to a boil and cook at low heat for 4 to 5 minutes, mixing with the whisk to avoid scalding. Season to taste with salt, pepper and nutmeg. A thin sauce will take approximately 2 teaspoons each of flour and butter per cup of milk. A thick, heavy sauce (for soufflés) will take up to 3 tablespoons each of flour and butter.

5. When the sauce is cooked, cut a little bit of butter and put it on top.

6. As the butter melts, smear it onto the whole surface of the sauce with the point of a fork. This will form a coating of fat on the surface of the sauce and will prevent a skin from forming. At serving time, stir in the butter which is on top.

LEMON-PARSLEY BUTTER
(Beurre Maître D'Hôtel)

1. The *maître d'hôtel* butter is the most frequently used of the many compound butters. It is sliced and used on broiled steak, chops, liver, or on boiled potatoes, cauliflower or even poached fish. To 2 sticks (½ pound) of softened sweet butter, add the juice of ½ lemon, 2 tablespoons chopped parsley, 1 teaspoon salt and 1 teaspoon ground white pepper.

2. Mix thoroughly until all the ingredients are well blended. Spread into a strip on the width of a piece of wax paper.

3. Roll the butter back and forth to make it smooth and equal all over.

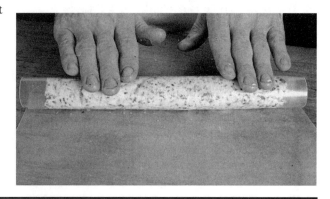

4. Close both ends of the butter tube and place in the refrigerator. Cut into slices as needed. The same method is used to make *béarnaise* butter, *Colbert, anchovy* and so on.

23. Mayonnaise

MAYONNAISE IS, PERHAPS, the most useful cold sauce in the world. The word may come from the medieval French word *mayeu,* meaning egg yolk, or, according to Grimod-de-la-Reynière, from the verb *manier,* meaning to knead. Mayonnaise lends itself to an infinite number of variations.

Mayonnaise is usually served with cold foods such as hard-boiled eggs, cut vegetables, salad, cold fish, shellfish, cold meat and pâté. (Its sister, hollandaise, made with egg yolk and butter, is served warm with fish, eggs and vegetables such as asparagus, broccoli and the like.) In French cooking, when the ingredients of a particular salad are bound with mayonnaise, it becomes: mayonnaise *de volaille* (chicken salad), mayonnaise *de homard* (lobster salad) and so on. Though according to classic French recipe books, mayonnaise is not made with mustard, I have rarely seen it made without. Mayonnaise made in the food processor or blender will keep longer when refrigerated than the handmade counterpart because the elements are more finely bound together.

Mayonnaise can become sauce *verte*, a green sauce made with mayonnaise, watercress, tarragon, parsley and spinach; sauce *gribiche,* mayonnaise with hard-cooked eggs, French sour gherkins, capers and shallots; sauce *tartare,* mayonnaise with parsley, chives, chervil and sour pickles; sauce *La Varenne,* mayonnaise with a purée of fresh mushrooms; sauce *russe,* mayonnaise with fresh caviar; and, of course, the well-known *aïoli,* known as the butter of

Provence and made with a very substantial amount of pounded garlic and olive oil. Of course, mayonnaise can be done with olive oil (the best is a virgin oil), or peanut oil, or a mixture of both; it is just a question of personal taste. Buy vinegar of the best possible quality, such as *vinaigre d'Orléans*. Use good mustard. The quality of the ingredients is sine qua non to the end result. Be sure that the ingredients are at room temperature. If the oil is too cool, the mayonnaise will definitely break down. If kept refrigerated, the mayonnaise must come to room temperature slowly before it is stirred or it will break down. This recipe yields about 2½ cups of mayonnaise. The same recipe can be made without the mustard for a milder taste; however, the mixture will be more delicate and more likely to break down.

2 egg yolks
1½ teaspoons Dijon mustard
1 tablespoon tarragon or wine vinegar
Dash of salt
Dash of freshly ground white pepper
2 cups oil (peanut, olive, walnut or a mixture)

1. Place all ingredients except the oil in a bowl and stir with a wire whisk. Add the oil slowly, whisking at the same time.

2. Keep mixing, adding the oil a little faster as the mayonnaise starts to take shape.

3. Consistency of the correct mayonnaise.

4. To serve, scoop the mayonnaise into a clean bowl, being careful not to smear the sides of the bowl. (Place the mayonnaise in the middle of the bowl.)

5. Smooth the top with a spatula by turning the spatula in one direction and the bowl in the other direction.

6. When the top is smooth, move the spatula in the same circular and reverse motion, going up and down to make a design on top of the smooth surface.

7. With your finger, push out the mayonnaise left on the blade of the spatula in the center of the decoration.

8. Mayonnaise ready to serve.

9. When the oil is added too fast, or when the ingredients are too cold, the mixture breaks down. It looks like a broken-down custard. Mayonnaise can be put back together with egg yolk, mustard, vinegar, or a small amount of hot water. Place 1 teaspoon of vinegar, if vinegar is used, in a clean vessel. Add 1 teaspoon of the broken sauce and whisk thoroughly. When smooth, add another teaspoon, then another, and when the mayonnaise starts to hold together, you may add the broken sauce at a faster pace.

10. For another method, pour the vinegar or hot water directly into the broken mayonnaise in one place along the edge of the bowl. Using the tip of your whisk, without getting too deep into the mayonnaise, mix the liquid with the top layer of the broken sauce until you see that it is getting together. Keep mixing, pushing your whisk deeper and deeper into the mayonnaise. Then, whisk larger and larger circles until all of the sauce is back together.

24. Larding: Strips and Leaves (Lardons et Bardes)

T HERE ARE BASICALLY TWO KINDS of larding needles: the large grooved needle *(lardoire)* for pot roast and other large pieces of meat and the small butterflied needle *(aiguille à piquer)* used for small cuts, such as filet mignon or rack of hare. The process of larding smaller cuts with fat was once common but it is rarely done nowadays. In our lighter and healthier contemporary cooking, one tries to reduce rather than increase the intake of fat. *Piquage* of meat is not necessary and I do not recommend it. It is shown only as part of a known technique.

Because meat is always cut against the grain, larding is done with the grain of meat. Otherwise, one might cut through whole strips of fat while carving.

Lard leaves *(bardes)* are used to line terrines and pâtés, or to wrap dry meat or game such as partridge or woodcock, and give moisture and enrich the meat during cooking.

LARDING A SMALL CUT OF MEAT

1. The fat used is fat back *(lard dur)* because it is firm and white and is not inclined to disintegrate as easily as fat from other parts of the pig. It is the layer of fat closest to the skin. Keep the piece refrigerated so it can be easily cut into strips. Flatten the piece with a large cleaver.

2. Turn upside down and, with a long, thin knife, start cutting the rind off.

3. With one hand pressing tight on top of the fat back, cut the rind off by keeping your blade flat, moving in a jigsaw fashion.

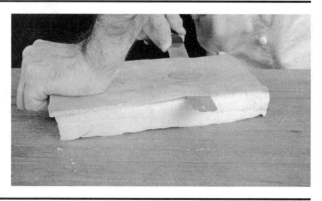

4. Cut the fat in long strips about ½ inch wide for the pot roast. Place in iced water to keep the fat firm.

5. Cut in small strips to lard the small cuts. Keep in iced water.

6. Place the fat strips inside the split end of the *aiguille à piquer* as far as it will go.

7. With one hand, keep the split end closed on the fat and insert the needle through the meat.

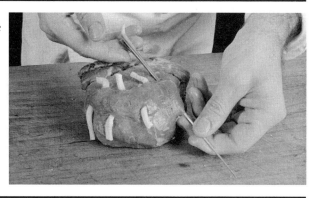

8. Pull with the other hand, leaving a small strip dangling on each side. The meat is larded on a bias in that case.

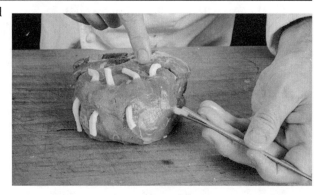

LARDING A LARGE CUT OF MEAT

1. Cut ½-inch slices of fat back.

2. Cut the slices into long strips and keep refrigerated, or in iced water to firm up.

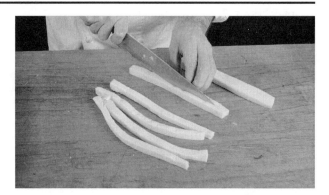

3. This is a plain grooved larding needle. Before placing the fat in it, push the needle through the meat to make an opening. Remove the needle, place the fat into the opening, and insert it into the premade hole, twisting as you push the needle in. Lift the end of the fat, and hold with your finger as you withdraw the needle, or the entire strip may come out.

4. This is another type of larding needle. It is easier to use because of its hinged tip.

5. With this needle, you place the fat into the groove and close the tip on top of it.

6. Insert the needle, twisting it through the meat (go with the grain of the meat). Lift up the tip and,

7. holding it between your fingers, pull off the removable handle.

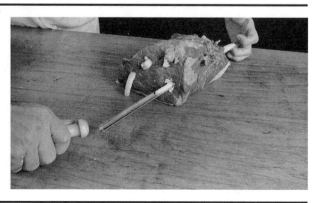

8. Holding the end of the fat with your thumb, pull the needle through in the same direction it went in.

9. Repeat until the entire piece of meat is larded every 1½ to 2 inches.

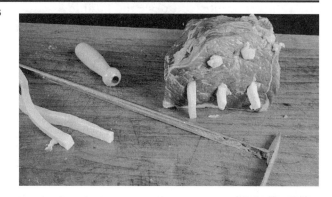

LARD LEAVES FOR TERRINES AND PÂTÉS

1. To make *bardes* or lard leaves, flatten the fat back with a cleaver. Place skin side down on the table. Stick one or two pointed knives through the rind to keep the fat back from sliding during cutting.

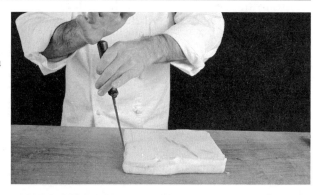

2. Using a long, thin knife, cut "leaves" as thin as you can, holding your blade horizontally.

3. This technique requires a certain amount of practice. You could ask your butcher to cut the leaves with his electric ham slicer.

25. Separating Eggs *(Séparation des Oeufs)*

WHEN YOU ARE SEPARATING EGGS, you often end up with an excess of yolk or white. The egg whites, almost pure albumin, freeze well. Defrosted egg whites whip even better than fresh egg whites, and they do not pick up odors. The yolk, however, high in fat, does not freeze well. Unless the temperature goes as low as −20 degrees, bacteria will grow in the egg yolk. In addition, yolks easily become freezer burnt. However, they can be kept for a couple of days in the refrigerator covered with a layer of water to prevent a skin from forming on top. Pour the water off before using.

1. To separate the yolk from the white, crack the egg on the edge of the bowl. Open the egg, keeping one half upright to hold the yolk. Let the white drop into the bowl.

2. Pour the yolk into the empty half shell, letting more white drop into the bowl as you are transferring the yolk from one shell to the other.

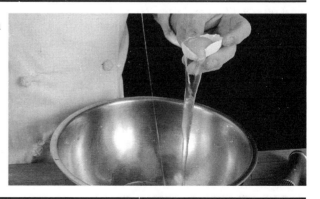

3. An alternative method is to pour the egg into your hand and let the white drip through your fingers.

26. Poaching Eggs *(Oeufs Pochés)*

WHEN MAKING POACHED EGGS, the fresher the eggs the better. The older the eggs, the more the whites will tend to spread in the water. A dash of vinegar (white vinegar preferably, to avoid discoloration of the eggs) is added to the water to help firm the egg white. Salt is omitted because it has the reverse effect and tends to thin down the white. Poached eggs lend themselves to an infinite number of combinations, from the very simple poached egg on toast, to the sophisticated eggs Benedict, served with ham, hollandaise sauce and truffles. Eggs can be poached several hours, even a day, ahead (as most restaurants do), eliminating any last-minute panic when you want to serve several people at once.

1. To poach 6 eggs, place 2½ to 3 quarts of water and ¼ cup white vinegar in a large saucepan. Bring to a boil; then, reduce to a simmer. Break one egg at a time on the side of the saucepan. Holding it as closely as you can to the water (to avoid splashing), open it with both thumbs and let it slide into the water. Drop your eggs at the place where the water is simmering so that they don't go down into the water too fast and stick to the bottom.

2. If you are afraid of burning your fingers, break the eggs in a saucer or bowl and slide them into the water. Go as fast as you can so that the difference in cooking time is not too great between the first and the last egg. Keep the water at a bare simmer, or let it "shiver," as it is said in France.

3. As soon as all the eggs are in the water, drag the bottom of a large slotted spoon across the surface of the water to move the eggs about a bit and keep them from sticking to the bottom of the pan. Once some of the whites have hardened, the eggs will not stick any more.

4. Large eggs take approximately 3 to 4 minutes of cooking. If you like them more runny or more set, the timing should be changed accordingly. Check the eggs by lifting them, one at a time, with a slotted spoon and pressing them slightly with your fingers. The whites should be set, but the yolks soft to the touch.

5. As soon as an egg is cooked, transfer it to a bowl of iced water. This stops the cooking and washes the vinegar off.

6. When the eggs are cold, lift each one from the water and trim off the hanging pieces with a knife or a pair of scissors. Place in a bowl of fresh cold water.

7. Drain well if you use them cold, or keep refrigerated in cold water. They will keep for at least a couple of days. To use hot, place in a strainer, lower into boiling water for approximately 1 minute, drain and serve immediately.

27. Eggs in Aspic *(Oeufs en Gelée)*

THIS IS A PERFECT FIRST COURSE for a summer dinner. The bottom of the molds can be garnished with ham, chicken, tongue, or decorated with tarragon, tomato, truffles and the like. Poach the eggs, technique 26, and make a strong, crystal-clear aspic, technique 21.

1. Place a bowl of melted aspic in an ice-water bath to accelerate the coagulation process. Stir until it becomes syrupy. Pour about ⅜ inch of aspic in the bottom of small individual molds and let it firm up in the refrigerator. Decorate the top of the aspic to your fancy. The eggs pictured here are decorated with blanched tarragon leaves and little pieces of tomato skin.

2. Place the well-drained, cold poached eggs on top of the decoration. Cool some more aspic and, when it becomes syrupy, pour enough on top and around to cover the eggs completely. Refrigerate. When cold, and set, unmold and arrange on a platter with chopped aspic around the eggs. See finished oeufs en gelée, page 123.

28. Omelets *(Omelettes)*

OMELET MAKING is both very simple and very difficult. A perfect omelet is golden in color on top, delicate and creamy in the center. In addition to fresh eggs and sweet butter, there are three other major ingredients: the right pan, practice and high heat. It is essential to have an 8- to 10-inch omelet pan, "well seasoned" to inhibit sticking, with rounded, sloping shoulders that give the omelet a nice shape and help it slide easily onto the plate when cooked. Be sure to use the highest possible heat, be careful not to overbeat the eggs and do not use too much butter, or the omelet will be wrinkled. The whole operation should not take you more than 1 minute.

PLAIN OMELET

1. Using a fork, beat 3 whole eggs with salt and freshly ground pepper until well mixed. Add 1 tablespoon water (optional) to lighten the omelet. Place 1 tablespoon sweet butter in the pan on high heat. When the foaming has subsided, and the butter has a nice hazelnut color, pour in the eggs. They should sizzle. Let the eggs coagulate for about 6 to 8 seconds.

2. With the flat side of a fork in one hand, stir the eggs in a circular motion. Simultaneously, with the other hand, shake the pan back and forth in a continuous movement so that the eggs coagulate uniformly. Lift up the pan slightly while the eggs are cooking so that the "scrambled" eggs end up piled up toward the front of the pan. If the pan is kept flat, and the whole surface is covered with a uniform layer of eggs, then the omelet will roll like a jelly roll or a carpet, and it will not be moist inside.

3. Fold the lower "lips" back onto the omelet, shaping it in a nice half-moon shape as you go along.

4. Run your fork along the side of the pan under the front of the omelet.

5. Tap the handle of the pan to encourage the omelet to lift up in the front

6. and, using the fork, fold the upper lip onto the center, taking care to see that it comes to a point at each end.

7. At this time, the omelet can be stuffed. Arrange the solid pieces, whether you use chicken livers, creamed chicken, spinach or whatever, in a line along the center of the omelet.

8. Changing hands, hold the serving plate vertically against the side of the pan and invert the omelet onto the plate. Pour the sauce, if any, around the omelet.

ALTERNATE WAY TO STUFF AN OMELET

9. Make a plain omelet and turn it onto a plate. With the point of a knife, make an incision lengthwise in the center of the omelet. Using a spoon, stuff the opening. Pour sauce, if any, all around the omelet.

10. From left to right: stuffed, flat and plain omelets.

29. Stuffed Eggs *(Oeufs Mimosa)*

STUFFED HARD-BOILED EGGS ARE an excellent garnish for cold salmon or other fish. They can also be served as a luncheon first course, or as an hors d'oeuvre for a buffet.

1. Be careful when cooking hard-boiled eggs. They should be lowered into boiling water and allowed to barely simmer for 10 to 12 minutes, depending on size. Then the eggs should be placed in cold water to stop the cooking and avoid the greenish discoloration around the yolk. Trim the eggs at both ends, cut into halves and "seat" the pieces on their cut ends. (Very fresh eggs are hard to peel because of their acidity but this diminishes after the eggs are 2 days old.)

2. Remove the yolks (without breaking the whites) and push through a metal sieve with the help of a sturdy spoon.

3. Add 1 tablespoon of soft sweet butter or mayonnaise for every 3 egg yolks. Season with salt and pepper and mix well. The mixture should be soft and homogenous. Fit a pastry bag with a fluted tube, technique 62, and fill up the white halves with the mixture.

4. Decorate the tops with capers. Refrigerate until serving time.

30. Eggs with Black Butter *(Oeufs au Beurre Noir)*

YIELD: 1 serving

Here are a few different ways of preparing eggs. The egg may well be the most versatile of foods. It can be prepared at least one hundred different ways. Eggs in aspic, for example (page 68), make a very nice first course for an elegant dinner. The skillet eggs pictured on page 74 are served with black butter that adds a special nuttiness to the eggs. Black butter is also served with poached brains, poached fish, etc.

1 teaspoon sweet butter, plus 1 tablespoon
2 large fresh eggs
Dash of salt
Dash of freshly ground white pepper
1 teaspoon drained capers
About 1 teaspoon red or white wine vinegar

1. A clever way to control the flow of vinegar or soy sauce or other liquid seasoning and to allow you quick access without screwing bottle tops on and off all the time is to store the seasoning in a wine bottle topped with a cork "pour spout." To make the spout, remove a strip on each side of the cork and then replace the cork on the bottle. To use the liquid (we are using vinegar here to make the black butter), shake the bottle directly over the bowl or skillet.

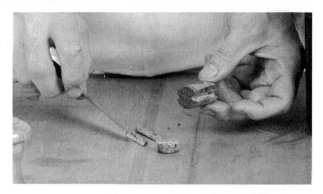

2. Break the eggs in a saucer. Melt 1 teaspoon of butter in a skillet and when it is foaming lightly, slide the eggs into the skillet. Cook for approximately 1 minute on very low heat. The edges of the whites should not curl. At the last moment you can cover the eggs with a lid for 10 to 15 seconds, to cook the top slightly and give them a shine. (Eggs cooked this way are often called "mirror eggs.") Slide the eggs onto a plate and sprinkle them lightly with salt, pepper and the capers.

3. Add the 1 tablespoon of butter to the skillet and cook until it turns dark brown and is smoking. Pour directly on top of the eggs. Add the vinegar to the hot skillet, swirl around to warm it up and pour the few drops left on top of the eggs. Serve immediately.

31. Eggs "Cocotte" with Cream
(Oeufs Cocotte Bressane)

YIELD: 6 servings

THESE EGGS are very easy to make. Unfortunately they are not served too often. The eggs are cooked in small soufflé molds or ramekins and eaten as a first course for dinner or for a light breakfast or brunch.

6 *large eggs, very fresh*
Salt
Pepper
6 *tablespoons heavy cream*

1. Use small ramekins or soufflé molds, no more than ½ cup in size. Butter the molds and sprinkle salt and pepper in the bottom.

2. Break an egg into each ramekin.

3. Place the ramekins in a skillet with tepid water around (a *bain-marie*) and cover. Place on top of the stove and let the water boil for approximately 1 to 1½ minutes. Uncover. The eggs should be barely set and still soft in the center.

4. Note that the eggs are shiny and glazed on top. Remove from the *bain-marie* and serve garnished or plain. With a bit of heavy cream on top, they are called eggs Bressane; with peas, they will become eggs Clamard, etc.

5. Sometimes the garnish is placed in the bottom of the mold and the egg is broken directly on top. In our case, put 1 tablespoon of heavy cream in the bottom of the mold, break the egg on top and cook, covered, as indicated above. The time of cooking will have to be increased by at least 30 seconds to a minute.

32. Scrambled Eggs *(Oeufs Brouillés)*

YIELD: 2 to 3 servings

IN CLASSIC FRENCH COOKING, the scrambled eggs are whisked into a very smooth purée and finished with cream and butter. They can be cooked in a double boiler using a wooden spatula, or on a low to medium heat using a whisk. Use a heavy, sturdy saucepan to obtain even heat. The eggs can be garnished with a bit of brown sauce or with a sauce *Périgueux* (a brown sauce with chopped truffles) as we have done here, or a fresh purée of tomatoes and grated Parmesan cheese, or peas, or sautéed chicken livers, etc. They can also be served plain. The eggs acquire a different name with each different garnish. They can be served as a first course, as well as for breakfast or lunch.

5 large eggs, very fresh
1 tablespoon, plus ½ tablespoon sweet butter
Salt and freshly ground white pepper to taste
1 tablespoon heavy cream

1. Break the eggs in a bowl and beat with a whisk. (Reserve the nicest half shells if you will be using them in your presentation.) Add the salt and pepper. Melt 1 tablespoon of butter in a large saucepan and add the eggs.

2. Cook on low heat, stirring all the time to mix well. Be sure to move the whisk in the corners of the saucepan where the eggs tend to set first. As soon as they begin to hold together but are still creamy, remove from the heat. Keep mixing. Remember that the eggs will continue to cook for a while after they are removed from the heat. Beat in 1 tablespoon of heavy cream and ½ tablespoon of sweet butter in pieces until smooth. Taste for seasonings and add salt and pepper if needed.

3. Spoon eggs onto individual plates, reserving enough to fill the egg shells. Fill the shells, embed in the center and garnish with a sauce *Périgueux*.

33. Deep-Fried Eggs *(Oeufs Frits Américaine)*

YIELD: 3 servings

THIS IS ANOTHER UNCOMMON WAY to prepare eggs. Instead of poaching them in water, we poach them in oil. The center comes out runny and soft, just like regular poached eggs. Only one egg can be done at a time, and it must be cooked very fast so that the white is wrapped around the yolk and nicely browned. Deep-fried eggs are usually served with bacon and fried tomatoes for lunch.

2½ to 3 *cups vegetable oil*
6 *large eggs, very fresh*

1. Place the oil in a 2-inch-deep non-stick skillet. (There should be at least 1½ inches of oil so the eggs can be immersed.) Heat to 360 degrees and warm two wooden spatulas in it (to prevent the eggs from sticking to the spatulas). Break one egg at a time into the oil, or break in a cup and slide it into the oil if you are afraid of being splashed with hot oil. Then, use the two spatulas to gather the egg white around the yolk.

2. "Squeeze" the egg slightly (between the spatulas, against the side of the skillet) for a few seconds to keep the egg white contained—so it doesn't spread as it cooks. If the egg sticks to one spatula, scrape it off with the other spatula. Turn the egg in the oil and cook it approximately 1 to 1½ minutes altogether.

3. Remove the egg with a slotted spoon, drain on paper towels and serve immediately. When the egg is taken out of the oil it will be nicely puffed. If kept a few minutes, it will deflate slightly.

4. Serve on toast with a slice of fried tomato and one or two slices of bacon. Like the preceding egg recipes, this dish can be served with a variety of garnishes and with each different garnish, it changes its name.

34. Butter Decoration *(Décoration en Beurre)*

1. To make hollow butter shells, you need a special tool with small teeth and a curved blade. The success depends entirely on the consistency of the butter. If the butter is too hard, the "peel" will not curl up, and you will be scraping shavings off the stick. If the butter is too soft, the blade will dig into it and make a mush. It is a trial and error procedure. Place each *coquille* (shell) in iced water.

2. For an attractive butter piece to put on a cheese tray, cut a stick of butter in half. Decorate each half, top and sides, with the tines of a fork.

3. The most difficult and the fanciest way of serving butter is to make flowers. The temperature, hence, the consistency, of the butter is the key. (See step 1.) Using the point of a small paring knife, scrape the top of the butter several times to build up a long bank of butter on top of the blade.

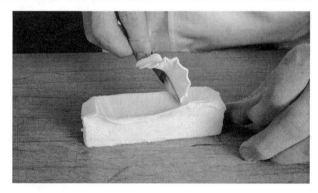

4. Curl the butter on the tip of the knife—jagged surface inside the "flower"—into one large corolla.

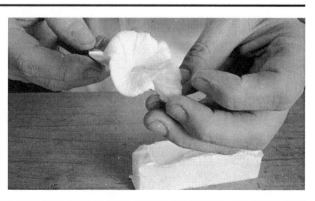

5. Curl another strip tighter and

6. place the curled strip in the center of the first corolla

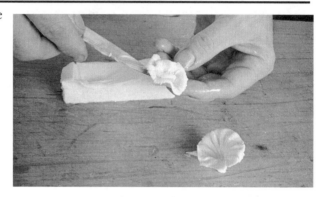

7. to form the heart of the flower.

8. Different butter decorations.

35. Potato Rose *(Rose en Pomme de Terre)*

OFTEN RESTAURANTS GARNISH with flowers sculpted from potatoes, carrots or white turnips. To avoid discoloration, the potatoes, after being carved, should be blanched in boiling water for 1 minute and cooled off under cold water. Then they can be soaked in a mixture of red food coloring and water to obtain a nice pink color. Carve a whole "bouquet" of these flowers and stand each one on a toothpick in a carved orange or grapefruit basket (technique 48). Surround with curly parsley.

1. Using a small sharp knife, cut a pointed shape from a peeled potato. Trim the shape to make it look like a child's toy top.

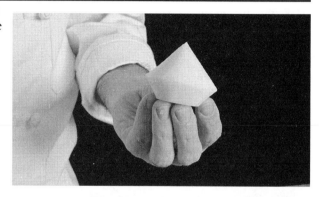

2. Make slits all around the base to simulate petals.

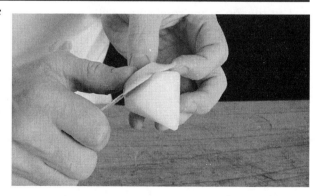

3. Using the tip of the knife, trim the edge all around above the petals.

4. Pull out the strip of potato, exposing the bottom layer of petals.

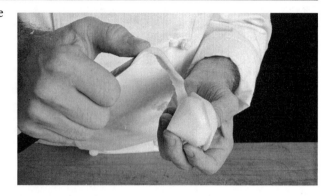

5. Keep cutting layers of slits, alternating the petals to get the right effect.

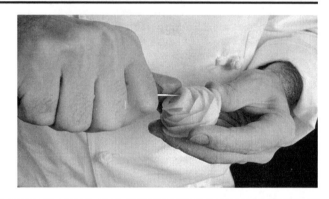

6. Cut the top of the rose, which will be too pointed, and blanch as indicated above.

36. Black Truffle Flowers *(Fleurs en Truffles)*

BLACK TRUFFLES are subterranean mushrooms that grow in the seedlings of "contaminated" trees, mainly oak and birch. Available fresh in season or canned, they are used often for decoration. With 1 truffle sliced very thin, one can do a lot of decoration. The rugged skin is peeled off and usually chopped and used in sauces, stuffing or pâté. A decoration made with real truffles is sober and elegant and particularly nice for a pâté or mousse like the one used to illustrate this technique.

1. Slice 1 truffle with a truffle slicer or a knife; it should be very thin. Cut little patterns and triangular pieces and make a decorative border on top of the mousse.

2. Use your imagination and make one or two central flowers with the pieces of truffle. Make an aspic. If you are making the mousse pictured here, mix 1 envelope of plain gelatin with the poaching liquid. Beat 1 egg white lightly until foamy and add to the mixture. Bring to a boil, stirring constantly to avoid scorching. As soon as the liquid boils—a crust will be forming on top of the liquid—turn off the heat. Let the mixture settle for 5 to 10 minutes. Strain through a sieve lined with a paper towel.

3. You should have about ¾ cup of aspic. Cool the aspic on top of ice, mixing with a spoon. As soon as the mixture becomes "oily," pour on top of the decorated mousse. If you are making another mousse or pâté, see the directions for aspic in technique 21.

4. Cool at least 2 hours in the refrigerator. Serve by scooping the mousse with a spoon. Serve with thin toast as a first course for an elegant dinner.

37. Tomato Rose and Other Vegetable Flowers *(Rose en Tomate et Autres Fleurs en Légumes)*

YOU DO NOT HAVE TO BE a professional to excel in decoration. The spectrum of color that you can choose from is enormous: truffles, black or green olives, tomatoes, scallions, leeks, carrots and so on. Only eatables should be used and they should be "tasteless." Raw orange or lemon peel on top of a mousse or a poached fish might impart some bitterness to the dish. Beets discolor after a while. You may or may not want the effect.

1. To make a tomato rose, start by cutting a "base" from a tomato. Do not sever from the tomato.

2. Continue cutting a narrow strip about ¾ inch wide, tapering it into a point. Use your knife in a jigsaw, up and down motion to give a natural edge to the petals of the flower. The strip should not be too thick.

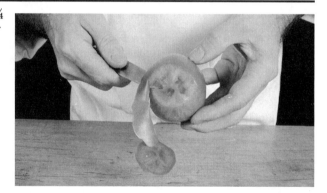

3. Cut another straight strip as long as the first one.

4. Curl the first strip of skin onto its base with the flesh side on the inside of the flower.

5. Roll the second strip into a tight scroll and

6. place it in the middle to make the heart of the rose.

7. To make stems and leaves, blanch the green part of a leek or scallion by plunging it into boiling water for about 30 seconds and cooling it immediately under cold water. The boiling water makes it greener and soft, and the cold water stops the cooking and keeps it green. Dry and lay the green flat, and, on the table, cut long strips following the grain of the leek. To make leaves, cut a wider strip with a pointed end.

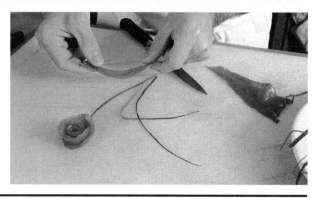

8. Cut lozenges of green and arrange around the stems to make small leaves. Use pieces of black from olives, the red of a tomato and

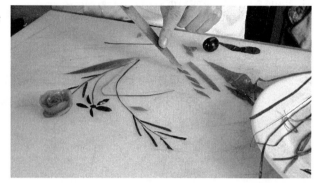

9. the yellow of a hard-boiled egg. Let your imagination help your fingers.

10. Create a nice bouquet to decorate a salad, a cold fish, a ham or a chicken.

38. Egg and Tomato Mushrooms
(Champignons en Tomate)

AN EASY AND EFFECTIVE WAY to decorate a cold dish, such as chicken or fish, is to garnish it with egg and tomato mushrooms.

1. Begin by cutting thick wedges from a nice, ripe tomato.

2. Squeeze the seeds out and "push" the flesh in to make a hollow cavity. Cut 1 hard-boiled egg diagonally, one piece bigger than the other. Place the tomato "caps" on top of the egg pieces.

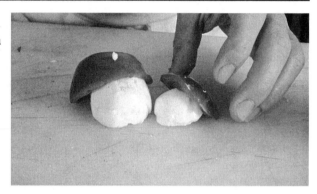

3. Fill up a paper cornet, technique 66. with soft butter or mayonnaise and decorate the top of the mushrooms with little dots so it resembles the cap of a speckled mushroom such as *amanita muscaria*.

39. Hard-Boiled Eggs Clown-Style
(Oeufs Durs en Clown)

YIELD: 6 servings

BEFORE YOU HARD-BOIL EGGS, make sure they are not cracked. Take two eggs and tap them gently close to your ear. The sound should be crystal clear. If one of the shells is slightly broken, even if the crack is invisible, it will sound cracked, and if placed in hot water this way, the egg white will seep out.

Place the eggs in a sieve and lower into boiling water or place the eggs in a saucepan and pour boiling water on top. Bring to a boil and simmer for about 10 minutes. Immediately run the eggs under cold water until cold. Crack the shells on the side of the sink and "roll" gently on a hard surface so the shell gets cracked all around. Peel under cold water so the water runs between the egg and the membrane (between the egg and the shell). If the eggs are not cooled immediately, the yolk becomes greenish and acidic.

This plain hard-boiled egg preparation is nice for children's parties, easy to prepare in advance and fun. It can be served with the peppery dressing we describe, or with a simple mayonnaise or oil and vinegar dressing.

Eggs

6 to 8 hard-boiled eggs
1 cucumber
1 slice boiled ham
A few black olives
1 tomato

Dressing

1 can (2 ounces) flat anchovy fillets with oil, cut into small pieces
2 tablespoons capers

1 hard-boiled egg, diced, and the trimmings of the other eggs
¾ cup finely diced boiled ham
⅓ cup coarsely chopped black olives, preferably the oiled, cured type
¾ cup olive oil, preferably virgin
About ⅓ cup lemon juice
¾ teaspoon salt
½ teaspoon freshly ground black pepper
⅓ cup diced red peppers

Combine all the dressing ingredients and arrange in a flat serving dish.

1. Trim the eggs on both sides.

2. Cut a "nose" in the middle of the egg by outlining a "triangle" and lifting it from the egg on one side. Make two little holes on each side of the nose for eyes, and place a piece of black olive in them.

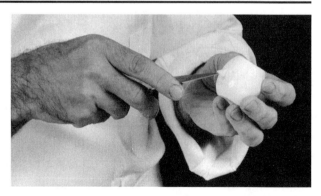

3. Make an opening to simulate the mouth and slide a piece of boiled ham in it, for the tongue. Cut the cucumber in thin slices and place on top to simulate the brim of a hat.

4. Slice a tomato in 6 to 8 ¼-inch slices. Place the tomato slices on top of the dressing as a base for the eggs. Top with the eggs and finish the hat with olive halves. Serve.

40. Mushroom Fish *(Champignon Sculpté en Poissons)*

1. Start with a large mushroom that's very firm and very white. Cut the top of the cap off the mushroom. The newly formed surface will become the background for the fish. Starting at the center of the mushroom, make 3 curved cuts at spaced intervals. These will be one side of the fish.

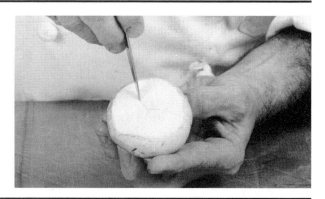

2. Then, starting at the edge of the mushroom, make 3 corresponding cuts to form 3 ovals. Each oval represents the body of a fish, minus the tail.

3. Pretending that the fish are interwoven, "draw" a tail at the end of each body.

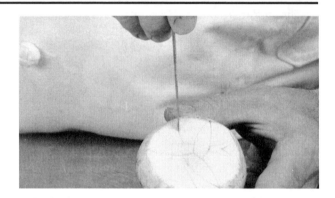

4. To set the fish in relief—to make them raised—you have to remove a thin layer (⅛ inch or less deep) of mushroom all around them. Slide your knife into the mushroom, in between each cut, and gently lift out the pieces of mushroom. Work slowly all around the mushroom until the fish are in relief.

5. If you want to make a more elaborate carving, cut a small triangle between each fish and remove the piece of mushroom. Within that triangle, cut another triangle and remove the piece of mushroom. Then, within the second triangle, make a third one and so forth, making a sort of triangular steps which form designs in all the free spaces around the fish.

6. With the point of a knife make the eyes, the gills and the scales, then trim the mushroom around.

7. Slice the decorated part off the cap, coat with lemon juice to keep it white or poach in a mixture of lemon juice and water for a few seconds, and use to garnish the top of a fish dish or a cold salad.

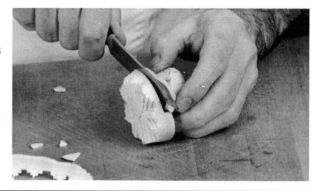

41. Fluted Mushrooms *(Champignons Tournés)*

To "TURN" OR FLUTE a mushroom means, in cooking vocabulary, to cut out strips from the cap of the mushroom in an elegant, spiral pattern. It is a difficult technique to master, and it may cost you a few hours of frustration before you get any results. You need a small, sharply pointed paring knife. Use firm, white, fresh mushroom caps. There are several methods or positions of the knife to turn mushrooms. Here is the method I use.

1. Hold the blade of the knife loosely in your fingers on a bias, cutting edge out. Place the side of your thumb behind the blade, on top of the mushroom.

2. Using your thumb as a pivot, push the blade forward and down in a smooth motion by twisting your wrist. The slanted cutting edge should carve a strip out of the mushroom cap. The rotation should be smooth and regular.

3. If the center is not perfectly formed, make a star by pushing with the point of the knife into the center of the cap. Separate the carved cap from the stem with the knife.

4. Making a relief from a mushroom cap is much easier than fluting. Slice off the crown of the mushroom. "Draw," in this case a little fish, with the point of your knife. Cut about ¼ inch deep into the flesh.

5. Cut the flesh around the outline so that the little fish comes out in relief. Mark the head, eyes and scales with the point of the knife.

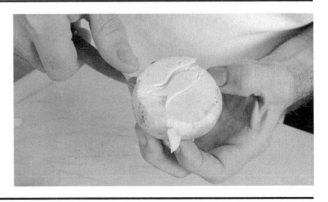

6. Trim the cap around the fish and

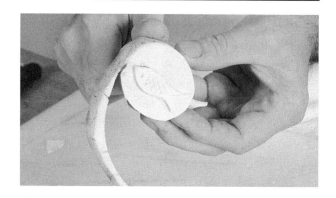

7. Slice underneath to make a nice "coin" shape with the relief on top.

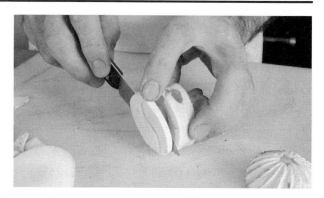

8. Different carved shapes. To stay white, the fluted and carved mushrooms should be cooked in water with a few drops of lemon juice, salt and butter. One minute of high boiling is sufficient to cook them. Mushrooms cooked in this manner are usually used to decorate fish dishes and cold dishes such as salads.

42. Cucumber Turtles *(Tortues en Concombre)*

CUCUMBER TURTLES ARE A FUN garnish for cold fish, cold salads, cold roasts, etc. Slice the cucumber lengthwise on both sides, discarding the center part with the seeds. Use only the fleshy part of the skin. Cut into chunks about 3 inches long.

1. With the point of a knife, start outlining a turtle on the green part of the cucumber.

2. Carve the turtle out; the head like a lozenge, the four legs and the small tail.

3. Mark the eyes on the head, score a criss-cross design on the back and carve out the toes. See finished Cucumber Turtles, page 102.

43. Vegetable Flowers *(Fleurs en Légumes)*

TO DRESS UP A BUFFET, there is nothing as colorful and festive as a bunch of flowers made of vegetables. They are fun to make and rewarding— follow the instructions below, but extend the idea and create on your own. Use your imagination since the possibilities of shape and color are practically endless. In the next technique we will show how to make vases to hold such flowers.

1. Peel a carrot. With this carrot, we will first make several flowers similar to a daisy. With the point of a knife, cut petals from the tip of the carrot. Cut into the carrot on an angle but don't cut through as you want the petals attached. Rotate the carrot as you carve so the tip of the carrot comes to a point as you cut. Be sure not to separate each petal.

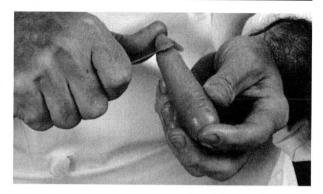

2. Rock the "flower" back and forth to gently separate it from the carrot in one piece.

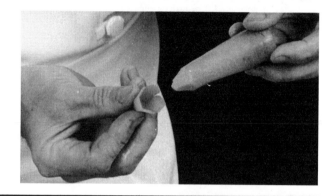

3. Place the flowers in a bowl of cold water to keep them crisp and bright until ready to use. Then finish with a little piece of black olive in the center of one flower, a caper in the center of another one and a piece of pimiento in the center of a third.

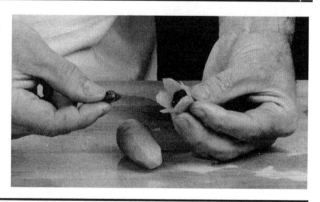

4. Proceed the same way with radishes. Choose oval radishes, if possible, and start cutting the petals.

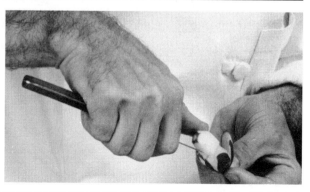

5. Place half a small olive upside down in the center of the radish. (A piece of red tomato or pimiento or green pepper can replace the olive for a different flower.)

6. Slice a piece of peeled carrot very thinly, without separating the slices. Turn the carrot so that all the slices are stacked one on top of the other. Cut into thin strips, which are still held by the core.

7. The carrot is now cut into thin strips held together at one end. Place in cold water overnight or for a few hours—the strips of carrot will curl and the "flower" will open up. Proceed as shown in the picture.

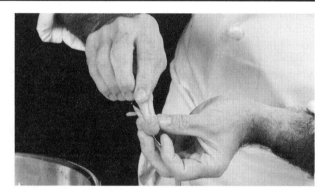

8. Peel a white onion but leave the root on. Start cutting it into slices held together by the root end.

9. Slice the onion across so all the slices are cut into strips held together by the root. Place in ice water.

10. On the right you have an onion that's completely cut and ready for immersion in ice water. On the left is an onion which has been soaked in ice water for a few hours.

11. Here is a variety of flowers made with radishes. The one being worked on is made the same way as the carrot and the onion in steps 7 to 9.

12. Taking an olive, green or black with the pit in it, insert your knife through the skin and cut around the pit to loosen. Remove the pit so you have a hollow receptacle.

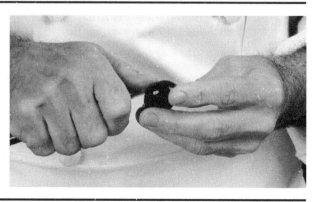

13. Cut the root of a scallion. Trim away the green. Insert your knife three quarters of the way down through the stem of the scallion and split it open. Turn it around. Keep pushing your knife through and pulling it up to split the scallion into fine strips.

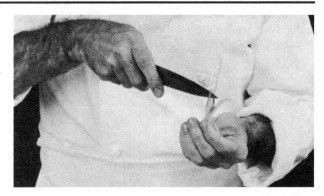

14. Scallions after having been crisped in ice water for a few hours.

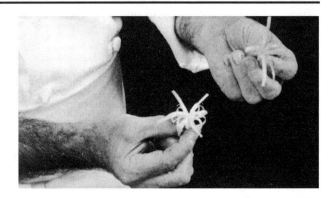

15. Place the crisped scallion into the cavity of an olive to make another flower.

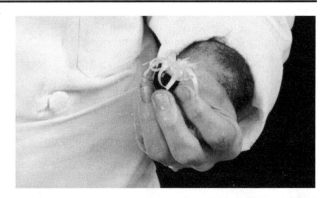

16. Slice a yellow turnip into very thin strips; roll a slice and fold it in half.

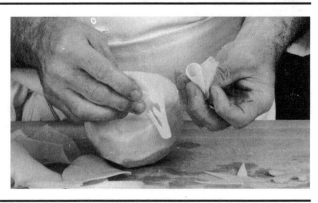

17. Hold the folded slice of turnip with a toothpick and insert a piece of feathered red pimiento, carrot or radish in the two holes. This forms another flower.

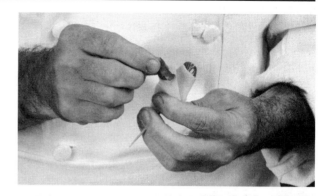

18. Using a vegetable peeler, make thin carrot slices. Stack them together and shred both ends.

19. Overlap several slices to form a large, shaggy, open flower. Stick half a radish, a piece of cherry tomato or a piece of olive in the center.

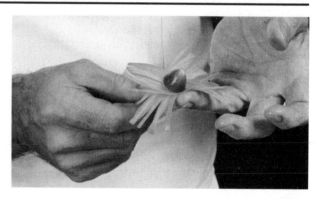

20. To form stems for your flowers, use thin pieces of wood such as long matches or pieces of wire cut from coat hangers. Use the green of scallions to shield and dress the wires. Insert the wire in the hollow of the scallion.

21. Once the wire is dressed, stick a cut radish on top or another flower. The green of the scallion should be longer than the metal stem so it can be turned under and around the bottom of the flower to form the chalice. Remember that these are only a few examples of the flowers that can be made with vegetables. Use your imagination to create new flowers—try working with lemon peel, pimiento, leeks, asparagus, etc. It is important that the flowers be kept in ice water for a few hours so they crisp into the right shape. See finished vegetable flowers, page 102.

44. Flower Vases with Squash

(Vases de Fleurs en Courges)

DIFFERENT TYPES OF VASES can be made from different kinds of squash. Simply hollow them out and decorate by feel. These hollowed squash can be used not just for vases, but to serve fruit salads in, vegetable salads, ice cream, etc. They can even be used as goblets to serve punch.

1. Cut out a duck from a piece of paper. Using the duck as a pattern, sketch its shape all the way around the squash with the point of a knife.

2. Cut out strips to outline the ducks. Carve out thin lines at the tail of the duck to simulate the feathers. Draw lines under the duck to imitate water. Cut a hat off the squash and outline a couple of lines to form a design near the opening. Hollow the squash and set it aside until ready to use (cover it lightly with plastic wrap and refrigerate it to prevent it from drying out).

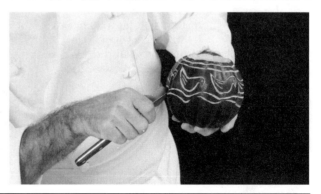

3. For another vase, use a butternut squash. Cut the cap off and with the point of your knife, outline long stems, flowers and leaves. Decorate all around the squash. Empty the squash if it is to be used as a receptacle. Leave the inside flesh if it is to be used as a vase.

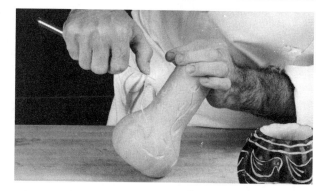

4. With another acorn squash, make a basket. Cut away one side. Now cut away the other side in the same manner to form a center handle.

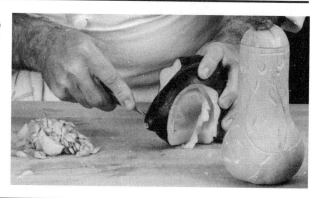

5. Using a spoon, remove the seeds from the inside of the squash. With a small, sharp knife, cut the flesh off the handle to make it very thin. Cut the flesh from the inside of the basket in the same manner so the squash is hollowed and thin all around.

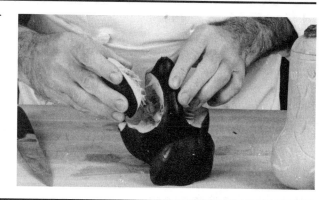

6. Cut away a decorative strip next to the edge of the basket to outline it. You can leave it plain or continue decorating. See finished flower vases with squash, following page.

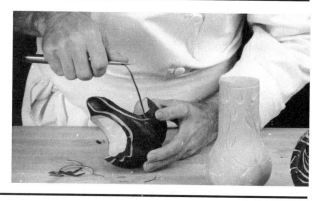

Vegetable flowers, flower vases with squash, apple swans, cucumber turtles

45. Olive Rabbits *(Lapins en Olive)*

A N AMUSING WAY TO TRANSFORM OLIVES into a decoration is to make little rabbits out of them. Choose extra large black or green olives with the pits in.

1. Cut a slice lengthwise from one side of the olive. Carve a small triangle from the slice.

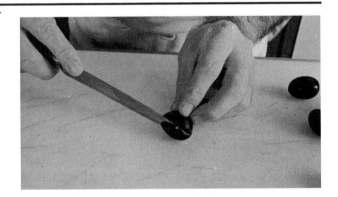

2. Place the olive cut side down. With a small knife, make an incision halfway down, close to the pointed side of the olive.

3. Twist the blade to open the cut. Insert the slice so that the pointed ears stand in the air.

4. Three little rabbits.

46. Apple Swans *(Cygnes en Pommes)*

APPLE SWANS ARE EASY to make and lovely to decorate a buffet, or a cold aspic dish or simply as a centerpiece, by arranging several of them in the center of a table.

1. Take a large apple (Greening, Red Delicious, etc.) and cut about a ½-inch slice off one side of the apple.

2. Place the slice flat side down and, using a small pointed knife, "draw" a head and neck in one piece the full length of the apple slice. Carve it out and set it aside.

3. The head piece can be done in a multitude of ways, with the head looking down or up. Use your imagination and try to make the most out of the shape and thickness of the apple slice.

4. With the point of a knife, "drill" a small hole on one side of the apple to hold the neck in place. Insert the neck and adjust until the neck fits snugly. Then set the neck aside, so it does not get in the way while you work on the wings and tail.

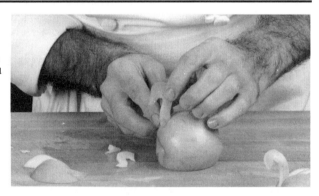

5. On one side of the apple cut wedges by first holding the knife vertically and slicing down and then holding it horizontally and slicing across.

6. You should remove approximately 5 wedges for each wing, keeping them as thin as possible (as the wedges get larger they become more difficult to cut out). Repeat the same procedure on the other side of the apple to make the other wing.

7. After the two sides have been carved for the wings, cut the back of the "swan" to make the tail. Four wedges are enough for the tail.

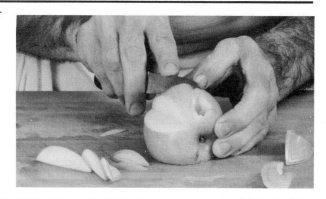

8. Now that all the cutting is done, the wedges are put back together to simulate the tail and the wings. Stagger the wedges at spaced intervals so it fans out. You will notice that the wedges stick to one another nicely.

9. Repeat the process with both wings and place the head on the swan. Sprinkle the whole apple with lemon juice to keep it from discoloring.

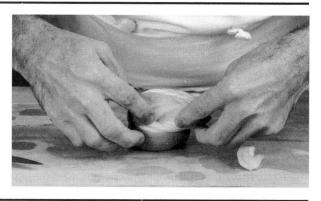

10. The "swans" are delicate and make an elegant decoration. Alternate green, yellow and red apples. See finished apple swans, page 102.

47. Cutting Citrus Fruits
(Quartiers et Tranches d'Oranges ou de Pamplemousses)

SECTIONS

1. Taking an orange as an example (always use seedless), hold the fruit flat in one hand. With a thin, sharp paring knife, cut a slice from the top to expose the flesh. Remove the skin in a strip, cutting deep enough to go right down to the flesh.

2. When the orange is "nude," remove each section by cutting with the knife right down to the core, as close to the membrane as you can. Arrange the sections as you go along.

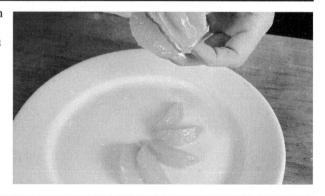

3. Squeeze the membrane over the orange sections to extract all remaining juices.

SLICES

1. Cut the top of the orange to expose the flesh. Place the cut top upside down at the other end of the orange and secure with a fork. This becomes a guard, preventing the knife from sliding and cutting your fingers.

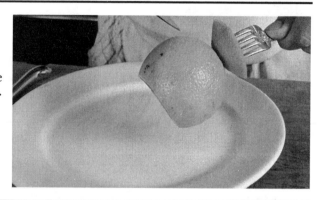

2. Cut the skin down to the flesh in strips, turning the orange as you go along.

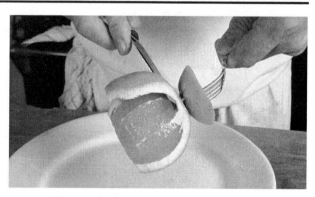

3. Place the peeled orange on the plate and cut into slices. Arrange the slices in a pattern as you go along. This method is principally used in the dining room.

48. Orange Baskets *(Paniers d'Oranges)*

ORANGE BASKETS MAKE a delightful garnish for compatible cold dishes, or for classic dishes such as duck *à l'Orange*. Baskets can be made with whole large navel oranges, or with halves. For large baskets, it is essential to have a stripper to strip the peel off the orange.

WHOLE ORANGE BASKET

1. Cut a thin slice off the blossom end to make a flat sitting surface. Using a stripper, start at the top and cut strips all around the orange, almost down to the flat surface. The strips should fly free, remaining attached to the orange.

2. Cut away wedges on both sides so you are left with a "handle" in the middle of the basket.

3. Carefully cut away the flesh from the handle.

4. Fold the strips over and onto themselves to make loops all around the orange. Fill the area underneath the handle with watercress or parsley to simulate a basket.

HALF ORANGE BASKET

1. Cut a thin slice off both ends of the orange to make a flat sitting surface. Using a round object as a guide, outline half-moons with a knife all around the orange. Cut with a knife, following the outline. Be sure to penetrate deep enough to the center of the orange. Pull apart and you will have two different orange baskets.

2. Cut a strip of skin just below and following the outline of the curve. Empty by scraping the inside of the basket with a spoon.

3. Fill up with orange sections, technique 47.

49. Orange Rind *(Pelures d'Oranges)*

Tʜᴇ ᴛʜɪɴ ᴏᴜᴛᴇʀ ʟᴀʏᴇʀ of the orange skin contains most of the fruit's essential oil and flavor and is very potent in cold Grand Marnier soufflés, orange butter creams, orange *génoise* and the like.

When a recipe calls for grated orange or lemon rind, be sure to grate only the bright orange or yellow part of the skin. The white part underneath is bitter and should not be used. Remove the grated rind from the grater by banging the grater on the table or use a dry brush to pry out the rind.

50. Orange Peel Julienne *(Julienne de peau d'Oranges)*

Aɴʏ ᴠᴇɢᴇᴛᴀʙʟᴇ, ᴍᴇᴀᴛ ᴏʀ ꜰʀᴜɪᴛ cut into thin, strawlike strips is called a julienne. The julienne of lemon or orange peel decorates dishes such as duck *à l'Orange* and galantine. The peel can also be cooked in sugar and the candied strips used in cakes, cold soufflés or as a garnish for fruit desserts.

1. Use a vegetable peeler to remove only the orange part of the rind. The white skin between the peel and the flesh is bitter.

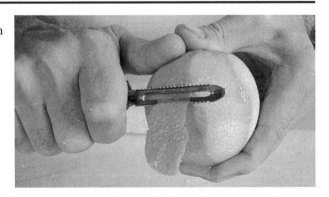

2. Stack a few peels together; fold the stack in half and cut into very thin strips. Whether used as a garnish or candied, the julienne should be blanched at least twice to remove the bitterness. Plunge the julienne in boiling water. Return to a boil and let cook for 1 to 2 minutes. Pour into a strainer and rinse under cold water. Repeat this process once more. Keep in cold water until ready to use.

51. Lemon *(Citron)*

THERE ARE INNUMERABLE WAYS of cutting a lemon, from the simple lemon wedge or slice to one of the more sophisticated ways shown below. Lemon is served with fish, shellfish, oysters, meat (veal or chicken), vegetables (such as asparagus, string beans), dessert (fruit salad), yogurt and cheese to name a few. Hence, it is well worthwhile to vary its preparation.

LEMON PIG

1. Choose a lemon with a nice pointed "nose." With the point of a knife, make one hole on each side of the nose and fill it with a black peppercorn or a piece of parsley or olive.

2. Cut a little wedge in the middle of the nose without separating the piece from the lemon to imitate the tongue. Cut both "ears" on each side of the lemon. Curl up a little piece of parsley to imitate the tail and place toothpicks underneath for the legs.

OTHER DECORATIONS

1. Cut a thin slice off both ends of the lemon to make a flat sitting surface. Cut the lemon into halves. Cut two strips of peel of equal size from the sharp edge of the half lemon.

2. Fold each strip around and make a knot to secure. Be careful not to break the strips.

3. Alternatively, cut one long strip of peel from the edge of the half lemon and make a knot with a loop. Place a piece of parsley in the loop.

4. For another treatment, cut both ends of the lemon. With a sharp-pointed paring knife (stainless steel is better with lemon), cut "lion teeth" all around the lemon. Cut deep enough to go to the core of the lemon.

5. For a slightly different look, repeat the same technique as described in step 4, but cut the teeth on a bias.

6. Decorate the different lemons with curly parsley.

LEMON SLICES FOR FISH

1. Trim the lemon, removing the yellow and most of the white skin underneath. Slice into ¼-inch slices, removing the seeds as you go along.

2. Fold each slice and dip into chopped parsley. By folding the slice, only the center gets covered with parsley. You can cover whole slices, half slices, and so on to vary your decoration. For an example, see technique 99, step 10.

52. Carving Watermelon
(Décoration d'une Pastéque)

A SIMPLE DESSERT, such as fruit salad, can become glorious when served in a carved watermelon. Choose a watermelon as dark green as possible and without too many variations of color so that the markings stand out.

METHOD 1

1. Fold a piece of wax paper in half.

2. Fold it in half again and cut with scissors to make a pattern for the handle of the basket.

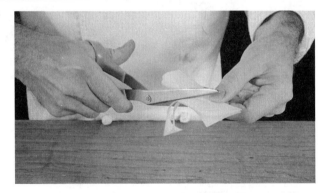

3. Pattern for the handle of the basket.

4. Place the pattern on top of the watermelon and outline it with the point of a knife. Sketch the shape of a lid on both sides of the handle with the knife.

5. Cut a decorative strip under the outline of each lid.

6. Remove the strip to expose the flesh of the melon.

7. Carve little petals with the point of a sharp paring knife.

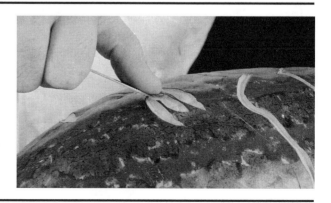

8. Cut out stems for flowers and leaves on the top and all around the melon.

9. Carve a butterfly, or any other object you fancy, on top of the lid. Following the outline of the lid, cut through the top of the melon with the paring knife.

10. Remove both lids and clean the insides with a spoon and a small knife.

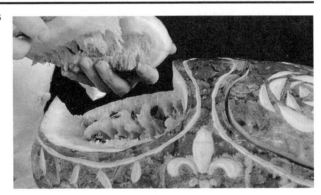

11. Cut the flesh away from the skin all around.

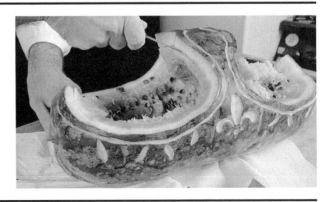

12. With a spoon, scoop the flesh out and pour into a bowl.

13. Replace the carved lids on top of the melon.

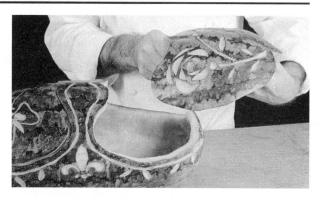

14. Watermelon ready to be filled with fruit salad.

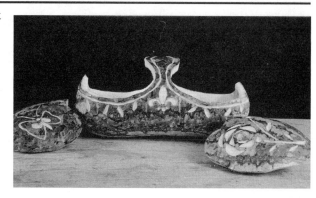

METHOD 2

1. Trim the melon on both ends. Trace waves around the melon using a glass or a small bowl as a guide.

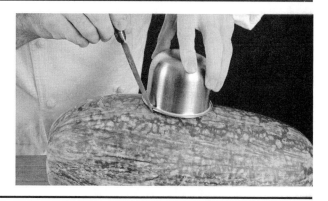

2. Following the contour, separate the melon into halves. Carve a freehand decoration around the melon. You can use small objects (round, square, triangular) as guides to outline a geometric design. Once the pattern is outlined, cut out strips of skin to delineate the design.

3. Scoop out the inside flesh. You may use some of it in the fruit salad.

4. Carved and uncarved halves of melon. Once the melon is carved, cover well with plastic wrap to keep the sculpture relief fresh and vivid looking. It will keep at least one week in the refrigerator. When you are ready to use your masterpiece, empty the melon of any liquid and fill up with fruit salad, using different colored fruits to give an artistic effect. It may also be used to serve a cold punch or ice cream.

53. How to Prepare Marrow *(Préparation de la Moëlle)*

B EEF MARROW IS OFTEN USED in French cooking. It is removed from the bone, poached and served on toast or served with a sauce, as we will here. It is sometimes used in place of butter in dumplings or quenelles. When the marrow is removed from the bone it is reddish and bloody. It should be placed in cold water in the refrigerator for at least a day and the water should be changed a couple of times to get rid of the bloody part of the marrow and make it white and firm. If the marrow is not soaked in water it will turn dark during cooking instead of being white.

1. Order a large marrow bone from your butcher and have it cut with a saw above or under the knuckles so as to have just the part in between, where most of the marrow lies. Use a hammer to break the bone. Be sure to do it on a butcher block or other heavy sturdy surface or else the vibration will cause the hammer to bounce.

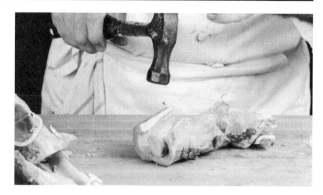

2. When the bone is broken open, use a small knife to remove the marrow, keeping the pieces as large as possible. Be careful not to cut yourself on the the very sharp pieces of bone. Place the marrow under cold water for about an hour, then in a bowl in water in the refrigerator, if possible over-night.

3. Slice the marrow in approximately ⅜-inch-thick pieces. Bring a pot of salted water to a boil and drop the marrow in it. Reduce the heat and simmer very gently for 4 to 5 minutes until the marrow becomes opaque, which indicates that it has been cooked throughout.

4. Using a slotted spoon, remove the pieces of marrow from the pot (they will be float-ing on top), and place in warm, cooked, artichoke bottoms.

5. Cover the artichokes and the marrow with the red wine sauce made from the recipe at the top of page 36.

54. Cornucopia Molds *(Cornets)*

Cornets are pastries, ham or salmon slices, or other foods shaped in the form of a horn. A tinned cornucopia mold is used to shape the food. The cornets can be stuffed with a variety of fillings. The stuffed cornets can be served on a *macédoine de légumes,* a vegetable salad, the recipe for which appears below.

HAM CORNETS *(Cornets de Jambon)*

1. Roll a square slice of ham so that one end is pointed. (Roll as you would a paper cornet, technique 66.)

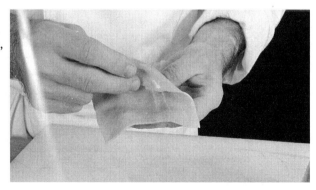

2. Slip into a cornucopia mold. Prepare your favorite stuffing or the one that follows. For 4 horns: 1½ tablespoons butter; ¾ cup chopped, cooked spinach; 1 hard-boiled egg, coarsely chopped; ⅓ cup chopped ham; salt, pepper and nutmeg. Melt the butter in a skillet until black and foaming. Add the spinach and cook, stirring for 1 minute. Remove from heat and add remaining ingredients. Let cool.

3. When cool, stuff the mixture into the ham cornet.

4. Trim the ham at the level of the stuffing.

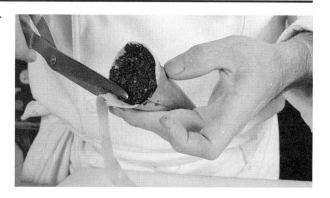

5. Remove from the mold; the cornet should slide out easily. Trim the ham for a neat, pointed cornucopia.

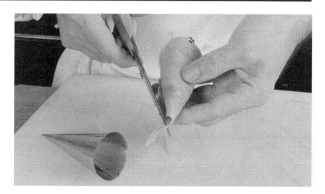

SALMON CORNETS (*Cornets de Saumon*)

1. Using slices of smoked salmon or *gravlax,* technique 87, twist the slices and fit them into the mold.

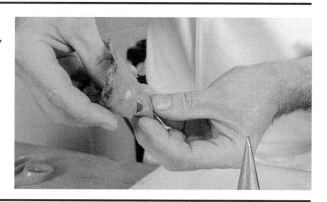

2. You may have to overlap slices to have the mold well lined. Stuff with a mixture of finely chopped hard-boiled eggs mixed with soft butter or mayonnaise and seasoned with salt and pepper.

VEGETABLE SALAD
(Macédoine de Légumes)

½ cup cooked peas
½ cup diced cooked carrots (¼-inch cubes)
2 cups diced cooked potatoes (½-inch cubes)
3 tablespoons finely chopped onion
¾ cup mayonnaise (preferably freshly made,
    technique 23)
½ tablespoon wine vinegar
Salt and pepper to taste

Mix together all the ingredients and arrange on a platter with the ham or salmon cornets on top and a tomato rose, technique 37. in the middle.

This recipe yields about 4 cups of *macédoine*.

DESSERT CORNETS *(Cornets à la Crème)*

1. Dessert cornets are shaped on the outside of the mold. Cut strips of puff paste, technique 269, ⅛ inch thick by about 1 inch wide and 18 inches long. Wet the strips with cold water on one side.

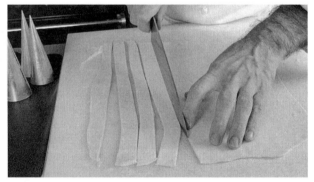

2. Squeeze the dough at the tip of the mold to secure it.

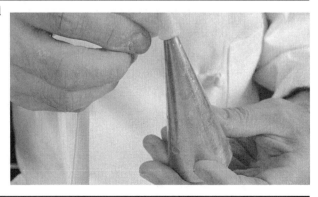

3. Wrap the strip around the mold, overlapping slightly, the wet side of the dough touching the mold.

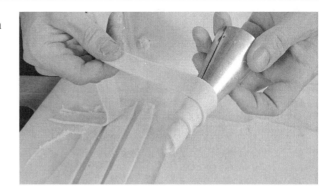

4. Trim the extra dough on the edge of the base of the mold. Holding the horn with your fingers inside, brush beaten egg over the dough.

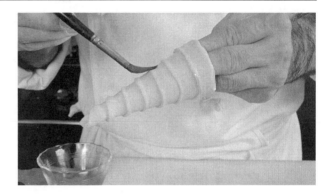

5. Place standing up on a cookie sheet and bake in a 400-degree preheated oven for 15 to 18 minutes. Let cool slightly before unmolding. You may have to run a knife between the dough and the mold to get the pastry loose, making it easier to slide off. Fill with sweetened whipped cream. See finished cornets below.

Clockwise from the top: dessert cornets, eggs in aspic, ham and salmon cornets.

55. Round, Square and Heart-Shaped Croutons *(Croûtons Ronds, Carrés et en Coeur)*

When bread is cut into a variety of shapes and fried, it is called a crouton. Round croutons are used as a base for filet, steak, poached egss and other dishes.

Small croutons cubes are used as a garnish for hot and cold soups and in stuffings and meat loaf. They may be fried or toasted in the oven. Heart-shaped croutons are served as a decorative garnish for coq au vin, puree of spinach and beef or veal stews. Trimmings are used to make bread crumbs.

1. Cut slices approximately ¾ inch thick.

2. For round croutons, use a glass or round crouton cutter to cut out circles. Fry in a saucepan in a mixture of butter and oil.

3. For square croutons, stack 2 or 3 slices of bread together and trim the edges. Cut into strips.

4. Cut the strips across to make cubes. Fry in butter and oil or dry in the oven.

5. For heart-shaped croutons, cut slices of bread into halves diagonally.

6. Trim each half to obtain a more pointed triangle.

7. Trim each piece into the shape of a heart.

8. Fry in a mixture of butter and oil. Dip the tip of each crouton in the sauce of the dish it is to be served with and then into a small bowl of chopped parsley. The parsley, which adheres to the bread because of the wet tip, forms a decorative point.

56. Bread Baskets *(Croûte en Pain de Mie)*

T HE CROÛTE IS USED as a receptacle. It is usually fried in oil and butter and filled with chicken hash, a poached egg and a sauce, or even with a small roasted bird such as quail or woodcock.

1. Cut a slice about 1½ to 2 inches thick.

2. Trim and, using the point of a small knife, cut halfway down the outline of the inside.

3. Cut pieces and scrape to hollow the *croûte*. Deep fry in oil, drain and spoon in a filling of your choice.

57. Melba Toast *(Toasts Melba)*

E SCOFFIER CREATED this super-thin toast for the cantatrice Melba. Though melba toast can be bought ready-made, you should try the real McCoy; it is easy to make and quite good.

1. Toast regular slices of bread under the broiler. Trim on 4 sides.

2. Keeping the slice flat, and using a thin knife, cut through the soft middle to split the slice into halves. It is relatively easy because both sides are crusty and will separate easily.

3. Place the slice, soft side up, under the broiler until dry and brown.

4. Slice the thin toast into halves.

58. Bread Socle (Socle en Pain)

T HE SOCLE IS USED PRINCIPALLY in classic cuisine as a stand for many garnishes, and as a decorative component around a dish.

1. Cut a thick piece from a loaf of bread and, using a long knife, cut off the crust.

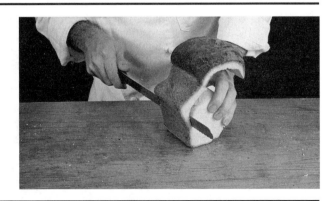

2. Carve the central cylinder according to your own fancy. It is fried in oil before being used. The socle as a decorative piece is not eaten.

3. In back, from left to right: diced croutons, *croûte,* socle, round croutons and heart-shaped croutons. In the front, melba toast.

59. Canapés

CANAPÉS ARE SMALL APPETIZERS made from plain and toasted bread, spread or covered with meat, cheese, caviar, anchovies and the like. They can be shaped and varied almost indefinitely, according to your own taste.

1. Make an incision straight down, close to the crust, on one side of a loaf of bread. This becomes a "guard" to protect your hands from the knife.

2. Cut wide slices about ⅓ inch thick.

3. You can use plain white bread as it is or you can toast it. Egg salad, tomato and the like, being moist, are better off on toast than on fresh bread which has a tendency to become soggy. Spread a thin layer of butter on the slices.

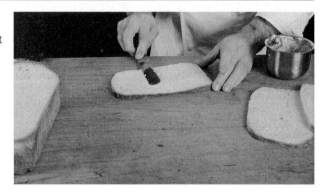

4. Cover the slices with ham, salami, prosciutto and so on.

5. To make lozenges, trim the slice all around and cut in half lengthwise.

6. Position the two strips side by side but stagger them slightly.

7. Cut into lozenges.

8. Cover another slice of buttered bread with smoked salmon, trim all around and cut into neat triangles. Cut square pieces of toasted and buttered bread and cover with caviar.

9. Fill a paper cornet with soft butter, technique 66. Cut a straight opening and pipe out a "G clef" on each of the salmon canapés. Decorate the prosciutto canapés with another butter design.

10. Cut the tip of the cornet on both sides to make open pointed lips, technique 66, steps 12 and 13. Pipe out small leaves or petals, three per canapé.

11. With the point of a knife, deposit a little dash of red paprika in the middle to simulate the pistil of the flower.

12. Arrange your canapés attractively on a platter and decorate with small pieces of curly parsley.

60. Folding in Ingredients
(Incorporation á la Spatule)

MANY RECIPES, primarily baking recipes, call for folding. The goal is to incorporate something delicate, usually whipped egg whites or cream, into a thicker mixture while retaining the fluffiness and airy quality in the mixture.

1. Use a wooden or rubber spatula, or even a metal one, and slide it flat on top of the mixture.

2. Then, cutting side down, go through the mixture and straighten out the spatula underneath it.

3. Twist the spatula again to come out on the top cutting side up. While you perform the whole circle with one hand, spin the bowl toward you with the other hand. The motions should be simultaneous. Do not overfold.

61. Coating a Cookie Sheet
(Plaque Beurrée et Farinée)

THERE ARE COUNTLESS RECIPES asking the cook to coat a cookie sheet, a soufflé mold, a tin cake pan and so on. The reason is primarily to avoid sticking and also to give whatever is cooking a nice golden crust and a buttery taste. In the case of a soufflé, it is even more important; it helps the soufflé slide up during cooking. There are basically three ways to coat a dish. Butter is first rubbed on the surface of the dish; then sugar is added for a sweet dessert, cheese for a cheese soufflé or flour for an all-purpose coating.

1. Rub soft butter all over the cookie sheet.

2. Add flour to the sheet and shake it thoroughly in all directions so that all the butter is coated with the flour. Pour the flour onto the second pan and repeat the operation. Give a bang to the back of the cookie sheet to get rid of any excess flour. The coating should be light and uniform.

62. Pastry Bag and Tube *(Poche et Douille)*

WHEN A COOK WANTS TO GIVE a professional look to his desserts, he uses a pastry bag. It simplifies the work and makes the decoration faster, cleaner and more uniform. Buy a plastic-lined pastry bag which is easy to use and to wash. A 14- or 16-inch bag is the all-purpose size most commonly used. Buy your pastry bag with a narrow opening at the point. If it is too small for your tube, you can always cut a piece off the tip to enlarge the opening.

1. Place the fluted or plain tube in the bag and push it so that it fits snugly and some of it shows through the opening.

2. If your batter is soft enough to fall through the opening by itself, it is a good idea to twist the bag above the tube

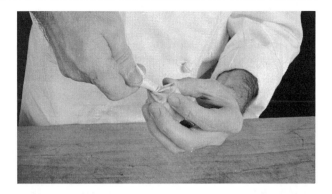

3. and push it inside the tube. This prevents the batter from leaking through.

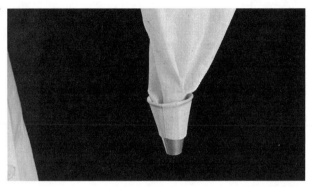

4. Fold the top of the bag approximately 2½ to 3½ inches down on the outside to avoid smearing the sides when filling the bag.

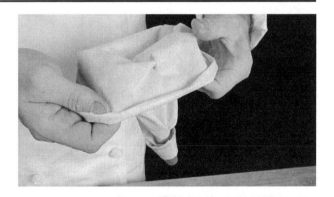

5. Place one hand under the fold to hold the bag and spoon some of the mixture into the bag, "squeezing" the mixture from the spoon with the hand under the fold. Do not fill the bag more than halfway.

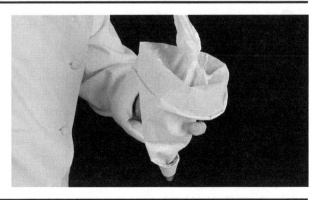

6. Unfold the pastry bag and fold the top in an orderly fashion.

7. Twist the top of the bag and "pull" it through the opening between your thumb and forefinger until your hand is against the mixture. The thumb and forefinger position is important and should keep the top of the bag tightly closed. If you open your fingers while pressing the mixture out, it will come up instead of going down through the tube.

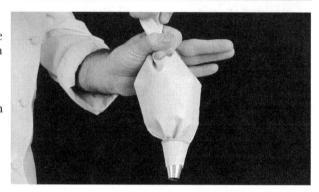

8. Pull the tip of the tube down and use your bag, "squishing" the mixture out by pressing with the palm of one hand and the tips of the fingers. The other hand can be used to control the direction of the bag if you are decorating, or to hold the cornet or other item being filled.

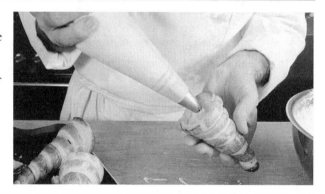

63. Lining Cake Pans (Garniture en Papier)

BEFORE BAKING PARCHMENT and wax paper were so widely available, cooks used brown wrapping paper to line cake pans. This served the purpose, but the modern papers which come on rolls are easier to work with. Not all cakes call for lined pans, but when they do, they are essential if the cake is to drop out of its cake pan intact.

ROUND CAKE

1. Cut a square piece of wax paper as wide as the diameter of the pan used, and fold in half. Fold the obtained rectangle in half to get a square. Fold the square diagonally, with the uncut corner as the point of the triangle. Fold the triangle onto itself in the same manner several times to obtain a thin, long triangle.

2. For a *savarin* mold, place the thin triangle point at the center of the mold and cut it off at the interior edge of the mold.

3. Cut it off at the other edge and

4. unroll. It should fit exactly.

5. For a round cake pan, fold the paper in the same manner as in step 1, measuring the radius of the pan and centering the point of the triangle at the center of the pan.

RECTANGULAR CAKE

1. Fold a long piece of wax paper in half the long way.

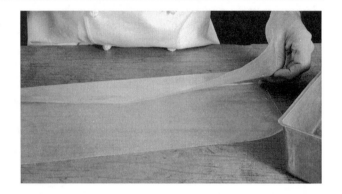

2. Turn the cake pan upside down. Place the folded paper so that the fold is at the center of the pan.

3. Crimp the paper on the lengthwise edge of the pan and

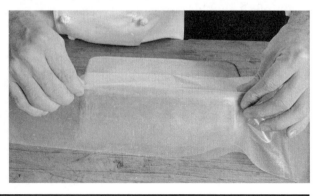

4. then at both ends to score the size of the cake.

5. With a pair of scissors, cut the paper on both sides of the pan extending the fold shown in step 3.

6. Paper cut and ready to be folded.

7. Bring the end and outside cut behind the center strip of paper on both sides.

8. The lining should fit perfectly in your cake pan.

64. Paper Casing *(Cuisson en Papillote)*

WHEN YOU SEE "PAPILLOTE" on a menu in a French restaurant, you can safely assume that it describes a dish served in an envelope of parchment paper, usually a veal chop or a filleted or whole fish. The paper is cut in the shape of a heart. The meat or fish is partially pre-cooked, then placed in the center and baked in the oven. When the papillote is folded correctly (it is sealed so that none of the aroma and steam can escape) it browns nicely, inflates, and the dish inside bakes in its own juices. The papillote is served directly on the serving plate and the guest opens it himself.

1. To cook en papillote, start by cutting a large rectangular piece of parchment paper. (In the olden times, cooks used brown paper bags.) Fold the rectangle in half.

2. Using scissors or a knife, start cutting from the folded side, following an imaginary line that resembles a question mark.

3. Open the heart shape and place the food on the bottom. The food should be partially cooked and all seasonings and flavorings added. Fold the top paper over the food.

4. Starting at the fold, fold the edge, overlapping the fold as you go along.

5. Fold the tip of the papillote several times to secure the closing.

6. Papillote ready to bake.

65. Paper Frill *(Papillote)*

IN ADDITION TO THE PAPER RECEPTACLE described in the preceding technique, the word papillote describes a frill—a delicate paper lace rolled into a "hat" and used to adorn the bone of a lamb chop or a ham. Its raison d'être is strictly aesthetic. A papillote is also a Christmas bonbon rolled in a piece of paper decorated with a drawing and a motto, then wrapped in colorful paper with frills at both ends. Another papillote, neither aesthetic nor edible, is a little piece of paper used by women to set their hair.

1. Cut a long rectangle of parchment or wax paper approximately 25 inches long by 5 inches wide. Fold lengthwise twice. Open the last fold. You now have a rectangle folded in half and scored down the center by the second fold. Using scissors, cut strips ¼ inch apart down the length of the paper. (Cut through the folded side to the score line.)

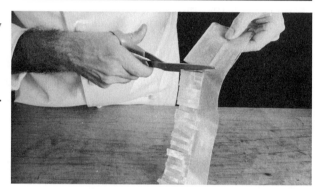

2. Open the rectangle completely and fold in half inside out to give the frills a nice roundness.

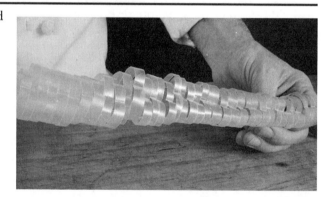

3. Secure with staples or plastic tape.

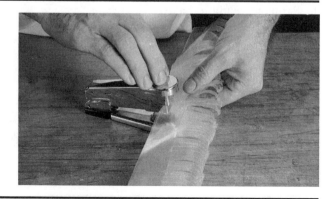

4. Roll the frill on your finger, or on a pencil if you are making small frills for lamb chops.

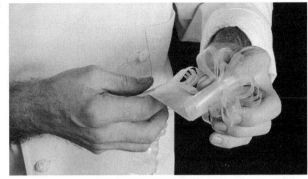

5. Secure the bottom part with a paper clip or a piece of tape.

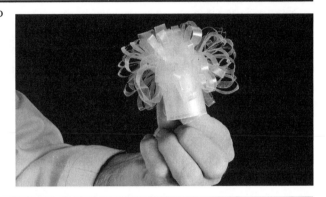

66. Paper Cone *(Cornet en Papier)*

A PAPER CONE OR HORN is an invaluable tool for fine and elegant piping. It gives a real professional touch to your decoration. Making cornets is not an easy technique to acquire, but it is well worth spending the time to master. They should be made with parchment, sulfurized paper or the best quality wax paper you can find.

1. Cut a triangle of strong paper with a pair of scissors.

2. Grab both ends with your thumbs and forefingers and twist onto itself to make a cone. Do not worry if the cone is not very pointed.

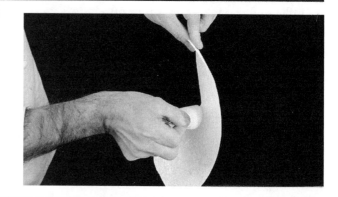

3. Holding the cone at the seam with both hands (thumbs inside and forefingers outside the cone), move the thumbs down and the fingers up to bring up and tighten the cornet making it needle sharp.

4. Hold the cone tight so that the paper does not unroll.

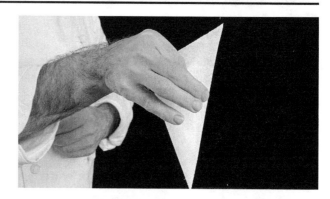

5. Fold the ends inside the cone to secure it and avoid uncoiling.

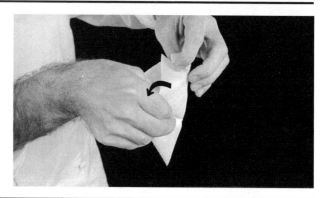

6. The cone is ready to be filled.

7. Place some filling in the cone, being careful not to soil the edges. Do not fill up more than ⅓ full.

8. Flatten the cone above the filling and fold one side.

9. Fold the other side.

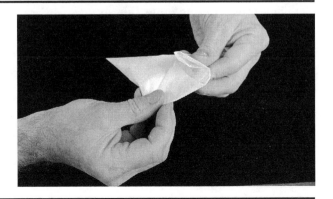

10. Then fold the center onto itself twice to secure the filling inside.

11. For a plain line, cut off the tip of the cone with a pair of scissors. The smaller the opening, the finer the decoration.

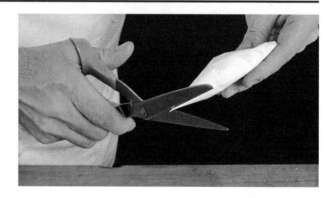

12. To make leaves, cut off a larger piece of the tip on a slant.

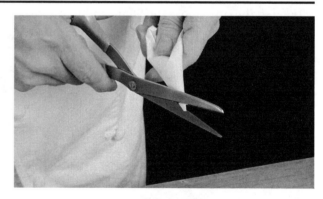

13. Then repeat on the other side so that the tip is open on two sides. For more about leaves, see technique 228, step 9.

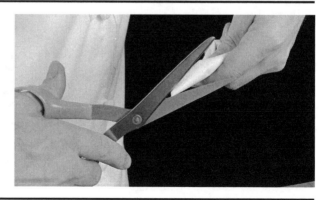

67. Collar for Soufflé *(Faux Col pour Soufflé)*

WHEN SERVED A FROZEN SOUFFLÉ, you may have wondered how it rose to such magnificent heights, sometimes 2 to 3 inches above the mold, without having been baked. It is very simple. Frozen soufflés are, of course, nothing more than whipped cream, a liqueur, egg yolks and sugar mixed together and then frozen. The "rising" of the soufflé is accomplished by the simple device of tying strong parchment paper around the mold and filling the mold up to the "collar." Collars are also used for hot soufflés to keep them from splitting and falling out during baking.

1. Cut a wide piece of strong baking parchment long enough to go completely around the mold and overlap slightly. Then fold the paper two or three times, depending on the width of the paper and on how high you want your soufflé to rise above the mold.

2. Apply your strip of paper to the outside of the mold, pulling the paper together securely and tightly so that the soufflé mixture cannot run down between the paper and the mold.

3. Secure the paper collar with a piece of string, tying it very tightly. For a frozen soufflé, fill the mold up only to the top edge. Place both the filled mold and the remaining mixture in the freezer for 15 minutes. By that time the surplus mixture will have become firmer and will not run. Add the mixture to the mold, filling the collar. Smooth the top surface. Return to the freezer and freeze until firm. At serving time, sprinkle some cocoa over the top to simulate browning in the oven. And don't forget to remove the paper!

68. Folding Napkins *(Pliage des Serviettes)*

THERE ARE AN INFINITE NUMBER of ways to fold napkins, whether they are used as a liner for food, or placed next to the dinner plate for a guest. The napkins should be large, square, of good quality linen, ironed, and possibly lightly starched. When the napkins are used as liners in the kitchen or dining room, technique 69, they can be folded very fancifully. Next to my plate, I like a napkin which has not been "handled" too much. It is fine simply folded in half or quarters.

1. Using a napkin already folded into a square, fold the opened corner three-quarters of the way up toward the pointed side.

2. Grab the opposite corners with both hands and fold underneath. The napkin can be used just the way it is.

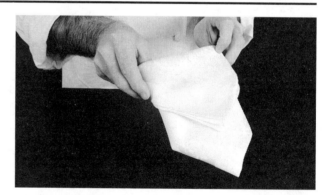

3. Or the opened corners can be folded back onto themselves.

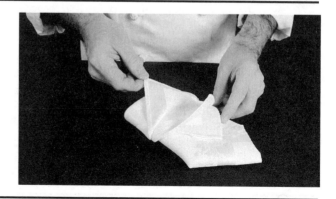

69. Flower, Artichoke and Gondola Napkins *(Serviettes en Tulipe, Artichaut et Gondole)*

FLOWER

1. This is the most commonly used napkin in food presentation. Start with a napkin that is perfectly square. Bring both corners of the same side toward the center.

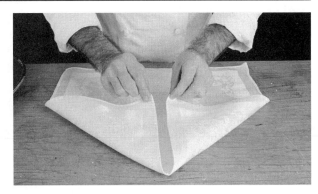

2. Then bring the two opposite corners to the center.

3. Holding the four corners in place, turn the napkin on the other side. Repeat the above operation by bringing the four corners toward the center.

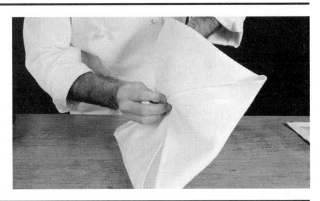

4. Turn the napkin on the other side and "unfold" the four centered corners onto themselves.

5. Folded napkin ready to use. Be sure to hold one hand underneath when transferring the napkin to a platter, or it will unfold.

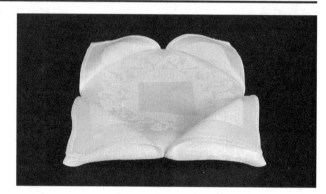

6. To make an eight-petaled flower, fold another napkin in the same manner, but give it one more turn and place it on top of the first one.

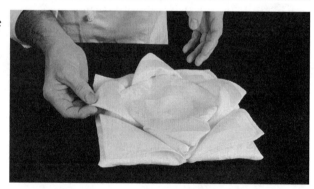

ARTICHOKE

1. To make a napkin into an artichoke, place a square piece of foil in the center of the opened square napkin. Bring the four corners toward the center.

2. Bring the four new corners toward the center.

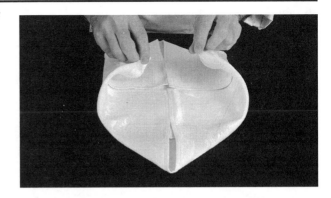

3. Repeat once more without turning the napkin (a total of three times).

4. Turn the napkin on the other side and fold the four corners toward the center.

5. Holding the four corners on the center, turn the napkin over a tall glass and press the napkin on the glass to round it slightly.

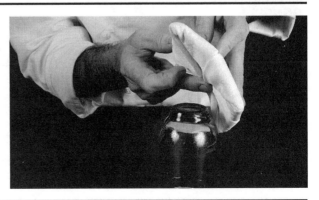

6. Pull the pointed pieces out, as if you were pulling off leaves of an artichoke.

7. Keep pulling the leaves until the last layer, where the aluminum foil is, is exposed.

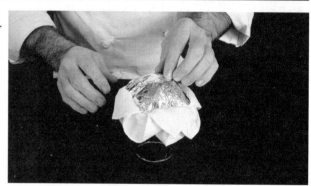

8. Turn the artichoke down on the middle of a folded flower napkin. Fill with *pommes soufflés,* technique 139, or *gaufrettes,* technique 137.

GONDOLA

1. To make a gondola, place a square piece of aluminum foil in the center of a square napkin (see step 1, artichoke). Fold in half to obtain a long rectangle. Fold one side into the center of the rectangle,

2. then the other side to form a triangular "hat."

3. Fold in the same manner, making the triangle thinner.

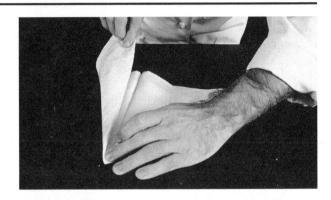

4. Fold a third time, making a long, narrow and sharply pointed triangle.

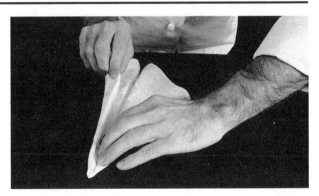

5. Then bring both sides together at the last fold.

6. Keeping the napkin in place with one hand, fold the point inward so it resembles the curved tip of a gondola. Fold a second napkin in the same manner.

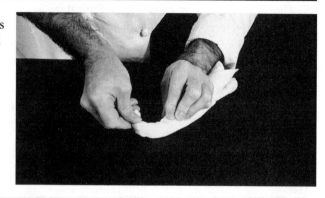

7. Open each gondola and arrange on a platter so that the curved side is on the outside of the platter. Cover the center with a square napkin. Use to present *coulibiac* of salmon, hot pâté in crust, cold fish or even asparagus or artichokes.

70. Iced Vodka Bottle *(Vodka Glacée)*

SPIRITS SUCH AS vodka, aquavit and pear or raspberry *alcools blancs* are often served ice cold and syrupy. The iced vodka is a must with fresh caviar. An unusual and attractive presentation is to serve the bottle imbedded in ice.

1. Place the bottle in a large empty can or a half-gallon milk carton. Fill with cold water and freeze.

2. Run the container under water and pull out the block of ice with the bottle.

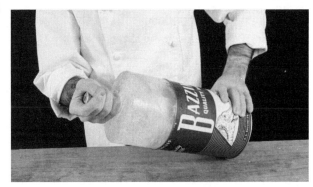

3. Serve it as is, or sculpt the ice with a pointed knife giving it some ridges and roughness, getting rid of the "molded look." Keep frozen.

4. At serving time, fold a napkin,

5. wrap it around the bottle, and secure with a knot.

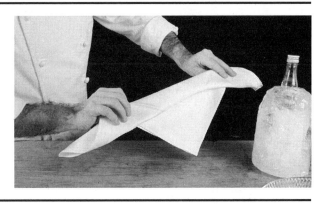

6. Fold the cover down to dress up the bottle. Keep in the freezer and refill the bottle as needed.

Shellfish and Fish

71. Oysters *(Huitres)*

AFICIONADOS PREFER OYSTERS RAW on the half shell with a dash of lemon, or a *mignonnette* sauce made by mixing together ½ cup good red wine vinegar, ¼ cup chopped shallots, ½ teaspoon coarsely ground black pepper and a dash of salt. (Crushed peppercorn is called *mignonnette;* hence, the name of the sauce.) These fine mollusks should be used, as all shellfish, only if they are alive and fresh. Despite the fact that restaurants sometimes wash oysters to get rid of any lurking bits of shell that might present problems to their patrons, once oysters are opened, they should never be washed. Their taste becomes flat and insipid. Oysters are usually larger and fatter in the United States than they are in France. The "green" flat oysters of France, the *Belons* and *Marennes*, are now grown in Maine. Oysters are usually poached in their own broth. Be sure not to overcook these delicate shellfish or they will toughen. As soon as the edges of the oyster whiten and curl up, they are cooked enough.

1. To open an oyster, only the point of the knife (and you need an oyster knife) is used. Hold the oyster with a thick potholder to protect your hand. With the oyster in the palm of your hand, push the point of the knife about ½ inch deep into the "hinge" (the pointed side of the oyster), between the "lid" and the body of the oyster.

2. Once the lid has been penetrated (this can take a considerable amount of pressure), push down. The lid should pop open. Lift up the top shell, cutting the muscle attached to it.

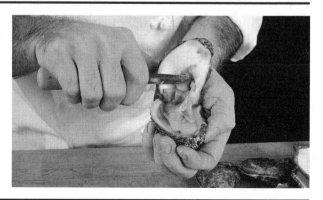

3. If the oyster is too hard to open at the hinge (the Malpeque from the cold waters of Canada are easier to open than the blue-points which are pictured here), insert the knife about 1 inch on the curved side of the oyster between the lid and the body. Twist the blade to pry the oyster open. Cut the muscle from the lid.

4. Slide your knife under the oyster to sever the muscle. The oyster is now loose in the shell. Place flat on a bed of chopped ice or directly on the plate.

5. Oysters and clams. Serve with buttered black bread, lemon wedges or *mignonnette* sauce.

72. Clams

WHERE THE OYSTER KNIFE is pointed and the tip is usually curved, the clam knife is straight, rounded at the tip, and sharp on one side. Personally, I prefer to use a regular paring knife to open clams. Cherrystones and little necks (the smallest of the hard clam clan) are commonly served on the half shell, although they are often cooked in the shell (clams casino and Rocke-feller), or outside the shell (clam fritters, spaghetti and clam sauce). Like oysters, clams should not be overcooked. There are only two alternatives when it comes to cooking clams: to poach them only a minute or so to avoid toughening, or to cook them a couple of hours to have them tender. Cooked in between the two, they will be very rubbery. This principle applies to meat as well. Beef should be cooked rapidly (a steak) or braised (a stew); in between, the meat is, paradoxically, overcooked and undercooked at the same time.

1. Holding the clam firmly in the palm of your hand, place the sharp side of the knife blade at the seam, slightly on the "bulged" side where it is easier to open, and, using the tips of your fingers in back of the blade, tighten your grip, "pulling" the blade up through the seam. The muscle has to be severed for the clam to open.

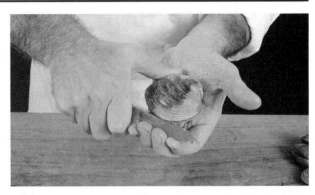

2. Force the clam open. Run the knife along the top shell to free the meat.

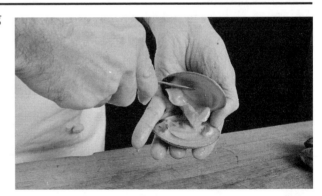

3. Break the top shell off by twisting it. Discard. You may work over a bowl to salvage the drippings.

4. To free the clam completely from the shell, run the knife under the meat and sever the muscle. Place on a flat plate. Do not wash. Serve with lemon, *mignonnette,* or a cocktail sauce and buttered bread.

73. Sea Urchins *(Oursins)*

UNFORTUNATELY, THIS SEA DELICACY is rarely available in fish stores or restaurants, even though it is commonly found off the coasts of the United States. They are popular in France, and are usually eaten raw with bread and butter. They exhale a prevalent odor of iodine, and the roe (the only part eaten) are reminiscent of nuts, butter and salt all together.

1. Bottom and top of a sea urchin.

2. The needles are straight and hard in fresh sea urchins.

3. Hold the sea urchin with a potholder. Insert the point of a pair of scissors into the "mouth" (the soft depression on one side). Cut one-third down the shell, then, turn the scissors and cut around the shell.

4. Lift up the "lid."

5. The mouth of the sea urchin is attached to the lid. Discard.

6. With a teaspoon, lift up the roe and eat with bread and butter. (They can also be used to make mousse or as a garnish.) Fishermen in France open the sea urchin and immerse it in seawater, shaking it to clean the inside. Everything washes out except the roe which is attached to the "wall" of the shell. They dip sticks of buttered bread into the roe and eat them.

7. Plate of sea urchins.

74. Mussels (Moules)

MUSSELS, SO PREVALENT IN FRANCE, are finally getting the popularity they deserve in this country. We have them in great abundance all along the New England and mid-Atlantic shores. The best mussels are the ones found in cold waters. They are sold by weight—about 12 average-sized mussels to a pound—and any aficionado can easily consume at least 1½ pounds.

There are a number of ways to serve mussels. The least sophisticated and easiest way to prepare them is *marinière* (sailor-style). This is how you frequently find them in the bistros in France—plain and in the shell. For something a little more sophisticated and richer, you can try them *poulette* (with a cream sauce). For this dish, the shell is separated and only the half shell with the meat in it is kept. In some recipes the meat is removed entirely from the shell after cooking and used to make a *pilaff de moules* or combined with a *rémoulade* or a light well-seasoned mayonnaise and served as a salad for a first course. Billi-bi, one of the best possible soups, can be made from the broth the mussels cook in, with the addition of wine, cream and herbs.

CLEANING MUSSELS

1. Mussels are attached to one another by a "cord" or "beard" which looks like old wet hay or grass. Nowadays, mussels are often sold half cleaned (that is, with the beard removed), even though they die rapidly without their life-sustaining cord. Even the live ones lose a lot of moisture and end up being small, dry and very yellowish, instead of plump, moist and pale beige in color. If you plan to keep them a few days, buy the uncleaned type.

2. With a small paring knife, scrape off the dirt and most of the encrustations that are on the shell. Cut off, or pull off, the beard. Place in cold water and rub the mussels against each other to clean the shells further.

3. Press each one on a bias to determine if it is full of mud or sand. If so, the shells will slide open and, obviously, these are to be discarded.

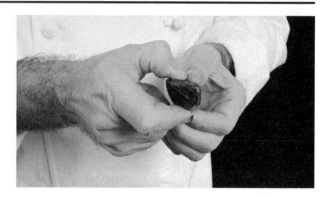

4. Certain mussels are open. This does not mean that they are bad. The spoiled ones smell strongly, contrary to the fresh mussels which smell pleasantly of iodine and seaweed. If you touch the inside muscle and edge with the point of a knife

5. the fresh mussel will close immediately. As long as the shell is moving the mussel is still alive. Place the mussels again in a lot of cold water with salt (a handful of salt per gallon of water), and let them sit for 1 hour so that they throw off any sand that escaped the first washing (there will always be a minimal amount of sand left in them).

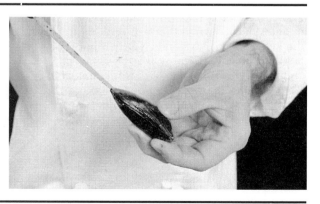

6. Wash again one or two more times. The mussels are now ready to cook.

MUSSELS SAILOR-STYLE *(Moules Marinière)*

5 pounds clean mussels
1 cup chopped onion
1 clove garlic, peeled, crushed and chopped
½ cup chopped parsley
½ teaspoon freshly ground pepper
Dash of thyme
1 bay leaf
Dash of salt
2 tablespoons butter
1 cup dry white wine

This recipe will serve 6.

1. Combine all ingredients in a large pot, cover, place on high heat and bring to a boil.

2. Keep cooking for approximately 10 minutes. Twice while they are cooking, lift the kettle with both hands, your thumbs holding the cover, and shake the kettle in an up-and-down motion to toss the mussels. They should all open. Do not overcook or they will toughen. Serve in large deep plates or in bowls with some of the broth on top.

MUSSELS WITH CREAM SAUCE
(Moules Poulette)

Cook as for *moules marinière*. Separate the shells, arranging the halves with the meat on plates. Melt 2 tablespoons butter in a saucepan and mix in 2 tablespoons flour. Add the broth, leaving any sandy residue in the bottom, and bring to a boil, mixing with a whisk. Let simmer 2 minutes. Add 1 cup heavy cream and bring to a boil again. Add salt and pepper if needed. Cook a few minutes and spoon sauce over the mussels.

PILAF OF MUSSELS *(Pilaf de Moules)*

1. Cook as for *moules marinière*. When the mussels are cooked, remove the meat from the shell and trim (optional, see trimming mussels). Prepare the sauce *poulette* and set aside. In a saucepan, sauté ⅓ cup chopped onion in 1 tablespoon butter for 1 minute. Add 1½ cups Carolina type rice, stir, add 3 cups chicken stock, salt and pepper and bring to a boil. Cover and cook in a 400-degree preheated oven for 20 minutes.

2. Butter a small bowl and place approximately 3 tablespoons of rice in the bottom and up the sides, making a "nest."

3. Add about 8 to 10 mussels, 2 tablespoons of the *poulette* sauce and

4. cover with more rice, enough to fill up the bowl.

5. Press the mixture with a spoon to pack it together well.

6. Place a serving plate on top of the bowl and

7. invert so the bowl now rests on the plate.

8. Remove the bowl, pour some of the sauce around the pilaf and decorate with a piece of fresh parsley.

9. From right to left: *pilaf de moules, moules poulette* and *moules marinière*.

TRIMMING MUSSELS

1. When serving mussels out of the shell, you might want to remove the brown edge all around the mussel.

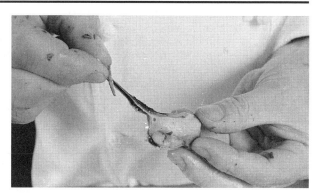

2. This border is tough, especially in large mussels. Pull it and it will come off easily. Discard. It is perfectly all right to serve mussels untrimmed; it's just not quite as elegant.

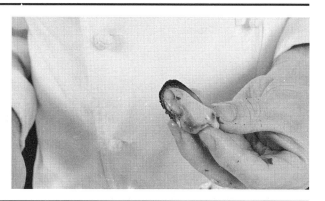

75. Crabs *(Crabes)*

Tʜᴇ ᴄᴏᴍᴍᴏɴ, ʙʟᴜᴇ ʜᴀʀᴅ-sʜᴇʟʟ ᴄʀᴀʙ is usually boiled in a well-seasoned broth and eaten on newspapers directly at the table. (In summer, when the crab discards his shell, the soft-shell crab is one of the best delicacies to be found in the United States.) Hard-shell crabs are inexpensive, tasty and readily available. They are also excellent in stew, sautéed with hot oil Chinese style, *provençal* with garlic and tomatoes, or *américaine* with a peppery wine and tomato sauce.

1. To prepare for stew, hold the live crab with a potholder and break the large claws off.

2. Turn the crab over. The crab pictured here is a female crab, which is considered the best. You can tell it's a female by the "skirt" which is wide and ends in a point. The male crab has a long, narrow tail instead of a skirt and doesn't have roe inside, but only the tomalley, or liver.

3. Lift the skirt up and twist to break it off. If the crab is dirty, brush under cold water.

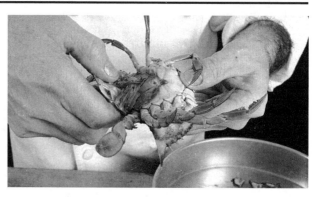

4. Starting next to the fin end and, using your thumb, pry open the shell.

5. If you find it difficult to pull apart, use a teaspoon to pry the shell open.

6. Separate the body from the shell.

7. Reserve the roe and tomalley attached to the front of the shell. The roe are bright orange and the liver is pale green.

8. Reserve the roe attached to the center of the body. Remove the spongy appendages that adhere to each side of the body.

9. Using your thumbs, break the body into halves.

10. The pieces should smell pleasantly, and the flesh should be white and plump. It is near the back fin that the largest morsel of meat is found.

11. Using a meat pounder, break the large claws.

12. Crab ready to stew or sauté. On the left, the two halves of the body, the cracked claws, and the roe and tomalley (used to season and thicken the sauce), and, on the right, the skirt and the shell to be discarded.

76. How to Prepare Shrimp
(Préparation des Crevettes)

SHRIMP (in the United States this refers usually to shrimp tails) are available in different sizes and prices. The large ones are very expensive. The smaller the shrimp, the less expensive they usually are. They always have the best flavor bought fresh, unshelled. For a shrimp cocktail, simply poach the shrimp with their shells in a vegetable stock (boiled water, carrots, onions, thyme, bay leaf, parsley, celery and black peppercorns) for about 10 minutes. Drop the shrimp into the boiling stock. Cover, barely bring back to a boil, then remove from the heat. Allow the shrimp to cool in the liquid where they will take on the flavor of the stock. The stock can be re-used to make a *consommé* of shrimp or a soup. To peel shrimp, hold from underneath, grab the appendage on one side of the tail, break it and pull it out. The shell should come out in sections, uncurling from around the flesh. Remove all the shell and keep only the tail part attached—if you want to present them this way for decorative purposes. What follows are a few different ways of preparing shrimp.

TO BUTTERFLY SHRIMP

1. To butterfly shrimp, put it flat on the table and cut the thick part of it with a knife to split it open. Do not cut through completely. At that point you may notice the intestinal tract which runs like a vein along the back of the shrimp. Its presence is not too important in a small shrimp, but in large ones it imparts a bitter taste and therefore should be removed. Sometimes shrimp have almost no intestinal tract and are very clean.

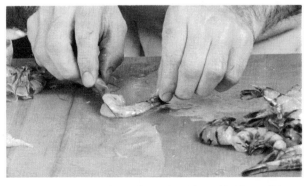

SHRIMP WITH GARLIC *(Crevettes à l'Ail)*

2. One attractive way to serve shrimp is to arrange them in a gratin dish alongside one another with their tails sticking up. During cooking the shrimp stiffen and retain that position. They can be sprinkled lightly with salt and pepper and covered with snail butter (see technique 78.) They can also be sprinkled with a few drops of lemon juice, butter, salt and pepper and cooked in a 425-degree oven for 4 to 6 minutes. Serve as a first course or main course for lunch.

SHRIMP SALAD *(Salade de Crevettes)*

1 *pound fresh shrimp, shelled (25 to 30 to the pound)*
½ *pound onions, peeled and very thinly sliced (about 2 cups loose)*
2 *tablespoons good red wine vinegar*
1½ *teaspoons salt*
1 *teaspoon freshly ground white pepper*

½ *teaspoon grated orange rind*
1 *cup Italian parsley, coarsely chopped*
½ *cup good olive oil, preferably virgin*

3. Place all the ingredients for the shrimp salad, except the orange rind, parsley and oil, into a large skillet. Cook for 2 to 3 minutes on medium heat, stirring with a wooden spatula. The mixture should not even reach a complete boil. As soon as the shrimp stiffen and whiten, remove from the heat and pour the whole mixture into a bowl. Add the rest of the ingredients, toss all together and let it cool and marinate for at least 1 hour before serving. The shrimp should be served at room temperature as a first course with toast or regular bread.

77. Shrimp Bread *(Pain aux Crevettes)*

YIELD: 6 to 8 servings

THE COMBINATION of bread, butter, shellfish, garlic and parsley is so good, why not put them all together—which is what we do here—for an attractive and unusual first course. We used a 1-pound *pain de ménage* type bread (technique 206). but other types of bread can certainly be used. In fact, individual rolls can be stuffed with 6 to 8 shrimp and served one per person. Scallops, crabmeat, snails, etc., can be substituted for the shrimp.

1 *pound round bread (see technique 206)*
3 *large cloves garlic, peeled*
½ *cup loose parsley leaves*
1 *stick (4 ounces) sweet butter, softened*
2 *teaspoons Ricard or Pernod or any other*
   anise-flavored apéritif
1 *teaspoon salt*
½ *teaspoon finely ground black pepper*

½ *pound fresh uncooked shrimp, peeled, about 25*
   to 30 to the pound (see technique 76)
Extra salt and pepper to taste

1. Remove the top of the bread and hollow it out. Chop the inside pieces in a food processor until finely ground. Set aside. Crush the garlic and chop it finely by hand or in the food processor along with the parsley. Add the butter, Ricard, salt and pepper and blend again until smooth.

2. Arrange a layer of shrimp in the bottom of the bread. Sprinkle lightly with salt and pepper. Spread one third of the butter mixture on top, then a layer of bread crumbs. Arrange what is left of the shrimp, salt and pepper, another third of the butter and the remaining bread crumbs. Dot the top with the remaining butter and bake in a 400-degree oven for 25 to 30 minutes, without the lid. It should be nicely brown on the top, cooked and very hot inside. The juice from the shrimp will be absorbed by the bread crumbs and the bread shell. Place the lid on the bread for the last 5 minutes to heat it up. Serve at the table cut into wedges. See finished shrimp bread, page 552.

78. Snails (Escargots)

Eaten by the Roman Sybarites who knew how to fatten them, escargots are a delicacy, unfortunately rarely available fresh in the United States. Although most snails come from snail farms, wild ones are still available at local markets in the countryside throughout France. The two varieties eaten are the succulent "big white" from Burgundy, called vineyard snails because of their fondness for grape leaves and vines, and the smaller garden snails, called the "small gray." The best and most tender snails are picked up at the end of winter. They are called *les dormants*, the sleepers, because they spend the winter in hibernation. Fresh snails are starved for at least 48 hours, in case they have eaten herbs which may be toxic to people. They are then soaked in a mixture of water, salt, vinegar and flour and allowed to disgorge for one hour. They are then washed in cold water, blanched in boiling water, and washed again in cold water. They are pulled from the shell and the lower part of the intestine, the cloaca, is removed. Finally, the snails are simmered in white wine, chicken stock and herbs for 3 to 4 hours. At this point, they are, more or less, at the state you find them in cans. The most popular way of serving snails is with garlic butter *à la bourguignonne*.

ESCARGOTS BOURGUIGNONNE

3 *dozen snails*
2 *sticks (½ pound) sweet butter, softened*
3 *cloves garlic, peeled, crushed and chopped very fine (2 teaspoons)*
4 *tablespoons chopped parsley*
1 *teaspoon Pernod or Richard (or another anise-flavored liqueur)*
½ *cup dry white wine*
1½ *slices fresh bread, crumbed in the blender*
1 *teaspoon salt*
½ *teaspoon freshly ground white pepper*

Mix together all of the ingredients except the snails.

You can vary the recipe by adding chopped shallots, almonds, chives and so on. You could omit the anise liqueur, the wine and the bread.

1. There are two kinds of shells, the real snail shells pictured in the foreground, and the porcelain imitations shown in the back, which are washed and reused in restaurants. The real shells are often washed and reused, but it is not an easy job to wash them properly, and they often smell rancid. Mushroom caps, as well as artichoke bottoms, are used as receptacles for snails.

2. Place ½ teaspoon of the butter mixture in the bottom of each shell and

3. push the snail in, rounded side first.

4. Cover with more of the butter mixture, at least 1½ to 2 teaspoons more.

5. When using the porcelain shells, proceed in the same manner.

6. Snails in porcelain and real shells, oven ready.

7. Place in a 400-degree preheated oven and bake for 12 to 14 minutes. Be extra careful not to burn the garlic butter. Bring the snails, bubbling hot, to the table.

8. The snails are served on a plate from the special *escargotière* (snail dish) in which they were cooked. To eat snails, a special fork and tongs are used.

9. Hold the snail shell with the tongs and pull the snail out with the thin, narrow fork.

10. Pour the extra butter left in the shell into the snail dish, and use your bread to soak up the butter.

79. Crayfish *(Écrevisses)*

THESE TINY SWEET WATER LOBSTERLIKE CRUSTACEANS are native to just about every part of the world except Africa. In the United States they come from Louisiana, well known for its crayfish, and California. The Pacific crayfish is usually quite clean, while crayfish from Louisiana sometimes require scrubbing to rid them of mud. There are many different species of crayfish, some too small to be eaten. To be edible they should be at least 4 to 5 inches from tail to head. Only the tail meat gets eaten (the body can be used to make soups, sauces and seasoned butter). Count on a dozen tails per person as a main course. Like all shellfish, crayfish should be handled live. Two different, classic ways of preparing crayfish follow—one in a hot broth, the other a crayfish au gratin—both are usually served as a first course. Crayfish can also be substituted for lobster in the Lobster Soufflé Plaza-Athénée (technique 83.

CRAYFISH IN BROTH *(Écrevisses à la Nage)*

YIELD: 2 servings

2 *dozen crayfish (about 2 pounds)*
1 *large leek (white part only), cut into julienne (see technique 4) (1 cup)*
1 *large onion, peeled, cut in half and thinly sliced (2 cups)*
2 *small celery ribs, peeled and cut in julienne (½ cup)*
2 *carrots, peeled and thinly sliced (1 cup)*
2 *cups dry white wine*

1 *cup water*
½ *teaspoon thyme*
3 *bay leaves*
4 *strips lemon rind (use a vegetable peeler)*
1½ *teaspoons salt*
½ *teaspoon freshly ground black pepper*
½ *teaspoon red pepper flakes or a good dash cayenne pepper (optional)*
1 *small bunch Italian parsley, stems removed, very coarsely cut (1 cup)*
2 *tablespoons sweet butter*

1. The central intestinal tract has to be removed or the crayfish will taste bitter. Hold the crayfish down as shown, grab the center flap of the tail and twist gently back and forth to loosen it.

2. Pull and the intestinal tract attached to it should come out. (If it breaks, try to pull it out with the point of a knife, but don't worry if you can't get it. The crayfish is still edible.)

3. Melt the butter in a large frying pan. Add the leek, onions, celery and carrots. Sauté on medium heat for 1 minute. Add the wine and water, thyme, bay leaves, lemon, salt, pepper and optional pepper flakes. Bring to a boil and boil on high heat for 2 minutes. Add the crayfish and parsley, stir to mix, cover and bring to a boil. Simmer gently for 1 minute. Remove from the heat and let the crayfish cool in the broth.

4. When cooled, arrange the crayfish on a platter with all of the vegetable garnish on top. *Troussé* a few crayfish to decorate the top of the dish. To *troussé*, take one of the front claws, turn it upside down being careful not to break the claw at the joint, and gently push the smaller "pincer" part into the shell of the tail to hold the claw in place.

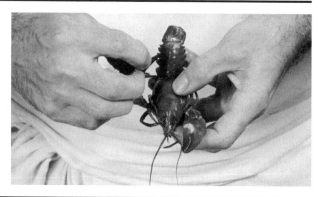

5. Repeat with the other claw. The crayfish are ready to be "seated." To enjoy the crayfish, you have to use your fingers, which means this is not a dish for a formal dinner party.

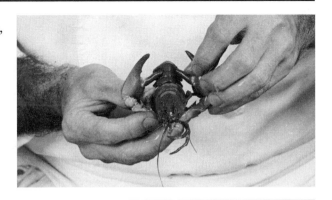

CRAYFISH TAILS AU GRATIN *(Gratin de Queues d'Écrevisses)*

YIELD: 2 servings

This expensive dish is served in some of the best restaurants of France. It is a time-consuming dish, very elegant and very rich. To make the crayfish go a bit further, you can reuse the shells to make a *bisque* of crayfish. (After you strain the crayfish in step 3, cover the shells and strained solids with water and boil for 2 hours, then strain. Adjust to 2 quarts and use as a base for sauces, *consommés* or thicken with tomatoes and cream for the bisque.)

2 *dozen crayfish (about 2 pounds), gutted (see*
    steps 1 and 2, previous technique)
2 *tablespoons sweet butter*
2 *tablespoons good Cognac*
3 *tablespoons chopped shallots*
½ *cup coarsely chopped leek*
1 *tablespoon chopped celery*
3 *tablespoons coarsely chopped carrots*
1 *large tomato, peeled and chopped*
1 *cup dry white wine*
2 *cups light fish stock*
½ *teaspoon thyme leaves*

1 *teaspoon salt*
½ *teaspoon freshly ground pepper*
1 *tablespoon tomato paste*
1 *cup heavy cream*

1. Separate the body from the tail of the crayfish. Melt the butter in an extra large skillet or saucepan, until very hot. Add the crayfish tails and sauté for about 1 minute, until they turn red. Remove from the heat and let cool.

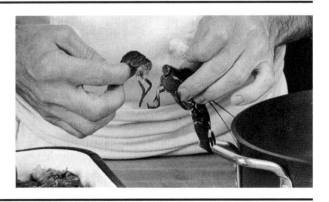

2. Remove the meat from the tails and set aside.

3. Chop the bodies coarsely. Place, with the tail shells, in the butter and continue sautéing on high heat for 2 to 3 minutes until the bodies turn red. Add the Cognac and ignite. When the flame subsides, add the shallots, leek, celery, carrots, tomato, white wine, fish stock, thyme, salt, pepper and tomato paste. Cover and bring to a boil. Lower the heat and simmer for 30 minutes. Remove from heat and strain through a food mill fitted with a large-holed disk. Press all the solids to extrude as much of the liquid as possible, then strain the juices again through a finer sieve. You should have approximately 1½ cups of liquid left. If not, reduce to right amount, or add water to adjust. Add the cream, bring to a boil and reduce by half. Arrange the tails in two small baking dishes (about 1 dozen per person) and heat in a hot oven for 1 or 2 minutes. Pour the hot sauce on top and serve immediately.

80. Stuffed Squid *(Calmars Farcis)*

YIELD: 4 servings

Squid is inexpensive, high in protein, low in calories and easily obtainable. Like a lot of other shellfish, it is tough only if overcooked. It should be either cooked very briefly or braised a long time in order to be tender. It's the in-between cooking that makes it as hard as rubber. The Basques as well as the Spaniards prepare calamari or squid using the ink that is contained in a bag inside the tentacles. The ink is not needed in our recipe. In fact, the small saclike appendage full of ink is usually removed before the squid reaches the marketplace. For our recipe, we used small tender squid about 6 inches long. After being cleaned as explained in the technique below, squid can be sliced, breaded and deep-fried or sautéed briefly, or blanched and marinated in oil, lemon or lime juice and served partially raw as a *seviche*.

Stuffing

8 *squid (about 1¾ to 2 pounds, not trimmed or*
    cleaned)
2 *tablespoons sweet butter*
⅓ *cup finely chopped onion*
2 *cloves garlic, peeled, crushed and chopped*
    fine (½ teaspoon)
1 *cup finely chopped mushrooms*
1 *teaspoon salt*
¼ *teaspoon pepper*
1 *cup fresh bread crumbs*

Sauce

2 *small ripe tomatoes, peeled, seeded and coarsely*
    chopped (¾ cup)
½ *cup finely chopped onions*
3 *to 4 cloves garlic, peeled, crushed and chopped*
    (1 teaspoon)
1 *cup dry white wine*
½ *teaspoon dried saffron pistils (optional)*

1. Separate the head and the tentacles from the body of the squid by pulling. Remove the purplish skin and fins from the central body—also by pulling. They should come off easily. Turn the saclike body inside out to wash it. You will notice that there is a soft bone or plasticlike piece, called the "pan," which you should also discard. Wash well and turn the body back into its original shape.

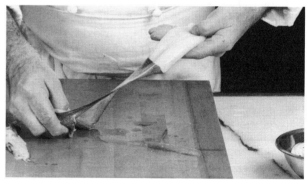

2. Cut the beak and head from the tentacles (the beak will pop out when you apply pressure to the head). Keep only the tentacles.

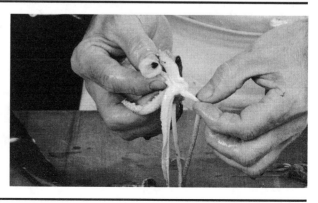

3. Coarsely chop the tentacles. To prepare the stuffing, sauté the onions in butter for about 1 minute. Add garlic, mushrooms and chopped tentacles and fins. Continue cooking for 2 to 3 minutes until the mixture of squid stiffens and the juices are reduced almost completely. Add the salt and pepper and allow to cool slightly. Add bread crumbs and toss lightly.

4. Spoon the stuffing into a pastry bag without any tube and stuff the bodies of the squid. Sprinkle the tomatoes, onion and garlic in the bottom of a large saucepan and arrange the stuffed squid on top. Place the stuffed squid one against the other so that the closed end or side of a squid is pushed against the open side of the next squid to block the opening and keep the stuffing from falling out while the squid cooks. Sprinkle with the white wine and saffron. Cover the squid with a piece of buttered parchment paper, place a cover on top and bring to barely a simmer on top of the stove (about 180 degrees). If the temperature is too high the squid will burst. It must not boil. Cook in this manner for approximately 15 minutes.

5. Remove the squid and arrange on a gratin dish or serving platter. Cover with the piece of parchment paper and set aside. Reduce the juices in the pan on top of the stove to about 1¼ cups. Taste and add salt and pepper if needed. Be sure to pour the juices that have accumulated in the gratin dish back into your sauce otherwise your sauce will be too thick.

6. Pour the reduced sauce on top of the stuffed squid, sprinkle with parsley and serve immediately.

81. Frog's Legs *(Cuisses de Grenouilles)*

YIELD: 2 to 3 servings

IN FRANCE, the green frog is commonly used and is about half the size of the bull frog that we use in the United States. The bull frogs are quite large and tender when young. The meat is usually pale beige and plump. If you come across darker-colored meat or stringy-looking flesh, it is likely that the frog is older and will be tough. Frog's legs are usually served as a first course for a dinner or as a main course at lunch. Two pairs of legs should be enough for a first course and 3 to 4 for a main course, depending on their size. Serve with plain boiled potatoes. Photographs 1 and 2 explain how to sauté frog's legs. Picture 3 illustrates two ways—one with *demi-glace* and the other with stewed tomatoes—to serve frog's legs once they have been sautéed. Notice that both recipes are finished with a garlic butter, photograph 3.

6 *pairs of frog's legs (approximately 1 pound), washed and dried*
1 *teaspoon salt*
¼ *teaspoon freshly ground white pepper*
½ *cup milk*
½ *cup flour*
1 *tablespoon vegetable oil*
2 *tablespoons sweet butter*
¾ *cup stewed tomatoes (make half of the sauce recipe in technique 144, omit the olive) or ½ cup demi-glace (technique 12)*
½ *stick sweet butter*

2 *tablespoons finely chopped parsley*
2 to 3 *cloves garlic, peeled, crushed and finely chopped (1 teaspoon)*

1. Cross the frog's legs by inserting one leg through the calf muscle of the other. Sometimes the hole is there, sometimes it isn't. You may have to cut between the muscle and the bone of one leg to be able to insert the other one. Put the legs in a dish, and add the salt, pepper and milk and let sit for ½ hour.

2. Place about ½ cup flour in a plastic bag. Drain the frog's legs from the milk, place them in the bag and shake vigorously. Pat the frog's legs gently to remove excess flour. For 6 pairs of frog's legs, place the oil and the 2 tablespoons of butter in a large skillet. Heat until the mixture is foaming and place the frog's legs flat in the skillet. They should not overlap. Cook over medium to low heat approximately 6 minutes on each side for large legs and a bit less for smaller legs. They should be browned on each side. Arrange on a serving dish.

3. Put the stewed tomatoes in the center of the serving dish (round platter in photograph) or pour ½ cup hot *demi-glace* around the legs (gratin dish in photograph). Melt ½ stick butter in a clean skillet and when it foams add the parsley and garlic. Cook for 5 to 10 seconds, shaking the pan. Spoon over the frog's legs.

82. Lobster *(Homard)*

FRESHNESS IS EXTREMELY IMPORTANT with lobster and other shellfish, and the only way to assure a lobster's freshness is to buy it alive. There are three basic ways of cooking lobster: boiling or steaming, stewing and broiling. The lobster is cut differently depending on which way you cook it.

BROILED LOBSTER

1. Place the live lobster on its back. Plunge a large knife right into the middle of the body and cut down the tail without going through the outside shell.

2. Using both hands, crack the lobster open.

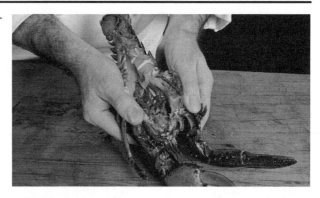

3. Remove sac (stomach) between the eyes and discard. This is usually full of gravel.

4. Save the liquid, the roe (if any), and the tomalley (liver).

5. Crack claws and big leg joints with a meat pounder or a hammer.

6. An alternate method is to place the lobster on its back and split the body without going through the outside shell. Split the tail into halves. Using both hands, crack the lobster open.

7. Roll each half of the tail back onto itself. Remove the sac, reserve liquid, roe and tomalley, and crack the claws.

STEWED LOBSTER

1. Holding the live lobster firmly with one hand, break off or cut the large claw and small legs on one side of the lobster.

2. Repeat on the other side. Move your knife down and out to separate the claws easily. Crack the claws with a hammer.

3. Insert the point of a large knife under the shell of the body and cut on each side to

4. separate the tail from the body. You can also just break it off.

5. Split the body in half, following the line on the middle of the back. Discard the sac and reserve the liquid, roe and tomalley. Cut the tail into three chunks.

BOILED OR STEAMED LOBSTER

1. After the lobster has been cooked in a strong vegetable stock and cooled in the stock, make a small incision with the point of a large knife between the eyes.

2. Let the liquid run out of the lobster through the opening.

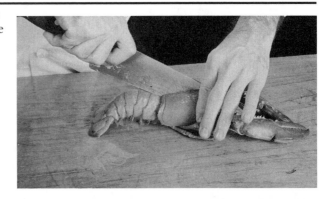

3. Plunge the knife straight down into the body and cut down, following the line on the middle of the back.

4. Split the tail in half, pushing with both hands on the blade of the knife. Remove the sac and the intestine (a small black thread along the tail).

5. From right to left: boiled lobster, lobster cut for stew and 2 lobsters cut for broiling. Boiled lobsters are usually served cold with mayonnaise, or lukewarm with butter or hollandaise. Lobsters cut for stew are used to make dishes like lobster Newburg and *américaine.* Broiled lobsters are usually seasoned with salt and pepper. The tomalley, roe and liquid are mixed with butter and paprika and spread on the meat. The lobster is then cooked in a very hot oven (450 degrees), or placed under the broiler for 8 to 10 minutes. Do not overcook.

83. Lobster Soufflé Plaza-Athénée

(Soufflé de Homard Plaza-Athénée)

YIELD: 8 main course servings or 12 first course servings

ONE OF THE BEST WAYS to enjoy lobster is simply broiled. However, a 2-pound lobster serves only one person whereas if you stuff it and glaze it with a sauce, it can serve two. In the soufflé Plaza-Athénée, a specialty of that famous hôtel-restaurant in Paris, the same lobster serves 4 people (and two lobsters, 8) as a main course for a lunch or 5 people as a first course for a dinner. The soufflé may be more complicated and sophisticated than a plain broiled or boiled lobster but it is far less expensive. Other fish or shellfish can be substituted for the lobster, such as scallops, shrimp, leftover fish, or other fillers can be added such as mushrooms. Dungeness crab, as well as spiny lobster and crayfish, also make an excellent soufflé. By following just steps 1 to 6 of the recipe you can make a *Homard Américaine* (or *Armoricaine*), a stewed lobster with wine, tomatoes and garlic, which can be served as is without the soufflé mixture on top. You can also make a lobster *consommé* from the carcass, claws, etc. (Add a carrot, onion and celery, and water or water and chicken stock, boiled for 1½ hours and strained, and use it as is, or with the addition of vermicelli or other pasta.) For the first part you will need:

2 live lobsters, approximately 2 pounds each
⅓ cup dry white wine
1 tablespoon flour
1 tablespoon sweet butter
1 tablespoon olive oil
3 cloves garlic, crushed, with skin left on
½ cup coarsely chopped parsley
¾ cup finely chopped onion
1 or 2 stalks celery, finely chopped (½ cup)
½ teaspoon thyme
2 tablespoons good Cognac
1 carrot, peeled and coarsely chopped (¾ cup)

1 sprig fresh tarragon or a small dash of dried tarragon leaves
2 medium to large ripe tomatoes, coarsely chopped
2 bay leaves
1 cup dry white wine
2 tablespoons tomato paste
½ teaspoon freshly ground black pepper
1 teaspoon salt
3 cups light fish stock, or chicken stock or water

To finish the sauce

1 *cup heavy cream*
1 *tablespoon Cognac*
1 *tablespoon sweet butter, cut into pieces*

Soufflé mixture (Read about soufflés on pages 760–761.)

2½ *tablespoons sweet butter*
3 *tablespoons flour*
1 *cup milk*
½ *teaspoon salt*
¼ *teaspoon freshly ground white pepper*
3 *eggs, separated, plus 3 egg whites*
2 *tablespoons grated Parmesan*

1. When choosing a lobster, pick one that is very active, an indication that it was recently caught. If the lobster is almost dead the meat in the tail and claws will have shrunk and the yield will be smaller. Like other shellfish, lobster spoils rapidly once dead, which is why it should be bought alive. (If you don't want to cut up the live lobster yourself, ask the fishmonger to do it for you, but insist that he save the liquid from the body as it is an essential ingredient for the sauce.) Hold the lobster and break off the large claws where they meet the body. It shouldn't take more than a split second. Using a meat pounder crack the claws so the meat will be easy to remove after cooking.

2. Separate the tail from the body by jerking the tail back and forth until it loosens enough to pull out.

3. With a heavy knife split the body in half along the middle of back and crack it open (See page 190 for more details about cuting up lobster). Discard the stomach (a bag usually full of gravel) which is near the eyes at the pointed end of the body.

4. Place all the liquid from the lobster plus the tomalley or the liver (the pale green part) and the roe—if it is a female—(the dark green part) into a bowl. Add ⅓ cup dry white wine and 1 tablespoon flour. Mix well with a whisk and set aside. This will be the thickening and flavoring agent for the sauce. Put the oil and butter in one extra-large or two medium-size saucepans and heat until very hot. Place all the lobster pieces in the saucepan and sauté for 1 to 2 minutes on very high heat until they begin to turn red. Add the Cognac and ignite.

5. When the flames die, add the onion, carrot, celery, thyme, bay leaf, tomatoes, tomato paste, white wine, stock, pepper and salt. Cover, bring to a boil and boil for 3 to 4 minutes. Remove the claws and tail from the stock (the meat won't be thoroughly cooked but gets cooked again later on) and continue cooking the rest of the mixture for 25 minutes more. When the claws and tail are at room temperature, remove the meat from the shells.

6. Butter a 4- to 5-cup baking dish, cut the meat into 1- to 2-inch pieces, and arrange in the baking dish. Return the shells to the stock for a few minutes or the remainder of its cooking time. When the sauce is cooked, strain through a food mill with large holes or through a colander into a clean saucepan. Press all of the solids to extrude as much of the liquid as possible. Add the flour/wine mixture and, stirring with a whisk, bring to a boil. Boil for 3 to 4 minutes and strain into another bowl through a fine strainer. You should have approxi-

mately 2 cups of sauce. Place 1¼ cups of sauce on top of the lobster meat. To the reserved sauce, add the cream, bring to a boil and reduce by half. Add the Cognac. Sprinkle the butter on top of the sauce to keep it from forming a skin. At serving time you will stir the butter into the sauce.

7. Melt 2½ tablespoons butter in a saucepan, add 3 tablespoons flour and cook, stirring, for 1 minute on medium heat. Add 1 cup milk and bring to a boil while stirring with a whisk. It will thicken. Let boil for about 10 seconds. Add ½ teaspoon salt and ¼ teaspoon white pepper and remove from heat. After 1 to 2 minutes, whisk in 3 egg yolks and 1½ tablespoons of Parmesan cheese. Beat 6 egg whites. Quickly whisk one-third of the beaten white into the mixture; fold in the remaining whites carefully. Spread on top of the lobster.

8. Even the mixture out with a spatula and sprinkle with the reserved ½ tablespoon of Parmesan. Score with a spatula to form a design and place on a cookie sheet in a preheated 375-degree oven for approximately 25 minutes.

9. This is what the soufflé looks like coming out of the oven. Serve immediately with the extra sauce on the side. This is a "double decker" soufflé—one layer of lobster meat with the sauce and one of cheese soufflé on top.

10. For a decoration, the legs, antenna and tail shells can be made into a butterfly. Take a thin leg and push the antenna into the hollow part of it to make a long tail.

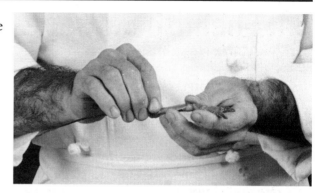

11. Remove the two pieces on either side of the lobster tail. These will be the wings of the butterfly.

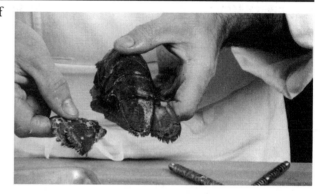

12. Force a toothpick through the joints of the butterfly "tail" and position a butterfly "wing" on either side. Place on top of the soufflé. (Remember these butterflies when you make a lobster or cold seafood salad—anytime you're cooking lobster).

Finished soufflé with "butterfly" decoration.

84. Shellfish Sausage *(Boudins de Fruits de Mer)*

YIELD: 8 to 10 servings

As its name implies, this is a purée of shellfish formed into the elongated shape of a sausage. The sausage can be small or it can be large—one sausage to serve one person or one sausage for 2 or 3. Sausage casings—whether small or large from lamb or hog or beef in size order—are often hard to come by and are delicate to work with. We chose not to use regular sausage casings and mold our sausage in foil. The foil allows you to choose the size and shape of your sausage, and because the sausage are skinless they are easier to manage on the plate. The sausage can be prepared ahead of time, kept in foil until ready to serve, then reheated in hot water in the foil. Serve with boiled salted cucumbers or tiny boiled potatoes.

Sausage

1 *pound fillet of sole, preferably gray or lemon sole, trimmed and cut into ½-inch pieces. Ask your fishmonger for a cup worth of trimmings. (See note.)*
½ *pound raw shrimp, with the shells*
½ *pound scallops*
1½ *cups heavy cream*
1 *teaspoon salt*
¼ *teaspoon freshly ground white pepper*
1 *tablespoon fresh herbs, chopped finely, a mixture of tarragon, parsley, chives, chervil, etc.*

(Note: The fish should be as fresh as possible so it has texture and albumin to hold the cream. If the fillets are burnt by ice or defrosted, the mixture will lack albumin and will bleed or separate.)

Sauce

2 *tablespoons butter*
½ *cup celery leaves*
¾ *cup onion, sliced thin*
1 *bay leaf*
¼ *teaspoon thyme leaves*
½ *teaspoon salt*
½ *teaspoon crushed peppercorns*
½ *cup dry Sherry*
3 *cups fish stock or water*
1¼ *sticks sweet butter*

1. Cut scallops into ¼-inch pieces. Peel the shrimp and cut into ½-inch pieces. Keep the shells to flavor the sauce. Purée the fish in the food processor for a few seconds. Push pieces of fish back into the purée with a rubber spatula, and blend again for a few seconds until you have a smooth mixture. Add ½ cup of cream and blend for a few seconds more. Whip the remaining cream until it holds a soft peak. (Do not overwhip.) Whisk the fish purée into the lightly whipped cream. Fold in the scallops, shrimp, salt, pepper and herbs.

2. Cut 3 large pieces of aluminum foil (about 14 inches long) and butter. Place one-third of the mixture in each.

3. Roll the mixture to enclose it and twist the ends to tighten.

4. Place the "sausages" in a large skillet. Cover with cold water and use a small lid as a weight to hold the sausages down and keep them immersed. Cover with a normal lid, bring to 180 degrees, and cook for about 15 to 20 minutes. (If you are making smaller sausages, cook for less time.) Don't let the water boil or even simmer. Remove from heat and let the sausages sit in the water for about 10 minutes.

5. Remove the sausages from the water and unwrap carefully. Transfer to a buttered dish, cover with wax paper and keep warm in a 160-degree oven while you make the sauce. (Discard any liquid that accumulated in the foil.)

6. Put the trimmings from the fish in a saucepan. Place the shrimp shells in the food processor and purée for a few seconds. Add to the trimmings with the celery leaves, onion, bay leaf, thyme, salt, peppercorns, Sherry and fish stock. Bring to a boil. Boil gently for 20 to 25 minutes. Strain, then reduce the liquid to ½ cup. Place on low heat and add the sweet butter, piece by piece, beating between each addition (read about emulsions, techniques 19 and 20). Add salt and pepper if needed. Coat the sausages and serve immediately.

85. Mousseline of Scallops with White Butter *(Mousseline de Coquilles Saint-Jacques au Beurre Blanc)*

YIELD: 6 to 8 servings

THE *mousseline* or "zéphyr" (named after the sweet, light wind of Greek mythology) is the lightest of those mousse-type concoctions made with fish, shellfish or meat. The *mousseline* is made with scallops and whipped cream, only. The ingredients have to be fresh and of good quality for the dish to work. Even though it is a sophisticated dish it is economical because ¾ pound of scallops will feed 8 people as a main course and approximately 12 people for a first course. The *mousseline* cooks in a water bath in an oven at fairly low temperature so the mixture doesn't expand while cooking and keeps a tight texture. (The same *mousseline,* cooked on a cookie sheet in the oven, puffs up like a soufflé and can be served as such.) It can also be cooked ahead, cooled off and reheated gently in hot water. In fact, pre-poached *mousseline* can be placed cold in a 400-degree oven and will puff like a soufflé in a few minutes. The *mousseline* can be made in a large soufflé mold as well as a savarin mold, or, as in our recipe, in small baba molds about ¾ cup each. If the scallops have been frozen, thaw slowly under refrigeration to lose the least possible amount of moisture.

The *mousseline* is served as a first course for an elegant dinner or as a main course for brunch or a light dinner accompanied by poached cucumbers or a purée of mushrooms.

Mousseline

¾ *pound cleaned sea scallops*
½ *teaspoon salt*
¼ *teaspoon freshly ground white pepper*
Pinch of curry powder
½ *cup heavy cream*
1 *cup heavy cream, softly beaten*

1. In Europe scallops usually have a roe or tongue left on top, which is bright orange (coral) and considered a great delicacy. In the United States, only the large center muscle is served. On that large center muscle there is a small sinew on one side which should be removed when they are to be sautéed briefly or eaten raw in a seviche. In our particular recipe, since the scallops are ground, the piece of sinew is left on.

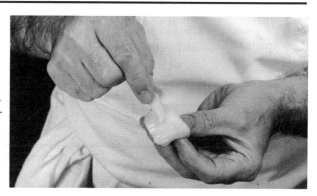

2. Butter the molds heavily and decorate as shown with blanched green of leek. (You can also use carrots, sliced thin and blanched, or a slice of truffle. Both the mousseline and the sauce are white so the addition of a touch of color makes the dish attractive.) Place the scallops in a food processor with the salt, pepper and curry powder. Purée the scallops for 10 to 15 seconds. Stop the motor and scrape the pieces that stick to the sides of the bowl back into the purée. Purée again for 5 to 10 seconds. Add the ½ cup heavy cream, and blend for

another 10 to 15 seconds until smooth. Beat the 1 cup of heavy cream until it holds a soft peak. Do not overwhip the cream or the *mousseline* will bleed and may break down. Gently whisk the scallop purée into the whipped cream.

3. If you have a lot of molds, fill them up with a pastry bag. Otherwise, place a heaping tablespoon in each mold and bang the bottom of the mold on a pot holder or folded towel so the mixture packs well and air pockets are removed.

4. Finish filling the molds, banging them again on the table. Smooth off the top with a spatula. Arrange the molds in a roasting pan.

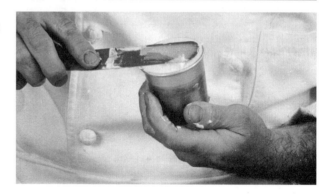

5. Cut a rectangular piece of parchment paper to fit the top of the pan. Butter half of the piece, fold the other half on top and open so the whole piece of paper is coated.

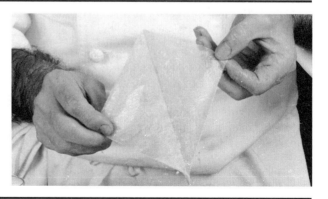

6. Place the paper on top of your molds. Fill the roasting pan with tepid water and place in a 350-degree oven for 15 to 20 minutes. If the *mousselines* raise about ¼ inch above the mold and are firm and springy to the touch, they are cooked. If you use a larger mold, you will have to increase the cooking time.

White butter sauce (Read about emulsions, techniques 19 and 20.)

1 *cup dry white wine*
½ *cup water*
¼ *cup finely chopped shallots*
1 *tablespoon good wine vinegar*
½ *teaspoon freshly ground white pepper*
½ *teaspoon salt*
2 *tablespoons heavy cream*
2 *sticks (8 ounces) sweet butter, softened*

7. Place all ingredients for the sauce—except the cream and butter—in a sturdy saucepan and place on medium heat. Bring to a boil and reduce until you have about ⅓ cup left. Force through a metal strainer, to purée the shallots, or purée in a food processor. Add the cream and place on low heat. (If possible, use an asbestos pad to diffuse the heat slowly.) Start adding the butter, beating with a wire whisk between additions. Add the butter slowly (it should take about 3 to 4 minutes to incorporate the two sticks of butter) and beat steadily to emulsify and add air to the mixture. The sauce should never boil. Keep warm on the side and reheat at the last moment before serving.

8. Unmold the *mousseline* on your hand, allowing any cooking liquids to drain through your fingers. Arrange the *mousse-lines* on individual warmed plates. If some of the design sticks to the bottom of the mold, pull it out and replace gently on the *mousseline.*

9. Heat the sauce just before serving and place about 2 tablespoons on top of each *mousseline.* Serve immediately.

86. Pike Quenelles *(Quenelles de Brochet)*

A QUENELLE IS A SUPERFINE DUMPLING usually made from fish, but sometimes made from veal or poultry as well as shellfish and potatoes. We will limit ourselves to fish quenelles here.

There are basically two different fish quenelles—the *quenelles mousseline* and the *quenelles lyonnaise.* The *quenelles mousseline* are made with heavy cream, egg white and the flesh of the fish (trout or sole is often used). They are quite light, akin to a fish mousse. The *quenelles lyonnaise,* from the city of Lyon, are made from essentially the same ingredients with the addition of a *panade,* a smooth thick paste used to give the quenelle its special velvety texture. The *quenelles lyonnaise* are made with pike and often with beef kidney fat, but in the version that follows butter is used. Sometimes chopped truffles are added to the mixture. The recipe calls for a 1½-pound fresh pike (the most common is the yellow pike from lakes) and yields 20 to 25 quenelles about 3 ounces each. The raw quenelle dough can be frozen. (Defrost slowly in the refrigerator when ready to use.) Quenelles are served in small earthenware casseroles (called Dutch terrines) all puffed up in their sauce, customarily with a *Nantua* (crayfish) sauce, or with a white wine sauce or a fish sauce.

THE PANADE

2 *cups milk*
½ *stick butter*
½ *teaspoon salt*
¼ *teaspoon freshly ground white pepper*
11 *ounces flour (about 2 cups)*

To make the *panade,* place the milk, butter, salt and pepper in a saucepan. Bring to a boil and add the flour all at once (see technique 264, steps 1 and 2). Mix. Cook a few minutes to dry. Place the *panade* flat on a dish, cover with plastic wrap and let cool.

THE FISH MIXTURE

1. Separate the head from a 1½-pound fresh pike, cutting underneath the gills on each side.

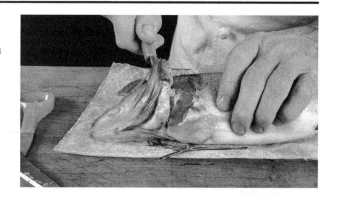

2. Cut along the back fins and follow the central bone with your knife. Repeat on the other side to lift up the second fillet.

3. Remove the skin by holding your knife at an angle and moving it left and right as well as forward as you pull on the skin with the other hand.

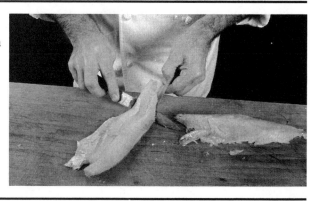

4. Cut the fillets into pieces and

5. blend in a food processor or blender.

6. Push the fish through a fine sieve to remove any leftover sinews or bones.

7. Scrape the flesh as it comes through the sieve. If you find steps 6 and 7 too tedious, they may be omitted.

6 *large eggs*
1 *pound sweet butter, softened*
1 *tablespoon salt*
¼ *teaspoon freshly ground white pepper*
⅛ *teaspoon grated nutmeg*

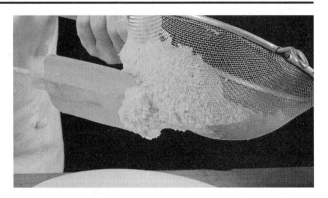

8. Cut the cool *panade* into pieces and blend with the eggs in the food processor until smooth. Transfer to a bowl and add the fish, butter, salt, pepper and nutmeg. Mix all the ingredients with a large spoon. Place the mixture, in several batches, back into the food processor and process to have it well homogenized. Refrigerate overnight covered.

9. There are a number of different ways to form the quenelles. One is to fill up a pastry bag, fitted with a large plain tube, with the quenelle mixture. Then butter a saucepan and pipe the quenelles directly into the saucepan.

10. Wet your fingers and push the "tails" of the quenelles down. Pour hot, salted water on top and bring to a simmer. Do not boil. The quenelles will rise to the surface of the water. Poach for a good 12 minutes without boiling. (If allowed to boil, the quenelles will expand and then deflate. At serving time they will not puff again.) Remove the quenelles with a slotted spoon and place into iced water.

11. In the method pictured here, the quenelles are "molded" with two spoons. Bring a pot of salted water to a boil. Reduce to a simmer. Fill one spoon with the mixture and shape it by rolling it up along the sides of the dish. Repeat several times to round the top of the quenelles.

12. Using the other spoon, scoop the dough from the first spoon, following the curved shape of the receptacle.

13. Repeat, changing spoons as many times as you need to in order to have a neat, well-shaped quenelle. Dip the empty spoon in the water as you go so that the dough slides easily from the spoon.

14. When the quenelle is shaped, hold your spoon very close to the water and let the quenelle fall. Poach following the directions in step 10.

15. A third method, and to my taste the best, is to roll the quenelle dough in flour and shape. Flour your board generously. Place the dough on the table and roll into a long stick. Roll the dough back and forth, moving your hands apart at the same time, to elongate the stick.

16. Dip the blade of a small knife in flour to avoid sticking and cut the stick at an angle into lozengelike pieces.

17. With your hand curved, use your palm to roll the quenelle back and forth to give it a smooth elongated football shape.

18. For tubular-shaped quenelles, roll the dough into a long stick and cut into pieces.

19. Flour your fingers and flatten the ends.

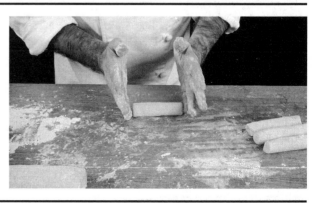

20. Hold a saucepan lid upside down by the handle. Place the lid at the edge of the table and roll the quenelles off the table and onto the lid.

21. Let the quenelles roll down into the salted, simmering water. As the water simmers, the quenelles will rise to the surface, and while cooking, will roll. Do not cover; do not boil; do not let the quenelles expand (see step 10).

22. Place in iced water when cooked. When cold, lift from the iced water and store in a covered container in the refrigerator. It is in this form that they are usually bought in the *charcuterie* in France. Reheat, covered, with your favorite sauce, or bake in the oven. Serve all puffed up, like a soufflé.

87. Salt-Cured Salmon with Green Peppercorns *(Gravlax à la Française)*

G RAVLAX, OR GRAVLAKS, was originally a Scandinavian salmon dish. Customarily made by boning out a fresh salmon and pickling it with lots of sugar and a dash of salt, it is heavily seasoned with dill. After a day or so, the fillets are sliced and served raw with a sweet mustard and dill sauce. Our version, *à la française*, is pickled with salt instead of sugar and is seasoned with a number of fresh herbs and a lot of green peppercorns. It is served sprinkled with capers, virgin oil and a dash of vinegar. One 7- to 8-pound salmon will serve about 30 persons.

1. Choose the freshest possible salmon with bright and glossy eyes and red, plump gills. Cut off the head, sliding your knife under the bone near the gills.

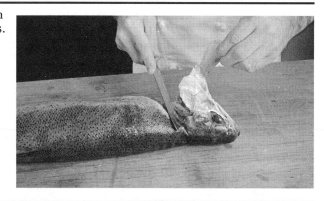

2. Using a sharp knife, start cutting along, and just above, the backbone.

3. Follow the central bone. Try to leave as little meat as possible on the bone.

4. Do not cut through, but follow the shape of the rib cage, sliding your knife, almost flat, along the ribs. Finish by "lifting up" the whole fillet.

5. Cut under the backbone and follow the same method as described in steps 3 and 4. The central bone is now on top of the knife.

6. Go slowly and be careful not to cut into the meat with your knife. Keep the blade almost flat. Separate the flesh and the rib cage, without going through the ribs.

7. Central bone completely separated. Note the rib cage.

8. Using small pliers, pull out the bones which go straight down in a line, almost in the center of each fillet. Start at the head. (This is the same technique used to clean smoked salmon.)

9. You can feel the bones by rubbing the tip of one finger from the head down to the tail of the fillet. The bones go about three-quarters down the fillet and there are about 30.

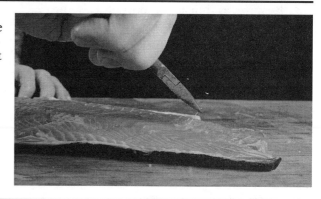

10. Using a large, stiff knife, begin to remove the skin.

11. Keep the blade on a 30-degree angle so you do not cut through the skin. Pull on the skin with one hand, and cut forward in jigsaw fashion, scraping the skin clear of all meat.

12. Remove the skin and discard.

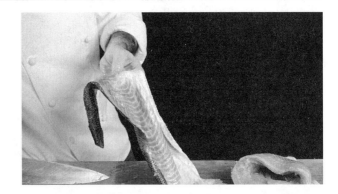

13. Remove, as thin as you possibly can, the white skin on the inside and thinner side of each fillet.

14. Turn the fillets over. All along the central line you will notice a dark brownish strip of flesh. Cut if off, going all the way down the center line.

15. Two fillets: in the foreground, the inside; in the background, the outside. The meat should be completely pink and cleaned of brown meat, bones and gristle. Seven to 8 pounds of salmon will yield two fillets between 2¼ and 2½ pounds each.

16. For each fillet, mix together ⅓ cup coarse (kosher) salt and 2 teaspoons granulated sugar. Place the fillets on a large piece of aluminum foil. Rub the salt and sugar mixture on both sides of the fillet. Reduce the salt and sugar mixture if the fillets are smaller.

17. Cover with another sheet of foil and fold the edges carefully.

18. The fillets should be well wrapped and tight in the foil. Place on a tray in the refrigerator for one day. Turn the fillet upside down and let pickle for another day. (If the fillets are smaller or thinner, cut the curing time to a total of one day.)

19. Unwrap the fillets. Mash 4 tablespoons green peppercorns (you need the soft green canned peppercorns from Madagascar) into a purée. Stir in one tablespoon of grated lemon rind and one tablespoon of good Cognac. Chop ¼ cup of fresh herbs (chervil, tarragon and thyme mixed together). Spread on both sides of the fillets (¼ cup for one fillet). (If green peppercorns are not available, you can use a tablespoon of coarsley ground black peppercorn instead.)

20. Wrap again in foil and place between 2 cookie sheets. Place about 8 to 10 pounds of weight on top of the cookie sheets to flatten the fillets. Keep refrigerated and pressed for 12 to 24 hours. Slice, technique 197, and serve. (The peppercorns and herbs may discolor the salmon in spots. This does not impair its flavor.)

88. Poached Salmon Glazed with Aspic *(Saumon Poché en Gelée)*

THERE IS NOTHING MORE GLORIOUS than a large, decorated, glazed salmon for a buffet. For a 6½-to7-pound salmon, the fish poacher should be 28 to 30 inches long. Make the vegetable stock and poach the salmon in it one day ahead. (If there's any salmon left over, the meat can be molded in aspic and served very attractively with vegetable garnishes as described in the next technique.)

2 cups coarsely chopped green of leek
2 cups diced carrots
2 cups coarsely chopped leafy celery
2 tablespoons salt
1 teaspoon black peppercorns
4 bay leaves
2 thyme leaves

Salmon with decoration

1. Place all the ingredients in a large kettle, cover with water and boil on a high heat for 30 minutes. Pour the stock and vegetables into the fish poacher.

2. Place the removable perforated rack on top of the vegetables. Lay the fish on top and fill with cold water, enough to cover the fish. The stock should be barely lukewarm. Bring to a simmer on medium to high heat. As soon as the stock starts simmering, reduce the heat to very low and let the fish poach (just under a simmer) for 30 minutes. (This is equal to 10 minutes per inch of thickness at the thickest point.) Remove from heat and let the fish cool off gently in the broth overnight.

3. Lift from the broth. (The salmon should be intact. If it is split, it boiled too fast.) Let it drain and set for a good hour. Then slide the salmon onto the working table. Cut through the thick skin in a decorative pattern near the head.

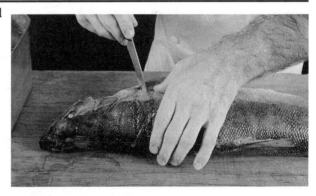

4. Pull the skin off. It should come easily.

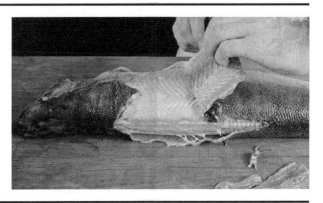

5. Using a small pair of pliers or tweezers, pull off the bones that stick out along the back of the fish.

6. Scrape off the top of the flesh, especially along the middle line to remove darkish brown fatty flesh. The salmon should be nice and pink all over. When the salmon is all cleaned, slide it onto a large serving platter. If you do not own a platter large enough to accommodate the salmon, cut an oval piece of plywood, pad with a towel, cover with a piece of white cloth and staple underneath.

7. Using vegetable flowers, technique 43, decorate the salmon. First, place long strips of blanched green of leeks near the head and tail to outline the edge of the skin. Next, place strips down both sides of the salmon to frame the area to be decorated.

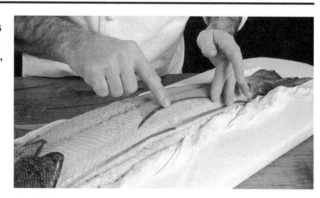

8. Make a flowerpot with thin slices of cooked carrots and green of leek.

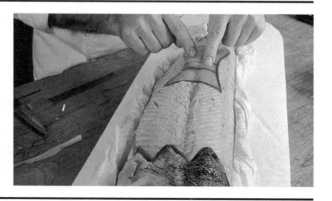

9. Make flowers using your imagination. Simulate the eye of the fish with the white of a hard-boiled egg and the black of an olive.

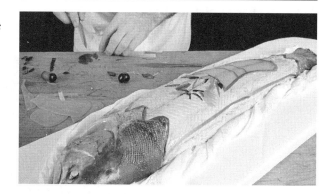

10. Make an aspic with the poaching broth by thoroughly mixing together 5 egg whites, 3 cups greens (a mixture of leeks, scallions, parsley and celery) and 5 to 6 envelopes of plain gelatin. Add 10 cups of strong, flavorful poaching liquid. Bring the mixture to a boil, stirring to avoid scorching. Let it come to a strong boil; then shut the heat off. Let the mixture settle for 10 minutes, then pour through a sieve lined with wet paper towels. Chill the mixture on ice until syrupy, and glaze the salmon. Repeat until the whole surface is coated with aspic.

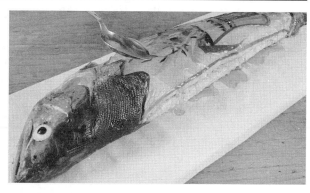

11. Prepare the garnishes. Fill artichoke bottoms, technique 110, with vegetable salad (for recipe, see technique 54, *macédoine*).

12. Slit, without going through, a large wedge of tomato. Pull open and

13. set a quarter of a hard-boiled egg in the opening.

14. Cut two tomatoes in half. Squeeze the seeds and some juice out. Compress the flesh inside to make a receptacle and fill it with the vegetable salad.

15. Decorate the top of the garnishes with strips or cut-outs of tomatoes, leeks, eggs and the like. Decorate around the salmon with lettuce leaves and the garnishes. Carve in the dining room, technique 198.

The salmon will serve 15 to 18.

89. Salmon Molded in Aspic *(Aspic de Saumon)*

THIS DISH IS AN ATTRACTIVE WAY to serve leftover poached salmon. The salmon pieces are suspended in aspic and garnished with eggs, tomatoes and a vegetable salad.

1. Poach a salmon and prepare the aspic following the directions in the preceding technique or use leftover poached salmon if you have it on hand. Pour 1 cup of melted aspic into a mold and roll it in a bowl filled with ice so the aspic coats the side of the mold as it hardens. (Alternatively, you could fill the mold with aspic—you will need a larger quantity—and set it into ice. The outside will solidify first. When the aspic is set all around, but slightly soft in the middle, scoop out the center to leave only an outside layer about ¼ inch thick.)

2. Note how the aspic coats the sides.

3. Add more aspic and keep twisting the pan to thicken the coating on the entire inside of the mold.

4. Garnish the bottom with some pieces of poached salmon and hard-boiled eggs.

5. Add a little more aspic and let it set.

6. Garnish the inside of the mold with salmon arranged on top of the aspic. Add hard-boiled egg, tomato and so on, to decorate to your liking.

7. Fill the center with a vegetable salad (for recipe, see technique 54, *macédoine*).

8. Cover the top with a layer of syrupy aspic. Let it set overnight, if possible.

9. To unmold, pull the solidified mass with the tips of your fingers all around the mold. It should detach itself easily from the side.

10. When the edges are loosened, turn the mold upside down on a platter and cover with a towel wrung in hot water.

11. After barely a minute, the mold should lift off easily.

12. Cut wedges with a thin sharp knife and

13. serve on individual cold plates. You may garnish the aspic with lettuce leaves and tomatoes and serve it with homemade mayonnaise, technique 23.

90. Preparing Sole *(Sole: Entière, Filets, Paupiettes)*

Y OU WILL FIND SOLE, especially Dover sole, featured in fine fish stores and restaurants, and rightly so, for this is probably the most versatile of fish. Dover sole is not found in North American waters and is imported, fresh or frozen, from Europe, the best being caught in the English Channel. It is the best of the small "flat" fish family (which includes grey sole, lemon sole, flounder, fluke and dab, to cite the most known), and it can be prepared in more than a hundred different ways. It is excellent broiled, poached whole or filleted, in mousses, *paupiettes*, sautéed in butter, deep-fried and baked, to give you a few examples. If Dover sole is not available in your market, apply the recipe to its kith and kin, especially the grey or lemon sole which are the firmest, though they are not firm enough to be char-broiled as the Dover sole could be. A 1-pound fresh sole will give you approximately 6 ounces of flesh after cleaning and filleting.

WHOLE

1. To prepare the Dover sole for poaching, broiling or sautéeing whole, place black skin up and cut the very tip of the tail. Loosen the black skin on the tail by scraping it enough so that you can take hold of the skin with your fingers.

2. Take a firm grip on the skin and

3. pull it off in one piece. Discard.

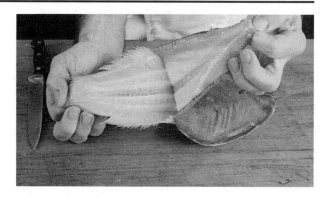

4. Detach the head close to the gills cutting on a diagonal.

5. Using sturdy fish shears, trim the protruding fins on both sides.

6. Using the handle of the knife, push out the roe. If you can, pull the roe out in one piece. Reserve to fry or sauté.

7. Using a regular knife, a fish scaler or an empty scallop shell, scale the white (also called the blind) side. When the fish is cooked whole, the white skin is left on because it is tender, and it makes a delicious and crusty surface when broiled or sautéed.

FILLETS AND PAUPIETTES

1. Remove the black skin and head as described in the preceding steps 1–4. Cut through the fillet to the bone to mark the contour of the flesh.

2. Slide a fillet of sole knife, which has a special thin, sharp and very flexible blade, under the central bone in the middle (apply pressure to flex the blade so that it slides along the central bone) and detach the fillet from underneath. Repeat with the other side, sliding the blade on the flat ribs. You now have 2 single fillets taken from the top of the sole.

3. Turn the sole over and fillet the other side. The correctly filleted sole yields 4 single fillets, 2 on each side. The cleaned, central bone and fins are excellent for stock or fish *fumet.*

4. For *paupiettes,* the fillets are rolled, starting with the thickest end. Be sure that the white, fleshy side which touched the central bone, is on the outside of the *paupiette.* Rolled this way, the *paupiette* will contract during cooking and keep its shape. Rolled the wrong way, it will open during cooking.

5. When served flat, the fillets are *ciselés* to retain their natural shape; i.e., little slits are made on top to prevent them from contracting while they cook.

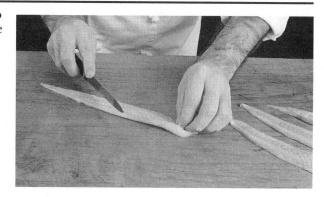

6. Cut only the top layer of the fillets on the sinewy side.

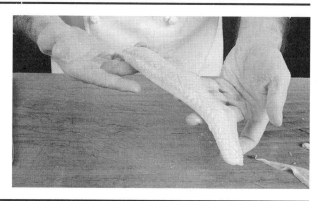

7. Fillets, stuffed or unstuffed, can be folded in half with the slits inside and served poached, with or without a sauce.

8. Fillets should be pounded when used to line a mold. Pound gently to avoid tearing the meat apart. The motion should be down and toward you (see technique 166, steps 4 and 5).

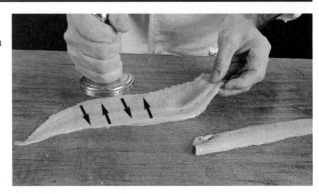

9. Arrange in a *savarin* mold to make a lining for a mousse or a quenelle mixture, technique 86.

91. Baked Sole with Mushrooms and Parsley (Sole Bercy)

1 1¼-pound Dover sole
3 tablespoons sweet butter
2 tablespoons chopped shallots
¾ teaspoon salt
¼ teaspoon freshly ground white pepper
4 large mushrooms, sliced (1 cup loosely packed)
3 tablespoons chopped fresh parsley
⅓ cup dry white wine
1 tablespoon flour
⅓ cup heavy cream
5 or 6 drops of lemon juice

Following technique 90, whole sole, steps 1–7, clean the sole, leaving the white skin on.

1. Rub a gratin dish with 1 tablespoon butter. Sprinkle shallots on top, along with salt and pepper.

2. Arrange the sole on top, and add another tablespoon butter.

3. Top with the mushrooms, 2 tablespoons parsley and the wine.

4. Place a buttered piece of wax paper on top and place in a 450-degree preheated oven for 10 minutes.

5. At this point, the sole should be done. Lift the sole up with a large spatula and place on a plate.

6. Using the blade of a knife, "push off" the bones on either side of the fillets. They should come off easily.

7. Lift up the top fillets of the sole from the central bone and

8. Place in a gratin dish or serving platter.

9. Remove the central bone in one piece and

10. Place the second half of the sole on top of the first half. The sole is now completely boned and reconstituted. Cover the sole with the wax paper and keep warm in the oven.

11. Melt 1 tablespoon butter in a saucepan, add the flour and cook for 1 minute on low heat. Add the drippings of the sole and bring to a boil, stirring with a whisk. Add the cream, bring to a boil and simmer for 2 minutes. Correct seasonings with salt and pepper, if needed. Add 5 or 6 drops of lemon juice to the sauce.

12. Remove the sole from the oven and coat with the sauce.

13. Sprinkle with remaining parsley and serve immediately.

This recipe serves 2 as a first course.

92. Sole Sautéed in Butter *(Sole Meunière)*

WHEREAS THE SOLE BERCY is cooked with the little side bones intact (they are removed after cooking, technique 91, step 6), *sole meunière* is cooked without them. The reason is that where the trimmings enhance the stock the *sole bercy* is cooked in, they just absorb the butter used to sauté the *sole meunière.* They do not add any extra flavor to the meat of the sole. Therefore, even though the sole will look smaller, it is preferable to remove the side bones before cooking.

1. Clean the sole (technique 90, steps 1–7), leaving the white skin on. With a pair of scissors, remove the bones on the side of the fillets.

2. Sprinkle the sole with salt and a small dash of pepper. Dredge in flour.

3. Melt ⅓ stick of butter in a skillet. Place sole in the hot butter, skin side down, and cook on medium to low heat for about 5 minutes on each side.

4. Bring the skillet directly to the table. Using a spoon and fork, lift up the top fillets and place on each side of the sole.

5. Remove the central bone and discard.

6. Place the bottom fillets on a hot plate and cover with the top fillets. The sole is reconstructed and completely boned.

7. Add 1 tablespoon of hot brown gravy all around (optional) and the drippings of the skillet.

8. Cover with slices of lemon dipped in chopped parsley (see lemon slices for fish, technique 51) and serve immediately.

This recipe serves 2 as a first course.

93. Goujonnettes of Sole *(Goujonnettes de Sole)*

GOUJON IS A SMALL fresh water fish that's called gudgeon in English. In France it is deep fried and eaten like French fries. *Goujonnette* is made from larger fillets of fish and cut into small *goujon*like strips and deep fried.

Fried fish is usually coated with flour or bread crumbs and either pan fried or deep fried. Deep-fried fish is usually soaked in beer and then flour or bread crumbs. Pan-fried fish is usually soaked in milk and then flour.

Fillet of sole is often used for *goujonnettes*. Serve with a hollandaise, *béarnaise*, *beurre blanc* or a lemon butter.

1. Cut the fillets in long strips about ¼-inch wide by 4 to 5 inches long.

2. Place the fish strips in a small bowl and cover with beer. Lift the pieces of fish from the beer and dip them into flour. Shake well.

3. Place the flour-coated strips of fish into a colander and shake well to eliminate excess flour. Heat vegetable oil to approximately 375 to 400 degrees and dip the *goujonnettes,* a handful at the time, into the fat. Fry for 6 to 8 minutes on high heat, until nicely browned all around.

4. Lift the *goujonnettes* from the oil with a slotted spoon and drain in a pan lined with paper towels. Sprinkle lightly with salt and arrange on a platter or in a folded towel. Serve with lemon wedges, lemon butter or a sauce.

94. Fillets of Sole in Lettuce Leaves

(Filets de Sole Claudine)

YIELD: 4 servings

THE FILLETS are topped with a purée of mushrooms, wrapped in lettuce leaves and then poached. Because of the salad wrapping, they stay quite moist, which makes them ideal for a party and the dish can sit for a while where normally fillet of sole would dry out. We generally use gray or lemon sole, though fillet of trout, striped bass and other fish will do as well.

This dish is served with a light *velouté,* rather than with a reduction of cream and fish juices. The sauce for the Stuffed Brill (technique 95) as well as for the Mousseline of Scallops (technique 85) or the Shellfish Sausage (technique 84) could be substituted.

1 *pound fillet of sole (about 4 ounces per person), split in half lengthwise with the small piece of bone between the halves removed*
1 *extra-large head iceberg lettuce, the leafy type*
1 *large carrot, peeled, sliced thin and cut into julienne (1 generous cup loose)*
1 *leek, white and light green parts only, cut into julienne (1 cup loose)*
6 *ounces mushrooms, finely chopped (about 2 cups loose)*
½ *teaspoon freshly ground white pepper*
1½ *teaspoons salt*

1 *cup dry white wine*
1 *tablespoon sweet butter*

Sauce

2 *tablespoons sweet butter*
1 *tablespoon flour*
1 *cup heavy cream*
2 *tablespoons chopped parsley*

1. Core the lettuce, then insert the tips of your fingers in the hole and spread the lettuce apart. This helps loosen the large outside leaves. Separate the leaves and pick out 6 to 8 of the largest ones. (Reserve the rest of the lettuce for another use.) Drop the large leaves in boiling water and as they wilt push them down gently into the water. Bring the water back to almost a boil, at which point the leaves will be soft. Place the whole kettle under cold running water until the leaves are cold. Gently lift the leaves out of the cold water and drain on paper towels.

2. Place the chopped mushrooms in a skillet over medium heat and cook until all of the liquid expelled from the mushrooms evaporates. This will take about 5 to 6 minutes depending on the freshness of the mushrooms and how much liquid they exude while cooking. Season with ¼ teaspoon salt and put an equal amount of the purée of mushrooms on top of each lettuce leaf.

3. Butter a large skillet and sprinkle with ½ teaspoon salt and ¼ teaspoon freshly ground pepper. Cover with the julienne of carrots and leek. Fold 2 single fillets and place over the mushroom mixture on each leaf. The white fleshy side of the fish should be on the outside or the fillets will unfold during cooking.

4. Fold the leaves over the fillets and place each package, seam side down, on the julienne of vegetables. (The purée of mushrooms is now on top of the fish.)

5. Pour the wine over the fillets, cover with a piece of buttered parchment paper and then with a lid. Bring to a boil and simmer gently for about 8 minutes, depending on how tightly the fillets are packed together. They can also be brought to a boil, then cooked in a preheated 425-degree oven for 8 to 10 minutes.

6. To make the sauce, melt 1 tablespoon of butter in a heavy saucepan and add the flour. Cook over medium heat about 1 minute stirring with a whisk. Holding the fillets in place with the lid, pour the cooking liquid from the fish into the *roux*. Mix carefully with a whisk. Bring to a boil and continue whisking until it thickens. The mixture is now called a *velouté*. Let simmer gently for about 5 minutes. You should have approximately ¾ cup of *velouté* left. Add the cream, bring to a boil and allow to boil for 2 to 3 minutes, until the mixture is reduced to about 1¼ cups. Taste for seasonings and add salt and pepper if needed. Break the remaining tablespoon of butter into small pieces and place on top of the sauce; it will melt and form a film which will prevent any "skin" from forming on top of the sauce.

7. Remove the packages from the saucepan and arrange the julienne of vegetables on a serving platter.

8. Place the packages on top of the julienne, cover with the piece of parchment paper used during the cooking, and set in a 160-degree oven until ready to serve (but for no longer than 20 to 30 minutes).

9. At serving time make sure you pour out or blot with paper towels the juices which have accumulated around the fillets of sole. If left, they will thin down the sauce.

10. Heat the sauce, stirring in the butter; add a few drops of lemon juice if desired and pour over the fillets. Dot with chopped parsley.

11. Cut in half, note how the sole is white and moist and has a light cover of mushrooms on top. Serve immediately with stewed cucumbers, zucchini or tiny boiled potatoes tossed with butter and parsley. Excellent as a main course for a light dinner, or in a smaller package as a first course for a dinner or as lunch.

95. Stuffed Brill *(Barbue Farcie)*

YIELD: 4 to 6 main course servings or 8 to 10 first course servings

T HE BRILL is a type of small turbot from the flat fish family. It is similar to an extra large sole which is what we used in this technique because brill, unfortunately, is not always available. Other kinds of flat fish can also be boned and stuffed in the same manner.

1 *brill or lemon sole, approximately 3 pounds, neither gutted nor trimmed*

Stuffing

½ *stick (2 ounces) sweet butter*
1¼ *cups fresh bread crumbs (3 to 4 slices white bread)*
2 *tablespoons freshly chopped parsley*
6 *shallots, peeled and finely chopped (⅓ cup)*
¾ *cup coarsely chopped shrimp, peeled, deveined and briefly cooked*
½ *teaspoon salt*

¼ *teaspoon freshly ground white pepper*

To cook the fish

¾ *stick (3 ounces) sweet butter*
1 *small leek, finely chopped (½ cup)*
2 *cups sliced mushrooms*
1 *cup dry white wine*
¼ *teaspoon freshly ground white pepper*
½ *teaspoon salt*

To finish the sauce

¼ *cup heavy cream*
½ *stick sweet butter (2 ounces)*
1 *tablespoon chopped fresh herbs (parsley, tarragon, chives, etc.)*
Salt and freshly ground pepper to taste

1. Trim away the outside bones of the fish and place it flat on a chopping board, white side up. With a sharp knife, cut along the central line.

2. Using a flexible bladed fish knife (in France this knife is actually called a *filet de sole*), separate the flesh from the bone by sliding the blade along the central bone. Repeat on the other side. Do not cut through the skin. You will notice that the flesh stops near another layer of bone.

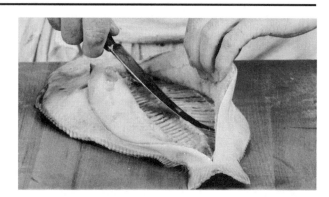

3. Turn the fish black side up and repeat the same procedure on this side. Using a large pair of shears, cut the bone away from the fish on both sides.

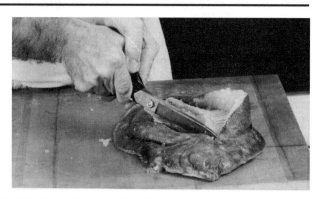

4. Cut the central bone as close as you can from the tail and from the head. It should come out in one piece.

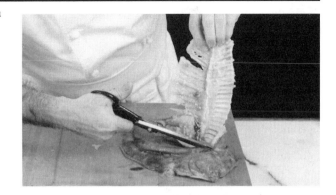

5. The fillets are now completely loose, but still held together by the head and the tail. To prepare the stuffing, melt the butter in a skillet and add the bread crumbs. Cook, stirring, until the crumbs are nicely browned. Place in a bowl and add the parsley, shallots, shrimp, salt and pepper.

6. Butter a roasting pan with 1 tablespoon of butter. Line the pan with the mushrooms and leek. Place the fish over this mixture, arranging the bottom fillets so they touch. Place the stuffing inside and cover with the two top fillets. Sprinkle with salt and pepper and pour the white wine on top.

7. Cover with a piece of buttered parchment paper and place the roasting pan on top of the stove. Bring to a boil and place in a preheated 425-degree oven for 20 minutes. Remove from the oven and, using a knife, remove the black skin and discard. Remove the solids around the fish and place in a bowl.

8. Using a small knife, pull away the layer of bones next to the fillets. It slides out easily. Discard the bones.

9. Holding the fish in place with the lid, pour the cooking liquid into a saucepan and set aside for the sauce. You should have about ½ cup of liquid.

10. Place a serving platter on top of the fish and turn upside down. Arrange the solids around the fish.

11. Pull off the skin on the white side and discard. Cover the cleaned fish with parchment paper and keep warm in a 160-degree oven while you make the sauce. Add ¼ cup heavy cream to the reserved cooking liquid and bring to a boil. Reduce, if necessary, to ¾ of a cup. Add the ½ stick of butter, piece by piece, whisking between each addition as you would for a *beurre blanc* (technique 19). Taste for seasonings and add salt and pepper if necessary. Remove the fish from the oven. Blot off any juices that may have accumulated around the fish.

12. Pour the sauce over the fish. Sprinkle with fresh herbs and serve immediately.

96. Whiting Breaded "En Colère"
(Merlan "en Colère")

UNFORTUNATELY CONSIDERED ORDINARY by most cooks, whiting is a very good, inexpesive fish. It has only a large central bone, which means it is easy to eat. It is extremely delicate provided it is well cleaned. Whiting can be served plain, poached or sautéed in butter, as well as deep-fat fried.

In our recipe, it is twisted into a crown shape called "en colère," "angry-style," so-called because its tail is secured in its mouth.

2 to 3 whiting

Breading

2 tablespoons flour
2 cups fresh bread crumbs

Batter (enough for 2 to 3 whiting)

1 egg, slightly beaten
1 teaspoon vegetable oil
1 tablespoon water
¼ teaspoon salt
Dash of freshly ground white pepper
Vegetable oil for frying

1. Each whiting should weigh approximately 1 pound before gutting. Make sure you remove the gill as well as the thin black skin inside the cavity on both sides of the wall of the abdomen. If the black veil is left in, it will make the fish bitter. Trim the fins, and wash under running water. Dry the whiting with paper towels.

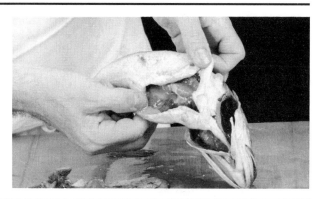

2. To prepare the batter, mix all the ingredients together. Coat the whiting lightly with flour and pat all over to shake off the excess. Dip into the egg batter to coat well and push off the excess with your fingers.

3. Roll the egg-coated whiting in the breadcrumbs. Pat gently so the crumbs stick to the fish. Twist the fish to place the tail between the jaws and squeeze them out to close and hold the tail in place.

4. Heat at least 2 inches of oil to about 350 degrees. Lower the fish into the oil and cook for 8 to 10 minutes. It should be well browned outside. To check if the fish is done, insert a fork or knife along the back bone of the thickest part of the fish—the flesh should separate from the bone easily. Drain the fish on paper towels and serve on a platter with fried parsley in the center (technique 124), lemon wedges and, if you wish, a piece of *maître d'hôtel* butter on top (butter seasoned with parsley, lemon juice and salt).

97. Cleaning and Boning Trout
(*Préparation de la Truite*)

T HE RIGHT WAY TO STUFF A TROUT WHOLE is to bone it and stuff it through the back. In this case, the trout shouldn't be opened and gutted in front as is usually done, but through the gill. If you are not a fisherman, it's not easy to come upon trout that haven't been gutted in the usual manner. However, a reliable fish store should be able to order them for you (usually alive) with some advance notice.

1. To gut the trout, insert your index finger into the opening of the gill, hook the gill and pull.

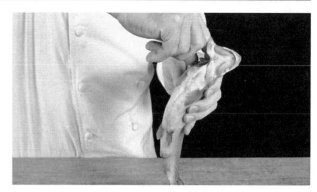

2. The gill will come out with the gut attached to it. Run water into the cavity to clean the inside of the fish as well as you possibly can without opening it.

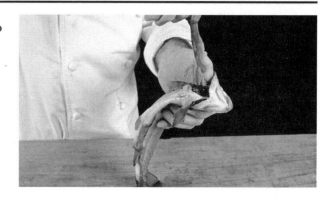

3. Trim the fins off.

4. Place the trout on the table and, holding it flat with one hand, start cutting along and just above the backbone.

5. Do not cut through, but follow the shape of the rib cage, sliding your knife, almost flat, along the ribs to detach the meat from the bone.

6. Repeat on the other side of the bone to detach the other fillet from the rib cage.

7. Sever the bone at the tail and pull to detach from the body. Sever at the head. Stuff and cook, following the recipe in technique 100, or use one of your own.

98. Rolled Trout *(Paupiettes de Truites)*

1. For *paupiettes* of trout, you can buy trout that has been gutted through the belly—the usual way. Separate the fillets from the bone, technique 87, steps 2–6, and sever from the tail end.

2. Remove the central bone near the head.

3. Roll each fillet so that the skin shows on the outside.

4. Rolled up trout, ready to cook. Trout are often prepared this way when they are to be poached and served cold in aspic.

99. Trout with Almonds *(Truite Amandine)*

1. In this technique, you can use trout that has been gutted in the usual way and boned through the opening of the belly. Slide the blade of a thin, sharp paring knife behind the rib cage, and detach the ribs from the flesh.

2. Repeat on the other side.

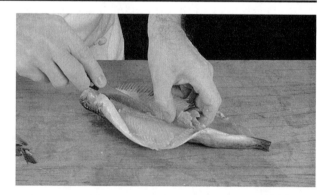

3. Continue to separate the meat from the central bone without going through the skin of the back.

4. Pull the bone loose, detaching it from the fish. Sever at the tail end and

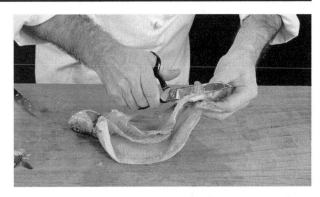

5. near the head.

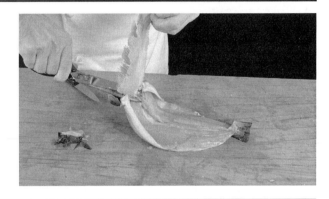

6. Fold the fish in half and

7. push the tail through the mouth.

8. Sprinkle the trout with salt, pepper and dredge lightly in flour. Melt 3 tablespoons butter in a heavy skillet, and when hot, place the fish in skillet, skin side down, and cook on medium to low heat for about 5 minutes on each side. The skin should be crisp and nicely browned.

9. Place the trout on a warm plate and add 1 tablespoon sliced almonds to the drippings. Cook the almonds for about 1 minute in the hot butter. Spoon almond and drippings mixture over the trout.

10. Sprinkle with a few drops of lemon juice and decorate with slices of lemon dipped in chopped parsley (see lemon slices for fish, technique 51). Serve immediately.

Serve 1 trout per person.

100. Stuffed Trout with Cream Sauce
(Truites Farcies à la Crème)

YIELD: This recipe well serve eight as a main course, with half a trout per person.

THE STUFFING

¾ *pound (12 ounces) fillet of fresh fish (it*
    can be sole, trout, pike or even whiting)
2 *egg whites*
1 *cup heavy cream*
¾ *teaspoon salt*
¼ *teaspoon freshly ground white pepper*
1 *tablespoon fresh tarragon (or ½ teaspoon dry)*
2 *tablespoons chopped fresh parsley*

Cut the fillets in small pieces. Place in the container of a food processor. Add the egg whites and blend until smooth. With the motor still on, add the cream slowly, letting the mixture blend well. Add the salt, pepper and herbs; blend well. Set aside and refrigerate.

THE TROUT

4 *1-pound trout*
10 *mushrooms*
½ *cup chopped shallots*
1 *cup julienne of carrots, blanched in boiling*
    water for 2 to 3 minutes, drained
2 *teaspoons salt*
½ *teaspoon freshly ground white pepper*
1½ *cups dry white vermouth*
½ *stick sweet butter, plus 2 tablespoons for the*
    roux

1 *tablespoon flour*
1 *cup heavy cream*
1 *tablespoon* glace de viande *(meat glaze),*
    optional

Bone and clean the 4 trout through the back following the directions in technique 97. Set aside. Preheat the oven to 400 degrees.

1. Cut the caps of the mushrooms into slices.

2. Stack the slices together and cut into juliennes. You should have about a cup. Use the stems for soup, stew, purée and the like.

3. Butter the bottom of a roasting pan generously.

4. Sprinkle with some of the mushrooms, shallots, carrots, salt and pepper.

5. Place the mousse in a pastry bag fitted with a plain tube. Stuff the 4 trout.

6. Arrange the trout on the bed of vegetables. To prevent the stuffing from moving, place a piece of wax paper against each trout.

7. Place the trout on top and fold the paper to cover the fish. If the trout is opened on both sides, wrap the paper all around to keep the stuffing inside.

8. Cover with the remaining vegetable garnishes, salt and pepper.

9. Add the vermouth. Butter half of a piece of wax paper. Fold the unbuttered half over the buttered half.

10. then unfold. The paper is now completely coated with butter. Place the ½ stick butter in pieces on top of the trout.

11. Cover with the buttered paper and bring to a boil on top of the stove. Place in the preheated oven for 15 minutes.

12. Lift the trout up from the poaching liquid and place on a serving platter. Pull the skin off from one side.

13. Turn and pull the skin from the other side.

14. Using a slotted spoon, place the julienne of vegetables on top of fish.

15. Cover with the wax paper and keep warm in the oven.

16. Melt the 2 tablespoons butter in a heavy skillet. Add the flour, mix and cook 1 minute on low heat. Pour the poaching liquid into the roux, mix well and bring to a boil. Let simmer for 2 minutes and add the cream. Bring to a boil and reduce the heat. Add the *glace de viande* and simmer for 2 minutes.

17. Remove the trout from the oven. You will notice that some liquid has accumulated around the fish. Add the liquid to the sauce and mix well.

18. Taste the sauce for seasoning. It may need salt and pepper. Coat the trout with the sauce.

19. Serve immediately, half a trout per person.

101. Sea Trout or Bass in Puff Paste
(Bar en Feuilletage)

YIELD: 8 to 10 servings

WHEN YOU BAKE *en croûte,* pick a large fish rather than a small one. You need a certain amount of time to cook the dough regardless of the size of the fish. With a large fish the dough will have enough time to cook without the fish getting overdone. Small fish tend to overcook by the time the dough is ready. Other crusts can be used instead of puff paste. In addition, the fish can be cooked boned or not boned, with or without a stuffing.

1 5-pound sea trout, whole, gutted with fin on, or 2 large fillets about 1½ pounds each
½ pound loose flesh of fish (use trimmings from the sea trout)
½ cup heavy cream
½ teaspoon salt
½ teaspoon freshly ground white pepper
½ cup finely chopped parsley
1 tablespoon minced fresh chives
1 tablespoon chopped fresh tarragon
1 teaspoon salt to sprinkle fillets
1½ to 2 pounds puff paste (technique 269)

1 egg with 1 egg yolk thoroughly beaten for glaze

Herb butter sauce
1 cup dry white wine
½ of the chopped herbs (⅓ cup) left from the mousse
2 sticks (8 ounces) sweet butter, softened and cut into small pieces
2 egg yolks
½ teaspoon freshly ground white pepper
½ teaspoon salt

1. Fillet the fish and remove the skin and sinews from both fillets and trim. Scrape any loose fish off the bone (you will need about ½ pound to make the mousse). Keep the bones to make a stock for a sauce or fish soup. To make the mousse: Purée the loose flesh in a food processor, add the cream, salt and pepper and blend again until smooth. Do not overblend or the cream may turn into butter.

2. Roll the puff paste ⅛ inch thick into two rectangles at least 2 inches wider and longer than the fish. Place a piece of parchment paper on a large cookie sheet and unroll a rectangle of puff paste on top. Place 1 fillet on the dough and sprinkle lightly with salt. Spread the fish mousse on the fillet and sprinkle half the herbs on top.

3. Lay the second fillet over the mousse. (A fish fillet is thicker at the head end than at the tail. When you position the second fillet over the first reverse direction so that you have thick over thin on one side and then thin over thick on the other.) Sprinkle lightly with salt. Brush the dough around the fillets with the egg glaze.

4. Unroll the second layer of puff paste on top of the fish and press all around the fish to make sure both layers adhere.

5. Trim around the fillets, trying to make the package look like a fish. Decorate with strips of dough and a round for the eyes. Brush with egg wash.

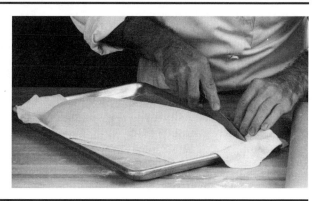

6. Using the tines of a fork, mark strips on the tail.

7. With the large end of a pastry tube (or the back of a spoon), make "scales" on the fish, cutting halfway through the dough, but not completely through. Place the fish in the freezer for 20 minutes or in the refrigerator for 1 to 2 hours.

8. Bake in a preheated 350-degree oven for 50 to 60 minutes. Let rest 5 minutes and with a large spatula, remove to a serving platter. Keep warm in a 180-degree oven while making the sauce (see below) or until serving time. Cut the fish into 1-inch slices and serve on hot plates with the sauce all around. See finished bass in puff paste, page 267.

To make the sauce: Bring the wine to a boil and boil for 1 minute. Add the herbs leftover from the mousse and bring again to a boil. Remove from the heat and pour the mixture in a food processor. Add the egg yolks, pepper, salt and about one quarter of the butter. Blend for about 15 seconds. (The boiling wine will cook the egg yolks enough.) Add remaining butter and blend for another 15 to 20 seconds to homogenize. This makes a very light foamy sauce, which should be served as soon as possible. If it cannot be served right away, keep warm in a double boiler and whip a few seconds before serving.

102. Pâté of Fish Tricolor

(Pâté de Poisson Trois Couleurs)

YIELD: 12 to 14 servings

This *pâté* of fish is particularly suited for a dinner party or a cold buffet. The contrast of colors makes it very attractive: the white of the whiting mousse against the green herb mousse; the orange salmon and the pale pink sauce. The *pâté* and the sauce—made with oil, tomato, cayenne and pepper—should be served cool but not too cold. We use three types of fish in this mousse. If one of the fish called for is not available, substitute another. The *pâté* can also be served hot with one of the hot fish sauces served with the brill, the bass in puff paste or the *mousseline* of scallops (techniques 95, 101, and 85, respectively).

Mousse

3½ pounds whiting, whole but gutted
2 egg whites
1 teaspoon salt
½ teaspoon freshly ground white pepper
2 cups heavy cream

Garnishes

¾ pound salmon
2 large fillets of sole (about 10 to 12 ounces each), separated into single fillets and each pounded to ¼ inch thick

Herb mousse

4 to 5 shallots, peeled and coarsely chopped (about ¼ cup)
1 cup dry white wine
¼ teaspoon freshly ground white pepper
½ teaspoon salt
1 small bunch watercress leaves (about 1 cup lightly packed)
1 small bunch cleaned spinach leaves (about 1 cup)
½ tablespoon fresh chopped tarragon or chives or any other herb
2 tablespoons chopped fresh parsley

Sauce

1 large tomato, peeled, seeded and coarsely chopped (approximately 1 cup)
½ teaspoon good paprika
Dash of cayenne pepper
1 teaspoon salt
¼ teaspoon freshly ground white pepper
1 tablespoon good red wine vinegar
1 egg yolk
1 cup good olive oil, preferably virgin, at room temperature

To prepare whiting mousse: Clean the whiting (technique 96), bone out, remove the skin as well as the black membrane in the inside cavity. You should have approximately 1½ pounds of flesh after the cleaning. Place the flesh in the bowl of a food processor and purée for approximately 40 to 50 seconds. Push through the fine screen of a food mill to remove any sinews left (*optional*). Put the mixture back into the bowl of a food processor with the egg whites, salt and pepper, and with the machine on, slowly add 1 cup of cream—it should take 10 to 15 seconds. Beat the other cup of cream to a soft peak and whisk the fish mixture into the cream.

To prepare the sauce: Combine all the sauce ingredients, except the oil, in the container of the food processor and blend for 30 to 40 seconds until smooth. With the motor still on add the oil slowly (it should take about 10 to 15 seconds), taste for seasonings and set the mixture aside. If it is too thick, which happens, thin down to a creamy consistency with 1 to 2 tablespoons of lukewarm water.

To prepare the herb mousse: Place the shallots, white wine, pepper and salt in a saucepan (preferably not aluminum because of discoloration). Bring to a boil, then reduce until there is approximately ⅓ cup left (about 5 minutes). Add the watercress and spinach, stirring. Cook covered for ½ minute, until the greens wilt. Uncover and keep boiling down until there is only about 1 tablespoon of liquid left. Set aside to cool. When cold, blend with the parsley and tarragon in the bowl of a food processor until smooth. Then combine with about 1 cup of the whiting mousse.

1. Line an 8-cup mold with approximately ½ inch of fish mousse on the bottom and the sides.

2. Cut the fresh salmon into thin, ¼-inch slices and line the fish mousse with a layer of salmon slices.

3. Sprinkle the salmon with salt and pepper and line the top and sides of the salmon with a thin layer of fish mousse and then the pounded fillet of sole.

4. Place the green herb mousse in the center.

5. Cover the green herb mousse with more fillet of sole and slices of salmon. Finally, cover the top of the salmon with a layer of the whiting mousse. Smooth the top with a spatula, cover with buttered parchment paper, then with aluminum foil. Place the mold into a pan of tepid water that comes approximately three-quarters of the way up the sides of the mold. Place in a preheated 275-degree oven for 1½ hours. At the slow temperature, the texture will be smooth. Cooked too fast, the *pâté* will develop tiny holes and the texture will be too airy.

6. Remove from the oven and let cool at room temperature for a few hours, Refrigerate overnight. Unmold and slice into ¼-inch slices. Place approximately 2 tablespoons of sauce in the bottom of each individual plate with a slice of *pâté* on top.

POACHED SCALLOPS WITH A GREEN
SAUCE *(Coquilles Pochées Sauce Verte)*

YIELD: 6 servings

For another easy, tasty and decorative shellfish dish, make this poached scallops with a green sauce.

1½ *pounds scallops (bay or sea scallops which should be very fresh)*
1 *cup dry white wine*
1½ *teaspoons salt*
2 *cups mushrooms, cleaned and cut into large chunks*
1 *cup watercress leaves*
2 *cups spinach leaves*

Remove the small muscle or nerve on the scallops. If you use sea scallops, slice into halves or three slices if they are large. Place the scallops, mushrooms, wine and salt in a large saucepan (not aluminum because of discoloration) and heat on a medium heat until it almost comes to a boil. Stir once in a while. You will notice that the scallops whiten and stiffen as they cook. They should just barely cook through and they do not even need to come to a full boil. Strain the mixture in a colander and cover to prevent too much drying. Place the juices back into a saucepan and add the watercress and spinach. Bring to a boil stirring; the greens should be wilted. Remove with a slotted spoon and place in the container of

a food processor. Reduce the juices to ½ cup and add to the greens. Blend for a few seconds until smooth.

Sauce

1 *egg yolk*
2 *tablespoons heavy cream*
1 *cup good oil (preferably virgin olive oil or a mixture of olive and peanut oil)*
¼ *teaspoon freshly ground white peppercorns*
Small strips of tomato skin for garnish

Add the egg yolks and the cream to the greens and blend for a few seconds until smooth. Add the pepper and the oil with blender on as you would make a mayonnaise. It should have the consistency of a salad dressing. Place some sauce in each individual plate with a few scallops in the center. Decorate with the tomato skin. The sauce should be cool but the scallops should be at room temperature.

103. Smoking Fish *(Fumage des Poissons)*

COMMERCIALLY SMOKED FISH is very expensive and often not as good as fish smoked at home. The commercial product is usually more salted and more smoked than the homemade product because the manufacturers want the fish to have the longest "shelf-life" possible.

Smoking your own fish is fun and rewarding. There are only a few smoked fish available on the market—such as white fish, sturgeon, trout and salmon—but you can smoke practically any type of fish at home. We have had great results with mullets, porgie, eel, pike, etc. There are two basic ways of smoking: the hot and cold methods. The hot method partially cooks the fish as it smokes. The cold method smokes the fish but leaves it raw.

If you have one of the small home smokers, often sold at camping equipment outfitters, you will be able to hot smoke but not cold smoke. If you have no smoker, you can make one yourself from an old refrigerator or metal locker. It can be used for both the hot and cold methods. Hot smoking is done at temperatures between 180 and 200 degrees. Cold smoking temperatures shouldn't go above 90 degrees.

Before you smoke—whichever way you choose—you have to cure the fish with salt. Here, too, there are two different methods: You can cure it in a liquid brine (salt and water), or with dry salt. The salt leeches all the moisture out of the fish thereby depriving the bacteria of the medium necessary for its survival. It is in this way that salting preserves. Use the kosher-type coarse salt which is a sweeter, better, more natural salt—without the additives put in regular salt to prevent caking.

Both meat and fish are smoked by being exposed to the smoke given off by smouldering wood chips. Different types of woods can be used—hickory, maple, alder, juniper and most woods from fruit trees. Resinous woods such as pine, spruce, etc., should be avoided. Herbs such as bay leaves or thyme can be added to the wood chips to flavor the smoke.

In the first technique we are hot smoking trout in a little home smoker. In the second, we will cold smoke salmon in a converted ice box smoker. Hot smoking is necessary with a tight, firm fleshed fish such as sturgeon, eel and even trout. The tougher the flesh, the higher the temperature should go; 180 degrees will be sufficient for trout, but it should go up to 200 degrees for eel. Because of its particular texture salmon is cold smoked. If subjected to temperatures above 90 degrees, it will cook through. The proteins coagulate around 120 degrees and force the moisture of the fish out (it is visible as a white custard-like sediment), the flesh will flake and the salmon cook.

SMOKED TROUT *(Truites Fumées)*

YIELD: 12 first course lunch or brunch servings

6 *trout, 12 ounces each, gutted and cleaned*
4 *cups water*
2 *cups kosher salt*
1 *tablespoon sugar*
Hickory or alder chips

1. Bring the water to a boil and add the salt and sugar. Mix to dissolve and let cool. (The saltiness of the brine can be checked with an hydrometer—the specific gravity should be 1155 at 60 degrees Fahrenheit—or by floating an egg on top of the brine; a bit of eggshell the size of a 50 cent coin should emerge from the water.) Place the trout in the brine for 2 hours. Remove, wipe dry with paper towels inside and out, and rub lightly with vegetable oil.

2. Skewer the trout, three at a time, through the gills and mouths. (We used sticks of wood as skewers.)

3. Hang the trout in the smoker. Plug in the hot plate, fill up the little tray with the wood chips, return to the smoker and put the cover back on the smoker. Leave the trout in the smoker approximately 2 hours. (It will take about 30 minutes before the chips are hot enough to produce smoke.)

4. After about an hour, replenish the tray with more wood chips. The temperature at this point will be between 160 and 180 degrees. After 2 hours, unplug the smoker and leave the trout in for another hour to cool and set.

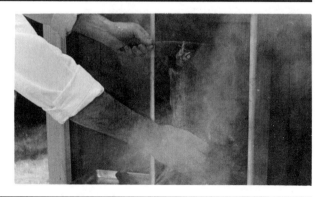

5. Take the trout out. They will have a nice yellowish color, be slightly warm to the touch and a little soft. Sometimes the weight of the trout causes it to break at the side of the head and fall.

6. Refrigerate for at least 1 day to allow the trout to set and the taste to develop. Then remove the skin: Start at the belly and "unwrap" to the back.

7. Continue unwrapping to the other side. The skin will come off in one piece.

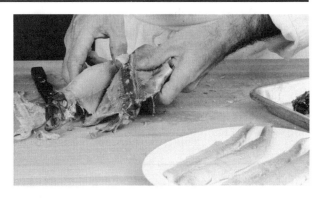

8. Remove the head and split the top fillet in half following the line down the center of the trout.

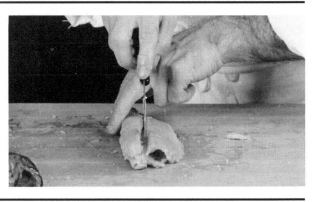

9. Pull out the back fillet, which is the thickest and the nicest. It should slide off the bone easily. Then push away on the other side to separate the belly fillet from the bone.

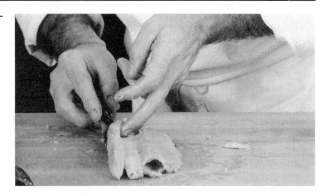

10. Remove the central bone which should come out in one piece. The trout is now ready and is usually served with toast and butter. For an elegant first course serve *La Truite Fumée Gloria*, which is a lukewarm, boned-out fillet of trout rolled and filled with scrambled eggs (see technique 32). See finished smoked trout Gloria, page 267.

SMOKED SALMON *(Saumon Fumé)*

Use a large thick salmon. Ours weighed 10 pounds (gutted, head on). If you don't want to smoke a whole fillet, you can smoke half a fillet as long as the flesh is thick. Take your piece in the thickest part of the fillet. The instructions that follow are for one side of salmon, 3½ pounds with skin on but boned, and head and tail removed.

½ *of a 10-pound salmon, scaled, washed and*
    filleted
2 *cups kosher-type salt mixed with 1 tablespoon*
    sugar
⅓ *cup vegetable oil*

1. Clean and fillet the salmon. Your fishmonger can do this for you or you can do it yourself following the instructions on pages 209-212.

2. Using a pair of tweezers or small pliers, pull out the tiny bones which run down the center of the fillet. The bones can also be removed after smoking, but if left they make carving difficult.

3. Spread some of the salt mixture on a large rectangular piece of aluminum foil and place the salmon, skin-side down, on top. Spread the rest of the salt mixture on top, sprinkling just a little on the tail because it is thin and shouldn't absorb too much salt. There should be about ⅛ inch of salt mixture on top of the fillet except for the tail end.

4. Pack the salmon tightly in the aluminum foil and refrigerate for 5 hours during which time the salmon will cure. Adjust the curing time for larger or smaller slabs of salmon. (If the salmon has been frozen, it will be more mushy and absorb more salt faster.) Remove from the aluminum foil, wash under cold water and dry carefully with paper towels.

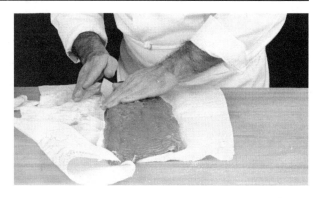

5. Place the salmon on a wire rack and let it dry for approximately 6 hours or overnight in front of a fan. A thin veil will form on top of the skin which should be dry to the touch. Rub the fillet generously all around with vegetable oil, place on a tray and let marinate in the refrigerator for 2 to 3 hours. (At this point the salmon should be served as gravlax.) To smoke the salmon, place in the smoker.

6. We use an electric barbecue starter to get the wood chips smoking. Note that an aluminum gutter elbow was fitted to go through the refrigerator. This leaves the source of heat on the outside so that only the smoke enters the refrigerator. With this method the temperature will not exceed 90 degrees inside the box. For hot smoke, place the barbecue starter and sawdust directly inside the refrigerator so that the temperature goes up to between 180 and 200 degrees.

7. Embed the barbecue starter into the wood chips. Wrap the opening of the aluminum elbow and the top of the flower pot with aluminum foil to contain the smoke and force it through the pipe into the refrigerator. Plug the starter in for 3 minutes. The chips will start smoking after about 1 minute. After 3 minutes of smoke, unplug. The chips will continue to smoke for a few minutes. Let the salmon "rest" (without opening the door) for 1 hour.

8. Repeat the same procedure twice more. This gives a total of 9 minutes of intense smoke and about 3½ hours in the smoker.

9. Let the slab dry and settle under refrigeration for at least 1 day before using. Slice thin on a slant and serve plain with a dash of lemon juice and thin, buttered slices of black bread. The salmon can also be seasoned with capers, olive oil and ground black pepper. If the salmon is frozen after smoking, the texture will be mushier after defrosting and will not cut into thin, transparent and elastic slices. See finished smoked salmon, page 267.

Smoked salmon, smoked trout Gloria

Bass in puff paste

Vegetables

104. Asparagus *(Asperges)*

ASPARAGUS HAS BEEN commonly cultivated in Europe from the seventeenth century on. The large white, fleshy Argenteuil is considered one of the best, although less available in the United States. The commonly found varieties are the Italian purple (with almost violet-colored tips) and the green Mary Washington type. There are countless ways of cooking and serving asparagus. The best is the simplest, boiled and served plain with vinaigrette, hollandaise or melted butter.

1. The fresh stalks are firm, not wrinkled, and the tips are tightly closed. To make the whole spear edible, the asparagus must be peeled. Use a small paring knife or a vegetable peeler.

2. Determine by scratching with your nail the place where the outer skin is getting fibrous and tough. It is usually 1 or 2 inches under the tip. Holding the asparagus at the root end, peel from the tip down toward the root until you touch your finger. Peel, rotating the asparagus as you go along so that the whole spear is peeled.

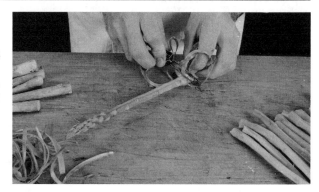

3. Cut or break the stalk at the end of the peel.

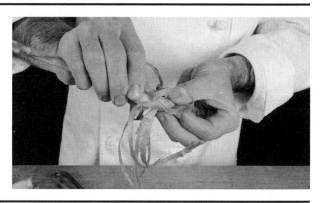

4. Asparagus are often bundled into a portion of about 10 or 12 thin stalks. Grab a handful and align the tips by leveling them on the flat table.

5. Holding the spears firmly in one hand, wrap your middle finger with soft kitchen string.

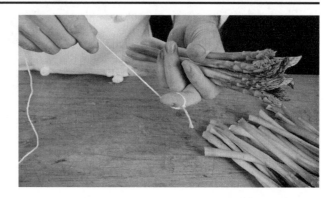

6. Start bundling the lower part of the bunch. Be sure to make it tight. (This is one reason why you should not use string that is too thin and might cut.)

7. Come across, still holding the bundle tight and

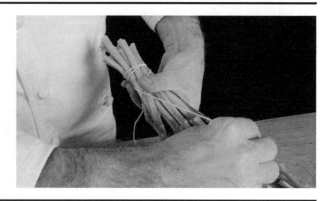

8. tie the front, lower than the tips. Secure with a double knot.

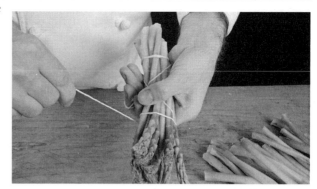

9. Trim the spears at the root end. The asparagus are now the same length. Bring a large pot of salted water to a rolling boil. Lower the asparagus into the water and cover them until it starts boiling again; uncover. If the cover is left on during the whole cooking time, the asparagus will turn yellowish. Boil, depending on size, from 6 to 10 minutes. They should still be crunchy, but cooked enough. Lift the bundle from the boiling water and serve immediately.

10. If cooked ahead or served cold, as soon as the asparagus is done, place the whole kettle under cold water to stop the cooking. To prevent breaking the asparagus, place a spoon across the pot to divert the force of the water so it falls gently on the tender tips. (If only a small amount of asparagus is to be cooked, place ½ inch water in a skillet. Spread the asparagus in one layer and cook, covered, for 4 minutes. Lift out the asparagus and let cool on a plate.)

11. Drain the asparagus on paper towels. To serve warm, place a bundle, when needed, in a sieve and lower into boiling water for about 1 minute. Drain and serve immediately. To serve cold, arrange the spears on a large, oblong platter and

12. garnish the ends with a bunch of curly parsley.

105. Asparagus Stew *(Ragoût d'Asperges)*

YIELD: 4 servings

THIS IS A VERY SIMPLE, elegant and delicious dish. It can be served as a first course or as an accompaniment to broiled lamb chops, pan-fried veal steaks or to any sauceless meat.

2 dozen green asparagus
⅓ cup water
½ teaspoon salt
½ stick (2 ounces) sweet butter, cut into pieces
¼ cup finely chopped parsley

1. Peel the asparagus, then cut on the diagonal into 1-inch lengths. (Peeling asparagus makes them edible from head to stem. See pages 269-271 for more about preparing asparagus.)

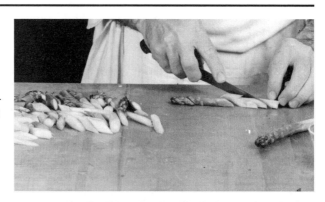

2. Place the asparagus in a skillet with the water and salt, cover and bring to a strong boil. Boil for 1½ minutes, uncover and add the butter and the parsley.

3. Return to a strong boil, shaking the pan to bind the ingredients together. Boil for 20 to 30 seconds until the sauce thickens and becomes foamy. The mixture will rise like milk ready to boil over. (To understand how and why the butter and water bind together, read the discussion on emulsion, techniques 19 and 20.

4. As soon as it foams, remove from the heat (further cooking will reduce the amount of moisture in the sauce and make the butter and water separate). Pour onto a serving dish and serve immediately. See finished asparagus stew, page 350.

106. Purée of Carrots *(Purée de Carottes)*

PUREE OF FRESH VEGETABLES makes an elegant accompaniment to saddle of lamb, creamed chicken, veal roast and other dishes.

1. Place 3 pounds of peeled carrots in a kettle. Cover with water and add 2 teaspoons salt. Bring to a boil and simmer for about 20 minutes. The carrots should be tender to the point of a knife. Drain. Line a bowl with cheesecloth.

2. Place the carrots in a food mill and strain on top of the cheesecloth.

3. Tie the four corners of the cheesecloth.

4. Push a stick through it and

5. let it hang in a deep vessel to drain the pulp of excess moisture. Let it hang for 2 hours.

6. Lift and press to extrude more liquid. Use the liquid for soup or vegetable stock.

7. Place the pulp in a saucepan. Add ⅓ cup heavy cream, 2 tablespoons sweet butter, 1 teaspoon salt and ¼ teaspoon freshly ground white pepper. Heat slowly on low heat and serve hot.

This recipe yields 6 to 8 servings.

107. Cauliflower *(Chou-fleur)*

Cauliflower is one of my favorite vegetables. It can be eaten raw with a spicy dressing, used in soup, pickled, combined with cream sauce and cheese or browned in butter.

1. In choosing cauliflower, be sure the heads are very white and very firm with small, compact flowers squeezed together. Separate the leaves from the stem with a paring knife.

2. Separate the flowerets from the central core by cutting around each one with your knife.

3. If the cauliflower is old, pull off the tough, outer layer from the stem of each floweret with a small paring knife. Drop the cauliflower into a large pot of salted water and boil 10 to 12 minutes until the stem can be pierced with the point of a knife. Immediately place the whole pot under cold, running water to stop the cooking. Protect the tender flowerets from the heavy stream of cold water by resting a large spoon on the kettle to divert the water's force. When cool, drain thoroughly and cover with plastic wrap.

4. To sauté cauliflower, place the cooked flowerets, head side down, in foaming butter. Sprinkle with salt and pepper. Bring to medium heat and cook for a few minutes, until the flowerets are nicely browned. Turn each piece on the other side and brown for a few minutes more.

5. Arrange the cauliflower on a platter in a circle so that the flowerets are facing the outside of the plate.

6. Keep piling up flowerets to reconstruct a whole head of cauliflower.

7. Cauliflower ready to serve. Sprinkle with parsley and serve immediately.

108. Broccoli and Cauliflower with Lemon Butter *(Choux Panachés au Beurre de Citron)*

YIELD: 10 servings

WHEN YOU SHOP FOR BROCCOLI, look for a head that's a beautiful deep green with tiny flowerets tightly packed together—a young broccoli, tender and very flavorful. In older broccoli, the flowerets start to open up, and the vegetable becomes softer, stronger in taste and is no longer crisp and tender. This versatile vegetable can be steamed briefly and served plain with lemon and salt or with melted butter and lemon, as well as with a white sauce. It can also be made into a purée or served crunchy in small pieces mixed with filets of anchovies, garlic and olive oil as a first course or part of hors d'oeuvre. Cauliflower can also be prepared these ways: The whole head can be cooked in one piece, as in our recipe, or in flowerets. It can be served with a cream sauce, or au gratin. It can be puréed or fried in butter "Polonaise style" with hard chopped eggs. Choose very tight, white, firm heads which are indications of youth and freshness. Older cauliflower is fibrous, slightly yellowish, softer and has a much stronger odor. Cauliflower and broccoli belong to the same family and are mixed together and served with a lemon butter sauce in the recipe below.

2–3 bunches broccoli (about 4 pounds)
1 large cauliflower (2 to 3 pounds)

Foaming Lemon Butter

1½ tablespoons water
1 tablespoon lemon juice
Dash of salt
Dash of white pepper
⅔ stick sweet butter, softened

1. Cut the broccoli into flowerets. Trim the stems. Peel away any fibrous skin.

2. Peel the pieces of stem.

3. Cut the peeled stems into pieces and combine them with the flowerets.

4. Place ½ cup water and ½ teaspoon salt in a large stainless steel pan and bring to a strong boil. The water should cover only the bottom of the pan. Add the broccoli in one layer. Pieces should not overlap. Cover and bring to a strong boil. Boil for approximately 4 minutes, covered. Remove the broccoli with a slotted spoon and place it on a tray. It should be green and crunchy. Set aside to cool until ready to use.

5. The cauliflower can be cooked whole after the green leaves and any bruised parts are removed.

6. Place 1 inch of water and ½ teaspoon salt in the bottom of a stainless steel saucepan. Bring to a strong boil and place the cauliflower in one piece in the boiling water. Cover and boil about 10 minutes. The cauliflower should be tender but still quite crunchy. (It could be served as is with a piece of fresh butter on top.)

7. For our recipe, separate the flowerets from the core. Heavily butter a large Pyrex or stainless steel bowl and sprinkle with salt. Line the dish with cauliflower, then broccoli, then cauliflower again, pressing the vegetables down slightly as you layer them.

8. Keep layering until the bowl is full. Sprinkle the top with salt and cover with a piece of buttered parchment paper. At serving time, heat the bowl in a *bain-marie* on top of the stove, or place it in a preheated 300-degree oven for 10 to 15 minutes, just long enough to warm the vegetables through.

9. Unmold on a serving platter and make a lemon butter.

10. Bring the water, lemon juice, salt and pepper to a strong boil and drop pieces of butter into the boiling mixture, bit by bit, shaking the pan with one hand as you do so. After all the butter has been added, the mixture will start foaming and will rise like milk about to boil over. As soon as it does, remove it from the heat and pour on top of the unmolded vegetables. Serve right away. This dish can be served by itself or as a garnish to meat, chicken or poached fish. See finished dish, page 350a.

109. Corn Crêpes *(Crêpes de Maïs)*

WHOLE EARS OF CORN are excellent poached (not boiled) in salted water, or cooked in aluminum foil on top of the barbecue. A puree of the pulp is very elegant served with veal or lamb. (Melt sweet butter in a saucepan, add the pulp, salt and pepper and simmer a few minutes, just enough for the starch to tighten and the puree to thicken into a creamy mixture.)
With the pulp, one can also make excellent crêpes.

6 *medium-sized ears of corn*
4½ *tablespoons flour*
4 *large eggs*
1 *teaspoon salt*
¼ *teaspoon freshly ground white pepper*
½ *cup milk*
½ *stick (4 tablespoons) melted sweet butter*

1. Holding the cleaned ear of corn in one hand, using a sharp knife, cut through the middle of each row of kernels. The object is to open each kernel so the pulp can be "pushed" out.

2. Stand the ear straight up. Using the back (dull side) of the knife, scrape the pulp out of the opened kernels, turning the ear as you go along. You should have approximately 1½ cups of pulp. Mix all ingredients thoroughly, starting with the pulp and the flour. Make the crêpes, technique 246, steps 2-6, using a non-stick pan if possible. Brown on one side only and roll up. The crepes will be very delicate and fragile to handle. Serve as soon as possible as a vegetable or as a garnish for your favorite meat. This recipe yields approximately 20 crepes.

110. Artichokes and Artichoke Hearts

(Artichauts et Fonds d'Artichauts)

ARTICHOKES have been widely cultivated in France since the middle of the sixteenth century (Rabelais mentions them). Cooked artichokes can be served cold as a first course, lukewarm with hollandaise or melted butter as a vegetable, or hot stuffed with meat or other vegetables. The small young artichokes, especially the Provence or the Tuscany violet, are eaten raw with salt and butter or with a vinaigrette.

WHOLE

1. A good-sized artichoke, Breton Stocky or Lyon Green, weighs about 8 ounces. Cut the stem off with a knife, or break it at the base (this helps pull out of the heart the stringy fibers that develop in overmatured artichokes).

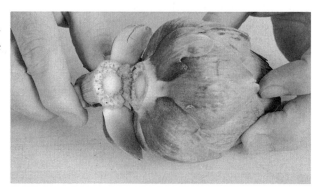

2. Cut off at least 1½ inches of the top.

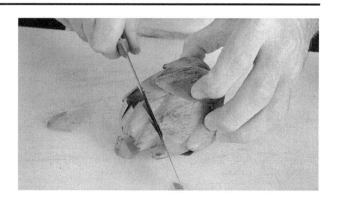

3. Cut off about one-third of the top of each leaf. The ends are very tough, bitter and often thorny. The reason is also aesthetic.

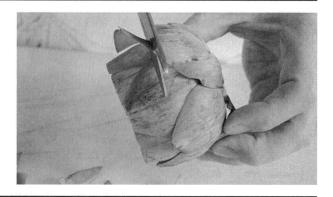

4. To prevent discoloration (artichokes turn dark very fast), tie a slice of lemon to the bottom of the artichoke where the stem is cut. Restaurants that cook artichokes several days ahead use this technique to keep the bottom white until serving time. The technique is optional.

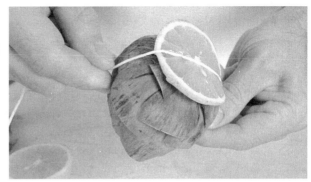

5. Place the artichoke in a large amount of boiling, salted water. Place a wet towel directly on top of the artichoke to keep it wet and immersed during cooking. Boil as fast as possible for 40 to 50 minutes, depending on the size. Do not cover. Artichokes tend to become bitter if covered during cooking. To test for doneness, pull out a leaf; if done, it pulls out easily. Do not overcook. Place under cold water (see step 10, technique 104) to cool.

6. Avoid refrigerating artichokes for it changes the taste. Serve not too cold. To serve lukewarm, lower into hot water for 2 to 3 minutes. Drain. Spread the outside leaves at the top enough to slide your fingers inside and around the center leaves.

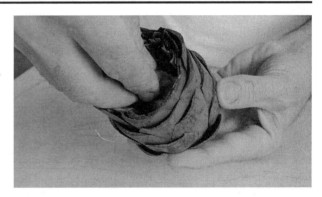

7. Pull out the central leaves; they should come out in one piece like a small funnel or cone. Now, the "choke" is exposed.

8. Using your fingers, or a teaspoon, remove the hairy choke from the cavity.

9. Replace the central leaves upside down on the opened top of the artichoke and garnish with curly parsley. Serve on a tulip napkin, technique 69, or directly on plate.

HEARTS

1. The artichoke bottom or heart is extensively used as a garnish or in the making of a dish. It can be filled with purée of smoked salmon or tomatoes, as well as with poached eggs or cooked beef marrow. Many restaurants use canned artichoke bottoms but the difference is like night and day. Break the stem and cut the leaves all around the base of the artichoke. Trim as closely as you can manage without taking "meat" from the heart itself. This is a delicate technique.

2. Cut the central core of the leaves just above the heart. Leave the choke attached; it will be removed after cooking.

3. Trim the remaining greenish leaves and pieces all around the heart.

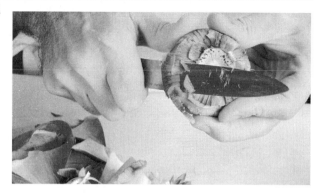

4. If you find it difficult to execute step 2, instead of cutting around the heart, you can break the leaves off at the base. Be careful not to pull out pieces of meat when breaking the leaves off.

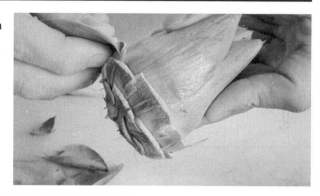

5. Trim all of the green off as evenly as you can manage.

6. Rub with lemon to avoid discoloration. If a recipe calls for pieces of artichoke bottom, separate the heart into 6 equal wedges and remove the choke, using a small paring knife. Cook according to your recipe. To cook 6 artichoke bottoms, place 3 cups water, 2 tablespoons vegetable oil, the juice of 1 lemon and ½ teaspoon salt in a saucepan. Bring to a boil. Add the heart and simmer for 20 to 30 minutes.

7. The heart should be tender when pierced with the point of a knife. Let cool enough to handle and remove the choke with a spoon. It should slide off easily if the artichoke is cooked enough. Cover the hearts with the cooking liquid and refrigerate. They will keep at least one week refrigerated. Use as needed.

111. Celeriac or Celery Root *(Céleri-rave)*

CELERIAC OR CELERY ROOT, usually available at certain times of the year, is not the root of the common stalk celery. Though it tastes like celery, it is a different plant. It is excellent cooked, but is commonly served raw in julienne with an oil and mustard sauce.

1. Peel the celeriac with a knife or a vegetable peeler.

2. Cut the celeriac in half through the root. Remove the spongy flesh in the center near the stem end.

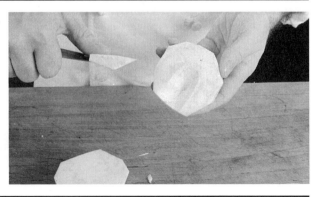

3. Using a knife or a *mandoline,* slice into ⅛-inch slices.

4. Stack a few slices together and cut into a fine julienne. Make a mayonnaise, technique 23, but triple the amount of mustard and double the vinegar. Mix with the celeriac and add more salt and pepper. Make the salad at least one hour in advance. Serve cool, but not ice cold.

112. How to Peel and Prepare Green Peppers *(Poivrons Epluchés et Farcis)*

PEPPERS CAN BE SLICED thin and eaten raw in a salad. They can be chopped, sautéed and served with eggs or fried with onions as a garnish, or served with hamburgers or steaks. However, if you are going to stuff them, the skin should be removed. Peeling them greatly improves their taste and texture. We have used the long tapered Italian pepper in the photographs that follow; they are sweeter, thinner and more tender than the ordinary ones.

TO PEEL AND SEED PEPPERS

1. Place the peppers on a rack under the broiler approximately 1 inch away from the heat. The Italian peppers will take approximately 10 to 12 minutes of browning and the regular type approximately 14 minutes. Turn them after 5 to 6 minutes of browning.

2. When they are charred all around, remove from the oven and place them in a plastic bag. Close the bag and let them steam and soften in the bag for about 10 minutes.

3. Steaming the peppers in a plastic bag makes the skin very easy to remove. Hold by the stem and pull the skin, which should come off easily.

4. Pull the stem and with it will come most of the seeds. Remove the seeds left inside with a teaspoon.

5. Another method is to open the pepper and spread it flat out on the table, scraping out all the seeds.

GARLIC PEPPERS *(Poivrons à l'Ail)*

8 *peppers, roasted, with skin and seeds removed*
6 *to 8 garlic cloves, peeled, chopped and crushed*
(1 tablespoon)
1 *teaspoon salt*
½ *teaspoon freshly ground white pepper*
½ *teaspoon red wine vinegar*
4 *tablespoons virgin olive oil*

6. Cut the peppers into ½-inch-wide strips. Combine with the other ingredients and let the whole mixture marinate for at least 2 hours before serving. Serve at room temperature with crunchy bread, or as a side dish or mix into a salad. The garlic peppers will keep in the refrigerator for at least 2 weeks.

STUFFED GREEN PEPPERS *(Poivrons Verts Farcis)*

8 *to* 10 *medium Italian-type peppers, peeled, seeded and opened*
½ *cup long grain rice (2 cups cooked)*
1 *tablespoon olive oil*
⅓ *cup chopped onions*
2 *cloves garlic peeled, crushed and chopped fine (about ½ teaspoon)*
½ *teaspoon freshly ground black pepper*
½ *teaspoon salt*

Pinch of thyme leaves
1¼ *cups finely diced boiled ham*
2 *tablespoons chopped parsley*
2 *tablespoons olive oil (for sprinkling on top)*

Boil the rice in 3 cups of salted water for 30 minutes and drain.

7. Heat the oil in a skillet, add the onions and sizzle for 1 to 2 minutes. Add the garlic, pepper, salt and thyme. (If you are going to serve the peppers cold, overseason the stuffing.) Remove from the stove and add the ham, parsley and cooked rice. Place 2 to 3 tablespoons of stuffing on each open pepper, fold and turn upside down so the seam side is underneath.

8. Place them side by side in an au gratin dish, sprinkle with the 2 tablespoons of olive oil and additional salt and pepper. Cover and place in a preheated 400-degree oven for ½ hour.

9. The stuffed peppers are also made with the regular, thicker-type pepper. Peel as explained previously and pull out the stem. You will notice that this pepper holds its shape better. With a spoon, remove the seeds without opening the pepper.

10. Use a pastry bag without any tube to stuff the pepper.

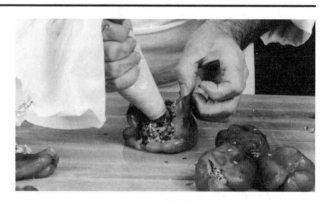

11. If the pepper opens, fold back on the stuffing and place seam side down in the au gratin dish. Cook in a preheated 400-degree oven for ½ hour. The stuffed peppers can be served warm as a vegetable, as well as a main course for lunch or as a first course for dinner. They can also be eaten cool, sprinkled with olive oil.

113. Patti Pan Squash with Tomatoes

(Patisson Blanc à la Tomate)

YIELD: 6 servings

THE SMALL PATTI PAN SQUASH has a beautiful scalloped shape that lends itself to some very attractive dishes. The young ones (washed, cut in half, seeded and sliced very thin) are excellent used raw in salads. They can also be cooked in water, made into a purée and finished with butter, salt and pepper. That same purée, with the addition of eggs, milk, salt, pepper and Swiss cheese, can be turned into a lovely gratin of squash. Served our way, it is a nice garnish for a roast of beef, a chicken or other roasted meats. The young squash don't have many seeds. The older the squash, the more seeds it will have. Seeds should be removed.

6 *small young patti pan squash*
2 *to 3 ripe tomatoes, skin and seeds removed and diced (about 2 cups)*
1 *teaspoon chopped onion*
2 *tablespoons sweet butter*
½ *teaspoon salt*
¼ *teaspoon freshly ground white pepper*

To make the tomato stew, heat the butter in a saucepan. Add the onions and sauté for ½ minute. Add the tomatoes, salt and pepper. Cover and cook 2 minutes. Uncover and cook an additional 2 to 3 minutes on high heat to reduce some of the moisture and thicken the mixture.

1. Cut a "lid" off the patti pan, preferably on the stem side.

2. Using a small coffee spoon, scoop out the inside seeds. Be careful not to go into the flesh itself.

3. Place ½ inch of water and ½ teaspoon salt in a saucepan and bring to a boil. Place the squash with their lids in the water, cover and bring to a strong boil. Boil for 3 minutes. Using a slotted spoon or a fork, remove the squash and set aside. Let cool until ready to use.

4. Sprinkle the inside of the squash slightly with salt and brush with melted butter if desired. Heat in the oven 1 to 2 minutes until warm. Fill the squash with the hot tomato stew, place the lids back on top and serve as an accompaniment or on its own with a poached egg.

114. Eggplant Custards *(Papetons d'Aubergines)*

YIELD: 8 servings

LONG, NARROW EGGPLANTS are usually more meaty and have fewer seeds than the large ones. Often large eggplants are baked in the oven, then the center is mashed with cooked onions, olive oil and seasonings and served as a dip that's known as "poor man's caviar." Slices of eggplant fried with skin on are used to line a mold filled with ground cooked lamb in the famous *moussaka* served with a tomato sauce. Eggplant is also good cut into little strips, dipped into a batter of beer or egg whites and deep fried. It is an essential ingredient of the famous *ratatouille* of Provence: a stew of eggplant, zucchini, onions, garlic, olive oil, etc., served hot or cold.

This dish is thought to have been created for the Popes when they lived in Avignon. It is from them that it gets the name *papetons*. It is a delicate dish, which can be made in large or small molds and is excellent by itself as well as with a roasted saddle of lamb or roast of veal. You will need 8 small baba molds, approximately ¾ cup each.

Eggplant custards

2 *pounds small, firm eggplant*
2 *teaspoons salt*
1 *cup peanut oil*
2 *medium-size cloves garlic, peeled and crushed*
6 *large eggs*
1 *cup heavy cream*
1½ *teaspoons salt*

Tomato sauce

2½ *pounds ripe tomatoes, cut into large chunks*
3 *tablespoons good olive oil*
1 *cup finely chopped onions*
3 *cloves garlic, peeled, crushed and chopped*

1½ *teaspoons salt*
½ *teaspoon freshly ground white pepper*
¼ *teaspoon sugar*
1 *tablespoon sweet butter*

Heat the oil in a heavy saucepan and add the onions. Sauté for 2 minutes on medium heat and add the garlic. Stir for a few seconds and add the tomatoes. Cover and cook for about 10 minutes on medium heat. Add the salt, pepper and sugar, stir well and remove from heat. Push the mixture through a food mill fitted with the fine screen. Add the butter bit by bit to the sauce, until well blended. Taste for seasonings and add salt and pepper if needed.

1. Peel the eggplant with a vegetable peeler keeping the skin as thin as possible. Blanch a few strips of skin for 1 minute in boiling water, then drain and cool under cold water. These will be used to decorate the molds. Slice the peeled eggplant into ½-inch slices. With the point of a knife, score both sides of the slice to form diamonds. Sprinkle with 2 teaspoons salt and spread the slices on a cookie sheet. Place another cookie sheet on top of the eggplant slices, and weigh it down with cans or other heavy objects. Keep pressed for ½ hour. The salt-

ing and pressing remove some of the bitter juices from the eggplant and prevent the slices from absorbing too much oil during cooking.

2. Blot the slices with paper towels. Heat about 3 tablespoons of oil in a skillet, and fry a few slices at a time on both sides until nicely browned. Set the slices in a colander after they are browned to allow some of the oil to drain. Place the fried eggplant in a food processor with the garlic and process until very smooth. (If the eggplant are very seedy, push the mixture through a food mill fitted with the fine screen.) Add the eggs and blend well. Stir in the cream and the 1½ teaspoons salt.

3. Butter several small molds or a large mold. Cut the strips of skin into flowers or different patterns.

4. Decorate the bottoms and sides of mold (the skin will stick to the butter). Fill with the eggplant mixture and place a piece of buttered parchment paper on top. Place the molds in a skillet with water around; cook in a preheated 375-degree oven for 25 to 30 minutes, until set. Remove and let sit for 15 minutes. If the decoration sticks to the mold when unmolding, remove and rearrange on top of the eggplant. *Papetons* also can be decorated after unmolding. Cover with the tomato sauce and serve. See finished eggplant custards, page 350.

115. Zucchini Puff Paste *(Feuilletés de Courgettes)*

YIELD: 4 servings

ZUCCHINI IS A VERY GOOD and very handy vegetable. It can be served in salad (see technique 126) as well as au gratin or just plain stewed or stewed in butter. With the addition of puff paste and a light butter sauce it can be made into a very elegant dish.

About ⅓ pound puff paste (technique 271)
¾ pound small zucchini, sliced into thin strips or
  wedges
½ cup water
4 tablespoons sweet butter, cut into pieces
1 teaspoon fresh lemon juice
Pepper and salt to taste

1. Roll out a strip of puff paste approximately ¼ inch thick. Cut 4 strips about 5 inches long by 1½ inches wide. Line a cookie sheet with parchment paper and place the strips of puff paste on it. Brush with egg wash, and score the top in a criss-cross pattern, for decoration. Place the tray in the freezer for 15 to 20 minutes, then in a preheated 375-degree oven for approximately 30 minutes, until well puffed, browned and crunchy. Set aside until ready to use.

2. Bring the zucchini, water and a dash of salt to a boil in a skillet. Cover and boil on high heat for 1 minute. Add the butter, lemon juice and a little extra salt and pepper and bring back to a boil, shaking the pan so that the butter binds with the liquid. Warm the puff paste strips in the oven and cut into halves. Arrange some zucchini strips across the bottom part of the puff paste, moisten with the butter sauce, cover with the second part of the puff paste and serve, hot, immediately. See finished zucchini puff paste, page 350.

116. Cucumber Salad *(Salade de Concombres)*

FIRST CULTIVATED more than 3,000 years ago, cucumbers are widely used in the United States as well as in many European countries and India. Cucumbers can be served raw as a salad, cooked or stuffed as a vegetable, or pickled to use as a condiment. However, it is raw in a summer salad (or as a salad ingredient) that cucumbers are most frequently served.

3 cucumbers
1 tablespoon coarse salt
4 tablespoons sour cream
1½ tablespoons lemon juice
½ teaspoon freshly ground white pepper
2 tablespoons peanut oil
2 tablespoons chopped fresh dill

1. Store-bought cucumbers are often coated with a chemical to retard spoilage, and it is better to peel them using a vegetable peeler. You don't have to peel the cucumber if you grow your own.

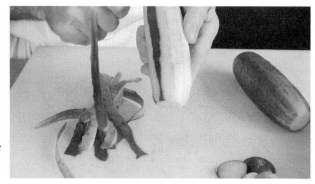

2. Cut into halves lengthwise. You may slice the cucumber with the seeds, season it and serve that way. However, it is more elegant to remove the seeds. Use a teaspoon.

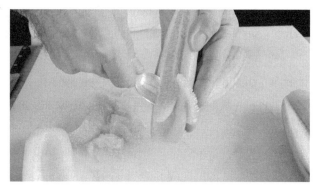

3. Slice into ⅛-inch or ¼-inch slices. You should have about 5 cups.

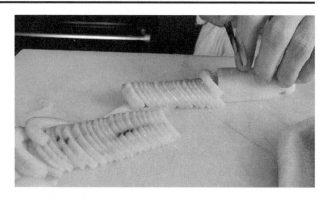

4. Place in a colander and sprinkle with coarse salt. Mix well. Let the cucumber macerate for at least 1 to 2 hours at room temperature. The salt, you will discover, draws the juices from the cucumbers, making them limp, and, paradoxically, very crisp at the same time.

5. Drain, rinse under cold water and press lightly to extract excess moisture. Combine the sour cream, lemon juice and freshly ground white pepper in a bowl. Add the peanut oil, beating with a wire whisk. Combine with the cucumber and the fresh dill. Do not use more salt. Prepared this way, the cucumbers will stay crisp for several days.

This recipe yields 6 to 8 servings.

117. Braised Lettuce *(Laitues Braisées)*

B OSTON LETTUCE makes a splendid and unusual cooked vegetable which goes well with veal, as well as chicken and beef. Although lettuce is customarily braised with carrots, onions and herbs, it is excellent boiled in water and finished with butter. One large head of lettuce will serve 2 as a garnish.

1. Remove any bruised leaves from the lettuce and wash in cold water, spreading the leaves gently under the stream of the water to remove any sand. Drop the lettuce into a large kettle of boiling, salted water and cover until it comes to a boil again. Uncover; if left covered, the lettuce will lose its vivid green color and turn yellowish. Place a wet paper towel on top of the lettuce; this will keep the lettuce underwater and help cook it evenly all around.

2. Let boil for 15 to 20 minutes, until the core of the lettuce feels tender to the point of a knife; it should be tender, not mushy. Immediately place the lettuce under cold running water. When cold, remove the lettuce.

3. Be sure not to disturb the natural shape of the lettuce. Squeeze gently to extrude the excess water.

4. Cut the smaller heads into 3 equal-sized pieces.

5. For a larger head, cut in quarters.

6. Place a piece, outside down, on the table and flatten the leafy end gently with a knife.

7. Turn the leafy green part onto the center of the lettuce and,

8. holding it with the point of the knife, fold the core end over it.

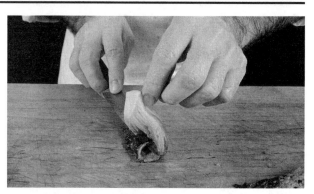

9. Trim the core. You should have a nice little package, slightly triangular. Sprinkle lightly with salt and pepper.

10. Melt some butter in a large skillet. When hot, place the lettuce pieces, folded side up, one next to the other, in the skillet. Do not crowd the skillet. Cook on medium heat 6 to 8 minutes until slightly brown. Turn gently and cook 4 to 5 minutes on the other side.

11. Arrange on a serving platter, folded side down. You may coat the lettuce with a good half-glaze (demi glace), 1 tablespoon per lettuce and sprinkle some butter cooked to a hazelnut color (*beurre noisette*) on top just before serving.

118. How to Prepare Endives
(Cuisson des Endives)

YIELD: 6 to 8 servings

BELGIAN ENDIVES make a great salad. (Separate the leaves, pile them together, cut into a fine julienne, then put in ice water to curl.) Endive are also good cooked. They can be served plain or in their broth or with a white sauce. (Wrap a slice of ham around each head or half a head, cover with a white sauce, sprinkle with cheese, and brown under the broiler.) Cooked endives can also be sautéed in butter, or covered with melted butter and chopped parsley (*meunière*) as well as puréed and finished with cream and seasonings. The basic way to cook endive follows.

3 pounds endive (medium size), approximately 12 to 15 pieces
½ tablespoon sugar
1 teaspoon salt
¼ stick (1 ounce) sweet butter
Juice of 1 lemon (approximately ¼ cup)
⅓ cup water

1. Wash and clean the root of the endive very lightly if brown and discolored. Do not cut enough to separate the leaves. Trim any discolored leaves. Rinse carefully under cold water and arrange in layers in a sturdy stainless or enameled pan.

2. Add the sugar, salt, lemon juice and water and cover the endive with a round of parchment paper. Place a plate on top of the paper and then the regular lid on top. The paper helps the endive steam better and the weight gently presses them down into their own juices. The top lid prevents the steam from escaping during cooking which would make the endive dry. Notice that the recipe has just a bit of liquid; the endive will render liquid of its own cooking.

3. Bring to a boil on top of the stove and either simmer on top of the stove or place in a preheated 400-degree oven for 25 to 30 minutes. The endives should still be firm when cooked. Let cool in the broth. When cool enough to handle, remove, arrange in a terrine or bowl, pour the juices on top, cover and keep in the refrigerator until ready to use.

119. How to Prepare Spinach *(Equeutage des Epinards)*

THERE ARE TWO BASIC WAYS of preparing spinach: in *purée*, when both leaf and stem are finely ground, and *en branches* (whole leaf), when the leaf is left whole and the stem removed. A *purée* of spinach is usually made with a light cream sauce, seasoned with nutmeg, salt and pepper and served with fried *croûtons* and hard-boiled eggs. It is a very good accompaniment to a roast of veal or a roasted chicken. Spinach prepared *en branches* is used in *timbale* or as a bed for poached eggs, fish, oysters or veal (called *à la florentine*).

LEAF SPINACH *(Epinards en Branches)*

1 pound fresh spinach
*¼ inch water in a large saucepan (not alumi-
    num) with a cover*
½ teaspoon salt

1. Note how the long stem runs along the underside of the spinach leaf.

2. Take hold of the leaf on both sides of the stem and pull the stem out. The stems can be used in soups or mixed with other whole leaf spinach if the whole mixture is to be used for a *purée*. Wash the spinach carefully.

3. Bring the water and salt to a strong boil and pile the spinach on top. Cover and cook on high heat for 2 to 3 minutes. The spinach will wilt but will still remain green.

4. Drain in a colander and run under cold water until cool enough to handle. Press into a ball, squeezing out the water, then cover with plastic wrap and keep in the refrigerator until needed.

SPINACH MOLD *(Timbale d'Epinards)*

YIELD: 6 servings

6 to 8 ½-cup soufflé molds, buttered
1 pound fresh spinach (prepared as above)
1 teaspoon salt
½ teaspoon freshly ground pepper
⅛ teaspoon freshly grated nutmeg
3 tablespoons sweet butter
2 teaspoons flour
¾ cup milk
½ cup heavy cream
3 large eggs
6 slices firm white bread, cut into 2½-inch
    rounds and fried in a skillet with butter and
    vegetable oil until golden brown

Cook spinach as explained in steps 3 and 4 and chop coarsely. Sprinkle with the salt, pepper and nutmeg. Melt the butter in a heavy saucepan and let it cook until it is dark brown. Add the spinach and mix with a fork. The dark brown butter gives the spinach a very nutty taste. Sprinkle the spinach with the flour, mix it in well, add the milk and bring to a boil, stirring constantly. Let it boil for ½ minute, take off the heat and let it cool off on the side for 10 to 15 minutes. Beat the eggs, mix in the heavy cream and stir the whole mixture into the spinach.

5. Fill the prepared molds with the mixture, dividing the solids and liquids equally, and place in a pan of tepid water. Bake in a preheated 350-degree oven for 25 to 30 minutes, or until set. The water should not boil. The timbale should rest for at least 15 to 20 minutes before being unmolded. To serve, run a knife around the inside of the mold to loosen the timbale. Unmold each timbale on a piece of bread and arrange around a roast, or serve, plain or with a light cream sauce. See finished spinach timbales, page 350.

120. Spinach Salad with Chicken Livers

(Salade d'Epinards aux Foies de Volaille)

YIELD: 6 servings

THIS SALAD can be made without the chicken livers and with or without the red peppers. The combination, however, makes it colorful, interesting and tasty.

8 cups (loosely packed) fresh spinach, stems
    removed (see technique 119)
5 to 6 chicken or duck livers, cooked in fat (see
    technique 153)
1 large sweet red pepper (green if red is not
    available), sliced
1 small clove garlic, crushed and chopped fine
1 teaspoon French mustard

2 teaspoons good red wine vinegar
Salt and pepper to taste
¼ cup good olive oil or peanut oil

1. Cut the red pepper in half lengthwise, remove the seeds and slice very thin. Wash the spinach and drain carefully in a salad dryer. Mix together the garlic, mustard, red wine vinegar, salt and pepper. Slowly add the oil, mixing carefully. Take 1 tablespoon of the mixture and combine with the sliced pepper. Set aside at room temperature until ready to serve. This can marinate for at least 1 hour.

2. At serving time, slice the chicken or duck livers on a slant into slivers. Mix the spinach with the remaining dressing and arrange in a bowl. Arrange the pepper around the spinach and sprinkle the livers on top. Serve immediately. See finished spinach salad with chicken livers, page 350a.

121. Escarole Soufflé (Soufflé de Scarole)

A SOUFFLÉ, from the verb *souffler* (to breathe, inflate or puff up), is nothing more than a thick white sauce into which egg yolks, flavoring and, finally, beaten egg whites are incorporated. The small air bubbles in the whites expand during baking, pushing it up to magnificent heights. To make this soufflé, you will need a 1½-quart soufflé mold.

4½ tablespoons sweet butter, plus 1 teaspoon to
coat the mold
¼ cup grated Parmesan cheese
3 scallions, cleaned, washed and sliced thin
1 head escarole, trimmed of most of the green
leafy part
1½ teaspoons salt
⅓ cup water
4½ tablespoons flour
1¼ cups milk
¼ teaspoon freshly ground black pepper
4 drops Tabasco sauce

3 egg yolks
½ teaspoon Worcestershire sauce
1 cup grated Cheddar cheese, plus strips, optional
7 egg whites

1. Butter the mold with 1 teaspoon soft
butter. Be sure it is well coated all around.

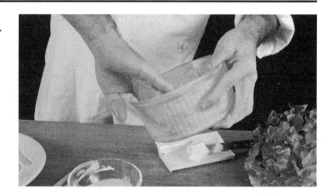

2. Add the Parmesan cheese and

3. turn the mold around so that the cheese
sticks to the butter. Let the extra cheese fall
into a bowl.

4. Refrigerate the coated soufflé mold. A very cold mold helps the soufflé rise straight. Keep your fingers out of the mold. If you smear the coating you may disturb the rising of the mixture.

5. Slice the trimmed escarole coarsley. (Trimmed escarole can also be braised in butter or served in a cream sauce.)

6. Melt 1 tablespoon butter in a saucepan and sauté the sliced scallions for 30 to 40 seconds. Add the escarole, ½ teaspoon salt and the water. Cover and cook for 5 to 6 minutes on high heat. Uncover and continue cooking for a few minutes until all liquid has been evaporated.

7. Melt the remaining butter in a saucepan and add the flour. Cook for 1 minute on low heat. Add the milk, 1 teaspoon salt, pepper, Tabasco sauce and bring to a boil, stirring with a whisk. As soon as it reaches the boiling point, the sauce will thicken. Boil on low heat for 1 minute, still stirring to avoid scorching. Add the yolks and mix well.

8. Add the salad mixture and

9. stir with a spatula. Add the Worcestershire sauce and the grated Cheddar cheese.

10. To whip the whites by hand, use a large balloon whip. It should be flexible, long, with a lot of wires, so that the whites are lifted up with each stroke. Use a copper or stainless steel bowl. The equipment should be immaculate. A greasy bowl or yolk particle in the whites will prevent them from whipping.

11. Beat with a strong motion, making a complete circle with each stroke, and lifting up the whole bulk of whites. (Cream is beaten more gently. If you beat cream as hard as you do egg whites, it would turn into butter.)

12. As soon as the whites hold a peak, but are still "wet," place about one-third in the white sauce–escarole mixture and mix with the whisk. Work as fast as you can, because as soon as you stop beating the whites, they start to break down and become grainy.

13. Using a spatula, fold the remaining whites and escarole mixture together.

14. Fill the soufflé mold to the edges. At this point, the soufflé can be refrigerated, and will keep for at least a couple of hours. At baking time, sprinkle the reserved Parmesan cheese on top and place on a cookie sheet in a 375-degree preheated oven. Reduce the heat to 350 degrees and bake for 30 minutes.

15. Five minutes before the soufflé is done, you may arrange strips of cheese on top, forming a decorative pattern, and place back in the oven to melt the cheese. Serve immediately.

16. A soufflé (especially if it is collapsed) can be served unmolded. Run a knife around the edges, pulling the soufflé into the mold at the same time, to free it from the mold.

17. Invert and remove the mold.

18. Serve in wedges with or without a light cream sauce.

This recipe serves 6 to 8.

122. Swiss Chard au Gratin (Côtes de Bettes au Gratin)

YIELD: 6 to 8 servings

ALTHOUGH COMMON IN EUROPE, particularly in Italy and France, Swiss chard and cardoon are not served often enough in the United States. Cardon stalks are peeled the same way as are the Swiss chard. The pieces of stalks are cooked in water or in a *blanc* (a mixture of water and flour) and sometimes served with marrow, in gratins or with cream sauce or red wine sauce. Swiss chard can be steamed and sautéed in butter or cooked in the juice of a roast. The green of the Swiss chard can be eaten and cooked like spinach. When the green is very tender it can be used in salads. The Swiss chard is often prepared with a *persillade* (parsley and garlic added at the last moment with butter and sautéed) and at other times in a gratin to serve with a roast chicken or broiled steaks—which is what we will make below.

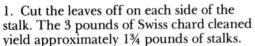

3 pounds chard with the widest possible stalks
1 tablespoon sweet butter
1 tablespoon flour
1½ cups milk
1 cup heavy cream
½ teaspoon salt
¼ teaspoon freshly ground white pepper
½ cup grated Swiss cheese

1. Cut the leaves off on each side of the stalk. The 3 pounds of Swiss chard cleaned yield approximately 1¾ pounds of stalks.

2. As you get toward the end of the stem, remove the green with the end of the stem. Keep the greens for soups or cook as you would spinach.

3. The stems are sometimes very wide and often not flat. Cut the stem in strips so the stalks are more manageable and easier to peel. To peel, cut a piece approximately 2 inches long from the stem. Do not cut completely through.

4. Break the "cut" piece and pull off. Note the fibers that hang from the large part of the stem.

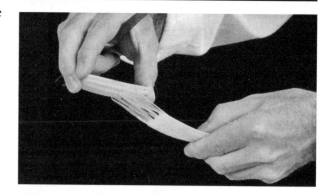

5. Take the fibers and pull them off so that a complete side of the stem is clean. Repeat the same procedure on the underside of the stem. Removing the fibers makes the chard much more tender and is especially necessary when the vegetable is large and a bit old. As they are peeled, drop in cold water to prevent discoloration.

6. Drop the white stems into salted boiling water. Bring to a boil and boil for approximately 6 minutes. Drain in a colander. The pieces should be tender but still firm. For our white sauce, melt the butter in a saucepan over medium heat and add the flour. Whisk and cook for about 1 minute, then add the milk and, still whisking, bring to a boil. Boil for about ½ minute. Remove from the heat and add the cream, salt and pepper. Mix well. Butter a 6-cup au gratin dish and arrange the chard in it. Sprinkle with the grated cheese and pour the sauce on top.

7. Place on a cookie sheet in a preheated 375-degree oven for a generous 40 minutes. If not brown enough after this time, place briefly under the broiler. Let the gratin rest at least 10 minutes before serving.

123. Braised Stuffed Cabbages *(Choux Farcis)*

YIELD: 6 servings

THE CABBAGE is excellent left raw and sliced very thin in salad. It is a great winter vegetable which blends well in soups or boiled with different types of sausages or pork or other meats. The cabbage can be stuffed whole (the stuffing is placed between the leaves) as well as made into small stuffed cabbage balls. To make 12 small stuffed cabbage balls, use one 3-pound cabbage, either regular or Savoy, the leafy, curly type.

Stuffing

1 tablespoon sweet butter
1 large onion, finely chopped (1 cup)
3 cloves garlic, finely chopped and crushed
1 pound reserved cabbage from the heart
1 cup water
1 pound ground pork (preferably from the
    shoulder or butt)
1 pound ground beef, not too lean
3 large eggs

2 teaspoons salt
1 teaspoon freshly ground white pepper
⅓ cup chopped parsley

Braising

2 medium carrots, peeled and coarsely chopped
    (1 cup)
1¼ cups coarsely chopped onions
5 cloves garlic, finely chopped (1 teaspoon)
2 cups good chicken stock

1. Cut off the core of the cabbage and spread out the leaves so they detach from the center. Try not to break the large leaves that are needed as wrappers for the stuffing.

2. The central part of the cabbage should be chopped finely and used in the stuffing. It will make approximately 1 pound.

3. Plunge the leaves into a large pot of boiling water, pushing them down gently as they get wilted. When they are all immersed, let the water come to a boil and boil gently for 5 minutes. Then place the kettle under cold running water. When cold, drain the leaves in a colander, place them flat on the table and remove approximately 2 inches of the toughest part of the stem. You should have about 15 to 20 leaves.

4. Make the stuffing: Melt the butter in a large skillet. Add the onions and sauté gently for 1 to 2 minutes. Add the garlic, stir, then add the chopped cabbage and 1 cup of water. Bring to a boil, cover and cook for 5 minutes on high heat. Cool to luke-warm. Place the meats in a mixing bowl. Add the eggs, salt, pepper and parsley and mix well with your hands. Combine with the cooked cabbage mixture and mix well again. Place one leaf in a ladle with sides overlapping and fill it up with about ½ cup of the stuffing mixture.

5. Cover the filling with the overlapping cabbage and press down to give the cabbage shape and make sure the stuffing is well packed and wrapped.

6. The cabbage should be well formed and round.

7. Another method of stuffing leaves is to lay a cabbage leaf out on a kitchen towel. If it is broken, add several pieces to form a large leaf. Place the stuffing in the center and bring the cabbage leaves over it.

8. Fold the towel into a ball and squeeze tightly to shape the cabbage into a ball. The cabbage can also be molded without the use of the towel, just by hand, but if you use the ladle or the towel, the cabbages will be more uniform in size.

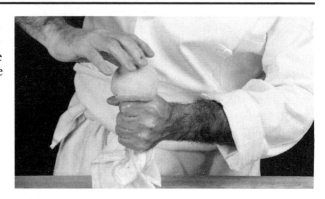

9. Place all of the braising ingredients except the chicken stock in the bottom of a roasting pan. Arrange the stuffed cabbages on top, side by side, with the folded side down, so they touch one another. Pour the chicken stock over. Cover the pan with a cookie sheet or aluminum foil and bring to a boil on top of the stove. Place in a pre-heated 350-degree oven for 2 hours. Remove the cover and arrange the cabbages on a serving platter, draining all the liquid. Place the liquid and vegetable garnish on top of the stove in a saucepan and reduce on high heat by about two-thirds. You should have approximately 2 cups of liquid left. Pour about 2 tablespoons of the sauce on top of each cabbage and serve. This dish is also excellent reheated.

124. Fried Parsley *(Persil Frit)*

Parsley should be fried in clean fat that is not too hot and there should be enough fat to cover the parsley completely. It should be fried fast or it will become dark and bitter. In classic French cooking fried parsley is served with fried fish, fried eggs, or fried croquettes.

2 cups curly parsley, washed and well dried
2 cups vegetable oil
Dash of salt

1. Bring the oil to 350 degrees and drop a handful of parsley at a time into the hot oil. Mix with your skimmer.

2. Fry for 10 to 12 seconds at the most. Lift out and dry on a paper towel. Sprinkle lightly with salt and serve immediately.

125. Dandelion Salad *(Salade de Pissenlits)*

YIELD: 6 servings

DANDELION SALAD announces the coming of spring and although there is some cultivated dandelion, it does not approach the taste of the wild one. Dandelion should be picked early in the season. Look for plants growing in gravel or soft earth; somewhere where the stem will have been covered half way up, and will have had a chance to get white like endive, with the same tender and slightly bitter and stringent taste. Although dandelions are commonly eaten in the French countryside, our recipe is a specialty of Lyon. The fat of the *lardons* is used instead of oil in the dressing for the salad. The salad is served on lukewarm plates with crusty bread and with a light Beaujolais.

1 pound cleaned, washed and dried dandelion
¾ cup pancetta, cut into small sticks (lardons)
2 slices of toast
1 garlic clove, peeled
2 hard-boiled eggs, shelled
2 cloves garlic, peeled, crushed and chopped fine
1 small can (2 ounces) anchovies in oil
1½ teaspoons good red wine vinegar
½ teaspoon salt

½ teaspoon freshly ground white pepper
2 tablespoons good olive oil, virgin if possible

1. The dandelion greens should be picked before the flower stage or they will be tough and bitter. Use your knife to dig into the ground and remove the whole plant along with the root. Scrape the root of any dirt, removing any black parts but preserving as much of it as possible so the dandelion leaves still hold together by the root. Split the large plants in half so they can be washed properly. Wash several times in cold water, drain well and dry.

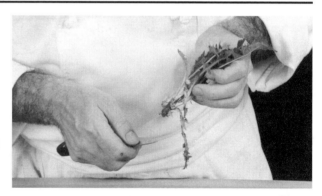

2. Cut the pancetta into ¹/₂-inch slices and then cut each slice into small strips (*lardons*). Place the *lardons* in cold water and bring to a boil. Boil for 1 minute, then drain and rinse under cold water. Set aside.

3. Rub the toasted bread with a whole peeled clove of garlic on both sides. In order for the bread to "abrade" the garlic it must be well toasted. Cut each slice of bread into 6 *croûtons*. Cut the 2 hard-boiled eggs into 6 segments each.

4. Place the anchovy fillets on the table and using the blade of a knife, crush and smear them down into a purée. Chop the 2 cloves of garlic very fine and add to the anchovies. Purée until smooth with the blade of a knife. Place the *lardons* in a skillet and fry them on medium heat until crisp. Meanwhile, place the purée of anchovies and garlic into a salad bowl, add the vinegar, salt, pepper and olive oil and mix well. When the *lardons* are ready, add them with their fat to the mixture and stir well.

5. Add the washed and dried greens and mix thoroughly. Sprinkle the *croûtons* and the eggs on top. The salad should be slightly lukewarm. Serve immediately. This is also good made from very thinly sliced red or white cabbage.

126. Vegetable Salads *(Salades de Légumes)*

VEGETABLE COOKERY has progressed considerably in recent years. Vegetables are usually cooked differently in restaurants than at home. In a restaurant most green vegetables—asparagus, spinach, string beans, peas, broccoli, etc.—are cooked in a lot of salted boiling water and, when cooked enough, plunged into cold water for a few minutes to stop further cooking and keep them green. This system destroys a certain amount of the vegetable's vitamins, which is why steaming or cooking in a tiny bit of water is preferable. However, it is the only practical way to cook great quantities of vegetables.

A small amount of vegetables will cool fast and retain its color without being plunged in cold water. Just undercook them a little, as they continue to cook for a few minutes after being strained.

Certain vegetables such as string beans and asparagus are excellent steamed and served right away. However, if they are allowed to sit a while exposed to the air they shrivel and begin to look wrinkled. If they are not to be served immediately, it's better to cook the vegetables in a little bit of water (less moisture gets pulled out of the vegetables while cooking) or cover them with a wet towel after cooking to prevent shriveling.

Cooked vegetables, besides being an accompaniment to meat, make very good salads. They usually improve in taste if they marinate in the dressing for 30 minutes before serving. Vegetable salads should not be served too cold and thought should be given to the combination of vegetables for the taste as well as color. Recipes for a few vegetable salads follow.

STRING BEAN AND TOMATO SALAD
(Salade de Haricots Verts et Tomates)

YIELD: 4 servings

Choose the thinnest string beans you can find. They should be firm, green and long. Remove both ends taking with them the string, if any. Wash the beans in cold water.

1 *pound string beans*
1 *tablespoon good red wine vinegar*
3 *tablespoons good peanut or grape-seed oil*
Salt and pepper to taste
3 *large tomatoes with or without the skin*

1 *tablespoon red wine vinegar*
⅓ *cup virgin olive oil*
⅓ *cup thinly sliced onions for garnish*
15 *to* 20 basil leaves

1. Place approximately ½ inch of water in a wide stainless steel saucepan and add ½ teaspoon salt. Bring to a strong boil. Add 1 pound cleaned string beans. They should cover the bottom of the pan in one layer. Cover and bring to a strong boil. Keep boiling, covered, over high heat for about 5 minutes, depending on the size of the beans and how fresh they are.

2. Using a skimmer, lift the beans from the pan and spread them on a large plate to cool off. They should be crunchy but cooked and a beautiful green in color. Toss the beans with the wine vinegar and oil. Season and set aside.

3. Peel the tomatoes if desired and slice crosswise very thinly. Place the seasoned string beans in the center of a large platter and arrange the slices of tomatoes around. Sprinkle generously with salt and pepper. Tomatoes require a lot of salt. Then sprinkle with the vinegar and the oil.

4. Wash the fresh basil and separate the leaves. Pile the largest leaves together.

5. Roll the leaves into a tight bundle and cut them into a very thin chiffonade.

6. Cut the onion into very thin slices and separate the slices into individual rings.

7. Sprinkle the onions on top and border with the julienned basil leaves. See finished string bean and tomato salad, page 350a.

BEET SALAD *(Salade de Betteraves)*

YIELD: 6 servings

4 to 5 fresh beets
1 teaspoon French mustard
2 tablespoons heavy cream
Freshly ground white pepper to taste
Salt to taste (beets require a lot of salt)

1. Cover beets with cold water and add salt. Bring to a boil and cook covered approximately 1¼ hours, or until tender when pricked with the point of a knife. Remove from water and allow to cool. Peel.

2. Slice in ¼-inch slices, stack slices together, a few at à time and cut into ¼-inch strips. Add dressing, toss and let sit until ready to serve.

ZUCCHINI SALAD *(Salade de Courgettes)*

YIELD: 4 to 6 servings

2 to 3 *small zucchini, washed*
1 *tablespoon good peanut or olive oil*
1 *teaspoon good red wine vinegar*
¼ *teaspoon ground black pepper*

1. Trim both ends of each zucchini. Cut into 2-inch chunks. Split each section lengthwise in four. Remove the piece in the center where the seeds are. Slice all the pieces in 2 to 3 sticks, depending on size.

2. Spread on a cookie sheet, sprinkle lightly with salt and place in a preheated 425-degree oven for 3 to 4 minutes until the zucchini starts to "sweat." Remove from oven and allow to cool. Add the dressing ingredients, mix well and serve at room temperature. See finished zucchini salad, page 350a.

CARROT SALAD *(Salade de Carottes)*

2 *large carrots, peeled and cut into* 1½-*inch chunks*
¼ *cup slivered almonds*
1 *tablespoon olive oil, preferably virgin*
Dash of salt and pepper

Cut each carrot chunk into slices. Stack the slices together to cut into strips about ⅛ inch thick. Place in cold water. Add a dash of salt, bring to a boil and boil for 2 minutes. Drain. Combine with other ingredients. Serve at room temperature.

MUSHROOM SALAD *(Salade de Champignons)*

1 *cup sliced mushroom caps*
1½ *teaspoons lemon juice*
1 *tablespoon good peanut or grape-seed oil*
Salt and freshly ground pepper to taste

Combine all ingredients, mix well and serve immediately.

127. Stuffed Mushrooms *(Champignons Farcis)*

MUSHROOM CAPS can be stuffed with meat, fish, shellfish, vegetables or most anything. Snails with garlic butter are often served in mushroom caps. The caps are cooked before they are stuffed.

24 large mushrooms
Salt and freshly ground black pepper
1 tablespoon peanut oil
3 to 4 shallots
3 tablespoons butter
⅓ cup fresh bread crumbs
1 tablespoon grated Parmesan cheese
½ teaspoon paprika
1 tablespoon melted butter

1. Break the stems off 20 large mushrooms. Place the caps, hollow side up, on a cookie sheet. Sprinkle with salt and peanut oil. Place in a 425-degree preheated oven for 10 to 12 minutes. Remove from the oven and turn the caps, hollow side down, to empty them of any liquid.

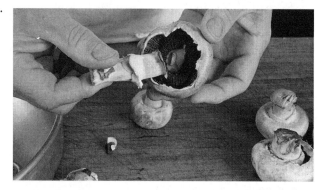

2. Chop the stems and the extra mushrooms very fine. You should have a good 3 cups. Chop the shallots (about 1½ tablespoons chopped). Place 3 tablespoons butter in a saucepan, add the shallots and cook for about 1 minute. Add the chopped mushrooms, salt and pepper and cook until most of the liquid has evaporated and the mixture is dry enough to hold a shape. Let it cool for 10 minutes.

3. Using a spoon, fill the caps so that each cap is rounded on top. Mix together the bread crumbs, Parmesan cheese, paprika and 1 tablespoon of melted butter.

4. Press some bread crumb mixture on top of the stuffed caps,

5. or dip the caps, stuffed side down, into the mixture so that the whole top is heavily coated with the mixture. Place the mushrooms, stuffed side up, under a hot broiler for 3 to 4 minutes, or until nicely browned.

This recipe serves 6 as a garnish.

128. Fried Potato Balls *(Pommes Parisienne)*

THE POTATO IS PROBABLY the greatest food contribution that the New World made to the Old. It was introduced in France in the second half of the sixteenth century, but was first used as a decorative plant. It was popularized by an agronomist named Parmentier during the eighteenth century. Hence, in classic cooking, any dish *Parmentier* includes potatoes. The potato is a versatile vegetable; it can be boiled, sautéed, baked, fried, steamed, broiled, stewed and so on.

1. Peel large baking potatoes. Keep in cold water to avoid discoloration. Push a round melon ball cutter down into the potato with your thumb as far as it will go.

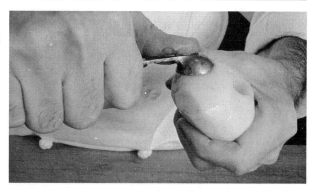

2. Still pressing the tool into the potato, pivot the cutter in a downward motion to scoop out a ball. Repeat, using as much of the potato as you possibly can. Place in cold water again to avoid discoloration. Use trimmings for soup or mashed potatoes. Blanch the balls in boiling water for 2 minutes, drain and fry in a butter and oil mixture.

129. Sliced Potato Cake *(Pommes Anna)*

1. This is a very presentable dish for a party. Begin by trimming the potatoes all around to make long cylinders.

2. Use the trimmings in soup or croquettes or mashed potatoes.

3. Slice by hand or machine into ⅛ inch slices. Saute the slices in butter and oil for a few minutes, so they are well-coated with fat but still firm. Butter an ovenproof skillet (preferably nonstick) or a cake pan.

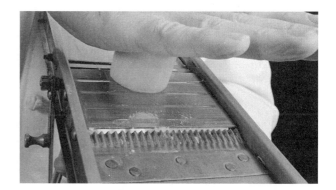

4. Arrange the slices in the bottom of a frying pan or cake pan. Place the potato slices any old way on top of the bottom layer. Season with salt and pepper and bake in a 425-degree preheated oven for 30 to 45 minutes. Let rest a few minutes, run a knife around the potatoes and unmold. Remove any slices that stick to the bottom, and replace where they belong on the "cake."

130. Potato Balls *(Pommes Poisson)*

The french name for this dish, which translates literally to "Fish Potatoes" comes from the fact that they are usually steamed or boiled and served with fish.

1. If you don't have small potatoes, cut medium-sized potatoes in half or large potatoes into chunks.

2. Trim all the edges (use trimmings for soup and the like).

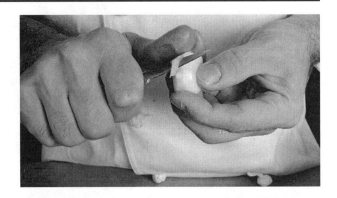

3. These potatoes are basically the same as the *pommes à l'Anglaise* (see page 327). but they are rounded and hold their shape better when boiled. They can also be sautéed or fried.

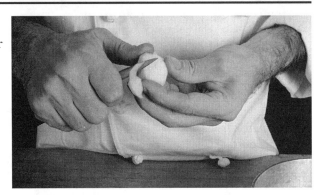

131. Potato Ovals *(Pommes Cocotte et Anglaise)*

COCOTTE

1. Cut large potatoes in half. Cut each half into two pieces.

2. Cut the quarters into equal elongated pieces.

3. Trim or "turn" each piece into a little football-shaped potato. These are *pommes cocotte*. They are blanched for 1 minute in boiling water, drained and sautéed in butter and oil and served as garnish for roast, steak and the like.

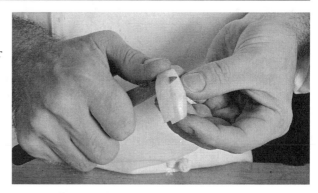

ANGLAISE

1. Trim potatoes at both ends and cut into large elongated chunks.

2. Trim each piece into a football-shaped potato. These potatoes can be steamed or boiled *(pommes à l'anglaise)*, blanched and fried *(pommes château)*, or cooked with butter and a little bit of water *(pommes fondantes)*.

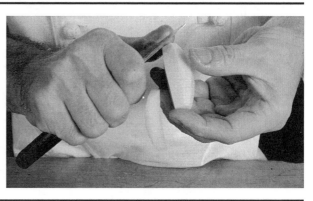

3. Left to right: groupings of *pommes poisson, pommes cocotte, pommes à l'anglaise, pommes parisienne*. Shaping the potatoes ensures proper cooking but is essentially done for aesthetic reasons. These kinds of potatoes should be cooked as closely as possible to the moment they will be eaten. If cooked ahead, they will taste reheated.

132. Potato Sticks *(Pommes Pailles, Allumettes et Pont-Neuf)*

DEEP-FRIED POTATOES take on different names depending on the shapes they are cut into before cooking. Though three kinds of potatoes shown here are all cut into sticks, the sizes are different and hence, the names.

1. Peel each potato and trim to look like a parallelepiped.

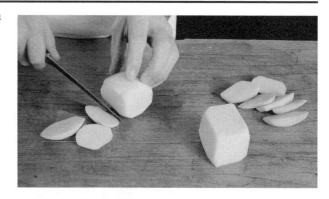

2. Cut it into ⅜-inch slices.

3. Stack the slices together and cut into ⅜-inch sticks for matchstick potatoes (*allumettes*) or into ¾- to 1-inch sticks for the *pont-neuf*.

4. The straw potatoes (*pommes pailles*) can be cut by hand or with a *mandoline*.

5. Left to right: straw, *pont-neuf* and matchstick potatoes.

133. Soap-shaped Potatoes *(Pommes Savonnettes)*

YIELD: 4 to 5 servings

THE *pommes savonnettes* make a very nice garnish for a roast filet of beef, roast chicken and most roasted meats. The slices of potatoes looking like little cakes of soap are placed flat into a saucepan, and cooked with water and butter on very high heat. The potatoes get very moist by absorbing some of the water and when the water evaporates they start to brown in the butter that is left behind. They get beautifully brown on the outside and soft in the center. These are based on the same principle as *pommes fondantes* (melting potatoes), which are cooked with butter and chicken stock and when three-fourths of the way cooked, when almost all of the liquid has been absorbed, the potatoes are cracked with a spoon lightly, so they finish absorbing the rest of the liquid. They are not browned further, but served at that point.

Pommes savonnettes remain at their best for 15 minutes, but they quickly acquire reheated taste, so serve them as quickly as possible. Choose large Idaho potatoes of the same size.

5 large potatoes (about 15 to 18 slices)
2 tablespoons butter
1½ tablespoons vegetable oil
¾ cup water

1. Peel the potatoes and trim into long, even cylinders. Use the trimmings to make soups, potato croquettes, mashed potatoes, etc.

2. Cut the potato cylinders into 1-inch disks.

3. Bevel the edges for a more finished look and to keep them from getting battered during cooking.

4. Take a heavy non-stick skillet or sauce-pan and arrange the potatoes snugly in the bottom, without overlapping. Place the nicer side of the slices face down in the skillet. Add more potatoes if necessary to fill the skillet. Add the butter, oil and water. The water should come three-fourths of the way up the slices. Bring to a strong boil on top of the stove, then place on the lower shelf of a preheated 475-degree oven or directly on the floor of the oven. The water must continue to boil so it will evaporate. If the water doesn't boil, the potatoes will cook and end up falling apart. If your skillet has a plastic handle, be sure to cover it with several layers of aluminum foil so it doesn't get damaged during cooking. Cook for 35 to 40 minutes, until the potatoes are very tender and brown. After about 25 to 30 minutes, the water should have completely evaporated and the potatoes should have begun to brown. The top will brown only slightly, but the bottom will be a beautiful dark brown in color. Let the potatoes rest for 2 to 3 minutes, then flip each one over.

Arrange them with the nicest side up on a platter, brush with butter and serve immediately. See finished soap-shaped potatoes, page 350a.

134. Straw Potato Cake *(Pommes Paillasson)*

YIELD: 4 to 6 servings

POMMES PAILLASSON (which translates to "doormat") are made from potatoes that are peeled, washed and then cut into a fine julienne with a *mandoline* (a slicer) or by hand. Once the potatoes have been cut into julienne, they have to be cooked right away or kept in water to prevent discoloration. The water bath washes off some of the potato's starch. If the potatoes are not kept in water but are cooked right away, the starch left in the potatoes will make them "cake" or hold better. On the other hand, they will be slightly gooey inside. If they have been washed they will be less starchy in taste but more fragile in construction—the potatoes will be more likely to disentangle. The starch acts like a glue. Whichever method you use, the taste is the same, only the texture is slightly different. Use large Idaho potatoes. One large potato will give you approximately 1 cup. Pommes paillasson should be served immediately as should most fried potatoes or they will take on a reheated taste. These potatoes are known as *rosti* in Switzerland and also *Darphin* potatoes in France.

4 cups julienned potatoes (use baking potatoes)
2 tablespoons sweet butter
4 tablespoons vegetable oil
¼ teaspoon salt
Dash of white pepper

1. Peel and wash the potatoes then cut into julienne. Wash the julienne and dry in paper towels or cook right away. In a non-stick skillet, heat half the butter and oil. When very hot, add half the potatoes, salt and pepper and coat well with fat by stirring. Use a fork to spread the potatoes around.

2. Use a large, flat spoon to press the potatoes down so the strips cohere together into a cake. Cook on medium heat for 4 to 5 minutes, pressing once in a while. Flip the pancake over and cook another 4 to 5 minutes on medium low heat. The pancake should not be more than ½ inch thick, crunchy on the outside and soft in the middle. If you cannot flip it in one stroke, place a plate on top, turn it upside down and slide back into the skillet. Repeat with the rest of the butter, oil and potatoes. Serve as soon as possible. See finished potato cake, page 350a.

135. Straw Potato Nest *(Nid en Pommes Paille)*

T HE POTATO NEST is done with julienne potatoes and is usually used as a garnish filled with tiny *pommes soufflés* or potato croquettes. To make the nest you need a special double wire basket available in specialty stores. For each nest you need approximately 2 cups of loose julienne potatoes. Washing the potatoes julienne will give you a nest which won't hold together as well as the one with unwashed potatoes which, however, won't release as well from the metal nest because the starch will stick to the metal wires. However, it works both ways. (See technique 134 for more about washing potatoes.)

1. Using a knife or a *mandoline* (vegetable slicer), slice the potatoes into slices ¹/₁₆-inch thick. Pile them together and cut into a thin julienne. Wash and dry, if desired.

2. Dip the wire basket in the hot oil. Then fill the bottom part of the basket with potato strips. Make a hole in the center and place the smaller part of the nest in the basket.

3. Secure both parts with the clip.

4. Drop the potatoes in 400-degree vegetable oil and cook for 4 to 5 minutes on high heat. Be sure that the potato nest stays completely immersed during cooking by holding it down into the oil.

5. To unmold, remove the clip and trim away the pieces of potato sticking through both the outside and inside of the nest. This makes it easier to release the potatoes from the mold.

6. Jiggle the wire basket and lift it up from the potatoes.

7. The potatoes may still be hard to remove. Turn upside down, and using a towel, press the mesh to bend it and help the potatoes release. Use a small knife to pry it out.

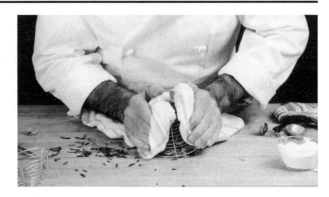

8. The potato nest released, and ready to be served. See finished straw potato nest, page 350a.

136. Waffled Potatoes *(Pommes Gaufrettes)*

1. The *gaufrettes* potatoes are cut with the *mandoline* which is a special vegetable cutter. Using the side with the wrinkled or "teeth" blade, hold the potato with the palm of your hand and cut straight down.

2. Turn the potato 90 degrees. Your fingers are now facing the other direction. Cut straight down. Turn the potato 90 degrees for the next slice. You are crisscrossing the slices.

3. *Gaufrettes* potatoes ready to be deep fried. If the holes are not evident, the slices are too thick. If the potato slice does not hold together, but is all stringy, the slices are too thin. Adjust the thickness accordingly. Wash the potato slices, dry and deep fry in 375-degree oil. Unlike *pont-neufs* or *allumettes*, which are cooked twice, *gaufrettes* are cooked only once, until nicely browned and very crisp.

137. Waffle Potato Nest *(Nid en Pommes Gaufrettes)*

1. Using the *mandoline*, cut the waffle potatoes. (See page 336 for more information on how to cut waffle potatoes.) Arrange slices of waffle potatoes in the bottom layer of the wire basket to simulate a tulip. (See the introduction to technique 135 for more details about this metal nest.)

2. Place the smaller nest on top, secure with the clip and dip in 400-degree vegetable oil. Make sure that the whole nest is immersed. It will take approximately 3½ minutes to cook. Remove from the oil, unclip and start jiggling the two parts of the nest to separate them. The nest may remain attached to the top part or may stick to the bottom part. (In our case the nest stuck to the top.)

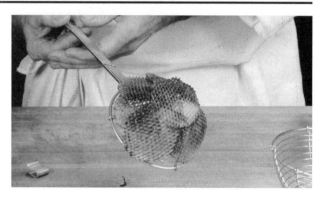

3. Using a knife, pry all around and trim the inside to release the nest. The waffle nest is even more fragile than the straw potato nest.

4. The potato nest can be filled with straw potatoes or soufflé potatoes and served as a garnish for roasted poultry. See finished waffle potato nest, page 350a.

138. Cream Puff Potatoes *(Pommes Dauphine)*

DAUPHINE OR CREAM PUFF POTATOES are made from equal amounts of *pâte à choux* (cream puff dough) and plain mashed potatoes. They are truly excellent served soon after being fried but soften if they're held too long. The *pâte à choux*, technique 264, can be made several days ahead, leaving you with just the potatoes to do.

1. Place the peeled potatoes in cold salted water. Boil and cook until done. Drain and push through a food mill. Mix the plain mashed potatoes with an equal amount of the *pâte à choux*. Fit a pastry bag with a fluted tube and fill, technique 62.

2. For potato crowns, lay out strips of wax paper or parchment paper and pipe circles onto the paper.

3. Dip the sheet of paper in the hot oil (340 degrees) and the potatoes will slide off into the oil. Cook, turning the potatoes every 2 minutes, for about 8 to 10 minutes. Dry on paper towels and sprinkle with salt.

4. For potato sticks, rest the tip of the pastry bag on the edge of the fryer. Squeeze the dough out, cutting it into strips by sliding the blade of a knife across the opening of the tube. Dip your knife in the hot oil to prevent sticking. Cook for 5 to 6 minutes in 340-degree oil. Drain on paper towels and salt.

5. For potato cream puffs, use a teaspoon to scoop some dough. Get as close as you possibly can to the hot oil (to avoid splashing), and push the dough off the spoon with your fingers.

6. Scrape the dough from the tip of your finger with the spoon, pushing it into the hot oil. Cook for 8 to 10 minutes in 340-degree oil, drain on paper towels and salt.

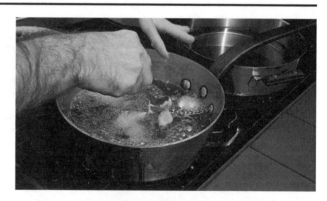

7. Three different shapes of *pommes dauphine*. Serve as soon as cooked to prevent softening.

139. Puffed Potato Slices *(Pommes Soufflées)*

M AKING THE PUFF, OR INFLATED, POTATO, called *pommes soufflées,* is a delicate operation. If the potatoes have too much moisture, as new potatoes often have, they will not puff. If they are soft and marbled, as old potatoes frequently are, they will not puff either. Often 15 to 20 percent of any one batch stays flat. In restaurants, the flat ones are served to the help as regular fried potatoes.

According to *Larousse Gastronomique,* the recipe was discovered accidentally in 1837 at the inauguration ceremonies for a railroad service to a small town near Paris. A local restaurant prepared a meal, including fried potatoes, for the official delegation. The train was late and the chef removed the potatoes from the fryer half cooked. At serving time, he was stupefied to see they puffed as he dipped them back in the hot oil. The chemist Chevreul worked out the chemical reasons and a recipe was compiled.

1. In restaurants, the first cooking of the potatoes takes place during the morning or afternoon preparation. They are dipped again in hot oil just before serving. Peel the potatoes and trim each one into the shape of a cylinder. (They can also be trimmed into a tube or a rectangle.) Use the trimmings in soup, puree, hash browns and the like.

2. Trim the ends of the potatoes. The slices should be the same size and shape to insure proper cooking, and for aesthetic reasons.

3. Using a slicer or a knife, cut the potatoes into ¼- to ⅜-inch-thick slices. Wash the potato slices in cold water and dry well with paper towels.

4. Pour vegetable oil, about 2½ to 3 inches deep, into two saucepans. Heat one to 325 degrees and the other to 375 degrees. Drop 15 to 20 slices into the 325-degree fryer and shake back and forth on the heat for 6 to 7 minutes (an asbestos pad will make the shaking easier by helping the pan to slide). Be careful not to splash oil on your hands while shaking the pan. You have to get a rhythm going. After 4 to 5 minutes, the slices should come to the surface and blisters should start to appear on them. Keep shaking another minute.

5. Stop shaking the pan. Using a skimmer, remove a few slices at a time. Let drain and soften for 5 to 6 seconds, then dip into the 375-degree fryer. The potatoes should swell instantly. Do not let them brown unless you are serving them at this point. As they puff up, transfer to a pan lined with a paper towel to drain. Finish the whole batch in this manner.

6. You will notice they deflate as you place them on the towel. Pick out the ones that puffed up and arrange them on the pan. Eat or discard the other slices. Covered with a paper towel, the good ones will keep at room temperature for several hours.

7. At serving time, drop the slices in the 375-degree fryer, moving them around with a skimmer so that they brown evenly. They should be very crisp to stay puffed. (During the first cooking, the surface of the slices becomes watertight. When the slices are dropped into hot oil, the water "imprisoned" inside tries to escape, pushing from the center, making the potato puff up.) Sprinkle with salt and serve immediately on folded napkins, technique 69.

140. Roman-Style Gnocchi *(Gnocchi Romaine)*

YIELD: 6 to 8 servings

THERE ARE THREE TYPES of gnocchi—*gnocchi Parisenne, gnocchi Romaine,* and *potato gnocchi.* The Parisian gnocchi is made from cream puff dough seasoned with Parmesan cheese, formed into small dumplings, poached in water, then usually baked in a white sauce and served au gratin all puffed up like little quennelles. The Roman gnocchi is made into a polenta from semolina and milk, cooled, cut into shapes and either friend or baked with butter, cream and cheese. The potato gnocchi are make with potato, flour, and egg and are poached and served with a sauce.

3 cups milk
2 tablespoons sweet butter
2 teaspoons salt
½ teaspoon freshly ground white pepper
⅛ teaspoon freshly grated nutmeg
1 cup semolina or farina (granulated hard
    durum wheat flour)
3 large eggs
1 cup heavy cream
1 teaspoon vegetable oil

¼ stick (1 ounce) sweet butter, melted
¾ cup grated Swiss cheese
1½ cups heavy cream

1. Place the milk, butter, salt, pepper and nutmeg in a large, heavy kettle, and bring to a boil. Pour in the semolina, mixing vigorously with a whisk. Reduce the heat and cook for 2 to 3 minutes, stirring with a wooden spatula until the mixture becomes very thick and lifts up from the sides of the pan. Set aside for 15 minutes until it cools slightly.

2. Beat the eggs in a bowl until well homogenized, then add the cream and
combine. Add the egg and cream mixture
to the semolina in one stroke and mix
thoroughly with the whisk. Be sure to work
fast or the basic mixture will lump. Place
the mixture back on medium heat and
bring to a boil, mixing constantly with the
whisk. Remove from the heat as soon as it
boils and thickens more.

3. Oil a cookie sheet (about 12 by 16
inches) and pour the mixture on it.

4. Spread the mixture out wjth a spatula
that's been wetted in water. The mixture
should be about ½ inch thick. Cover with
plastic wrap and refrigerate until cold and
set, at least 2 to 3 hours.

5. Using a round cookie cutter about 3
inches in diameter, cut rounds from the
cold semolina mixture. Butter an au gratin
dish and arrange the pieces overlapping
slightly.

6. Pour the melted butter on top of the rounds. Sprinkle with cheese and place the dish on a tray in a preheated 425-degree oven for about 15 minutes or until slightly browned.

7. Meanwhile, gather all the trimmings into a solid flat piece so that more rounds can be cut out of it.

8. When the gratin is slightly brown, pour the cream on top and place back in the oven for about 10 to 12 minutes, until glazed and beautifully browned. If not brown enough, place the tray under the broiler for a few minutes. Let the dish rest for 5 to 6 minutes before serving.

141. Green Noodles *(Nouilles Vertes)*

PASTA IS NOT COMPLICATED TO MAKE. Although it is made here by hand, the small pasta machines make the process quite easy and give very good results too. Use 3 cups of flour instead of 2¾ if you are using a machine. Green noodles, usually made with spinach, and sometimes Swiss chard leaves, are beautiful with a cream sauce and tomatoes. The spinach does not give much taste to the pasta. Pasta can be made with all-purpose flour, although a mixture of unbleached, hi-gluten flour and semolina flour gives a better texture and bite to the pasta.

1 *pound fresh spinach*
About 2 cups flour (semolina, semolina and
high glutten, or all-purpose). Depending
on moisture in the flour, measurement
might change by a few tablespoons.
3 *large egs, lightly beaten*
½ *teaspoon salt*
2 *tablespoons good olive oil*

Cook the spinach in salted, boiling water for 6 to 8 minutes. Strain and cool off under cold water. When cold, press with your hands to extrude as much water as possible. Chop, blend or mash into fine pieces. You will have between ½ and ⅔ cup of spinach purée.

1. Place the flour in the middle of the work table and create a well in the center. Add remaining ingredients to the well. Start mixing with your fingers.

2. Using a dough scraper, gather all the ingredients into a solid, compact mass.

3. Knead the dough with your hands for 2 to 3 minutes until nice and smooth. Place in a plastic bag and let "rest" in the refrigerator for at least 30 minutes.

4. Flour the table generously. Divide the dough into 4 pieces.

5. Roll each piece into a thin wheel, pushing on the rolling pin to spread the edges of the dough.

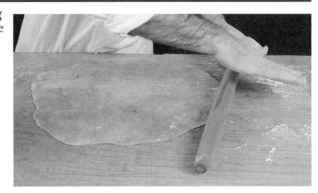

6. Keep rolling with one hand, "pulling" the dough with the other hand to stretch it.

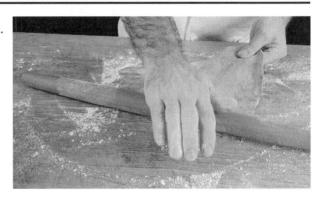

7. When thin enough (no more than ⅛ inch), hang the dough on the rolling pin or

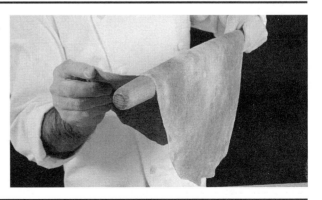

8. on a broomstick, or on the back of a chair lined with wax paper, and let it dry and stretch for a good 30 to 45 minutes.

9. Sprinkle the table with flour and stack the four pieces of dough on top of one another, being sure to flour generously between each layer.

10. Roll the layers into a cylinder and

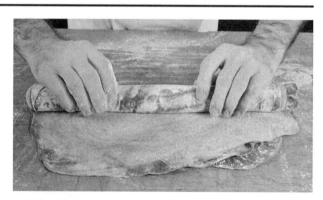

11. cut into ¼- to ½-inch slices.

12. Separate the noodles. Cook in a lot of boiling salted water for no more than 3½ to 4 minutes. Serve with butter, cheese or your favorite sauce. If you don't use right away, let them dry on a towel to absorb the moisture. Keep in mind that the longer they dry the longer they will need to cook.

142. Onion Soup *(Soupe à l'Oignon)*

YIELD: 6 servings

ONION SOUP is widely served all over France, sometimes *gratinée,* that is with a crust on top, sometimes just as a broth. It can be served in a large terrine, as well as in individual crock pots. After an evening at the theater, it is usually served *gratinée.* The onions are sometimes sautéed lightly and left in the soup, as in our recipe; other times they are browned to a dark stage then slightly singed with flour, cooked, then pushed through a food mill as in the Lyonnaise version which is made with water rather than stock.

4 *cups thinly sliced onion (3 to 5 onions, depending on size)*
1 *pound good Swiss cheese, grated (Emmenthaler or Gruyère)*
3 *tablespoons sweet butter*
10 *cups chicken stock, or a mixture of chicken and beef stock, or a mixture of water and stock*
1 *clove garlic, crushed, peeled and chopped very fine*

1 *teaspoon salt (to taste)*
1 *teaspoon black pepper (to taste)*
2 *dozen slices of French bread, cut very thin and toasted under the broiler*

1. Use sweet yellow onions, making sure you remove all the skin and the roots. Cut them in half across and slice very thinly. Melt the butter and brown the onions on medium heat in a large saucepan for 5 to 6 minutes, until slightly brown. Stir in the stock, garlic, salt and pepper and boil for 30 minutes.

2. Place 4 to 5 slices of bread in each individual ovenproof bowl (use 12-ounce bowls).

3. Half fill each bowl with the stock. The bread will soften as it absorbs the liquid. Gradually keep adding liquid until the bowls are filled evenly and to the top. This is very important because the cheese crust must not sink into the bowl if it is to brown in the oven.

4. Sprinkle the cheese on top without pushing it into the liquid. You will need at least 2½ ounces of cheese per bowl or a good ½ cup (the drier the cheese the better).

5. Press the cheese around the edges of each bowl so that when it melts it sticks to the sides and forms a crust that will stay put instead of sinking into the liquid.

6. Place the bowls on a cookie sheet and bake in a preheated 400-degree oven for approximately 35 minutes, until nicely browned all around. Serve right away, one bowl per guest.

Zucchini puff paste, spinach timbales, eggplant custards, asparagus stew

Chicken stuffed under the skin, broccoli and cauliflower with lemon butter, straw potato cake, soap-shaped potatoes, straw potato nest, waffle potato nest

Spinach salad with chicken livers, mayonnaise of chicken, zucchini salad, string beans and tomato salad

Poultry and Meat

143. Trussing Chicken and Other Poultry *(Bridage du Poulet et Autres Volailles)*

WHAT, ESSENTIALLY, is the purpose of trussing a bird? It is so once properly tied, and I emphasize properly, the bird will keep its shape, will be easier to manipulate and will roast evenly throughout without getting dry. Here are several methods of trussing chicken and the like; the first is for ordinary chicken and the like; the second is for fowl; such as capons and turkey. Method 3 is a way of trussing without a needle. To eriscerate a chicken, see technique 156.

METHOD 1

1. Cut the tips of the wings.

2. Cut the other small tips at the first joint. The removal of these little extremities is more for aesthetics than anything else.

3. Tuck the first section of the wings under.

4. Push the legs toward the breast. If you keep the legs tucked tight on the side of the bird, they will push the breast up and make it plump.

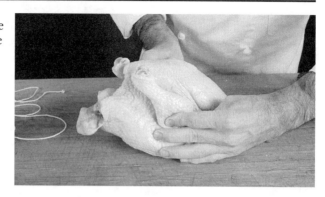

5. Thread the needle with a long piece of kitchen twine (not too thin) and make a knot at the eye. lift up the drumstick and insert the needle in the "soft" spot in the lower part of the thigh bone. Be sure to insert the needle in the right place so that the string is anchored into the bone rather than in the skin.

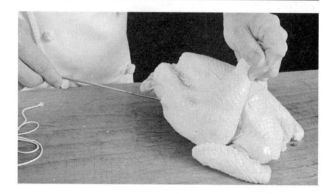

6. Come out at the point where the thigh and drumstick join.

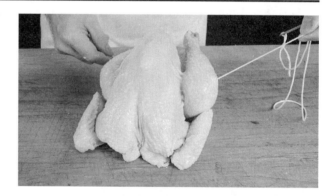

7. Turn the chicken on its breast. Push the needle through the wing section, the loose neck skin, the skin of the back and the other wing.

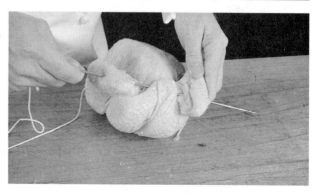

8. Place the chicken on its back and push the needle in the middle joint of the leg, through the lower back, a reverse operation of steps 6 and 5.

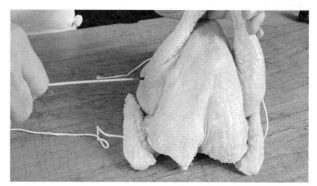

9. Lift up the skin of the tail end and push the needle through. It is important that the needle go through the lower part of the skin because it makes a small tight loop that holds the drumstick in place.

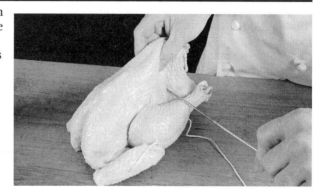

10. Pull both ends of string tight, securing with a double knot.

11. Chicken, trussed and oven ready.

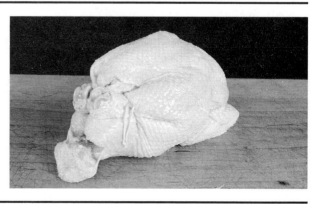

METHOD 2

1. This method uses two trusses but the needle goes through the same spots as the first method. Lift the drumstick and push the needle through the body at the joint of the thigh and drumstick. Come out at the corresponding joint on the other side.

2. Turn the capon on its breast and push the needle through one wing section, the loose skin of the neck and the back skin, then the other wing.

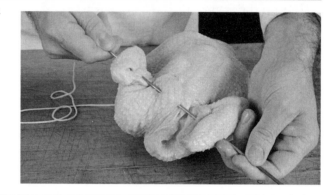

3. Pull the string tight and secure with a double knot. Cut the string. The front part of the bird is trussed.

4. Next, push the needle straight across through the hole in the lower part of the thigh bones.

5. Lift up the loose skin under the tip of the breast and go through with the needle. Secure with a tight double knot.

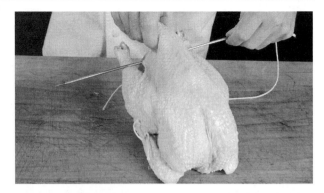

6. Capon trussed with two strings, oven ready. The two strings give a tighter-trussed bird.

METHOD 3

1. Cut the wings at the second joint. You may also remove the tips of the wings only, and tuck the first section under, as shown in the two preceding methods.

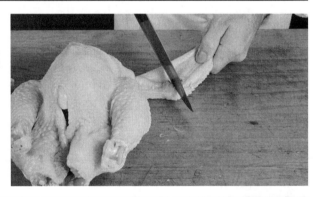

2. Slide the string under the back, next to the tail.

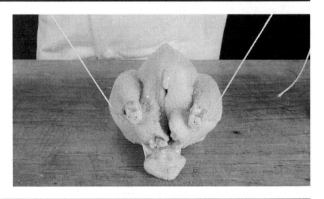

3. Lift the string on both sides and cross it over the top.

4. Slide the string under the tip of the drumstick and pull it tight.

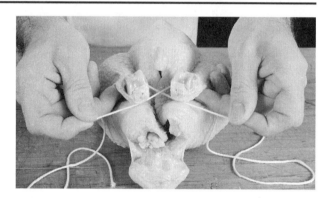

5. Bring the string along both sides of the chicken. Place your thumbs on both sides of the neck, and "push" the chicken forward, pulling up the string at the same time. This step is important; it pushes the breast up.

6. Place the chicken on the breast. Bring one end of the string above the wing and behind the bone of the neck, securing the loose skin of the neck as you go along.

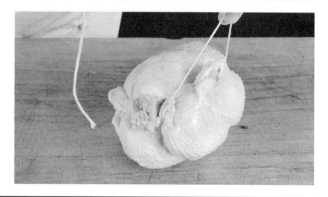

7. Secure tightly with a knot.

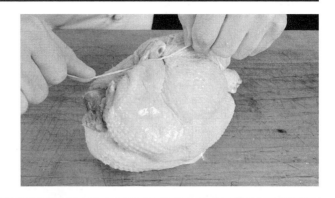

8. Chicken trussed without a needle, oven ready.

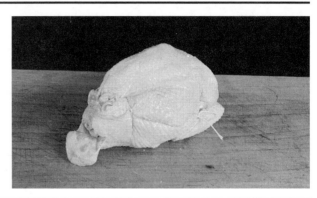

144. Chicken Stuffed under the Skin
(Poulet Farci sous la Peau)

YIELD: 4 to 6 servings

S TUFFING A CHICKEN between the skin and the flesh not only flavors the bird but keeps it moist as well.

Stuffing

1½ tablespoons sweet butter
6 ounces mushroom (about 3 cups loose), sliced
½ teaspoon salt
¼ teaspoon freshly ground black pepper
1 tablespoon chopped parsley
2 cloves garlic peeled, crushed and chopped fine
    (1 teaspoon)
1 3½-pound roasting chicken
1 tablespoon soft sweet butter to cook the chicken

Sauce

2 tablespoons finely chopped onion
2 to 3 cloves garlic peeled, crushed and chopped
    (1 teaspoon)
2 cups fresh, coarsely chopped tomatoes (peeled
    and seeded)
Salt and pepper to taste
½ cup oil-cured pitted olives
1 tablespoon chopped parsley or other fresh herbs
    (chives, tarragon, etc.)

1. Melt the 1½ tablespoons of butter in a saucepan, add the mushrooms, salt and pepper. Cook on medium heat for 4 to 5 minutes, until the liquid given off by the mushrooms has evaporated. Add the parsley and garlic and mix well. Let cool. Remove the wishbone from the chicken and slide your finger between the flesh and the skin to loosen the skin from the breast.

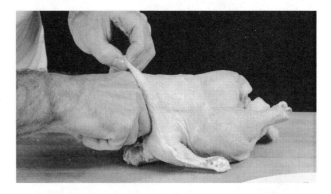

2. Keep pushing your fingers between the skin and the flesh to separate the leg meat from the skin. Slowly loosen the skin all around the chicken except along its back.

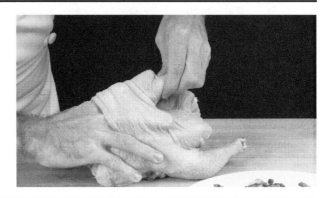

3. Lift the skin from the flesh and using a spoon or a spatula push the seasoned mushrooms inside.

4. Press the chicken back into shape and truss with or without a trussing needle. (You can find instructions for trussing beginning on page 353.)

5. Rub the skin of the chicken with 1 tablespoon softened butter, sprinkle lightly with salt and pepper and place the chicken on its side in a roasting pan or skillet. Roast in a preheated 400-degree oven for 1 hour, turning from side to side after the first 25 minutes and finally placing it on its back the last 10 to 15 minutes of cooking. Baste every 5 minutes during the last 10 to 15 minutes of cooking.

6. Lift the chicken from the roasting pan, trim the ends of the drumsticks and keep the chicken warm on a platter, uncovered in a 160-degree oven. Pour out most of the clear fat in the roasting pan; add the onions and sauté for 1 to 2 minutes on medium heat. Add the garlic and mix for a few seconds, then the tomatoes. Bring to a boil and simmer gently stirring with a wooden spatula to melt the solidified juices. Season the sauce with salt and pepper. At serving time, pour the sauce on top and around the chicken, sprinkle with the olives and the herbs and serve immediately. The chicken can be carved in the dining room or cut into portions in the kitchen and arranged on plates with the olives, sauce and herbs. (See finished chicken stuffed under the skin, page 350a.) The olives are not added to the dish prior to serving because they tend to blacken and make the sauce taste bitter.

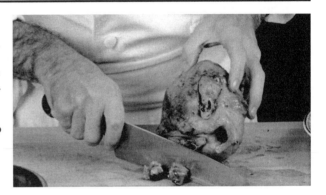

145. Preparing Chicken for Broiling
(Poulet pour Griller)

CHICKENS THAT ARE TO BE BROILED, barbecued or charcoal-broiled should be cut in the way that offers maximum surface to the heat.

1. Holding the chicken on its side, cut through the backbone on one side of the neck with a sturdy sharp knife.

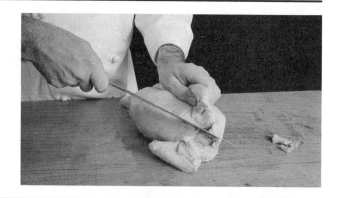

2. Pull the chicken open and

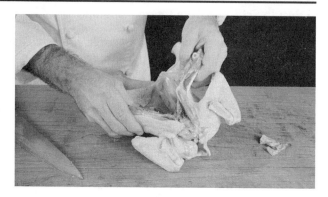

3. separate the backbone by cutting on the other side of the neck bone down to the tail. Reserve the pieces of bone for stock.

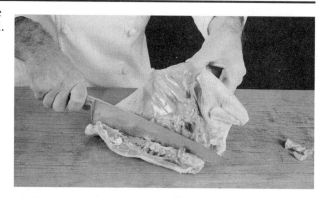

4. Place the chicken flat, skin side down, and using a meat pounder, flatten it.

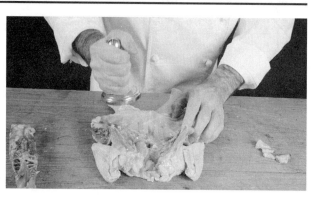

5. Remove the shoulder bones that stick up by cutting at the joint.

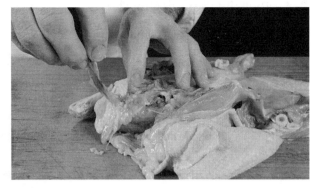

6. Remove the rib cage on each side.

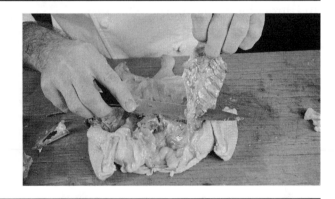

7. Make an incision at the joint which separates the thigh from the drumstick. This helps the chicken cook evenly (the thickest part of the leg would otherwise take longer to cook).

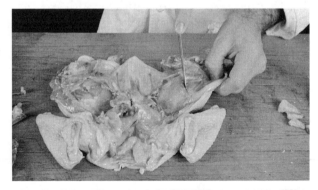

8. Cut a hole through the skin between the point of the breast and the thigh.

9. Push the tip of the drumstick

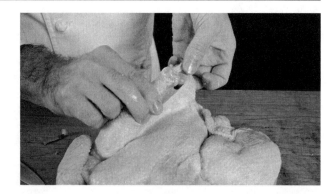

10. through the hole to secure the leg.

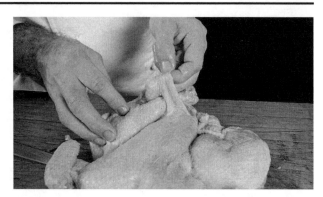

11. Chicken ready to broil. Sprinkle with salt and pepper and brush with vegetable oil before cooking. Cook skin side up. For chicken *grillé à la diable,* bake the chicken in a 450-degree preheated oven—a 3- to 3½-pound roaster won't take more than 35 minutes—coat with mustard and bread crumbs and finish under the broiler.

146. Preparing Chicken for Stews
(Poulet pour Sauter)

THERE ARE LITERALLY hundreds of recipes that call for cut-up chicken. Chicken can be cut "off the bone" (the backbone), which is the more elegant method, or with the bone in. The second yields more pieces and is, therefore, more economical.

OFF THE BONE

1. A chicken can be cut off the bone into quarters (2 legs and 2 single breasts), into 5 pieces (2 legs, 2 wings, 1 breast), or into 7 pieces, if the chicken is large enough (about 3½ pounds), by separating the legs into thighs and drumsticks. Begin by cutting the wing at the second joint, leaving only the first section attached to the chicken.

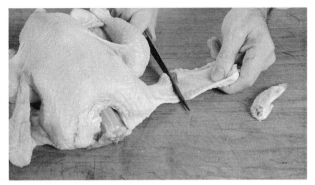

2. Place the chicken on its side and, with a small sharp knife, cut the skin all around the leg.

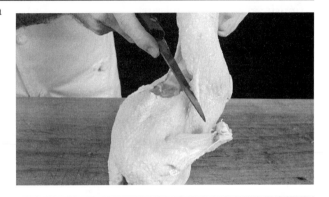

3. Open the leg to expose the joint where the thigh is attached to the body. Cut through the joint.

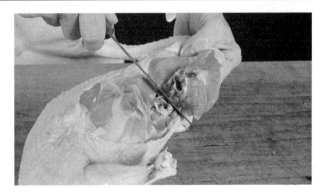

4. Holding the chicken firmly with one hand, pull the leg until it separates from the body.

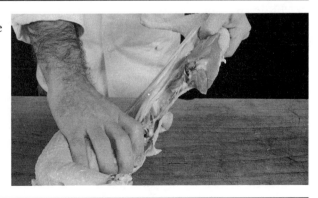

5. Cut off the tip of the drumstick and

6. push down on the meat to expose the bone. Separate the thigh and drumstick at the joint. Cut the other leg in the same manner.

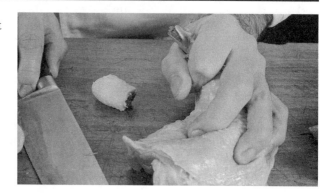

7. With the chicken on its side, pull back the wing. With your knife, find the joint where the wing is attached to the body and cut through with the point of your knife.

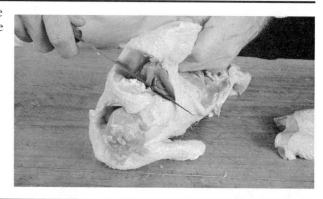

8. Cut down along the breast so part of the white meat is attached to the wing.

9. Then, holding the chicken firmly with one hand, pull the wing section out. Repeat on the other side.

10. Trim the end bone of the wings.

11. Separate the breast (in fact, the sternum; *bréchet* in French) from the carcass. Use the carcass, neck and tip of bones for stock or sauces.

12. Chicken ready to sauté.

BONE IN

1. Remove the first joint of both wings. Then, with a heavy knife, cut through the center of the breast and through the back on one side of the backbone to separate the chicken into halves.

2. Remove the backbone and tail from the half it is attached to.

3. Separate the leg from the wing, going right through the bones with the large knife.

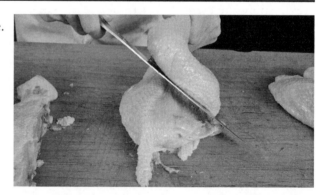

4. Cut each breast and leg into halves.

5. Chicken ready for stewing or frying.

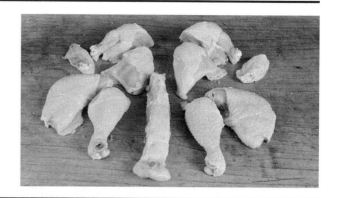

147. Cold Glazed Chicken *(Poulet Glacé Arlequin)*

T HIS COLD GLAZED CHICKEN is roasted, then cut into quarters, and the juices reduced to a glaze used to brush the chicken pieces. It is then glazed with a clear aspic and finally presented with a green pea and a red tomato aspic. It can be presented on individual plates or on a larger platter for a buffet. It makes a festive and elegant main course for an after the theater supper. We used a 3-pound chicken.

Aspic

YIELD: about 3½ cups

4 *cups good chicken stock or a mixture of chicken and beef stock*
3 *envelopes unflavored gelatin*
2 *egg whites*
1 *cup leafy part of celery green*
½ *cup coarsely chopped carrots*
¼ *cup coarsely chopped parsley*
1 *to* 2 *branches fresh tarragon coarsely chopped*
½ *teaspoon crushed black pepper* (mignonnette)
Salt to taste (depending on seasoning of the stock)

Combine all ingredients together in a sturdy saucepan. Bring to a boil, stirring occasionally, and let boil strongly for 4 to 5 seconds, then remove to the side of the stove and let it set 10 minutes. Strain through a fine sieve lined with paper towels. (For more information about aspic, see technique 21.)

Tomato aspic

YIELD: About ½ cup

1 *large or* 2 *medium ripe tomatoes*
½ *teaspoon paprika*
¼ *teaspoon salt*
Dash of white pepper
1 *cup melted aspic*

Peel the tomato, cut in half and press the seeds out. Put in a blender with the paprika and blend well. Place in a fine chinois or a paper towel and press most of the liquid out. Combine the tomato solids with remaining ingredients and set aside.

Pea aspic

1 10-ounce package frozen baby peas (see note)
2 cups water
½ teaspoon salt
¼ stick (1 ounce) sweet butter

Bring the water and salt to a boil. Add the peas and bring back to a boil. Boil uncovered for 2½ to 3 minutes. Drain immediately and place the peas in a food processor. Blend for 30 seconds. If the peas are allowed to cool or if the peas are not tiny baby peas, the skin will not liquefy properly and the taste will not be as refined or the color as bright. Therefore, it is important to process them immediately after cooking. Add the butter, a dash of salt and blend another 30 seconds. This yields 1 cup of purée. Combine ½ cup of the purée of peas with 1 cup of melted aspic. Set aside. This pea purée is a great vegetable dish by itself—a perfect accompaniment to roasts, poached eggs, etc. In this recipe it is just used incidentally and we only use ½ cup of the mixture.

(Note: Fresh peas from the garden are always the best. Unfortunately, so-called fresh peas in the pod bought at the market are often large and starchy. That's why we prefer frozen baby peas.)

1. Truss (see technique 143) salt and pepper the chicken and roast in a preheated 400-degree oven according to the instruction on page 391, step 5. When the chicken is cooked, drain it of its juices. You will notice that the juices run nice and clear. Let it mix with the drippings.

2. Pour out the clear fat—keep it to brown meat or sauté potatoes. (If the drippings are not separated into solidified juices and fat, cook the drippings on top of the stove to evaporate the moisture. When the moisture has evaporated, you will have solidified juice in the bottom and clear fat on top. Cook on medium low heat, being careful not to burn the juices. If the solidified juices are burnt, it will give a bitter taste to the sauce.)

3. When the fat is completely removed, retrieve the solidified juices by adding a little water to the pan and heating until the juices dissolve. Strain through a fine sieve and reduce to 2 tablespoons of *glace*. (To serve a regular roast chicken with juices, reduce less and add 1 or 2 tablespoons of fat back into the juices after stirring to enrich.)

4. Cut the chicken in half.

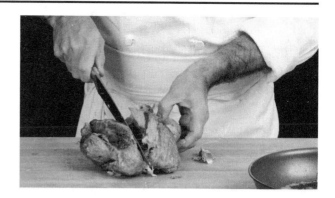

5. Separate each half into breast and leg. Remove the carcass from the breasts and legs.

6. Remove the shoulder bone from the breast and cut off the top of the wings. The thigh and drum bones get left in the leg.

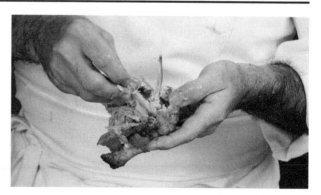

7. When the *glace* has reached the concentration of jam (thick and dark without being burnt), place the chicken on a wire rack and brush with the *glace*. The glaze is an extremely concentrated, strong reduction, and is used as a flavoring agent.

8. Place the chicken with the *glace* in the refrigerator to cool it off. Meanwhile, take 2 cups of liquid aspic, place on ice, and stir until almost solidified and syrupy and ready to set. Glaze the chicken, using a spoon. If the aspic solidifies too fast and you don't have enough coating on your chicken, place the tray of chicken back into the refrigerator, remelt the aspic drippings, place on ice again until syrupy, and glaze another time. The chicken may have to be glazed several times. Aspic is slow to take on chicken because of the fat in the skin.

9. Cover the plates with a layer of pea aspic. When the aspic is set, cut two triangles and remove from the plates.

10. Clean with a towel so as to have two neat triangles opposing each other.

11. Set the tomato aspic in ice and when it is ready fill the two empty triangles. You now have two green and two red triangles.

12. If you want the dish to be even more decorative, cut two rounds with an upside-down pastry tube.

Fill each empty round with aspic of the opposite color. Then place your plates back in the refrigerator. When cold, place your piece of chicken on top and a bit of chopped aspic around. Serve well chilled. See finished cold glazed chicken, below.

Chicken pie

Cold glazed chicken

148. Mayonnaise of Chicken *(Mayonnaise de Volaille)*

YIELD: 6 to 8 servings

A MAYONNAISE OF CHICKEN is an elegant chicken salad. The word mayonnaise, when associated with poultry, poached fish, shellfish, lobster, cold meats, etc. always denotes cold salad. It is delicate and decorative, ideal to serve at a luncheon or a buffet party. The chicken can be poached and the mayonnaise made as well as the ingredients for the decoration. However, the salad cannot be assembled much more than an hour before serving because the shredded lettuce will soften and the mayonnaise will darken and lose it's fresh look.

---

1 *chicken, about 3 ½ pounds*

Mayonnaise

2 *egg yolks*
½ *teaspoon salt*
¼ *teaspoon freshly ground white pepper*
1 *tablespoon good red wine vinegar*
1¼ *cups oil (preferably equal parts of virgin olive and peanut or grape-seed oil)*

Decoration

1 *or 2 heads Boston lettuce, cleaned and dried*
1 *tablespoon olive oil*
1 *teaspoon red wine vinegar*
Salt
4 *hard-boiled eggs, shelled and quartered*
1 *tomato, cut in wedges*
1 *tablespoon large capers*
1 *can (2 ounces) anchovy fillets in oil*
1 *carrot, peeled and cut into strips with a vegetable peeler*

---

1. To poach the chicken, put it breast side down in a narrow stainless steel pan. Add 4 cups tepid water, 2 teapoons salt, 1 teaspoon black peppercorns, 2 teaspoons herbes de Provence, 2 bay leaves, 1 cleaned leek, 1 peeled onion and 2 carrots. Bring to a boil, then simmer 30 minutes. Cool in the hot liquid for 30 minutes more, remove and let cool to room temperature. Strain the stock and freeze it for later use. Pull out the two legs which should separate easily from the carcass, and remove the skin of the breast and the legs.

2. Still using your fingers, remove the bone from the breast as well as from the thigh and drums. Slice the breast meat on a slant to have long, thin slices.

3. Slice then pound the leg meat slightly to extend it and have nice thin slices. Make the mayonnaise. Be sure that the egg yolks and oil are at room temperature or they will separate, especially since there is no mustard in this mayonnaise.

4. Whisk the yolks, salt, pepper and vinegar in a bowl (not aluminum as it will discolor the mayonnaise). Add the oil slowly while beating with the whisk. As the mayonnaise becomes harder, add the oil a bit faster. The mayonnaise should be a nice spreading consistency. Pile the slices of lettuce together and shred thinly with the heart. Season with 1 tablespoon of olive oil, the vinegar, salt, and place in the bottom of a large, open, preferably glass bowl. Drop the carrot strips into boiling water for approximately 30 seconds to wilt the slices so they can be folded. Refresh under cold water and set aside.

5. Arrange the slices of chicken on top of the lettuce. Be sure to cover all the lettuce. Alternate slices of dark and white meat.

6. Using a spatula, cover the top of the chicken with about ¼ inch of mayonnaise in a dome shape, making it smooth with the spatula.

7. Arrange the carrot strips as though they were ribbons around a package.

8. Outline the ribbon with anchovy fillets cut in half lengthwise to make thin strips.

9. Take a piece of carrot strip and fold as shown in the picture to make a loop of a bow. Place four loops in the center of the salad.

10. Fold, roll or twist another carrot strip and place in the center of the bow. Decorate salad with hard-boiled eggs, tomato wedges and capers. Serve as soon as possible. See finished mayonnaise of chicken, page 350a.

149. Small Ballotine of Chicken

(Ballottines de Volailles Fine Champagne)

YIELD: *4 ballotines*

A BALLOTINE is meat, poultry, game or fish that has been boned, stuffed, tied and roasted. The leg meat is ground and stuffed into the breasts. The ballotines are then braised, and served with a sauce and *glace* of chicken.

Ballotine

2 *chickens 2½ pounds each*
⅓ *cup crushed ice*
⅔ *cup heavy cream*
½ *teaspoon salt*
¼ *teaspoon finely ground white pepper*

Cooking ballotine

¼ *stick (1 ounce) sweet butter*
½ *teaspoon salt*
¼ *teaspoon pepper*
1 *cup dry white wine*

Stock

Carcass, gizzard and neck of chicken
1 *large onion, peeled*
4 *cloves*
1 *leek, cleaned*
3 *bay leaves*
½ *teaspoon thyme*

Sauce

2 *cups stock (step 5)*
1 *cup dry white wine*
2 *teaspoons butter*
2 *teaspoons flour*
1 *cup heavy cream*
1 *teaspoon fine Champagne Cognac*

1. Place the chicken on its breast and cut the skin alongside the backbone. Separate the skin from the carcass on one side, following the bones.

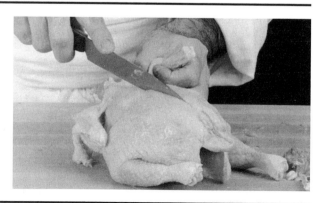

2. After the skin and meat have been separated from the bones, turn the chicken on the other side, remove the wishbone and cut alongside the breastbone.

3. Place the chicken on its side and cut through the joint of the shoulder. Start pulling the skin and meat from the central carcass.

4. The meat and skin of the entire half chicken should come off. It will still be attached at the joint of the thigh bone. Cut through the joint of the thigh and pull the chicken half off. The chicken half will still have the bone of the wing and the leg in it.

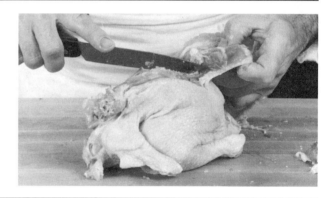

5. Pull out the leg meat and bone from the skin. The object is to keep the breast meat and the skin of the entire half chicken intact to use as a wrapper. Bone out the meat from the leg and set aside (the meat gets chopped later in the food processor). Place the bones, gizzard and neck in water and bring to a boil, then skim the top. Add the onion, cloves, leek, bay leaves and thyme. Bring back to a boil, lower the heat and simmer for 1 hour on medium heat. Strain. You should have approximately 2 cups of liquid. If more, reduce to 2 cups.

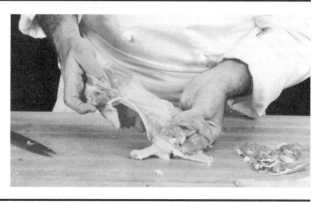

6. To make the stuffing, clean the leg meat of sinew and cut into 1-inch pieces. (You should have approximately 14 ounces of meat left from the 4 legs.) Place in the food processor with ⅓ cup of crushed ice and process for 15 to 20 seconds until smooth. Slowly add the cream, then the salt and white pepper. It should not take longer than a minute to make the mousse. Set aside. Spread out the skin with the breast meat attached.

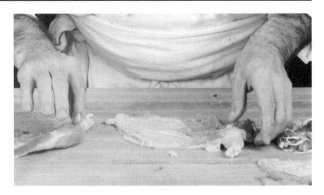

7. Remove the sinew from the small filet of the breast. Lift the meat of the breast from the skin—it will still be attached by the wing bone—and place the filet underneath.

8. Divide the mousse between the four breasts, place directly on the skin and cover with the breast meat.

9. Fold the skin over the meat to encase meat and stuffing together.

10. Tie the little ballontine carefully on the top and around with kitchen string. (This is covered in technique 168, pages 438–439.) Melt butter in a heavy saucepan, sprinkle the meat with the salt and pepper and brown the pieces gently on medium heat on both sides for approximately 6 minutes altogether, 3 minutes on each side. Add white wine to mixture, cover and simmer very slowly for 15 minutes.

11. Place the *ballotine* on a platter. When cold enough to handle, remove the string and trim off the extra skin. Keep warm uncovered in a 160- to 180-degree oven while you make the *glace* and sauce.

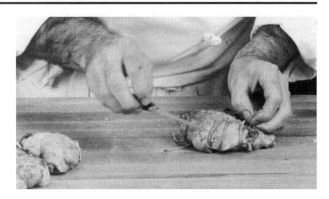

12. Strain the cooking juices into a small saucepan. If there is no juice left, add some water, stir to dissolve all the solidified juices and strain into a clean saucepan. Reduce on low heat to obtain 2 to 3 tablespoons of glaze (see technique 147.) At some point during the reduction the sauce may separate into fat and juices. If this happens, pour the fat out, add 1 or 2 tablespoons of water to the mixture left and boil to combine together. You should have approximately 2 to 3 tablespoons of *glace* of chicken.

13. While the *glace* is cooking, make the fine champagne sauce. Take the 2 cups of stock, add the white wine and reduce the whole mixture on high heat to 1 cup. Melt the butter in a saucepan and add the flour. Cook for 30 seconds, stirring with a whisk and add the cup of reduced stock, stirring constantly with the whisk and bring to a boil. Add the cream, bring to a boil again and reduce for 3 to 4 minutes while boiling. You should have approximately 1⅓ cups of leftover sauce. It should be smooth and creamy but not too thick. Season with salt and pepper and finally, add the Cognac. Place ¼ cup of sauce on very warm plates, and using the *glace,* make two circles in the sauce.

14. With the point of a knife, pull through the *glace* and the sauce to make a streaky design. Place the *ballotine* in the center with about 1 tablespoon of sauce on top and some drippings of *glace* on top of that. Serve immediately. The *ballotine* is good served with rice pilaf, or *pommes savonnettes* (technique 133), and a green vegetable.

150. Chicken with Morels *(Poulet aux Morilles)*

THE MORELS are wild mushrooms that can be found along the edges of the woods and on hillsides in early spring. Fresh-picked morels can be toxic eaten raw in salad. They can also be toxic when cooked if you eat large quantities of them at frequent intervals. However, they are perfectly safe after they have been dried which is the way they are usually bought in specialty stores. Dry morels are very expensive but 1 ounce goes quite a long way. Use the tiny, pointed black-headed type which is the best morel.

1 3½-pound chicken
1 ounce dried morel mushrooms
5 to 6 shallots, peeled and finely sliced (2 table-
    spoons)
2 tablespoons sweet butter
½ teaspoon salt
¼ teaspoon freshly ground black pepper
½ cup dry white wine
⅓ cup dry Sherry
1 cup heavy cream

1. One ounce of tiny dried black-headed morels, usually imported from Europe.

2. Soak the morels in water for at least 15 to 20 minutes. If they are whole, split them in half lengthwise to dispose of the sand. The inside is like a very hollow furrow. Cut off the tips of the stem.

3. Discard the soaking water as there will be sand at the bottom of it. Wash the morels again, several times if necessary, in luke-warm water, until there is no sand left in the bottom of your bowl. Lift the morels gently out of the water so as not to take the sand with them. Drain and press gently to extrude some of the water.

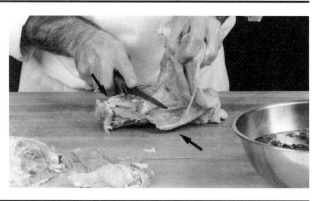

4. Cut the legs from the chicken and sepa-rate into drums and thighs. Pull the skin off the meat. Remove the wishbone from the breast. Cut at the shoulder joint (arrow) and along the breastbone (arrow). Pull the breast meat off in one piece. Repeat on the other side.

5. Remove the skin from the breast. Trim the wings. (Use the carcass, trimmings, etc., to make a stock for future use.) Cut each individual breast into 2 pieces. You now have 8 pieces of chicken with all fat and visible skin removed. Sprinkle the chicken pieces with salt and pepper.

6. Melt the butter in a skillet. When foaming, place the pieces of chicken in it. Gently sauté on medium heat for 4 minutes. The chicken should be browned lightly, but a crust shouldn't form on the flesh. After about 2 minutes on one side, turn and brown 2 minutes on the other side. The butter should be foaming nicely, but not burning. Add the white wine, cover and simmer another 2 minutes, then remove the lower 2 pieces of the breasts. These boneless pieces of white meat will get cooked first. After another 2 minutes, remove the other 2 pieces of white meat where the wing is attached. Leave the dark meat simmering gently for another 5 to 6 minutes, then remove and set aside with the breast meat. Add the shallots to the pan drippings for about 1 minute. Add the Sherry, bring to a boil and reduce on high heat for 2 to 3 minutes, or until the mixture is almost completely reduced.

7. Add the morels, stir and add the cream. Bring to a boil and reduce about 1 minute on high heat. The sauce should be glossy and should just coat a spoon. Add salt and pepper to taste and a small cube of *glace de viande* (see technique 12) if you have any. If not, reduce the sauce for another 1 to 2 minutes. Pour over the chicken and serve immediately. This is a quick, elegant dish, ideal as a main course for a dinner served with braised endives or potatoes and green vegetables.

151. Chicken Pie *(Fricassée de Poulet en Feuilletage)*

YIELD: 6 servings

THE CHICKEN PIE IS a stew made of boned chicken combined with a vegetable garnish and a cream sauce, topped with puff paste, and baked.

Braising the chicken

1 3½-pound chicken, quartered
½ cup thinly sliced onions
1 pinch thyme leaves
1 cup dry white wine
1 cup chicken stock

Garnishes

2 carrots, peeled and cut into 2-inch chunks, split into ¼-inch-thick sticks, blanched 3 to 4 minutes in boiling water and drained
½ cup frozen baby peas, blanched 30 seconds in boiling water and drained
1 or 2 stalks celery, peeled, cut into 2-inch chunks and then into ¼-inch sticks, blanched 1 minute in boiling water and drained
1 cup fresh snow peas, cleaned, blanched 1 minute in boiling water and drained (Note: The vegetables can, of course, be varied at will.)

Sauce

1 teaspoon sweet butter
1 teaspoon flour
1 cup heavy cream
Salt and pepper to taste

Crust

1 pound of puff paste (technique 269)
2 beaten egg yolks, for the wash

1. Sprinkle the chicken with salt and pepper. Brown in a saucepan, skin side down, without fat on medium heat for 8 to 10 minutes. There is enough fat in the skin to brown the pieces, without adding extra fat. Add the onions, bay leaf, thyme, wine and stock to the chicken. Cover and simmer for 25 minutes. Remove from heat and, when cold enough to handle, remove skin and take the meat off the bones. Cut the meat into 1- to 2-inch chunks.

2. Reduce the juices left in the pan to 1 cup. Knead the butter and flour together (a *beurre manié*) and, using a whisk, whip the mixture into the juices vigorously. Bring the sauce to a boil stirring and simmer 5 minutes. Add the cream, bring to a boil again, taste for seasonings, and add salt and pepper if needed. Divide the meat and all the vegetable garnish among the crocks and pour the sauce over. The crocks should not be more than two-thirds full.

3. Roll the puff paste dough into ⅛-inch-thick rounds, and brush them with the egg yolk.

4. Place the dough on top of the crocks, egg-washed side down. Be sure to stretch the dough on top of the terrine so it does not sink in the center. Press to assure that the dough adheres firmly to the sides of the dish.

5. Brush the top and sides of the dough with egg yolk. Refrigerate for 1 hour, or place in the freezer for 15 to 20 minutes to firm up the dough.

6. Place the crocks on a cookie sheet in a preheated 375-degree oven and bake for 30 minutes. Serve immediately one crock per person or a large one for several people. For a large terrine, make a hole in the crust and serve the stew from the crock, with a piece of puff paste and some vegetables in each portion. The chicken pie is a complete main course with crust, vegetables, meat and sauce. See finished chicken pie, page 373.

152. Chicken Sausage *(Poulet en Saucisse)*

A GALANTINE is a boned bird, usually a duck or chicken, filled with a force-meat mixture and alternate layers of liver, truffles and the like. The boned, stuffed bird is poached in broth, cooled off and served with its own aspic. A *ballottine* is essentially the same except the stuffed bird is roasted instead of poached and served hot with a sauce. A simplified version, the *poulet en saucisse,* is not quite a galantine or a *ballottine,* but it partakes of both. The most tedious part of the preparation is boning the chicken. The meat is completely separated from the carcass and left in one piece.

BONING THE CHICKEN

1. Using a 3- to 3¼-pound roasting chicken, remove the wings at the second joint and reserve. Lift up the skin of the neck to expose the flesh and, using the point of a small knife, follow the contour of the wishbone to get it loose.

2. Pull the wishbone out.

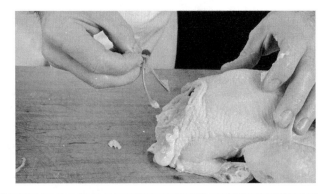

3. Place the chicken on its breast, and cut down the backbone to expose the meat.

4. Following the carcass with your knife, begin cutting the meat from the bone. Cut the joint at the shoulder (see arrow). Cut on top and around the breastbone and down on the other side. This is not really complicated; you simply separate the meat from the bone as you go. Do not worry about the leg, shoulder and wing bones.

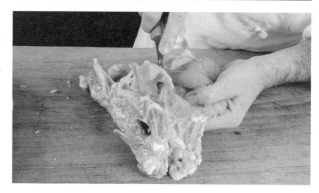

5. Remove the carcass in one piece.

6. Cut around the bone of the thigh to free it of meat. Holding the tip in one hand, scrape with your knife, "pushing" the meat from the bone. Separate the thighbone at the joint between the thigh and drumstick. The drumstick bone is left in.

7. With a large knife, cut the tip of the drumstick and

8. "push" the flesh back to expose the bone.

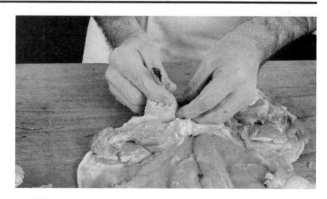

9. Cut the tip of the wing bones.

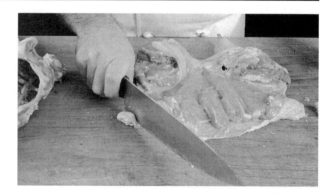

10. You will notice that there are 2 fillets loose on the breast. Pull them off and position them lower than the breast, where there is no meat on the skin. Most of the surface should be lined with meat.

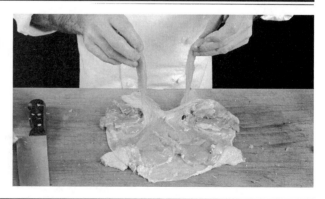

THE POACHING BROTH

Wings, bones, neck and gizzard from chicken
1 carrot, peeled and coarsely sliced
1 onion, peeled and coarsely sliced
1 celery rib, coarsely sliced
2 bay leaves
¼ teaspoon thyme
½ teaspoon salt

Place the wing pieces, bones, neck and gizzard in a kettle, cover with cold water and add the remaining ingredients. Bring to a boil and simmer for 1½ hours.

STUFFING AND COOKING

2 tablespoons sweet butter
½ cup chopped onion
5 ounces mushrooms, chopped fine (1 cup)
1½ teaspoons salt
½ teaspoon freshly ground white pepper
2 large chicken livers
Same amount or weight of chicken fat as of
   chicken livers (lumps from inside the bird)
8 ounces ground pork
1 tablespoon sherry

Melt the butter in a saucepan, add the onion and sauté for 1 minute. Add the mushrooms, ½ teaspoon salt and ¼ teaspoon pepper. Cook until all the liquid is evaporated from the mushrooms and the mixture starts to stick in the pan (about 5 minutes). Set aside and let cool. Cut the livers and chicken fat in small pieces. Place in a food processor and process until smooth. Add the ground pork, remaining sherry. All ingredients should be well blended and the mixture should be smooth.

11. Spread the purée of mushrooms equally on the meat.

12. Then place the liver mixture on top, spreading it with wet fingers. (Wet your fingers by dipping them into cold water.)

13. Bring both sides of the skin toward the center.

14. Pull the skin of the neck to enclose the stuffing.

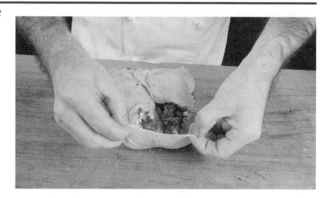

15. Place the chicken on a piece of cheesecloth and

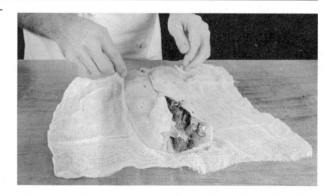

16. wrap carefully. Tie with a string and secure both ends, technique 168.

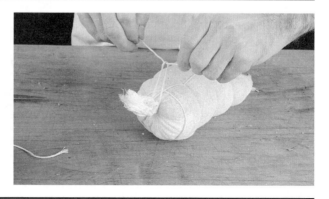

17. Using 2 tablespoons butter and 1 tablespoon vegetable oil, brown the chicken (it will brown through the cheesecloth) in a large skillet on medium to low heat. It will take about 20 minutes.

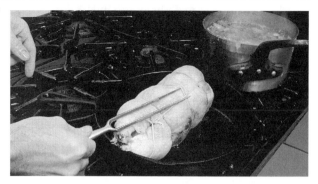

18. Strain the poaching broth. You should have 5 to 6 cups. If you don't, add water as necessary. Place the browned bird in a deep casserole and pour the stock on top. It should come almost to the top of the bird.

19. Bring to a boil, lower the heat and simmer very slowly (it should barely simmer) for 1½ hours. Let the chicken cool in the stock, overnight if possible. Remove from stock

20. and unwrap.

21. Trim the meat around the drumstick bone and pull the drum up. (This is just for appearances; note photograph 24.)

22. Twist and pull off the bone from the wings.

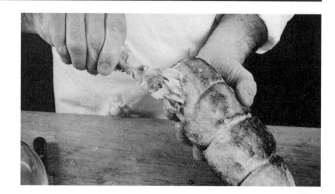

23. Strain the cold stock through a fine sieve to remove the fat. Bring to a boil and reduce on medium heat until you have about 1¼ cups left. It should be reduced enough to make a concentrated natural aspic. Place the reduced stock on ice and mix while cooling. Cut the "sausage" into ½-inch slices.

24. Arrange on a large tray and coat with the aspic when it is oily and almost set. Place paper frills on the legbones, technique 65. See finished dish, page 392a.

The *poulet en saucisse* serves 6 to 8.

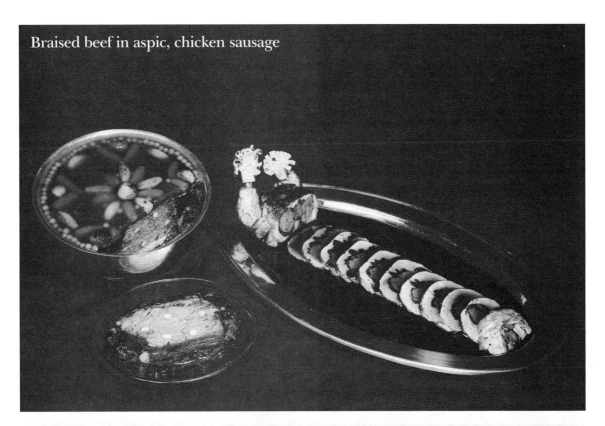

Braised beef in aspic, chicken sausage

Sweetbread terrine, pheasant pâté in crust, pork liver pâté

153. Braised Chicken Livers
(Foies de Volailles Braisés)

YIELD: About 25 slices

Braised chicken livers can be served on *croûtons* (small pieces of toast) for hors d'oeuvre, or sliced thin and added to a salad (see technique 120). They can also be served as a garnish in *vol au vent* or with a brochette. Duck, as well as turkey or goose, livers can be substituted for the chicken livers just as successfully.

8 *ounces large chicken livers, cleaned of large*
   sinews
1½ *teaspoons kosher-type coarse salt*
¼ *teaspoon freshly ground white pepper*
1 *clove garlic, crushed and chopped fine*
½ *teaspoon Cognac*
¼ *teaspoon sodium nitrite (see note*
   technique 181)
8 *ounces chicken fat, coarsely chopped*

1. Toss the chicken livers with the salt, pepper, garlic, Cognac and sodium nitrite. Cover with plastic wrap and let macerate in the refrigerator at least 24 hours. This will cure the livers. Chop the chicken fat coarsely (see picture) and place over medium heat and render slowly for about 15 minutes. Place the livers in a saucepan in one layer and strain the melted fat on top. The livers should be covered with the fat. Place the livers in a preheated 275-degree oven for 15 minutes. Remove from the oven and allow the livers to cool in the fat. If the chicken livers are to be kept for awhile, let them cool in the fat overnight. Remove from the fat and place in a jar. You will notice that the fat contains some liquid. Remove the hard fat. Melt. Do not use the juices at the bottom of the pan. Pour the melted fat on top of the livers and let harden in the refrigerator. If the juices are left with the livers for a period of time, they will turn the livers sour. At serving time, remove the livers from the fat, using paper towels to wipe off any fat that clings to the livers. Then cut on a slant in thin slices and serve on toast or in a salad.

154. Chicken Liver Custards

(Gâteau de Foies Volailles)

YIELD: 6 to 8 servings

THE CHICKEN LIVER custard is a specialty of the French area of Bresse, which is known for the superiority of its chicken, and the pale, pink, fatty livers which are considered the best. The custard is a refined dish which is generally served as a first course for an elaborate dinner or as a main course for a brunch or a light dinner. You can make it in individual molds or in a large one with or without the carrots on top. The sauce is a reduction of chicken stock with cream. A tomato sauce with a mushroom garnish is excellent with it, too.

Custard

3 *chicken livers, cleaned of filaments and any greenish parts*
1 *large clove garlic, crushed, or 2 small cloves*
1 *teaspoon sweet butter*
½ *teaspoon freshly ground white pepper*
1 *teaspoon salt*
1 *teaspoon cornstarch*
1 *cup milk*
6 *large eggs*
1 *cup heavy cream*
2 *to 3 large carrots, peeled*

Sauce

2 *cups good chicken stock*
1 *cup good beef stock*
1½ *cups heavy cream*
1 *tablespoon sweet butter*
1 *tablespoon coarsely minced fresh chives*

1. Blend the livers and garlic in a food processor until smooth. In a skillet, melt the butter until hot and add the liver mixture. Using a rubber spatula, stir the livers briefly until they solidify and hold. Place the mixture back in the food processor and blend again with pepper, salt and cornstarch and then add the milk. Blend until smooth and add the eggs and the cream. When well blended, strain into a bowl through a fine sieve.

2. Butter several small soufflé molds or a large 4- to 5-cup mold. Fill the molds with the liver mixture and place in a pan with tepid water.

3. Bake at 350 degrees for about 35 minutes for the small molds, 60 minutes for the large mold. The water around the custard should not boil. If it gets too hot, add some cold water or some ice cubes during the cooking. Remove from the heat and let the custard set for at least 20 minutes before unmolding.

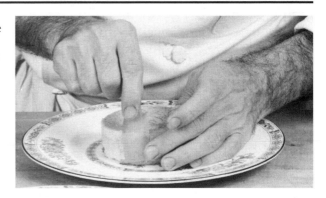

4. Slice the carrots very thin either with a vegetable peeler, a *mandoline* or with a knife, as explained in technique 4. Slice some of them into rounds and some of them into long strips. Drop the carrots into boiling water, bring back to a boil and boil for ½ minute until wilted. Lift out into a bowl of cold water to stop cooking and retain color. Drain the carrots and place on a paper towel to dry. Set aside until ready to use. Start decorating the custard. Use the strips around.

5. Reduce chicken and beef stock in a saucepan to about ½ cup to obtain a strong, dark *glace*. Add the heavy cream and boil on high heat for 2 to 3 minutes until it reduces to about 1½ cups and is slightly syrupy. Add salt and pepper to taste and place the butter, in small pieces, on top of the sauce to prevent skinning. Set aside. At serving time brush with butter to shine the top and heat slightly in the oven. Arrange sauce around each custard and sprinkle with the chives. Serve immediately. See finished chicken liver custards, page 529.

155. Goose Liver Pâté in Aspic

(Foie Gras Truffle en Gelée)

YIELD: 8 to 10 servings

Fresh fattened goose or duck livers are now available from upstate New York, California, and Canada as well as France. The canned "pure foie gras," studded with truffles, costs a small fortune but is a real delicacy. It is fattened, overfed liver of the goose, or duck, poached in Cognac, stock and different spices, cooked slowly in the fat of the goose, or simply just sterilized in tin cans. There are many ersatz, so-called *pâté de foie*, which are made with trimmings of goose liver, pork and different seasonings. The *pâté* featured in this technique is called "block"—it is whole goose-liver *pâté*, cooked with seasoning. It comes in small as well as large cans (ours weighed 1 pound).

1 *fresh cooked duck or goose foie gras,*
  or a canned "block"

Aspic

1 *cup coarsely chopped celery (leafy part)*
⅓ *cup parsley leaves*
½ *cup carrots, peeled and coarsely chopped*
1 *or 2 branches fresh tarragon or a dash of*
  dry if not available fresh
1 *cup coarsely chopped green of leek*
½ *teaspoon crushed peppercorns*
4 *egg whites*
½ *cup good Port wine*

4 *envelopes unflavored gelatin*
6 *cups good strong chicken or beef (or a mixture*
  of both) stock
Salt and pepper to taste

1 *fresh poached or canned truffle for*
  decoration

1. For the aspic: mix all vegetables, egg whites, geletin and Port wine in a stainless steel enameled saucepan. Add the cold stock and season highly with salt and pepper. Bring to a boil, stirring the mixture almost constantly to avoid scorching. As soon as it boils, a crust will form on top. Reduce the heat, let set for about 10 minutes. Do not stir or disturb the stock anymore at that point. Remove from heat, let set for about 10 minutes, then strain through a fine strainer lined with paper towels. Place half of the liquid in a large shallow glass

bowl. You should have about a 2-inch thickness of aspic. Place in the refrigerator to set.

2. Cut the *foie gras* into 1-ounce slices. Slice the whole block or slice only part of it and leave the rest whole. You will need one truffle to decorate the *foie gras*. Peel the rough surface of the truffle and keep the peel in a jar with either Cognac or Madeira. This can be kept for months in the refrigerator and used as needed, for *pâtés,* sauces, etc. Using a knife or a truffle slicer, slice the peeled truffle as thin as possible. Make little cutouts to simulate the flowers or strips to make the stems and push down to embed into the *foie gras* to decorate.

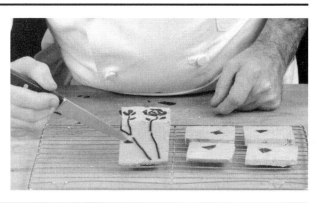

3. If the remaining aspic has set, melt and place on ice. Arrange the slices and the uncut *pâté* on a wire rack over a tray and chill. The *pâté* has to be cold for the aspic to stick to it. Gently stir the aspic with a spoon as it sits in the ice. When it starts looking oily, use a spoon to quickly coat the *pâté*. If the aspic becomes too hard, place the *foie gras* back into the refrigerator, remelt the aspic (including the drippings), and again stir over ice until oily; coat the *foie gras* again. If needed, coat several times to obtain an even color. Keep refrigerated.

4. Arrange the slices on the set aspic with the remaining *pâté* in the center.

5. If there's any set aspic left over, cut it into small strips, then into little cubes. Arrange around the slices. (Aspic should not be put through a pastry bag as is sometimes recommended in recipes.) Keep refrigerated until serving time. Serve very cold, with thin toast and a sweet Sauterne which goes very well with it. It is served as a first course as well as before the salad after the main course in a very elegant dinner. See finished goose liver pâté in aspic, page 529.

156. Cleaning Squab and Other Poultry
(Préparation du Pigeon et Autres Volailles)

THE SQUAB is a young domesticated pigeon about 4 weeks old, which has not yet flown and has been specially fed to be plump and tender. An older pigeon is tougher and should be braised but a dove (which is a wild species of pigeon) is quite tender.

This technique of cleaning can be applied to all poultry; it is illustrated with squab because squab usually comes uncleaned. Most birds you encounter in butcher shops and supermarkets are completely cleaned.

1. Cut the feet off the squab just under the joint. Holding it on its back, cut the tips sticking out at the first joint of each wing. This is primarily for aesthetics.

2. Holding the skin tightly squeezed around the neck, make a long incision to expose the bone.

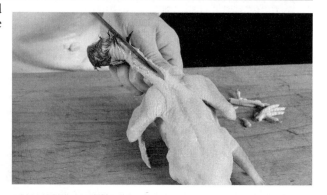

3. Separate the neck from the skin and crop (the loose saclike first stomach) by pulling with both hands.

4. Cut the neck at the base, near the body, and the skin next to the head. Separate the neck from the head.

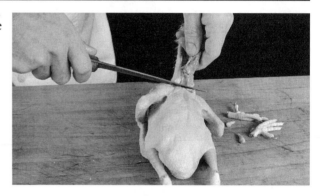

5. Pull out the crop and the viscera from the skin of the neck.

6. Lifting up the crop and viscera in the direction opposite the backbone, slide one finger underneath the crop. Slide the finger along and on each side of the backbone to get the guts and lungs loose.

7. Sever the crop near the opening and fold the neck skin onto the back of the bird.

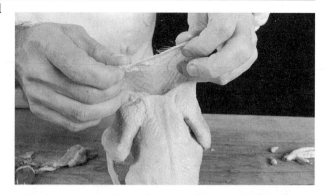

8. Cut a piece from the opening above the tail and

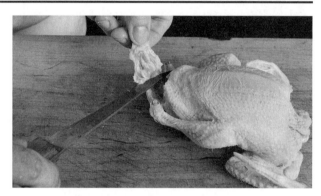

9. slit the skin open to the tip of the breastbone.

10. Pull the insides out. All the entrails should come out easily in one long piece.

11. Reserve the little lumps of fat on each side of the opening. Separate the heart and the liver. For a chicken, remove the gall—the green part of the liver. (Squab liver does not contain gall though most other poultry does.) The gall is in a pouch attached to the liver. Do not break it open. Remove in on piece and discard. Slit the gizzard (the second stomach) on the thick and fleshy side until you feel the inside which is harder.

12. Open it and remove the pouch inside.

13. Make a hole on each side of the opening and slide the tip of the drumstick inside to hold the leg.

14. Squab trussed, technique 143, and oven ready. From left to right: fat, cleaned gizzard, heart and neck. (The liver is in front.)

157. Toadlike Squab *(Pigeon Crapaudine)*

SQUAB CRAPAUDINE is usually served with deep-fried potatoes and garnished with watercress. Clean the squab following the directions in the preceding technique.

1. Holding the bird on its back, cut above the legs, alongside the breastbone. Do not cut through the backbone.

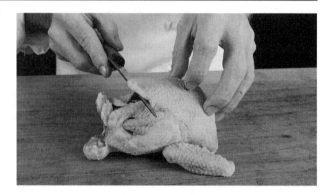

2. Separate the bird at the cut and

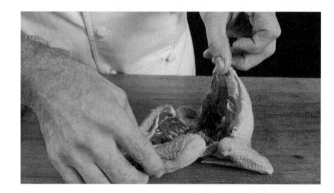

3. crack the back open.

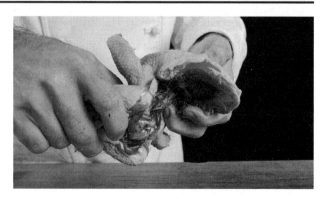

4. Turn the squab cut side down and flatten it with the heel of your hand.

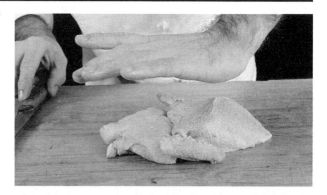

5. The tip of the drumstick can be secured through the skin of the back or it can be held upright by positioning a skewer through the wing and thighs. Place the squabs on a roasting pan. Sprinkle with salt and pepper and place in a 450-degree preheated oven. For 1¼- to 1½-pound squab, bake 25 minutes, about 12 minutes on each side.

6. Brush the squabs with 1 teaspoon of good mustard (Dijon-type) and sprinkle each with 1 tablespoon fresh bread crumbs. Baste with the drippings to moisten the bread and place under a hot broiler for 4 to 5 minutes until nicely brown. Make the "eyes" with pieces of hard-boiled egg whites and pieces of black olive.

158. Boned Stuffed Squab *(Pigeons Désossés et Farcis)*

YIELD: 4 servings

The squab is a good transition between regular poultry and real game, such as pheasant, woodcock, etc. It is dark meat and though it doesn't have a gamey taste, it is probably as close as you can get to game if you have never had it. Squab liver, unlike other poultry livers, does not have a gallbladder (the little green sac filled up with bile which is removed from the liver). Squabs weigh from approximately 10 to 18 ounces. The squabs here weighed 1 pound each, cleaned. It is easier to eat the squabs if they are boned out, particularly if you are going to stuff them. The same instructions for boning squab also apply to cornish hens and other small birds such as quail or woodcock. Serve on squab per person with broccoli and cauliflower mold (technique 108) and potato cake (technique 134).

Stock

Carcasses, necks, gizzards, wings
½ cup sliced onion
½ cup coarsely sliced carrot
2 cloves garlic, skin on
¼ teaspoon thyme
1 cup dry white wine
4 quarts water (approximately)

Sauce

½ teaspoon salt
¼ teaspoon freshly ground white pepper
½ teaspoon arrowroot, diluted with 1 table-
    spoon water

Stuffing

(You may change the fruits in the stuffing, using
figs, dates, raisins, etc.):

3 slices French bread, well toasted and blended
    into fine crumbs (about 1 cup)
¾ cup finely chopped mild boiled ham
1½ cups loose, finely chopped mushrooms (about
    4 ounces)
½ cup (about 4) sliced dry pitted prunes
½ cup (about 4) sliced dry pitted apricots
¼ cup melted sweet butter
½ teaspoon salt, depending on the saltiness of the
    ham
¼ teaspoon freshly ground white pepper

1. Trim the wings of the squab and eviscerate if needed. Lift the skin at the neck and cut around the wishbone. Remove the bone by pulling.

2. Put the squab on its side and push the piece of wing that remains back and forth to help locate the joint of the shoulder. Cut, twisting the blade back and forth, so it slides into the joint. Cut through. Repeat on the other side. Most of the boning from now on can be done with your fingers.

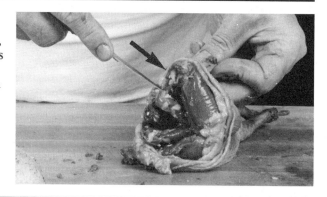

3. With the bird still on its side, push your thumb through the cut joint to release the meat from the carcass. Repeat on the other side.

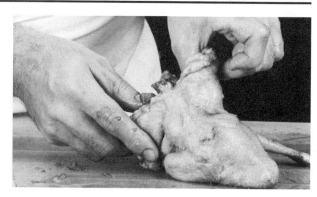

4. With the squab on its back push your finger between the flesh of the breast and the carcass to loosen the meat on both sides of the central breast bone (sternum). The skin will still be attached to the long cartilage part of the central bone.

5. Place the squab on its breast. Now separate the skin from the back bone. Be careful when pushing with the tip of your finger, not to go through the skin. (If you make a hole, it is not crucial, but try not to.) Keep pushing gently but firmly with your finger until you are close to the tail of the squab. All the skin should be loose.

6. Put the squab on its back and separate the meat from the long cartilage of the breast. Use your thumbs as levers to tear the skin from the central bone (arrow). Notice that some of the cartilage will still be attached to the skin.

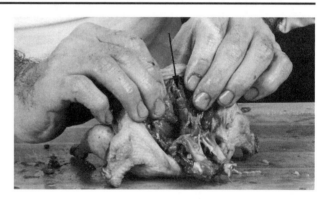

7. Now, with the skin completely loose from the central carcass, turn meat and skin gently inside out.

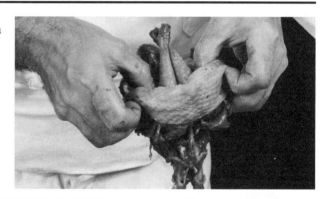

8. The only part of the squab still attached to the carcass is at the joint that joins the thigh bone to the body. Twist the bone at the joint (arrow) to tear it out of its socket on both sides.

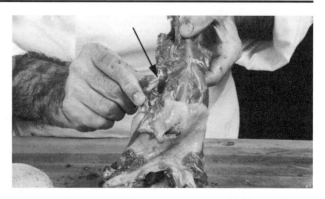

9. Keep pushing the skin from the bone and cut it off at the tail which should be left with the carcass. The carcass is now completely free from the rest of the squab.

10. Remove the thigh bones from the leg on each side. With your knife scrape the bone free of all meat and cut at the joint where it meets the bone of the drum.

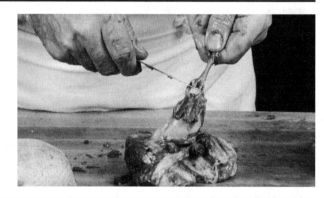

11. Turn the squab right side out again. The only bones left are little pieces of the drum and the first joint of the wing. Place the neck, gizzards, heart, carcass, trimmings, etc., in a large saucepan without any fat. Brown on high heat for 1 to 2 minutes, then on medium to low heat for 25 minutes, stirring once in a while with a wooden spatula. (There is enough fat in the skin to brown the bones.) The saucepan should be large enough to hold the bones in one layer.

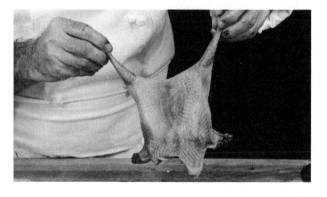

12. When the bones are nicely browned all around, and a nice crust of solidified juices has formed at the bottom of the pan (do not cook to fast or the juices will burn and the sauce will be bitter), add the onions, carrots, garlic and cook, still browning for another ten minutes. Add the white wine, thyme and approximately 2 quarts of water. Bring to a boil, lower the heat and simmer slowly for one hour. Remove the scum with a skimmer. After another hour, add another 2 quarts of water and cook for another hour. Strain the liquid through a fine strainer. You should have approximately 4 cups left. Remove as much fat as possible then reduce the liquid to 1 ¼ cups. This reduces stock will be the base of the sauce.

13. While the stock cooks, prepare the stuffing. Toss all the ingredients of the stuffing gently and using a pastry bag, your finger, or a spoon, stuff the four squabs.

14. Cover the opening at the neck and tail by wrapping the loose skin under. Gently press the squab back into its original shape.

15. To truss, place a piece of string under the squab at the tail opening and cross above the drums.

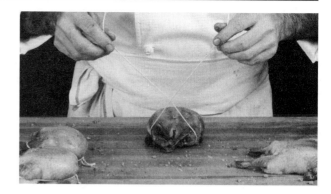

16. Bring the string back under the tip of the drumsticks in a figure 8. Pull gently on both ends of the string to close the opening at the tail and bring around the sides of the bird to tie in front.

17. Make a knot under the breast. Trussing holds the squab in shape while cooking. Sprinkle the squabs with the salt and pepper and place in a roasting pan breast side up. To brown properly, the squabs should not touch one another, and the sides of the roasting pan should not be too high. Because squabs are fatty enough, you don't have to rub them with butter before roasting. Roast in a preheated 400-degree oven for 30 minutes. After 15 minutes, baste with the fat which has melted from the birds, then baste every 5 minutes.

18. Untie and trim the ends of the drumsticks and the ends of the wing bones. Place the squabs on a platter and keep warm uncovered in a 160-degree oven while you finish the sauce. If the pan drippings are separated into solidified juices and clear fat, pour the fat out and retrieve the solidified juices by dissolving with stock. If not, cook the juices on top of the stove until the fat separates completely from the solidified juices. Then pour the fat out and add the 1¼ cups of stock. Boil the mixture for a few seconds while stirring with a spatula to dissolve juices. Strain into a small saucepan and add the arrowroot, stirring. Season with salt and pepper. You should have a generous cup of sauce. Serve on a large platter or on very hot individual plates. Coat each squab with about 2 to 3 tablespoons of sauce.

159. Trimming and Cooking Meat
(Préparation et Cuisson des Viandes)

To ascertain the exact degree of doneness when roasting or broiling meat, you need a thorough, practical knowledge of cooking. The professional chef knows by touching, or rather pushing into the meat with his fingers. How the meat springs back clearly reveals the degree to which the meat is cooked. An underdone roast feels soft and mushy; when rare, it feels soft with some bounce; when medium, it feels hard and springy; and when well-done, it feels hard with almost no bounce. However, variations due to differences between cuts, quality and method of cooking make this system difficult for the untrained.

Another method—cooking meat so many minutes to the pound—is also unreliable because it doesn't take into account the temperature of the oven, or the cut, shape, quality or preparation of the meat. For instance, a 6-pound rib roast will take close to 2½ hours in a 325-degree oven to be rare and about 1½ hours in a 420-degree oven. At the same temperature, a 3-pound piece of top round will take twice the time required for a 3-pound flank steak because of the difference in shape. One meat may be porous, another may be tight; one may be fatty, the next one may be lean; one is boned out, another is cooked bone in, and so on and on. All these factors modify the cooking of the meat and alter the timing.

A reliable modus operandi is the thermometer, one as thin as possible to avoid making big holes in the meat. Plunge the thermometer into the thickest part of the meat and wait approximately 45 seconds before reading the dial. (Do not use the kind that is left in the meat during the whole cooking time.)

The cooking figures given by manufacturers or the U.S.D.A. are invariably too high. Beef and lamb should be removed from the oven when the internal temperature reaches 110 to 115 degrees for rare, 115 to 120 degrees for medium rare, 130 to 135 degrees for medium, and 155 to 160 degrees if you want it well-done. Veal should be cooked to an internal temperature of about 150 degrees. Poultry and pork should be removed at 160 to 165 degrees. Trichinea, the parasite worms found in pork, are killed at a temperature between 138 and 140 degrees.

It is *imperative* that the meat "rest" before being carved (from 5 to 10 minutes for a small rack of lamb, to 25 minutes for a large rib roast) so the juices can settle, ensuring a nice pink color throughout the meat. A roast beef sliced as soon as it comes out of the oven will be mushy, lukewarm, practically raw in the middle, and grey and dry 1 inch all around the outside. The same piece of meat will be uniformly pink throughout if allowed to settle in a lukewarm place for 15 to 20 minutes.

You will really come to understand meat once you begin trimming it yourself, relying less on your butcher and more on your own skills. It requires some practice, but it will save you money and you will be able to have your meat trimmed the way you like it without extra expense. When it comes to trimming meat the cook and the butcher have different goals. The cook trims differently and trims more.

Once you get to know the principal cuts in one animal, they become quite easy to recognize in other animals, even if the cuts are handled differently. For example, after you have worked on a saddle of lamb, you will know that the lamb loin chops come from the saddle. You will also recognize veal saddle, veal loin chops, pork loin chops, and, in the beef, the shell steak, the tenderloin and the porterhouse steak, all of which come from the same part of the animal. Whether you are served a saddle of venison or a "rabble" (back) of hare, you will recognize where it comes from in the animal.

Spring lamb—the 8- to 12-month-old animal—is preferred for *selle d'agneau.* It has more taste and flavor than baby lamb and hasn't yet acquired the strong flavor of mutton. Baby lamb (which weighs under 20 pounds with skin and head) is usually served around Easter and is always cooked medium, unlike mutton which is cooked well, and spring lamb which should always be served pink.

1. A saddle, the piece between the ribs and the legs, comprises the T-bone with the two loins and two tenderloins. The kidneys are underneath the saddle. This saddle is 9½ pounds, untrimmed.

2. Remove the kidneys, including their lump of fat, by cutting and pulling.

3. Remove each kidney from its envelope of fat.

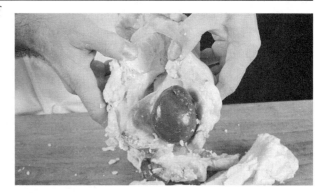

4. Cut the flank or skirt on both sides of the saddle.

5. With the saddle still upside down, trim the strip of sinews and fat along the central bone.

6. Keep trimming the fat on both sides of the tenderloin.

7. Turn the saddle right side up and trim the fat off the back.

8. Keep trimming on both sides of the loins, leaving only a very thin layer of fat on top of the meat.

9. Turn the saddle upside down and fold the skirt back onto the tenderloin. (This protects the choice tenderloin from drying during cooking.)

10. Place the saddle right side up and using the point of a knife, prick the large sinew all the way down the spine so that the meat does not contract during cooking.

11. Tie the saddle to secure the skirts underneath.

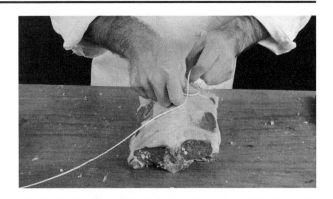

12. Saddle, oven ready. The trimmed saddle weighs 3½ pounds, and the trimmings and kidneys combined weigh 2 pounds. The trimmings make a delicious stew. The kidneys can be broiled or sautéed (technique 177). The fat is discarded.

160. Boning a Saddle of Lamb
(Désossage Selle d'Agneau)

THE SADDLE is comprised of the two loins, the two tenderloins, the flanks and the kidneys. An expensive cut of meat, it can be roasted whole and carved (see page 541), as well as boned out and cut into small médaillons (technique 165) or stuffed (technique 169). The loin (which is a half sadde) can be cut into loin chops or boned out and stuffed. The lamb fat is strong and cannot be used in any dish. The bones can be used for stocks or soups.

1. This photograph shows one saddle and one loin (half saddle). Place the saddle on its back to expose the filets. Remove the filet on each side, cutting along the central bone.

2. Keep your knife flat and cut along the T-bone on each side to expose the loins.

3. Turn the saddle and cut on each side along the backbone, to release both loins.

4. Trim the loins and tenderloins of all fat and sinew. Bone the half saddle in the same manner.

5. The saddle of lamb with the two loins and two filets, and the half saddle with its loin and tenderloin, all boned out. The bones can be used for stocks and the meat can be cut into scallopini and sautéed, or roasted whole, as well as stuffed.

161. Saddle of Lamb in Crust

(Selle d'Agneau en Croûte)

YIELD: 8 servings

A 5½-pound saddle of lamb yields about 2 to 2½ pounds of meat, completely trimmed and boned. In this technique, the boned-out meat is re-formed into a saddle with spinach replacing the bone. It is encased in puff paste and baked. The pink of the meat contrasts beautifully with the green of the spinach and the golden color of the crust. The spinach-stuffed saddle *en croûte* makes an elegant dish for a dinner party.

Roasting

1 *boned saddle (technique 160)*
2 *tablespoons (1 ounce) sweet butter*
½ *teaspoon salt*
¼ *teaspoon freshly ground black pepper*

Stuffing

2 *pounds spinach, cleaned and cooked (technique 119)*
½ *teaspoon salt*
¼ *teaspoon freshly ground black pepper*
2 *tablespoons shallots, chopped fine (about 3 to 4 shallots)*
1 *clove garlic, crushed and finely chopped*

To finish the dish

1 *pound puff paste for the crust (technique 269)*
1 *egg yolk mixed with 1 tablespoon milk or cream for the wash*

Melt the butter in a large skillet and when hot, salt and pepper the meat and brown on high heat for about 1 minute on each side to sear. Set the meat aside to cool. Heat the drippings until they turn dark brown and add the spinach with salt and pepper. Stir with a fork to separate the leaves and add the shallots and garlic. Sauté on medium heat for about 1 minute, stirring occasionally. Remove the spinach to a plate and cool. Roll out the puff paste into a large rectangle about ⅛ inch thick.

1. Set the two loins in the center of the dough. The meat, as well as the stuffing, should be cool.

2. Arrange the spinach between and on top of the loins, and place the two tenderloins on top with more spinach in between. The meat and spinach are arranged to reconstruct the saddle. Brush the sides of the dough with egg wash and fold one side over the meat carefully. Bring the other side on top so it overlaps slightly.

3. Trim the dough to leave only a bottom flap on each end of the saddle. Fold the flap back on the meat to enclose the saddle tightly.

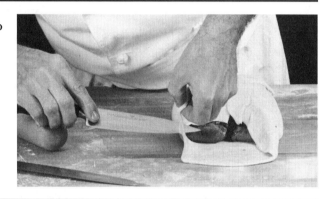

4. Place the saddle, seam side down, on a parchment-lined cookie sheet. Brush again with egg wash and decorate with strips of dough in a crisscross pattern. Brush the decorations with egg wash and let set in the refrigerator for 1 hour before cooking, if possible, or in the freezer for 15 to 20 minutes.

5. Place in a preheated 425-degree oven for 30 to 35 minutes for a medium-rare saddle. Remove from the oven and let the saddle rest in a warm place for at least 15 minutes before carving. The carving is a little tricky. Use a long, thin, sharp knife and cut ½-inch slices to reveal the two pieces of loin and two pieces of tenderloin. To help carve, place a large flat spatula against the slices to keep them from breaking apart. Serve with the sauce (see step 6, page 420). See finished saddle of lamb in puff paste, page 420a.

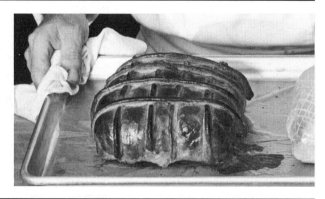

Loin of Lamb in Crust *(Demi-selle d'Agneau en croûte)*

YIELD: 4 servings

1. This variation on the lamb *en croûte* uses just one loin—not the whole saddle—and a "ham dough" instead of puff paste. The ham dough (the recipe appears in technique 184) is easier to make than puff paste and is less fragile. It is not as flaky as puff paste and won't brown quite as deeply. Bone-out one loin as explained in technique 160. Prepare half of the stuffing and sear the meat in butter. Prepare about 1 pound of ham dough. Roll into a rectangle and arrange the loin, spinach and tenderloin on top.

2. Bring one side of the dough on top of the meat and brush the top and sides with egg wash. Overlap the other side on top and trim both ends of the dough.

3. Brush the ends with the wash, fold and press gently on top. Turn the loin upside down and place it on a parchment-lined cookie sheet.

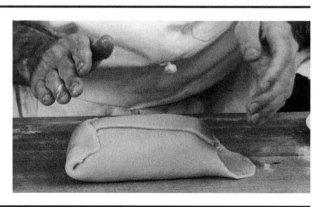

4. Decorate the top with a rose made of dough: Wrap a thin strip of dough around a lump of dough.

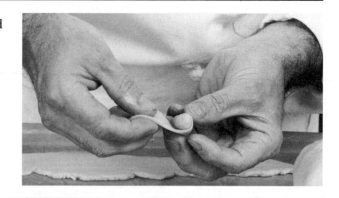

5. Make thin "petals" and wrap one after the other around the flower. Turn the edge of the petals outward to make them more lifelike (see technique 307).

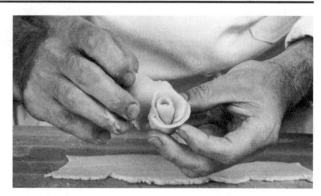

6. Place the flower in the middle of the loin with one leaf on each side. Brush the dough with the egg wash and mark crisscross lines with the back of a knife. Cook in a preheated 425-degree oven for about 25 minutes. Let the meat rest at least 10 to 15 minutes before carving. The single loin is easier to carve than the whole saddle. For a sauce to serve with the saddle or loin, cut the bones and sinew in 1-inch pieces. Place in a large saucepan and brown over medium heat for 25 minutes, without adding fat. Add 1 quart brown stock (see technique 12) and 1 quart of water. Cook slowly for 2 hours, removing the scum as it rises to the top. Strain and reduce to about 1¾ cups *demi-glace* of lamb. Test for seasonings and add salt and pepper if needed. Serve with the carved saddle or loin. See finished loin of lamb in crust, page 420a.

Loin of lamb in crust, saddle of lamb in puff paste

162. Trimming Rack of Lamb
(Préparation du Carré d'Agneau)

1. The double rack of lamb, the piece between the saddle and the shoulder, is not as lean on the shoulder side

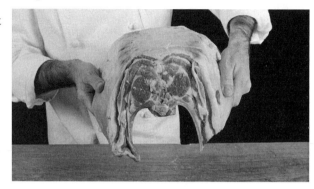

2. as it is on the saddle side. This double rack is 7½ pounds, untrimmed.

3. The double rack can be split into halves in a few different ways. One is to insert a skewer into the spinal cord and,

4. using it as a guide, split the double rack in half with a cleaver. However, this method leaves the meat of each rack attached to the backbone, and makes it hard to carve at the table.

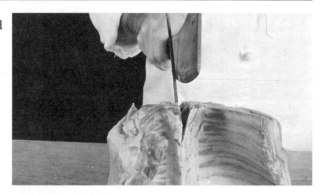

5. Although slightly more involved, this method for splitting the rack is better by far. Using a sturdy sharp knife, cut down on each side of the backbone. Keeping your knife tight along the bone, go as deep as you can. The tip of the knife should go down to the T-bone.

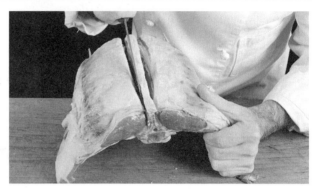

6. Holding the double rack with one hand and working with a cleaver from the inside of the rack, begin to sever one of the racks where it joins the backbone. Do not sever entirely; just make an incision. Stop and go to the other side of the backbone and sever the second rack entirely. Use only the tip of the cleaver and be sure not to cut into the meat which should stay attached to the rack.

7. Go back to the incision on the first side and separate with the cleaver. The incision makes the job easier.

8. Two single racks with the detached central backbone.

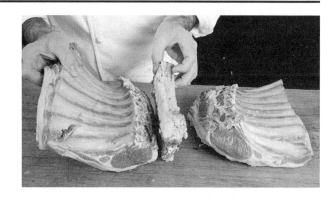

9. Trim the ends of the ribs (trimmings are used in stew).

10. Trim the fat along the rib cage.

11. Trim the fat from the top of the rack and

12. remove the shoulder blade.

13. Then trim the big sinew near the loin.

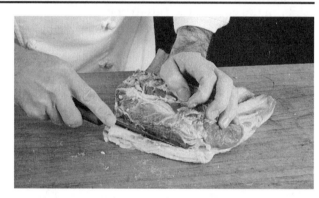

14. Rack, oven ready, 1½ to 1¾ pounds each.

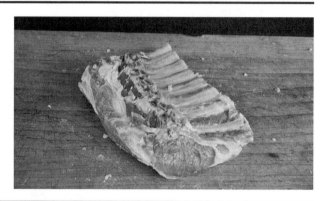

15. You can trim about an inch and a half of fat and meat from between each rib to dress up the rack.

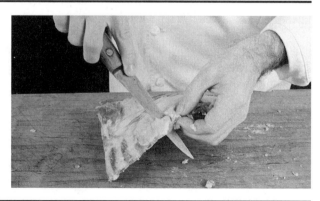

16. Paper frills, technique 65, can be placed over each trimmed bone at serving time.

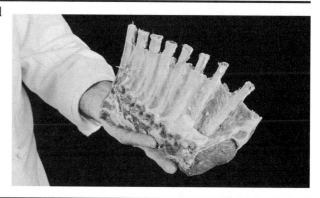

163. Lamb Chops *(Côtes d'Agneau)*

1. Trim and separate a double rack as explained in the preceding technique. Separate each rack into individual chops by cutting between each rib.

2. For thin chops, make one chop from each rib. For thicker chops, cut one chop with 2 ribs, then remove one of the ribs.

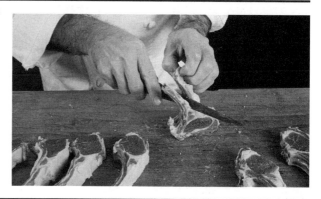

3. Cut the layer of fat along the rib.

4. Holding the chop in one hand, cut the fat above the "eye" all the way around the rib.

5. "Scrape" it off with your knife to expose a clean bone.

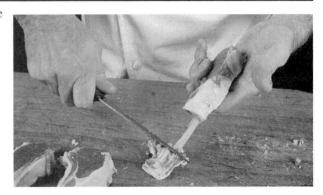

6. Flatten the chop slightly.

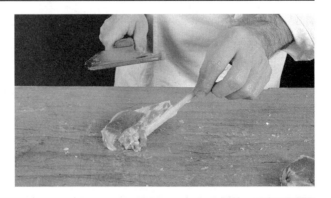

7. Trim a chunk of the fat above the eye.

8. Chops from one rack. Note that the 2 chops on the left in the back row are nicer. They are cut from the end of the rack that is near the saddle. These are called the "first" or "prime" chops. The other chops in the same row are cut toward the shoulder and are called "second" or "lower" chops. It is customary, as shown in front, to serve one first and one second chop to each guest.

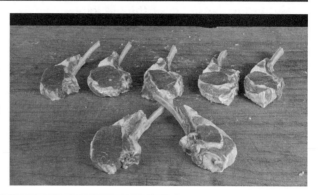

164. Trimming Leg of Lamb
(Préparation du Gigot)

1. A whole untrimmed leg of lamb with the hipbone weighs approximately 7½ to 8 pounds. Use a spring lamb, i.e., a lamb from 8 to 12 months old.

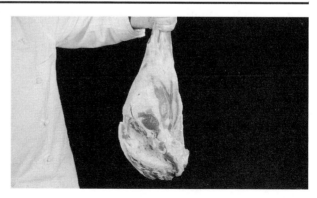

2. Place the leg on its back and insert a thin, sharp, sturdy knife along the hipbone. Follow the bone as closely as you can.

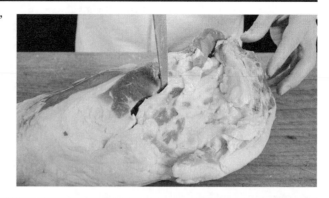

3. Cut inside the socket of the hip joint (you will see the tip of the femur). Remove the tail and the hipbone in one piece. Discard or keep for stock.

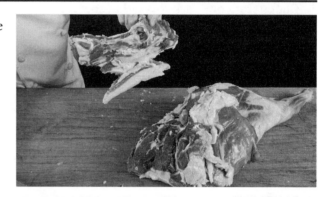

4. Trim the fat along one side of the leg.

5. Then trim the fat along the other side.

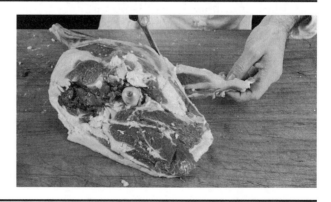

6. Holding the leg by the shank, cut the meat all around the bone.

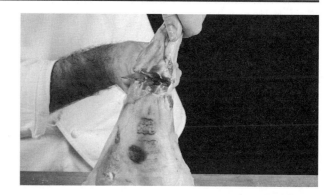

7. With the leg flat, remove the meat from the tip of the bone. You should have 2 or 3 inches of exposed bone.

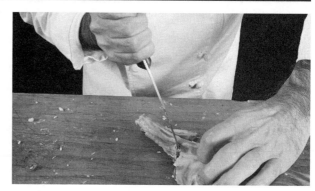

8. Using a saw, cut off the knotty tip of the bone. The bare bone is decorative and serves as a handle, which makes carving easier.

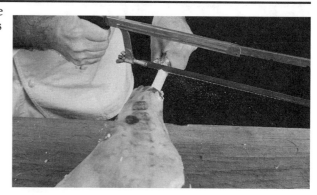

9. Trim the top of the leg of fat, leaving a layer about ¼ inch thick.

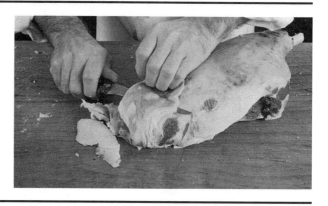

10. The leg can be roasted whole oɪ a piece can be removed and used for stew. (This shortened leg is called *gigot raccourci* in French.)

11. Leg of lamb, oven ready.

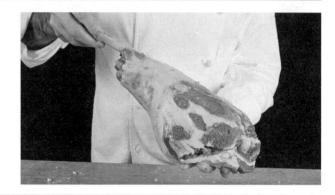

165. Loin of Veal *(Carré de Veau)*

IN TECHNIQUE 188 we trim and slice a rack of pork. Here we are trimming a loin— in this case a loin of veal. The loin is divided by a "T" bone with the tenderloin (filet) on one side and the loin on the other. The loin as well as the tenderloin is the choicest, tenderest and most expensive piece of veal. The loin is sometimes roasted whole, stuffed or unstuffed. It is also boned out, trimmed of all fat and sinew and divided in small mignonnettes (small scallopini) or grenadins (larger steaks). The filet is usually roasted whole or used in pâtés. The bones and trimmings should be kept for stalk and the sinewy piece of the flank steak used in stews, pâtés or stuffing.

1. Lift up the flank to expose the filet. Trim off most of the fat on top of the filet.

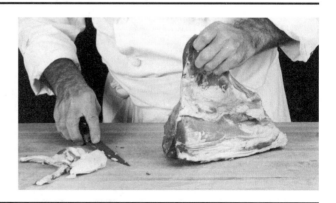

2. Place the rack on the table, loin side down, and cut along the bone to loosen the filet. Note how the bone forms a "T" and the filet can easily be scooped out from one side.

3. Remove the loin by cutting along the center bone and backbone.

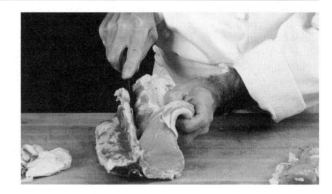

4. Cut underneath to separate the loin from the backbone in one piece.

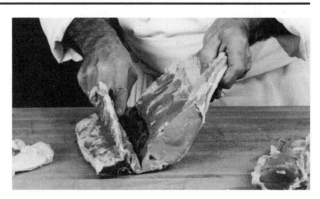

5. Cut the flank at the tail end of the loin. Trim the top of the loin of sinew and fat.

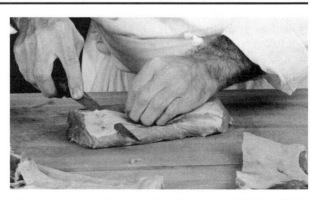

6. Clean the filet of all sinew and fat. Use the sinew in stocks and the flank in stews.

7. Cut small *médaillons* of veal (*mignonnettes*), about 1 ½ ounces each. *Mignonnettes* take only a few seconds to cook. They should be served three per person. Cut the loin into 4- to 5-ounce steaks (*grenadins*), to be served one per person with sauce and garnishes.

8. Pound the *mignonnettes* and the *grenadins* gently to make them of equal thickness and shape.

9. The whole loin carved: 5 *mignonnettes*, 3 *grenadins,* and the filet left whole. Be careful not to overcook the veal. *Mignonnettes* should be sautéed in butter that's not too hot for no more than 30 to 40 seconds on each side. The *grenadin* steaks will take 3 to 4 minutes, and the whole filet about 12 to 15 minutes.

166. Breaded Veal Scaloppine
(Escalope de Veau Viennoise)

FOR VEAL SCALOPPINE, you should use first-quality veal *(plume de veau)*, usually the cuts from the top sirloin or the loin. The meat should be without fat or gristle. Each scaloppine should weigh about 5 to 6 ounces and should be pounded paper thin into a slice about 10 inches in diameter.

1. Use a long sharp knife. Holding your hand flat on the meat to direct the knife, and cutting on a slant,

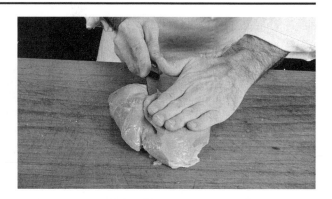

2. slice about ¼ inch down the meat. Do not separate the slice from the meat.

3. Open the first slice and cut another slice through, separating it from the bulk of the meat. Both scallops should hold together. (You can also cut a ½-inch-thick slice, place it flat on the table and butterfly it to obtain the same result.)

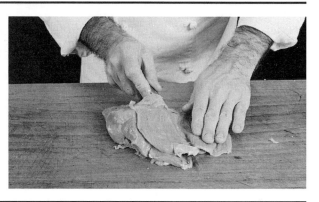

4. Using a meat pounder, thin out the veal by pounding down and out from the center toward the edges. The meat should not be crushed, but thinned down. Wetting the pounder with cold water helps it slide on top of the scallops without making holes in the meat.

5. Pounding is the most delicate operation in the recipe. If you do not have a good meat pounder, or if you do not feel confident about the procedure, ask your butcher to prepare the scallops for you. After it is pounded, dip in flour lightly, shaking off any excess.

6. Beat together 1 egg, 1 tablespoon vegetable oil, 1 tablespoon water, salt and pepper and dip both sides of the scallop in the mixture. Squeeze out excess with your fingers.

7. Prepare fresh bread crumbs in the blender and spread on the table. Dip the veal on both sides, pressing on it slightly to make the crumbs adhere well. Shake off any excess.

8. Pat the breaded veal with the flat side of a large knife.

9. Mark a crisscross lattice on top with a knife. Refrigerate until cooking time. The breaded veal is cooked in a large frying pan in a mixture of butter and vegetable oil. Start with the marked side down. After 3 to 4 minutes on medium heat, turn and cook for the same amount of time. In the *viennoise* style, it is served with melted butter and decorated with chopped hard-boiled eggs, capers, lemon slices and anchovies.

167. Rolled Veal *(Paupiettes de Veau)*

A PAUPIETTE is a thin piece of meat or fish that is pounded, rolled and usually stuffed and then braised. *Paupiettes de veau* are sometimes called *oiseaux sans tête* (headless birds) because of the resemblance to stuffed quail or woodcock. This recipe serves four.

THE STUFFING

1 *tablespoon sweet butter*
½ *cup chopped mushrooms*
½ *cup chopped onion*
¼ *cup chopped celery*
1 *clove garlic, peeled, crushed and chopped fine*
1 *pound ground pork shoulder*
2 *tablespoons chopped parsley*
½ *teaspoon salt*
¼ *teaspoon freshly ground black pepper*

Melt the butter in a saucepan, add the mushrooms and cook for 1 minute on medium heat. Add the onion and celery and sauté for 2 minutes. Remove from the heat and stir in the remaining ingredients. Stuff and cook the scaloppines as described below.

THE VEAL

1. Holding your hand flat on the meat to direct the knife,

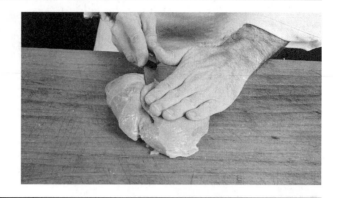

2. cut 8 scaloppines, about 2½ ounces each. Pound each piece into a paper-thin slice about 6 to 8 inches in diameter. (See steps 4 and 5 in the preceding technique.)

3. Place 2 tablespoons stuffing in the middle of each scaloppine.

4. Wrap the stuffing carefully and

5. tie with string. Cook according to recipe below.

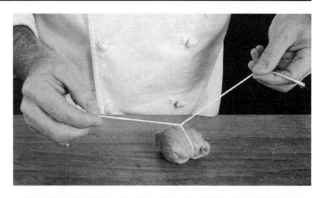

6. *Paupiettes* ready to cook and scaloppine ready to sauté or to bread.

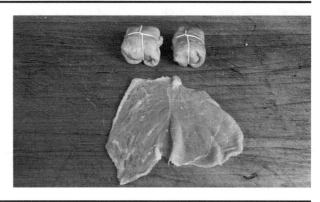

TO COMPLETE THE DISH

4 *tablespoons sweet butter*
1 *cup thinly sliced onion*
3 *cloves garlic, peeled, crushed*
    and chopped
½ *cup dry white wine*
1 *teaspoon salt*
½ *teaspoon freshly ground black pepper*
1 *teaspoon arrowroot*
2 *tablespoons cold water*
1 *tablespoon chopped parsley*

You will need a large casserole with a cover. Melt 2 tablespoons of butter in the casserole, brown the *paupiettes* on all sides and set aside. In a skillet, melt the remaining 2 table-spoons butter, add the onion and sauté for 3 to 4 minutes. Add the garlic and sauté 1 minute longer.

Pour the onion mixture over the *paupiettes*, then deglaze the skillet with the wine and add this liquid to the casserole with the salt and pepper. Bring to a boil, then reduce heat and simmer, covered, over low heat for 25 minutes. With a slotted spoon, transfer the *paupiettes* to a platter and remove the strings. Keep warm.

Mix the arrowroot and the cold water into a smooth paste and stir into the braising liquid. Bring to a boil and taste; add salt and pepper, if needed. Pour the sauce over the *paupiettes*, sprinkle with parsley and serve immediately, two to a person.

168. Tying a Roast *(Ficelage du Rôti)*

THERE IS NO REASON to tie a roast if it is a solid piece of meat, such as a bottom round. However, to fasten lard leaves around a piece of meat, or to assemble loose pieces of meat, tying is necessary if the meat is to hold together while cooking and after.

1. Gather or roll the meat into the desired shape.

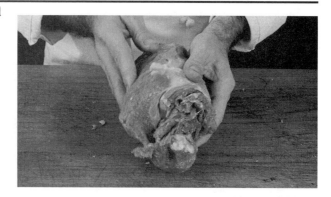

2. Slide thick, soft kitchen string (thin thread will cut through meat) under the roast and tie at the end close to you. Do not cut the string off.

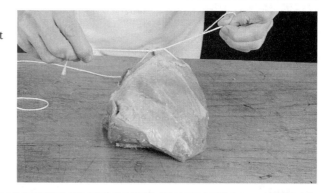

3. Make a loop around your opened fingers and

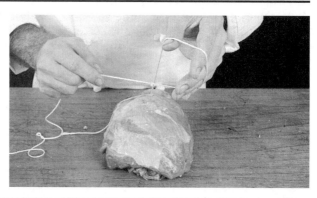

4. slide the opened loop under the roast about 2 inches in front of the first ligature.

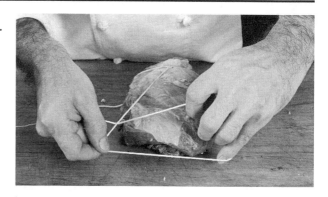

5. Pull the string up to tighten the loop. Repeat, making a loop every 2 inches.

6. Slide the string under the roast and make a single loop at each ligature to fasten the roast underneath.

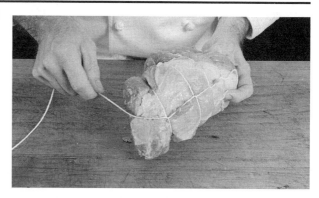

7. Bring the string around and make the last knot at the first ligature. Cook according to your favorite recipe. Remove the string before serving.

169. Stuffed Veal Breast

(Poitrine de Veau Farcie)

VEAL BREAST is an inexpensive and versatile cut of meat. It can be roasted; it can be divided into short ribs *(tendrons)* and braised; and it can be stuffed as shown here. Most recipes for stuffed veal call for a boneless piece of meat. However, the meat is easier to bone after cooking. The ribs slide off effortlessly, which helps you recognize when the meat is cooked. They also keep the roast from shrinking and add to its flavor.

A veal breast can weigh from 4½ to 8 pounds and run from about 18 to 25 inches long. The stuffed veal can be braised in the oven or cooked, covered, in a large, deep roasting pan over a flame. If you do not have a pan large enough to accommodate the breast, you may cut it in half. Each piece is then stuffed and tied before braising. Use your favorite stuffing, or the vegetable stuffing suggested below. This recipe will serve 8 to 10.

1 *10-ounce package fresh spinach*
1 *3-ounce piece fresh salted pork (called sweet pickle or corn belly), cut into ¼-inch sticks (small* lardons)
2 *carrots, peeled and coarsely chopped (1 cup)*
2 or 3 *onions, chopped (1½ cups)*
1 *celery rib, peeled and coarsely chopped (1 cup)*
1 or 2 *small eggplants, peeled and cut into ½-inch slices (4 cups)*
1 *green pepper, seeded and cut into ½-inch slices (1 cup)*
½ *cup water*
2 *teaspoons salt*
1 *teaspoon freshly ground black pepper*
¼ *teaspoon thyme leaves*
4 *hard-boiled eggs, coarsely chopped*
3 to 4 *cloves garlic, peeled, crushed and chopped fine (1 tablespoon)*
⅓ *cup chopped parsley*
9 *cups fresh bread crumbs*

Cook the spinach in salted, boiling water for 8 to 10 minutes. Drain, run under cold water and press to extrude the water. Chop coarsely.

Place the lardons in a large saucepan and cook on medium heat until the pieces are browned and crisp and all the fat is rendered (about 5 minutes). Add the carrots, onion and celery and cook for 3 to 4 minutes. Add the eggplant, green pepper and water. Mix well, cover and let cook until all the water is evaporated and the mixture starts to sizzle again (about 5 to 6 minutes). Add the salt, pepper, thyme and mix well.

Remove from the heat. Add the chopped eggs, spinach, garlic, parsley and bread crumbs. Stir just enough to blend the ingredients together.

1. Use the best veal you can find, pale pink (flesh colored) with white fat. This large breast weighs 7 pounds, bones in.

2. Use a small knife to enlarge the opening on the larger side of the breast.

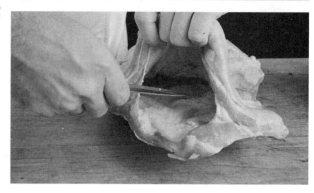

3. Push your hand inside the cavity to loosen the top layer. Push your fingers to the edges all around, but do not go through. You should have a nice deep pocket.

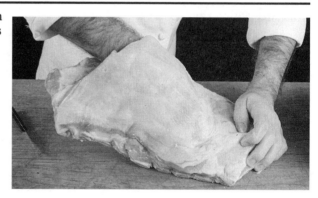

4. Place the stuffing in the cavity.

5. Push and pack it with a large spoon.

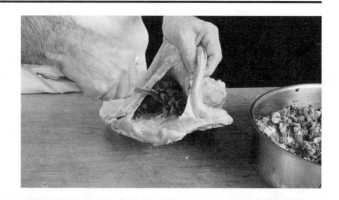

6. Sew the opening with soft kitchen string.

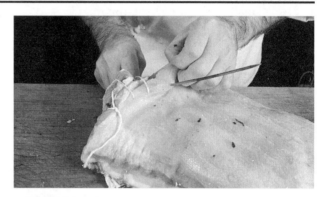

7. Secure with a double knot.

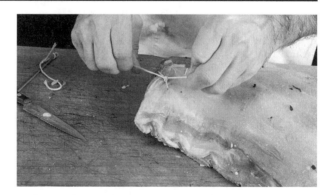

2 tablespoons butter
1 tablespoon olive oil
1¼ teaspoons salt
1 teaspoon freshly ground black pepper
3 medium onions, peeled and halved
1 cup water

In a large roasting pan, melt the butter and add the olive oil. Sprinkle the breast all around with salt and pepper. Brown on all sides on medium to high heat (about 10 minutes). Add the onions. Cover tightly, reduce the heat to very low and cook, covered, on top of the stove for 1½ hours Add a generous cup of water to the pan. Cook, covered, for another hour. You may also place the meat, covered, in a 325-degree preheated oven and bake the same amount of time. At this point, the meat should be tender, and there should be just enough natural juices to serve with the veal. Let the meat "rest" for 15 minutes before carving. Remove the string and slice, following the ribs, into nice portions. You may remove the bone, or serve it with the meat. Pour some of the juice on the slices and serve immediately.

170. Rib Roast (Côte de Boeuf)

1. This rib roast has 4 ribs and weighs about 9 pounds untrimmed. A rib roast is fatter on the large side which is closer to the "chuck" or the neck.

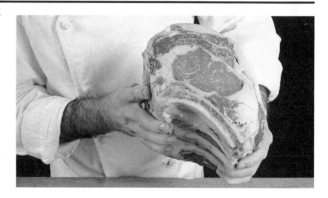

2. It is leaner on the smaller end which goes toward the "sirloin" or the lower back. Hence, it is preferable to buy the ribs closest to the sirloin.

3. Using a sturdy sharp knife, lift up the top layer of fat from the whole roast.

4. Keep cutting down the back of the roast to remove the flat bones. The only bones left should be the ribs.

5. Remove the nerves and large sinews covering the meat.

6. Place the top layer of fat on the roast to keep it from drying out during cooking.

7. Tie it with string. When the meat is cooked (110 degrees internal temperature), remove the layer of fat and brown the top of the roast under the broiler for a few minutes. Carve following the directions in technique 203.

171. Trimming Shell Steak

(Préparation du Contre-filet ou Faux Filet)

1. The shell steak is cut from the beef loin. With a sturdy knife, follow the bones under and behind the loin and separate the "shell roast" from the bone. A 7½-pound bone-in yields 6 pounds boneless.

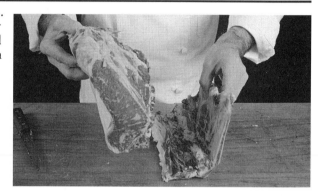

2. Place flat on the table and, using your knife horizontally, trim the large nerves off the meat.

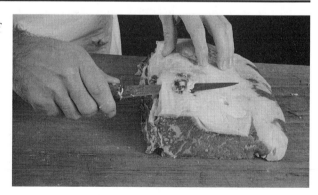

3. Keep trimming until the top of the roast is cleaned of fat and gristle.

4. Cut the fatty end off, leaving some of the fat attached.

5. The roast is 4¼ pounds completely trimmed. You could roast it at this point and serve it rare with its juices, or with a *bordelaise,* truffle or other sauce. Or you can slice it into 8- to 10-ounce steaks.

6. Notice that the "chain"—the sinewy strip along the back of the roast—is left attached to the steak.

172. Pepper Steak (Steak au Poivre)

PEPPER STEAK is usually made with an expensive cut such as a shell steak from the beef loin. However, it is quite good made from a hip steak or a shoulder blade steak (also known as a "chicken steak"). An 8- to 10-ounce boneless, well-trimmed steak serves one.

1. If the shell steak is bought ready-cut, trim the fat all around the meat.

2. The choice meat is as tasty as the prime, which is often too fatty and rich to sauté.

3. Crush whole peppercorns with a rolling pin or the edge of a heavy saucepan by spreading them out and pushing down and forward. You can hear them crack. Repeat until all the little corns are broken. Crushed peppercorn is called *mignonnette* in French cooking. Black peppercorns are preferred, being more flavorful and less pungent than white.

4. Salt the steak on both sides. Spread the *mignonnette* on the working surface and press the steak onto the pieces on both sides. Sauté the steak in hazelnut colored butter, 3 or 4 minutes on each side. The classic way to prepare steak *au poivre* is to deglaze the skillet with cognac, add some brown sauce and finish it with little bits of fresh butter. However, red wine is often added, as well as shallots and sometimes cream. Find your own variations.

173. Trimming Fillet or Tenderloin

(Préparation du Filet de Boeuf)

1. The whole fillet or tenderloin is one of the choicest parts of the beef. Untrimmed, this fillet weighs 9 pounds.

2. Start in the front of the fillet (the larger end), cutting and lifting the fat from the meat.

3. When the top layer of fat is loose, pull to separate it from the meat.

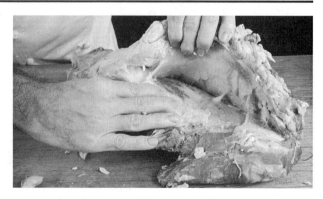

4. Keep pulling the thick layer open.

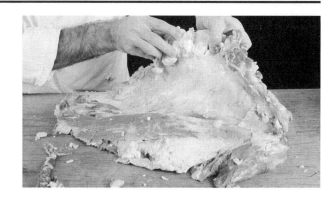

5. Then trim it off as closely as you can to the meat.

6. The "chain," a long, thin piece of meat that is full of gristle, should be removed although many restaurants and butchers leave it attached.

7. Pull the large lump of fat under the "head" of the fillet and

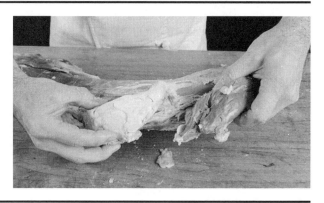

8. sever with your knife.

9. Turn the fillet upside down and pull the long, thin, fatty strip of gristle

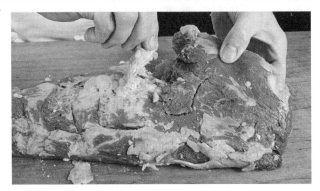

10. from the corner under the head to the tail of the fillet. Sever.

11. Placing the fillet back in its upright position, pull off the thin, veil-like layer on top to expose the large sinews.

12. Using a sharp knife held on an angle, remove the sinews which cover the meat.

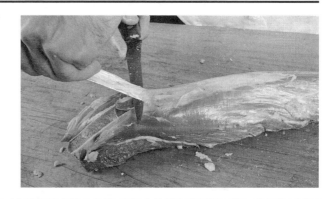

13. The meat, fat and sinew free, is completely nude. Fold the narrow tail underneath and

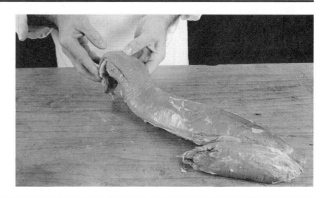

14. secure with a piece of string. Tie up the loose part of the front, also.

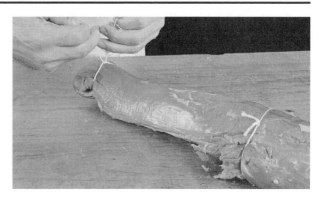

15. Trimmed fillet, oven ready. This fillet weighs 3½ pounds trimmed, a loss of almost two-thirds of its untrimmed weight. Sprinkle with salt and pepper. Melt half a stick of butter in a roasting pan and sear the meat on all sides for about 5 to 6 minutes on high heat. Place in a 425-degree preheated oven for 18 to 20 minutes, basting every 5 minutes. Let "rest" 10 minutes before carving.

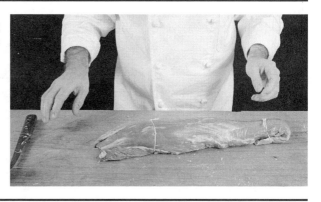

174. Cuts of Fillet *(Division du Filet de Boeuf)*

1. When a trimmed beef fillet, technique 173, is not roasted whole, it is cut into a variety of steaks. The tail is cut into tidbits for fondue, or for sautées like stroganoff. Then, the tip of the head and

2. the thinner part of the tail are cut into small (4- to 5-ounce) filets mignons.

3. The center is cut into *tournedos* or *coeur de filet* (heart of fillet), 8 to 9 ounces each.

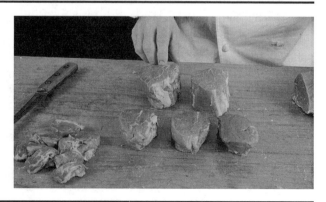

4. Then the last piece, which weighs about 1¼ pounds, is used as a *chateaubriand* to serve 2 to 3. Place the *chateaubriand* on a kitchen towel.

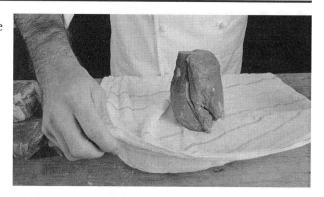

5. Wrap the towel around and, holding it tight,

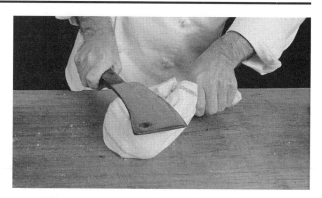

6. pound it with the flat side of a cleaver to mold it into a thinner and rounder shape.

7. The whole 3½-pound trimmed fillet gave 8 ounces of tidbits, 3 filets mignons, 2 *tournedos* and 1 *chateaubriand*.

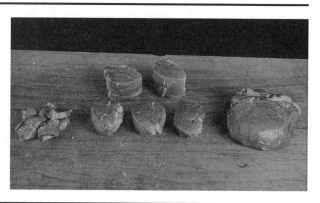

175. Stuffed Flank Steak *(Bavette Farcie)*

FLANK IS A POPULAR CUT OF MEAT and not too expensive. It is usually roasted or charcoal broiled and served thinly sliced, as London broil, technique 205. The meat is fibrous and will be tough if not cut against the grain. However, properly prepared, flank is tasty and juicy. This stuffed flank is served hot, but it is also good cold, cut in thin slices and served without the sauce on a bed of lettuce decorated with tomato wedges, sour French pickles *(cornichons)* and good mustard. A 3- to 3¼-pound untrimmed flank steak (about 2¼ to 2½ pounds trimmed) when stuffed will serve 6 people.

THE STUFFING

¼ cup vegetable oil
3 tablespoons sweet butter
2½ cups ¼-inch bread cubes, made with white bread
1 pound lean ground beef
2 eggs
1 onion, peeled and chopped (¾ cup)
½ celery rib, chopped (½ cup)
2 cloves garlic, peeled, crushed and chopped fine (1 teaspoon)

2 tablespoons chopped parsley
1½ teaspoons salt
½ teaspoon freshly ground black pepper
¼ teaspoon crushed thyme or savory

Heat the oil and butter in a skillet and brown the bread cubes. Combine the remaining ingredients in a large bowl and then add bread cubes, mixing in lightly to avoid making a mush. Stuff the flank steak, salt and pepper all around, and cook as directed below.

1. You will probably buy the flank trimmed, or ask the butcher to trim it for you. However, if you buy it untrimmed, your first step is to pull off the thin "skin" on one side and

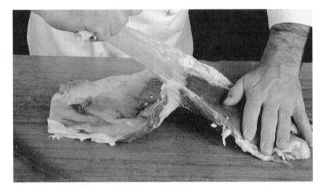

2. then the fatter skin on the other side. Trim off excess fat at the end.

3. Keeping the flank flat with one hand, cut into the steak lengthwise with a small, sharp paring knife to make a pocket for the stuffing.

4. Lift up the upper "lip" and cut, keeping your blade horizontal. Be careful not to come out at either end.

5. Cut deeper into the steak, but do not cut through to the other side.

6. If you cut through the flank by accident,

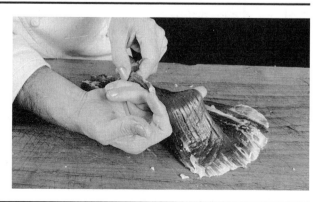

7. slice a thin piece off an end where it won't affect the pocket

8. and use it as a patch to plug the hole; the stuffing will keep it in place.

9. Once your cavity is ready, push the stuffing (your recipe or ours) into the opening, making sure the corners are filled.

10. Bring the lower lip of the flank against the stuffing.

11. Then bring the upper lip down on top to form a nice loaf.

12. Tie the roast, technique 168.

COOKING THE STUFFED FLANK STEAK

1 tablespoon butter
1 tablespoon oil
1 medium carrot, peeled and diced fine (about
    ¾ cup)
1 onion, chopped (about ¾ cup)
2 bay leaves
1 tomato, coarsely chopped (about 1 cup)
1 teaspoon thyme leaves
1 cup water or stock
1 cup dry red wine
2 tablespoons arrowroot
¼ cup cold water
Salt and pepper

You will need a deep, heavy casserole with a cover. Heat the butter and oil in the casserole, and then brown the stuffed meat on all sides. Add carrot, onion, bay leaves, tomato and thyme and cook over moderate heat, uncovered, for 5 minutes. Add water or stock and wine, bring to a boil, cover and braise on a very low heat on top of the stove, or in a 350-degree preheated oven for 1½ hours. Lift meat to a platter, remove strings and keep warm while making the sauce.

Spoon out most of the fat from the surface of the braising liquid in your casserole. Mix the arrowroot with the cold water and then stir into the liquid left in the casserole. Bring to a boil and cook, stirring constantly, until the sauce thickens slightly. Add salt and pepper to taste.

To serve, cut the meat in ½-inch slices (if cut too thick, the meat is tough), one per person, and arrange on a platter with the uncarved part of the roast. Pour 2 or 3 tablespoons of sauce over each serving.

176. Braised Beef in Aspic

(Daube de Boeuf en Gelée)

BEEF FOR BRAISING is usually taken from the bottom round which is part of the leg. The bottom round is divided into two pieces—the eye of the round and the "flat," which is the moister piece of meat and the cut used here. *Daube de boeuf* can be served hot with a sauce, but this recipe is for a cold *daube* in aspic—a beautiful summer buffet dish.

---

1 5-pound bottom round, studded with fat back
    (technique 24: larding a large cut of meat)
    or without larding
1 12- to 16-ounce piece piece pork rind
4 cloves garlic, lightly crushed with skin on
2 bay leaves
½ teaspoon thyme leaves
1½ cups coarsely sliced onion
1½ cups coarsely sliced carrots
¾ cup coarsely sliced celery
1 cups good dry red wine (good dry fruity wine is
    fine)
2 tablespoons butter
2 tablespoons salt

1 teaspoon freshly ground black pepper
3 cups water
2 tablespoons arrowroot dissolved in 1 cup
    cold water
2 envelopes plain gelatin moistened with ½ cup
    red wine
2 dozen small glazed onions (technique 11)
2 dozen small cooked turned carrots
2 dozen small cooked turned turnips, glazed in
    butter
1 tablespoon cooked peas
1 dozen cooked string beans

---

1. Place the bottom round in a large vessel. Add the next eight ingredients. Cover with plastic wrap and let the beef marinate for at least 1 day in the refrigerator (2, if possible). Remove the beef and vegetables from the liquid.

2. Melt the butter in a saucepan. Sprinkle the beef with salt and pepper and brown on medium to high heat for about 10 to 12 minutes. Brown thoroughly on all sides.

3. Transfer to a deep casserole.

4. Add the vegetables to the drippings and brown for a good 5 minutes. Add the vegetables and liquid to the meat. Pour the water into the saucepan and boil to melt all the solidified meat drippings. Add to the meat. Bring to a boil, cover and place in a 330-degree preheated oven for 3½ hours.

5. Remove the meat and place in a nice terrine, bowl or earthenware casserole. Strain the juices and scoop as much of the fat from the top as you can. (If you have the time, let the mixture cool and remove the fat after it hardens.) Discard the vegetables. Add the diluted arrowroot and gelatin to the sauce. Bring to a boil.

6. Place about one-third of the vegetable garnishes around the meat. Strain the sauce again and pour over the meat. It should barely cover. Push the vegetables down into the sauce if they rise. Cover the bowl with plastic wrap and refrigerate for a couple of hours until it hardens.

7. When set, arrange the remaining vegetables on top as artfully as you can.

8. Make some aspic, technique 21, with whatever poultry or meat stock you have on hand. Cover the top of the mold with the aspic. Let cool for a few hours before serving.

This *daube de boeuf* will serve 12 to 15. See finished dish on page 392a.

177. Kidneys *(Rognons)*

THE CHOICEST KIDNEYS are veal and lamb kidneys. The kidneys are enclosed in an envelope of fat near the tenderloin. Unfortunately U.S.D.A. regulations require veal kidneys be opened and freed of fat and skin before leaving the slaughterhouse. This means they can never be broiled or braised whole, like lamb kidneys. Beef kidneys are usually used for long-simmered stews such as kidney pie.

Veal Kidneys *(Rognons de Veau)*

1. One single veal kidney cleaned of its fat and skin.

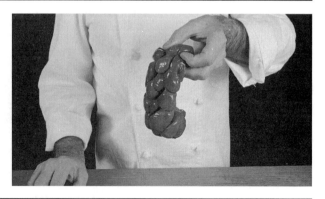

2. Butterfly the kidney into halves lengthwise.

3. Remove most of the strip of fat and gristle which runs through the middle.

4. Cut the kidney into slices if you want to sauté it.

5. On the left: kidney ready to broil or roast whole. On the right: kidney ready to sauté. Kidneys should be cooked a few minutes only at the highest possible heat. They should be pink in the middle. Drain the kidneys in a sieve for a few minutes (pink liquid will run out of the kidneys and should be discarded). After the kidneys are sautéed, a sauce is made with the drippings in the pan. Return the kidneys to the pan only long enough to warm them in the sauce. Do not boil; the kidneys will get as tough as rubber.

ROGNONS D'AGNEAU (*Lamb Kidneys*)

1. Lamb kidneys are usually broiled on a skewer and served with *beurre maître d'hôtel* (technique 22) and watercress. They can also be sautéed and served with a sauce. Remove the thin skin that covers the kidneys if it wasn't removed at the slaughterhouse. Cut the kidney in the middle and butterfly it.

2. Using a skewer, go into the kidney on one side of the center (the small lump of fat) and come up on the other side.

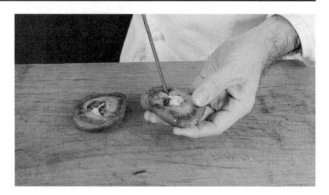

3. Kidneys ready to broil. Sprinkle with salt and pepper and broil (charcoal broiling is the best) on high heat for 2 to 3 minutes on each side. Let "rest" 1 to 2 minutes before serving. They should be pink in the middle.

178. Sweetbreads (*Ris de Veau*)

SWEETBREADS MAY WELL BE THE CHOICEST of the offals. The best sweetbreads are from lamb and calf, but only the calf is available and used in the United States. Sweetbreads are glands. The elongated sweetbread, the thymus, is at its best in young calves and almost disappears in older animals. The round sweetbread, the pancreas, is considered the better of the two. In old animals, it becomes mushy and pasty, but is still used by some cooks in stew. There are infinite ways of serving sweetbreads: breaded and sautéed *maréchal,* braised with a Madeira sauce, in champagne sauce, in puff paste, in pâté and so on.

1. Sweetbreads: pancreas (*la noix*) on the left; thymus (*ris de gorge*) on the right. Choose sweetbreads that are white and plump. Place the sweetbreads in cold water for several hours. Transfer to a saucepan, cover with cold water and bring to a boil. Let boil for 1 to 2 minutes. Place under cold running water until the meat is cold.

2. Pull off the sinews—the rubbery pieces that adhere to the meat—

3. on top and around the pieces.

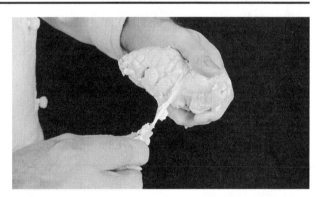

4. Line a cookie sheet with a clean towel, arrange the sweetbreads on top and cover with the towel.

5. Place another cookie sheet on top and place about 6 to 8 pounds of weight on top. Keep pressed for a few hours or overnight. Pressing the sweetbreads extrudes the undesirable pink liquid and gives white, compact and tender sweetbreads. Unpressed sweetbreads are always rubbery. Prepare the sweetbreads following your favorite recipe.

179. Brains *(Cervelles)*

IT IS UNFORTUNATE that brains are rarely featured in restaurants. They are excellent, nutritious, easy to prepare and inexpensive. The best brains are veal and lamb brains. (Pork brain is a bit mushy and not as flavorful.) Brains are often poached in a flavorful stock, then fried in butter and served with capers, parsley and lemon. They are also used in pâtés, salads and sauces, and are sometimes simply breaded and fried. Though this technique is illustrated with veal brain, lamb brain is handled in the same manner.

1. A veal brain weighs approximately 10 to 14 ounces. Soak in cool water for 1 or 2 hours.

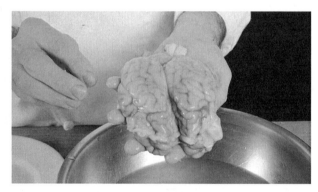

2. Pull off the fine membrane covering the brain. (You can loosen it by sliding the tips of your fingers through the crevices of the brain.) This is not done in all restaurants and is an optional step. I prefer to remove the membrane because it is tough and because the brain will be darker after cooking if the membrane is left on.

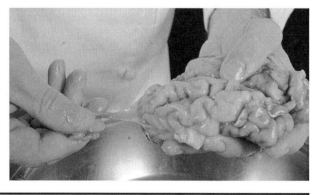

3. Work under water, cleaning up the whole brain. Place 2 cups water, 2 tablespoons good vinegar, 1 bay leaf, ½ cup sliced onion, 1 teaspoon salt and 1 teaspoon crushed peppercorns in a saucepan. Bring to a boil and simmer for 15 minutes. Add the brain to the stock and simmer slowly for 10 minutes. Let the brain cool off in the liquid. Refrigerate in the liquid. It is ready to be used when needed.

4. Remove the brain from the cooking liquid and separate into halves with a knife.

5. Split each piece open (butterfly).

6. One brain ready to be used. For brains in black butter, probably the most common way of serving it, sprinkle with salt and pepper, dredge in flour and sauté in butter and oil until crusted and nicely browned on both sides. Transfer to a serving platter and sprinkle with drained capers and ½ teaspoon vinegar. Melt some butter in a saucepan until dark and smoking. Pour over the brain and sprinkle with chopped parsley. Serve immediately.

180. Chitterlings Sausages *(Andouillettes)*

YIELD: 12 *andouillettes*

THE *andouillettes*—chitterling sausages—are a delicacy of French *charcuterie.* They are usually served grilled or baked accompanied by mashed or sautéed potatoes. The *Andouille de Vire* is an extra large *andouillette,* a specialty of Normandy, served cold in slices and recognizable by its thick black skin. *Andouille* or *andouillettes* are made from the fatty, small intestine (chitterlings) and stomach of pig or calf, or a mixture of both. In our recipe, we use only pig chitterlings because veal chitterlings are very rarely available.

6 *to 8 feet hog or beef middle casings, same size*
    as for **Boudins** *(technique 194)*
10 *pounds pork chitterlings*
1 *clove garlic, peeled, crushed and finely chopped*
8 *to 10 shallots, peeled and chopped fine* (¾ *cup*)
1½ *tablespoons unsalted butter*
1 *cup dry white wine*
3 *tablespoons good Dijon-style mustard*
1 *tablespoon salt*
2 *teaspoons freshly ground black pepper*

To poach

3 *cups good chicken, beef or veal stock or a*
    mixture of these
2 *cups dry white wine*
Dash of salt and pepper

1. If the chitterlings are frozen, thaw slowly in the refrigerator for about 48 hours. Chitterlings look like fatty casings. They are usually well cleaned and no further cleaning is necessary. Place the chitterlings in a large kettle, cover with cold water and bring to a boil. Lower the heat and simmer slowly for 2 hours. Drain and set aside. The chitterlings shrink considerably.

2. Cut the chitterlings into 1-inch chunks. Melt the butter in a large saucepan, add the shallots and sauté for 1 minute on medium heat. Add the garlic, mix well and remove from the heat. Combine with the chitterlings, then add the white wine, mustard, salt and black pepper and mix well together. The mixture is now well seasoned and ready to be stuffed in casings.

3. Clean the casings (see step 3, technique 181), then, using a large funnel and the back of a wooden spoon, push the chitterlings pieces through.

4. Massage the mixture down into the casing. Do not pack it too tight because the meat will expand during cooking and it will burst if it is too tight.

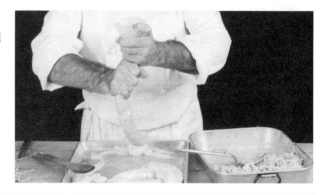

5. Separate the casing into 5-inch long sausages, as explained in technique 194, step 5, or by using a piece of kitchen string.

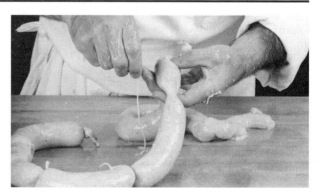

6. Prick the sausages with a fork. This will prevent them from bursting while poaching.

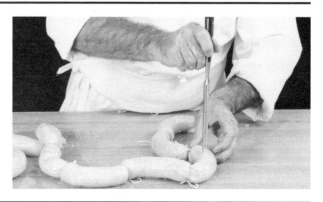

7. Use a large roasting pan or a saucepan which can accommodate the chitterlings in one layer. Add the stock and wine. It should cover the sausages by ½ inch.

8. Place an upside-down plate on top to keep the *andouillettes* immersed while cooking. Place on medium heat and bring the liquid to 170 to 180 degrees. Do not boil or the sausages will burst. Add a dash of salt, depending on the seasoning of the stock, and a dash of pepper. Remember that the cooking liquid should be well seasoned. Poach for 15 minutes. Remove from the heat and let the sausages cool in the liquid. When cold, remove from the liquid and refrigerate. This is the stage at which chitterling sausages are bought in a French *charcuterie*. The sausages will keep in the refrigerator for a week or can be frozen. The liquid can be frozen, used for other sausages, or made into an aspic.

To finish four sausages

At serving time, melt 1 tablespoon of butter in a skillet and brown the sausages over very low heat (or they will burst). Brown for 2 minutes on each side. Add ¼ cup white wine and simmer covered, very slowly, for 10 minutes. Serve as such with the juices. See finished chitterlings sausages, page 529.

181. Salami and Sausage (Saucisson et Saucisse)

THE WORD *saucisson* in French refers to large sausages that are usually dry, like salami. Like smoked salmon, prosciutto, and other cured meats and fish, these sausages are not cooked. *Saucisse* refers to smaller sausages, such as link sausages and even frankfurters and knockwurst. These sausages are cooked and then served. The recipe below can be used to make either sausage—sausage that can be cooked with potatoes, in brioche and the like, or that can be dried to make salami.

In this recipe, the sausage is cured by the addition of regular salt to the ingredients. It could also be salted and cured in brine for a day or two. Sodium nitrite is added to help the sausage achieve a nice pink color. It is used sparingly as it toughens the meat. If you omit it, the difference will be hardly noticeable (see note below). Fresh sausage is kept in the refrigerator for a good 2 or 3 days to cure before cooking (dry sausage cures while it dries) and in the process of curing it turns pink even without the sodium nitrite, though it takes slightly more time.

To dry, the sausage should be hung in a cool cellar or garage. The place should be airy, preferably dark and very dry or the sausage will spoil. The first few days of drying are the most important. The skin of the sausage will become whitish which is a sign that it is curing. After 6 weeks, the sausage can be consumed semi-firm *(demi-sec)*. However, dried it will keep for months.

The fresh pork butt, which is part of the shoulder blade roast, is an excellent cut for sausage, as it is readily available, and has the right proportion of lean to fat.

Note: The addition of a curing agent—like sodium nitrite, sodium nitrate, or potasium nitrate (saltpeter)—to homemade sausages or pâté is not essential, but the meat is a more attractive pink color if it is cured. Alternatively, you can use a good commercial curing or pickling salt (Morton Tender Quick Meat Cure, for example, which is available on request at most supermarkets or by contacting Morton Salt directly). Replace the regular salt in your recipe with the same amount of curing salt.

5½ pounds fresh pork butt

2¾ ounces salt (5½ tablespoons); this seems an enormous amount, but it is necessary

½ teaspoon sodium nitrite (optional)

2 teaspoons freshly ground white pepper (for fresh sausages, use 2½ teaspoons and omit the peppercorns)

1½ teaspoons whole black peppercorns (only for dry sausage)

1 large clove garlic, crushed, peeled and chopped fine, technique 2 (1 teaspoon)

4 tablespoons dry red wine

1. For a coarse sausage, the meat can be cut by hand into ¼-inch pieces. If you are using an electric meat grinder, use a large screen with the holes about ⅜ inch wide. Position the vice first, then the knife (flat side out) and the screen. Screw the lid on. Grind the meat. Then mix thoroughly with the other ingredients. (The red wine can be replaced with white wine or omitted, as you prefer. The garlic can also be omitted.)

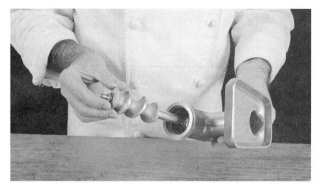

2. Natural casings come from pig, sheep and beef. Pork casings are 1½ to 2 inches in diameter and are used for Italian sausage. Sheep casings are about 1 inch in diameter and are used for link sausage. The beef casing pictured on the right is about 2½ to 3 inches in diameter and is the best for large sausages. It comes in bundles preserved in salt and can be kept almost indefinitely, packed in salt in a cool place.

3. Pull the length you need and wash under lukewarm water. Fit the end of the casing to the opening of the faucet and allow tepid water to run through the inside. Then let the casing soak in cold water for 10 minutes. Drain and squeeze the water out.

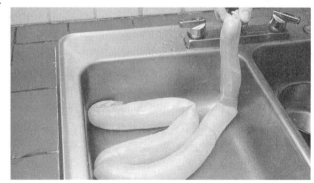

4. To use the meat grinder as a stuffer, you need a sausage attachment. Remove the knife and screen, leaving only the vice. Screw the funnel into place with the lid.

5. Gather the casings on the funnel.

6. Leave a small piece hanging so air can be "pushed" out of the casing. If air pockets form in the sausage, you will find when you slice it that there are "holes" in the meat and the meat will be gray. Fill the casing, holding the tip of the casing lightly so that it does not unroll too fast.

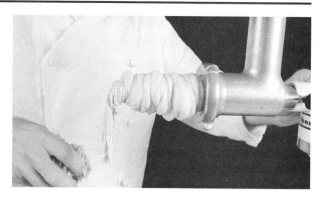

7. To fill the casing by hand, use a large pastry bag with a large plain tube or a funnel with a large opening (at least 1 inch). Slip some of the casing around the tapered part of the funnel to have a good grip. Push the meat into the casing with your fingers.

8. Squeeze along the length of the casing to push the meat down.

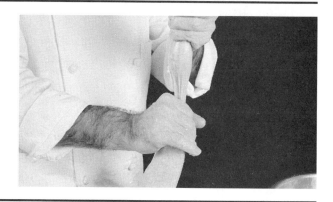

9. To tie the end, make a simple flat knot first.

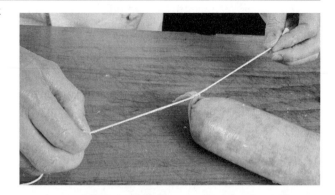

10. Then fold the tip of the casing on top of the knot and

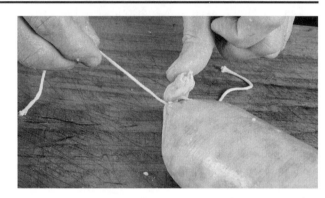

11. tie it again with a double knot.

12. Tie the string so that you have a loop to hang the sausage.

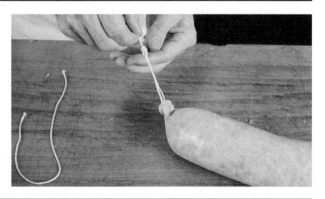

13. With one hand, push the meat toward the tied end. Squeeze the sausage where you want the end to be. Prick with a sharp fork or a skewer wherever you see a little pocket of air. Twist the sausage simultaneously. Be sure that there is no air trapped inside the meat.

14. Tie the end with a single knot.

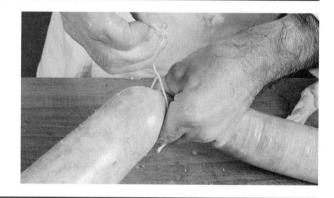

15. Then cut and tie as shown in photographs 10 and 11.

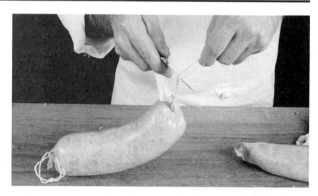

16. Sausage ready to dry. To cook the sausage, let it cure for at least 2 days in the refrigerator. Prick all over with a fork and cook in barely simmering water for 35 minutes. It can also be roasted with potatoes.

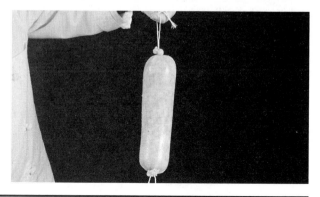

17. After 3 weeks of drying, tie the salami, if desired to make it more compact. Let dry another 3 to 4 weeks before using.

182. Cured, Raw Country Ham

(Prosciutto/Bayonne-style) (Préparation du Jambon Cru)

I**T ALWAYS COMES** as a surprise to people that prosciutto, as well as salamis, French *rosette,* or even the Swiss *bunderfleish* of the Grisons (cured dried beef), is just plain, uncooked, raw meat served cut into thin slices. The greatest hams in the world, such as Bayonne from the southwest of France, Westphalia and Czechoslovakia as well as Parma from Italy, are all uncooked hams, served raw in very thin slices with bread and butter or sweet fruits such as melon or figs. Great American hams, such as Smithfield, Virginia or the Nashville country ham, can be served the same way.

To make a prosciutto-type at home you have to cure a piece of pork, perferably the hind leg of the pig. A shoulder, a piece of the front leg, as well as a piece of chuck (used for Italian *coppa*), give excellent results. In many parts of Europe farmers cure and dry their own hams as well as smaller pieces of meat and use them either raw (cut in thin slices) or cooked with sauerkraut or beans for a country casserole dish.

There are two basic ways of curing ham: either you immerse it in a liquid brine (mostly salt, sugar and water), or you cure it in dry salt. The salt drains the liquid out of the meat, depriving the bacteria of the moisture it needs to survive, and therefore preserving the meat from spoilage. We prefer not to smoke our ham, just cure it then dry it. After the salting, the meat is sometimes smoked, then it's dried. Professional producers dry at exact temperatures with controlled humidity. Too much heat and humidity can spoil the ham. A home-cured ham—hung in a cellar, a garage or an attic—should be processed in winter so it has a chance to cure and start drying before the warmer, more humid months.

1 15-pound fresh ham with "quasi" (pelvic bone)
 removed
1 3-pound box kosher-type salt
½ cup granulated sugar
Cognac
Whole black peppercorns

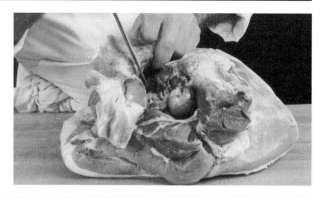

1. Buy the freshest and highest quality
hind leg, or fresh ham, that you can find.
Ours weighed 15 pounds with the pelvic
bone removed. Using a sharp, sturdy knife,
remove the pelvic bone attached to the joint
of the femur (or thighbone).

2. Make a hole around the tip of the femur
and massage the ham to help release some
liquid and blood (if any) through the opening. Pour some Cognac into the hole
around the bone and massage the meat
around it. (Although we have never frozen
the pork and have never had any problem,
at this point, some people recommend
freezing the meat for a few days to eliminate
any possibility of trichinosis.)

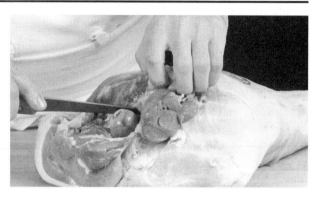

3. Mix the salt and the sugar together
(kosher-type salt is purer and sweeter than
table salt) and rub inside the ham around the
thighbone, forcing it into any openings,
then place the ham in a large plastic bag.
Pour plenty of salt under, around and on
top of the ham, using the whole 3-pound
box. Leave the bag slightly open so the meat
can breathe and place in a cool place, skin
side down. The ham should be completely
saturated with salt and the holes around the
bones should be packed full of salt because
these areas are prone to souring. Check
every few days to make sure that the meat is
still entirely covered with salt. Some liquid
will be leeched out and absorbed by the salt.
Leave the ham curing in a cool place for at
least a day per pound. Try to avoid handling the meat too much with your fingers.

4. After 16 days, clean the salt off the ham with paper towels. Be sure that the ham is clean and well dried. Rub 2 large cloves of peeled garlic all over the ham. Then sprinkle one tablespoon of good Cognac on the meat. Place ½ cup of black peppercorns in a coffee mill for a few seconds to crush coarsely (*mignonnettes*). Cover the ham with crushed peppercorns, especially where there is no skin where it will adhere best.

5. Place the ham in a large canvas bag or wrap it in a large kitchen apron.

6. The cloth allows the air in so the ham will dry, but keeps flies or other insects out.

7. Tie with heavy kitchen string and make a loop at the end. Hang the ham in a cool, drafty place. There must be ventilation or the ham will spoil. If it is hung in a garage in the winter it may freeze slightly on the outside. This will not harm the ham in any way. (The salt lowers the temperature at which the ham will freeze and it will have to get very cold before the ham freezes through.) On the other hand, if the weather is warm and especially humid, the ham may get covered with mold. If this happens, unwrap, clean the ham, and re-wrap in a

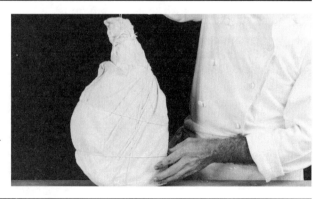

clean canvas. Place in front of a fan to dry. (In a humid climate, simulate a cold and drafty enviorment by placing the ham in a refrigerator with a fan for a couple of weeks so it gets a good start drying.) Let the ham hang for a minimum or 5 to 6 months. It will then be ready, although still slightly soft inside. The longer it dries, the harder it becomes and the more weight it loses. After approximately 6 months of drying the ham will have lost close to half its original weight.

8. When ready to eat, use a steel brush wetted with water and paper towels to brush and dry the ham. The thick rind will clean easily but the underneath may be covered with mold. Start trimming on the thickest side (the top round and meatiest part of the ham). The rind as well as the beautiful white fat underneath can be used to cook lentils, beans, soups, stews, etc. It is a wonderful seasoning.

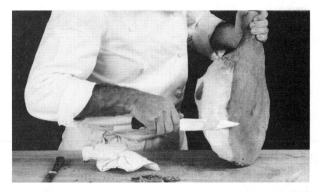

9. There is a special piece of equipment used to hold the ham in place during carving—a stainless steel metal strip on top of a piece of marble. Unless you have it, the best way to keep the ham in place is to put it in a long pâté mold or squeeze it in a drawer.

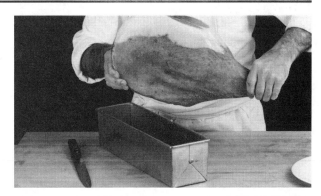

10. Using a long, thin knife, cut out the thinnest possible slices. Do not apply too much pressure on the knife. An electric knife makes the carving easier. Serve the slices plain with cornichons, mustard and crunchy bread. Or fry with eggs in what is called a *pipérade* in the south of France. Once the ham has been started, it is advisable to go through it fairly quickly, though it will last a few weeks. Cover the cut end with a piece of plastic, secure it with a rubber band and keep it hung in a cool place or refrigerated. If not used for one to two

weeks, the first slice will discolor but will still be perfectly edible. This home-cured ham makes a beautiful centerpiece and is enough for a buffet of 40 to 60 people. See finished cured raw country ham, page 529.

183. Ham in Aspic *(Jambon en Gelée)*

A WHOLE HAM is the ideal centerpiece for a large party. It can be served lukewarm, studded with cloves, beautifully glazed with apricot or pineapple jam, or hot in a crust with a Madeira sauce. However, on a hot summer night, cold ham, glistening in aspic, makes a stunning presentation. The troublesome matter of having someone carve a whole ham in the dining room in view of all the guests is eliminated by pre-cutting the ham and reforming it in its original shape. Buy the best quality "York" type that you can afford, a fully cooked (so called) and very lightly smoked ham. The one shown here was 19 pounds at purchase. Although called fully cooked, it greatly improves when recooked. You need an extra-large kettle. Cover the ham with cold water and bring to a boil. Lower the heat and simmer very gently, the water barely "shivering," for 2½ hours. Let cool in the poaching liquid. This step is better done a day ahead.

1. Remove the cloth, if any, which wraps the ham.

2. Place the ham on its back and cut along the hip bone, or pelvis, to get loose (see technique 164, steps 2 and 3).

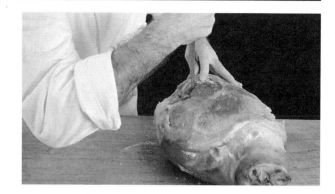

3. Keep cutting, following the outline of the bone and pulling until the hip or pelvis bone comes off. It has to be severed where it is attached at the tip, inside the socket of the hip.

4. Trim, as thin as you possibly can, the dry bottom "skin" of the ham and the top skin all around the ham.

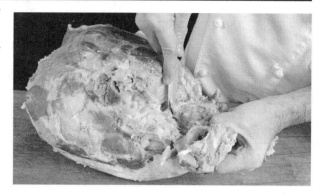

5. Trim around the shank bone (see technique 164, steps 6 and 7).

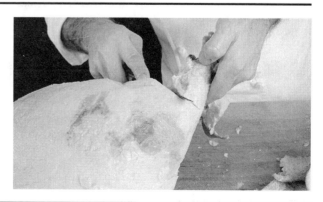

6. Saw the bulky tip of the bone. You will notice that there is a thin bone (part of the fibula) on top of the larger tibia bone.

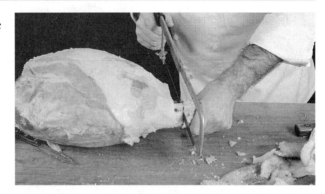

7. Pull the thin bone out. If it comes out without tearing the meat, the ham is properly and sufficiently cooked.

8. Trim a layer of the nice, white fat from the top of the ham. (You should have approximately a ¼-inch layer of fat left on the ham at the thickest part of the fat.) Cut the fat into pieces.

9. Place the pieces in a food processor or blender. Blend until pureed smooth. Refrigerate to stiffen it.

10. Cut straight down to the bone, a good inch or so in from the edge of the ham. This will give the slices a clean edge and will protect your hand during the carving in case the knife slips.

11. Start cutting at a slant, not quite parallel to the bone.

12. Be sure to arrange your slices in order as you are cutting.

13. When the ham gets too wide, alternate cutting your slices on the right, then on the left. Keep cutting until you see the long femur bone.

14. Start replacing the slices on top of the ham. They should go back in the same order they came off.

15. Keep building the ham back, trying to reform the original shape as closely as you can.

16. Spread a layer of the puréed fat on top to hide the cut of the slices.

17. Make it as smooth as possible. At this point, the ham should be refrigerated for a few hours (possibly overnight) so that the fat stiffens and sets.

18. Using green of leek, tomatoes, carrots and the like, decorate the ham to your fancy (see technique 37). Cover the cut end near the shank with carrots or leek. Refrigerate.

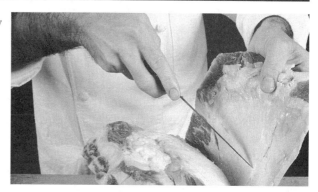

19. Glaze with an aspic, technique 21, making sure the aspic is almost set and the ham very cold.

20. Repeat several times (the aspic does not stick easily on fat), recovering the aspic between glazings and remelting it.

21. Pour enough cold aspic to cover the bottom of a large platter. Let it set until hard. Place the ham on top of the aspic carefully, and fit a frill at the end bone, technique 65.

184. Ham in Crust *(Jambon en Croûte)*

YIELD: 18 to 20 servings

A WHOLE HAM in crust makes a beautiful presentation for a buffet or an Easter or Christmas dinner. It is very difficult to slice a ham into thin slices without the crust crumbling which is why we cook the ham first, slice it, then wrap the dough around it and bake. The crust is used to encase the completely carved ham.

What in the market is called a "fully cooked ham" greatly improves when recooked. Place in a large kettle, covered with cold water, and bring slowly to a simmer. Keep the water barely "shivering" for 1 hour at about 185 to 190 degrees. Do not boil or the meat may split open. Let the ham cool in the stock for at least 3 hours at room temperature, or preferably overnight. Using the tip of a small sharp knife, remove the hip or pelvic bone from the ham (see step 1, technique 182). Try not to cut too deep into the meat. Remove the skin and most of the fat from the top, which can be kept for other uses, leaving at the most a ¼-inch layer of fat on top of the ham. Trim all around, especially underneath, where the surface may be a little tough.

Cooking the ham

1 *10- to 12-pound fully cooked, lightly smoked ham, with pelvic and shank bone in, re-cooked for 1 hour and trimmed according to above instructions*
3 *tablespoons good apricot jam*
1 *tablespoon dry mustard*
3 *tablespoons brown sugar*

Dough

1 *pound unsifted flour (about 3 ½ cups)*
1½ *sticks (6 ounces) sweet butter, softened and cut into pieces*
2 *tablespoons vegetable, peanut, grape-seed or almond oil*
½ *teaspoon salt*
1 *teaspoon sugar*
3 *egg yolks mixed with ⅓ cup cold water*
1 *egg, plus 1 egg yolk for the wash*

Sauce

4 *cups concentrated* demi-glace *(see technique 12)*
¾ *cups dry Madeira wine or dry Sherry if Madeira is not available*
⅓ *stick (1⅓ ounces) sweet butter, cut in small pieces*
Salt and pepper to taste

To make the sauce, reduce the wine and stock on medium to high heat for about 20 minutes. You should have about 3 cups of liquid left and the mixture should be just thick enough to coat a spoon and be glazy. Add the butter piece by piece, stirring with a whisk to make a smooth and shiny sauce. Add salt and pepper to taste and keep warm until serving time.

1. Blend together the jam, mustard and sugar and spread on top of the ham. Place the ham on a cookie sheet in a preheated 425-degree oven for 30 minutes. Let the ham reach room temperature and carve in thin slices on a slant, arranging the slices neatly on the table as the carving progresses. (At this point the ham could be served just as is.) Keep carving until the central bone is exposed. Do not carve out whole slices from the center of the ham because the slices would be too large. Slice on one side of the bone then on the other side. To re-form the ham, arrange the slices back on the ham in their proper order. Do not worry if they are not exactly in order or not perfectly neat, since they will be covered with the dough.

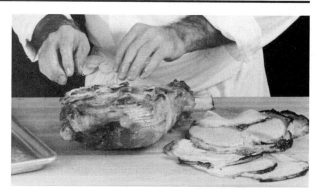

2. To make the dough, place all the ingredients in a mixer, and using the flat beater, mix on medium speed until smooth and well combined—about 1 minute. It can also be made by hand using the technique of *fraisage* (technique 237). Roll the dough to ¼-inch thickness into a large circle and brush with egg wash.

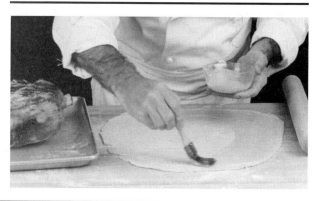

3. Place the carved ham on a cookie sheet lined with parchment paper and cover it with the dough, wet side touching the ham.

4. Press the dough all around the ham so it adheres and trim the excess dough. The ham at the shank should be well encased in the dough. We don't encase the whole ham but only cover the top and sides. It makes it easier to handle and moisture released during cooking can escape without the dough becoming soggy underneath.

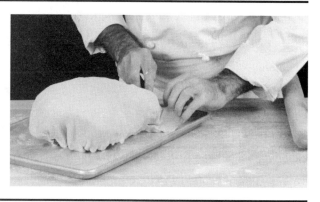

5. Brush the dough all over with egg wash and decorate with strips of dough. Arrange two strips on top to outline the lid. When the ham is cooked a lid will be created by cutting between these two strips.

6. Decorate the lid with flowers made of dough. Make a long, thin strip and let it fold on itself to imitate the petals and stem of a flower.

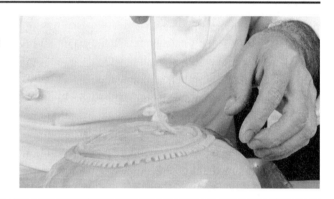

7. Cut stems, leaves and other patterns and place to your fancy on top of the lid.

8. Decorate the outside of the lid by making a relief of cherries. Shape rounds with a pastry tube and arrange with stems.

9. Cut leaves and place them in relief all around the cherries. Press the top and bottom of each leaf to keep them in position. The egg wash helps the decorations adhere.

10. Place another piece of dough with "teeth" around the shank.

11. Brush the top of the decoration with more egg wash and place the ham in a cool place to let it set for an hour.

12. Place the ham in a preheated 425-degree oven for 10 minutes. Reduce the heat to 400 degrees and cook another 30 minutes. The ham should be beautifully glazed and shiny. Let the ham rest for 30 minutes in a lukewarm place before serving. Cut the lid following the outline of the dough. See finished ham in crust, page 490.

13. Lift up the lid to expose the meat. Place the lid back loosely on the ham. Place the ham on a serving platter and secure a frill to the end of the bone. Serve one or two slices of ham per person with some of the Madeira sauce spooned on top. The ham goes well with a purée of spinach as well as with the little papetons of eggplant or the cauliflower and broccoli mold (technique 108).

185. Savoy Sausage in Brioche

(Saucisson en Brioche)

YIELD: 4 to 6 servings

SAUSAGE CAN BE POACHED and served with a potato salad or roasted with tiny potatoes around. It can be poached then cooked in a puff paste as well as in a *pâte brisée.* Cooking it in brioche dough is a classic way of preparing sausage. The aluminum foil keeps the dough from separating from the sausage while cooking.

Sausage

1 *bought or homemade sausage (about 1¼ pound)*
1 *teaspoon vinegar*
1 *teaspoon salt*

To finish

1 *egg, plus 1 egg yolk*
1 *teaspoon butter*
1 *tablespoon bread crumbs*

Brioche (enough to make 2 sausages)

1 *package dry yeast*
¼ *cup lukewarm milk*
½ *teaspoon sugar*
1½ *sticks (6 ounces) sweet butter*
3 *cups flour*
4 *large eggs*
1 *egg yolk*
1 *egg plus 1 egg yolk for the wash*
1 *teaspoon salt*

Combine the yeast and the lukewarm milk in a small bowl and let the mixture work and bubble for 5 minutes. Place all the remaining brioche ingredients in the large bowl of a electric mixer. Start mixing slowly then add the yeast mixture and beat on medium speed for 5 to 6 minutes. After 2 minutes, scrape the bottom of the bowl with a large rubber spatula to combine all the ingredients and start beating again. At the end of the beating time the dough should be very elastic and should release from the beater easily when pulled. Remove the dough and place in a bowl in the refrigerator if not needed right away. You can keep the dough in the refrigerator overnight and use it the day after. Even though the refrigerator is cold, the dough will still work and develop slowly. The day after, push the dough down, and use as needed.

1. If you want to use the dough right away, let it rise in a lukewarm place, covered, for 2 hours. Knock it down by kneading it a few seconds. Cut the dough in half, dust with flour, and spread or flatten each piece with your hand to a thickness of ⅜ to ½ inch. The dough will make 2 sausages. If you are only making one sausage use the extra dough to make small brioches or freeze it for future use.

2. Prick the sausage with a fork, cover with cold water and add vinegar and salt. Bring to about 180 degrees barely simmering. It should not boil. Let the sausage poach for about 10 minutes and remove from heat. When cool enough to handle, take the skin off. Beat the egg and egg yolk together to make a wash. Brush the sausage with egg wash and dough. Sprinkle flour on the dough. The sprinkling of flour will mix with the egg wash and form a "glue," which will hold the sausage to the dough while cooking.

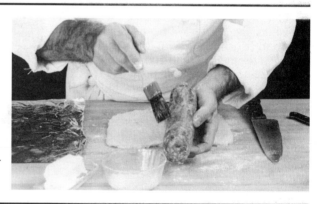

3. Lay the sausage on the dough and wrap the dough toward the top. Encase and seal the sausage tightly.

4. Spread butter on two-thirds of the surface of a square piece of aluminum foil. Sprinkle the buttered part with 1 tablespoon of fresh bread crumbs.

Place the sausage on the buttered part and wrap the foil around. Do not wrap too tightly so the dough has a little bit of space to expand.

5. Tighten both ends securely and place in a roasting pan, seam side down. Let the dough rise in the aluminum foil and "push" for about ½ hour in a warm (about 80 degrees) part of the kitchen. Roll the package seam side up and place in a preheated 375-degree oven for 40 minutes. Every 10 to 15 minutes, roll the sausage a quarter of a turn so the sausage does not sink into the dough on one side more than the other.

6. After about 40 minutes, take the sausage out of the oven, remove from the aluminum and brush again with egg wash. Raise the oven temperature to 400 degrees and bake for 5 to 8 minutes to brown better. Let set for 10 to 15 minutes before carving. If made ahead, the sausage can be reheated in a preheated 300-degree oven for 15 minutes. Serve in slices, as is, or with a little bit of melted butter on top. Excellent as a first course, or as a main course for lunch or brunch.

Savoy sausage in brioche, ham in crust

186. Pork Spread Rillettes *(Rillettes de Porc)*

YIELD: 12 first course servings

T HE WORD *charcuterie* implies different manners of cooking meat, but most particularly different pork preparations: pâtés, sausages, galantines, ham, etc. By extension the word *charcuterie* is also the store where these dishes are sold. In addition most *charcuteries* sell take-out food from pike *quenelles* to different salads of fish, shellfish, stuffed tomatoes, smoked fish, salami, *rillettes*, etc. The following techniques cover *rillettes*, pig's feet, headcheese, black pudding, chitterling sausages, tripes, parleyed ham—the typical preparations available from *charcuteries*.

Rillettes consist of seasoned pork cooked a long time, cooled and shredded into tiny pieces, bound together by fat and seasoned highly with salt and pepper. They are eaten cold with Dijon mustard and crunchy French bread as a first course or as a snack. The *rillettes* can also be made out of goose, rabbit or duck, but most of the time pork will be added to enrich the *rillettes* with fat and make it the right consistency. The *rillettes* are usually packed in small crocks and served as such with bread. *Rillettes* can be seasoned with wine or stock, thyme, bay leaf, etc., but the simple recipe given below and made with water retains the true taste of that country dish. The crocks should be covered tightly with plastic wrap and kept refrigerated up to 10 days. To keep longer the crocks have to be sealed with melted fat. When frozen the texture changes and the taste tends to grow rancid.

2¾ *pounds fresh pork from the chuck, butt or*
  neck (the meat should have about one-third
  lean meat to two-thirds fat)
1 *tablespoon salt*
½ *teaspoon freshly ground black pepper*
1 *clove garlic, peeled*
Water

1. Cut the meat into 2- to 3-inch cubes and place in a large heavy saucepan with the salt, pepper, garlic and enough cold water to reach 1 inch above the surface of the meat. Bring to a boil and cover. Simmer very, very slowly for 4 hours, covered. Uncover and cook another hour to evaporate the extra liquid. Skim the scum which comes to the top of the liquid every 20 minutes during the first 2 hours of cooking. The meat should poach gently in the liquid.

2. You may have to add water during the cooking process because if the water reduces completely and the fat melts, the meat will fry in the fat instead of poaching in the water. After 5 hours of cooking, nearly all water should have evaporated and the liquid in the pot should be fairly clear. Let the mixture cool overnight. The pieces of meat should be embedded in a nice, clear, white fat. If there's any liquid under the fat, pour it out.

3. Shred the pieces of meat between your fingers to separate the fibers of the meat. The *rillettes* are really meat fibers bound with fat. The easiest way to shred the meat into fiber is by hand.

4. Place in a bowl and mix with a wooden spatula until the mixture is smooth.

5. To make the mixture whiter and fluffier, place in the bowl of an electric mixer with the flat beater and beat for 30 seconds on slow speed. Do not overwhisk or the fat will become too white and two creamy. Add salt and pepper as you are beating. Remember that the *rillettes* should be well seasoned.

6. Divide the mixture into crocks. Smooth the top, cover tightly with plastic wrap and let set a few hours, preferably one day in the refrigerator before serving.

7. Just before serving, decorate with a fork. Serve very cold with crunchy French bread and cold white wine. See finished pork spread, page 529.

187. Cold Parsleyed Ham *(Jambon Persillé)*

YIELD: 10 to 12 servings

THE *jambon persillé*, a great way to use leftover ham, is pieces of ham imbedded in parsleyed aspic. The pink of the ham and the green of the parsley make a very attractive presentation as well as a delicious dish. It is usually served as a first course with a dry white wine or a light red wine, crunchy bread and *cornichons*.

Approximately 1 ³/₄ pounds ham (4 cups),
  cut into 2- to 3-inch chunks
1 cup chopped parsely
2 pig's feet (use the front leg which is fleshier,
  about 1 ¹/₂ to 2 pounds together)
2 cups good beef or chicken stock
2 cups of water
1 teaspoon salt
¹/₂ teaspoon freshly ground pepper
2 cups dry white wine

¹/₂ cup chopped shallots (about 6 to 8), chopped
  fine
¹/₂ cup finely chopped leeks

1. Separate the meat from the bone on the leftover ham and cut into chunks. Keep the bone to season lentils or bean soups.

2. Split the pig's feet in half by cutting through the middle of the hoof and around the bone.

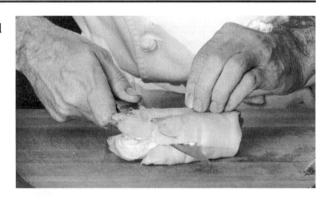

3. Use a cleaver to split the bones in half. Place the feet, stock, water, salt and pepper in a large saucepan and simmer for 1 hour, covered. Add the wine, shallots, leeks, ½ cup of parsley, cover, and simmer for another hour. Remove the feet from the liquid. There should be about 2 to 2½ cups of liquid left.

4. Pick the meat off the bones and chop coarsely. Be sure to remove all the tiny bones from the hoof.

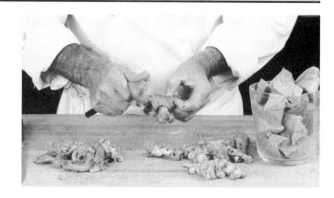

5. Strain 1 cup from the reserved liquid and set aside. Add the chopped feet and the ham to the remaining stock, cover, bring to a boil and simmer 5 minutes. Let cool, stirring occasionally until it starts to set.

6. Meanwhile, add the ¾ cup of parsley to the cup of strained stock and bring to a boil. Cool in a metal bowl over ice. As the liquid starts to set, twist the bowl and use a brush to spread the liquid so that a thin layer of parsleyed aspic coats the bowl all around. Roll the bowl on ice as you are spreading the aspic so the sides get cold and the aspic sticks.

7. Place the ham mixture (it should not be completely set) in the lined bowl, packing the pieces together tightly and making sure that the chopped feet and the loose mixture surround the pieces of ham.

8. Cover with a piece of wax paper, place a small plate on top and flatten with a weight. Cool overnight in the refrigerator.

9. Run the bowl lightly under hot water for a few seconds, run a knife around the bowl and, using a kitchen fork, pry the ham out.

10. Cut into wedges and serve cold as a first course. See finished parsleyed ham, page 529.

188. Stuffed Pork Chops with Sour Sauce (Côtelettes de Porc Farcies Charcutiére)

YIELD: 6 servings

ALTHOUGH in our recipe we use the pork chops from the rack, loin chops can be used as well. The chops do not have to be stuffed and can be broiled or sautéed in different ways; for example, Normandy-style with apples, cream and Calvados.

Stuffing

6 *pork chops, center cut (6 to 7 ounces each)*
1 *tablespoon (½ ounce) sweet butter*
1 *leek, cleaned and diced very thin (white and light green parts only) (¾ cup)*
1 *stalk celery, peeled and finely diced (2 tablespoons)*
1 *pound cooked leaf spinach (see technique 119), coarsely chopped*
½ *cup finely diced boiled ham*
½ *teaspoon salt*
¼ *teaspoon freshly ground black pepper*

Sauce Charcutière

2 *medium sized tomatoes, peeled, seeds squeezed out and coarsely chopped (1 cup)*
½ *cup finely chopped onions*
3 *cloves garlic, crushed and chopped fine (1 teaspoon)*
½ *cup sour French gerkins* (cornichons), *thinly sliced*
¾ *cup* demi-glace *(see technique 12)*
½ *cup dry white wine*
2 *tablespoons chopped fresh herbs (parsley, tarragon, chives, etc.)*

1. When you buy a whole rack or a piece of rack you will find that it usually comes with the backbone. This makes it difficult to cut into chops or to carve in the dining room if it is roasted whole. To remove the backbone, place the rack flat and cut all along the bone to separate from the meat.

2. Standing the rack up and using the front part of a cleaver, cut through the end of the rib to sever the whole backbone.

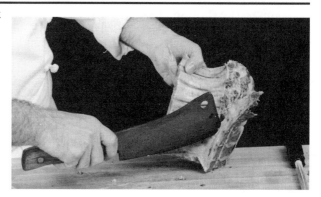

3. The backbone is now separated from the rack. The rack at that point could be roasted whole, seasoned with carrots and onions, and served with natural juices. Prepared this way, it is easy to carve in the dining room.

4. Cut in between each rib to make individual chops. The chops should weigh approximately 6 to 7 ounces each.

5. Trim each chop along the rib of sinews and fat. Trim if the pork is a few days old, as this is where the meat usually spoils first. In addition, trimming makes the chop a bit more elegant. However, if the pork is very fresh it is not absolutely necessary to trim it.

6. To make the chop still more attractive, clean the end off the rib. (Use the trimmings in stocks or soups.) Cut the meat all around the bone (it will be mostly fat), and scrape it off to expose the end of the rib.

7. Place the chop flat and holding it down with one hand, slice it through the middle with the point of a knife. Do not slice the ends. It should form a pocket. Cut deep enough to touch the rib with the knife.

8. Open the chop and flatten each half with a meat pounder to make it a bit larger so it can hold more stuffing and form a better pocket.

9. Melt the butter in a small skillet, add the leek and sauté for 1 minute on medium to low heat, then add the celery and sauté for a few seconds. Mix the spinach in with a fork and sauté for another minute. Combine with the ham and season with salt and pepper. Mix well. Let the stuffing cool, then divide among the chops.

10. Push the stuffing in the cavity and close the meat on top. If the chops are not over-stuffed and if the meat has been pounded nicely, it doesn't need to be tied or secured with a skewer.

11. Sprinkle the chops with salt and pepper. Melt 1 tablespoon of butter in a wide skillet with a cover. Add the chops and cook, uncovered, on medium heat, for 5 minutes on one side. When browned, turn, cover and cook on low heat for another 6 to 8 minutes on the other side. The pork chops should cook slowly or they will become dry and stringy.

12. Place the chops on a platter and keep warm, uncovered, in a 160-degree oven. Add the onions to the drippings and sauté for 1 to 2 minutes on medium heat, then add the wine. Boil for a few seconds, stirring to melt all the solidified juices. Add the tomatoes and garlic and cook for 1 minute. Add the *demi-glace*, bring to a boil and reduce for 2 to 3 minutes until it coats the spoon and has the consistency of a sauce. Add salt and pepper if necessary. Stir in the cornichons, pour the sauce over the chops, sprinkle with herbs and serve.

189. Pork Liver Pâté *(Pâté Maison)*

PÂTÉ, WHICH COMES FROM THE LATIN *pasta,* meaning paste or dough, is a forcemeat mixture wrapped and cooked in a crust and served hot or cold. The term pâté *en croûte* (pâté in crust), which is often seen on menus, is a redundancy though its usage is understandable as the word pâté has broadened in meaning to include most ground meat, game, fish and even vegetables cooked with or without a crust and served cold, as well as hot.

Pâté *maison* or pâté *de campagne* (country-style pâté) is usually a coarse, simple loaf made with pork and liver and served cold. It can be excellent or dreadful, depending on the honesty and professionalism of the restaurant. You can think of pâté *maison* as a glorified meat loaf.

There are a few important things to remember about pâté. It should be well-seasoned. The amount of fat should be correct to obtain a moist pâté, and it should cook slowly so that the fat does not melt away too fast, resulting in a dry loaf. Though it is recommended in many recipes, it is not necessary to "press" the pâté after it is cooked. If the proportions were correct, there is no need to press the fat out. For the recipe that follows, you will need two 1½-quart rectangular loaf molds.

2 *pounds fresh pork liver*
1 ³/₄ *pounds pork fat*
1 ³/₄ *pounds pork butt or shoulder*
Lard leaves, technique 24, or caul fat to line the molds
5 *bay leaves*
1 *teaspoons thyme*
2 *teaspoons black peppercorns*
3 *tablespoons salt*
3 *eggs*
1 *cup dry white wine*

2 *tablespoons cornstarch*
1 *cup chopped onion*
2 *cloves garlic, peeled, crushed and chopped fine*
1 *teaspoon sodium nitrite (see Note, technique 181) or other curing agent*
1 *cup aspic (optional)*

1. Trim the fresh pork liver, removing sinews and skin.

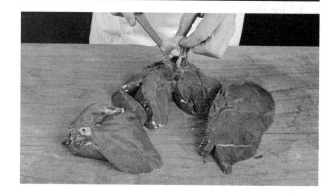

2. Cut into cubes. You should have about 1¾ pounds of trimmed cubes.

3. Weigh out the fat and pork butt. The liver, fat and meat should be used in equal proportions. Cut everything into 1-inch cubes. Process the liver and fat in several batches until liquefied in a food processor. Grind the meat in a meat grinder or by pulsing in a food processor until it is the texture of hamburger. Mix the liquefied liver and fat and the ground meat together in a mixing bowl. Line two loaf molds with lard leaves or caul fat.

4. Using a coffee or spice grinder, pulverize the bay leaves, thyme and peppercorns. Add the pulverized seasonings to the meat with the salt, eggs, white wine, cornstarch, onion, garlic and saltpeter. Mix thoroughly. Divide into two loaves.

5. Bring the lard leaves back onto the meat and cover with aluminum foil.

6. Place in a roasting pan and add enough cold water to come two-thirds the way up the molds. Place in a 325-degree preheated oven for 1 hour. Reduce the temperature to 300 degrees and bake 2 more hours. The internal temperature should read about 150 degrees when the pâté is done. The pâté shrinks while it cooks leaving space all around itself that fills up with fat. The pâté can be cooled and served in its present state or you can pour aspic over the pâté when you remove it from the oven to push the fat up and make it run over the mold.

7. The aspic will get absorbed into the meat during the cooling process and will set and make the meat moist. Either way, the pâté should set at least overnight and preferably for 48 hours. Run a knife around the cold pâté.

8. Unmold. If the pâté doesn't come out easily, run the bottom of the mold under hot water for a few seconds.

9. Clean the outside of the pâté gently with a wet towel.

10. Cut into ⅜-inch slices and serve with crusty bread, *cornichons* and a dry white or red wine. See finished pork liver pâté, page 392a.

190. Sweetbread Terrine *(Terrine de Ris de Veau)*

THE TERRINE, whose name comes from the dish in which it is cooked, is always served cold. The name evokes a more elegant and refined pâté, where the meats are arranged artfully inside the mold. It brings back memories of glistening aspic and the fragrance of cognac and truffles, where pâté *maison* (the preceding technique) brings back the taste of garlic, crusty bread and sour little *cornichons*. For the recipe that follows, you will need an earthenware, enameled or copper terrine or *cocotte*.

2 tablespoons butter
⅓ cup finely chopped shallots or onion
1½ pounds blanched and pressed sweetbreads,
    technique 178
Salt and freshly ground white pepper
Lard leaves to line the terrine, technique 24
1 pound lean veal
¾ pound pork fat
½ pound pork shoulder
2 tablespoons dry sherry

3 tablespoons dry white wine
2 egg yolks
¼ cup shelled pistachio nuts (optional)
1 teaspoon ground parisienne spices (a mixture
    of white pepper, ginger, cinnamon and clove)
1 tablespoon flour
½ teaspoon sodium nitrite (optional) (see Note, technique 181)
2 bay leaves
Thyme
Aspic, technique 21 (optional)

1. Melt the butter in a saucepan. Add the shallots or onion and sauté 1 minute. Add the sweetbreads, ¾ teaspoon salt and ¼ teaspoon white pepper. Roll the pieces in the butter and let cook gently on low heat, covered, for 10 minutes. Line the terrine with lard leaves.

2. The terrine should be well-lined with the leaves hanging on the outside. Using a food processor, chop the veal very fine. Chop the pork fat and shoulder meat in the same manner. Mix with the sherry, white wine, egg yolks, pistachios, 2½ teaspoons salt, 1½ teaspoons white pepper, parisienne spices, flour and sodium nitrite (see technique 181).

3. Place a layer (about 1 inch thick) of the meat mixture on the bottom of the terrine. Arrange sweetbreads on top. Be sure to stuff some mixture between the pieces of sweetbread. They should not touch but be bound together by the chopped meat.

4. Add more forcemeat, then more sweetbread, and, finally, cover with the forcemeat.

5. Bring the lard leaves onto the mixture. Place the bay leaves on top and sprinkle with thyme. Cover with foil, place in a pan of cold water and bake in a 325-degree preheated oven for 1 hour. Reduce the heat to 300 degrees and bake for another 2 hours. The internal temperature should be approximately 145 to 150 degrees when it comes out of the oven.

6. Remove from the oven when cooked. Pour ³/₄ cup melted aspic into terrine. Cool overnight. When cold, cover with plastic wrap. The terrine is more flavorful after it has set for 48 hours.

7. Cool some more aspic on ice.

8. When syrupy, pour some on the terrine to coat the top. Clean the mold before bringing it to the dining room. Serve from the mold. See finished sweetbread terrine, page 392a.

191. Pheasant Pâté in Crust

(Pâté de Faisan en Croûte)

Pâté of pheasant in crust is more time consuming and involved than the sweetbread terrine and pâté *maison*. The meat marinates with the spices and seasonings for 3 to 5 days. Then, the pâté is cooked and allowed to cool for a day. Next, aspic is poured in and finally, it can be served the following day. The process takes one week and though it can be accelerated somewhat, it is better when done step by step with the proper amount of time between each step.

THE FORCEMEAT MIXTURE

1 *(2-pound) pheasant*
6 *lard strips (see technique 24)*
1 *piece of caul fat (see photograph 3), or several lard leaves*
1 *pheasant liver plus 1 chicken or duck liver*
1 *black truffle, chopped coarsely (optional)*
1¼ *pounds pork butt or shoulder, chopped fine (it should be half lean, half fat)*
1½ *tablespoons very finely chopped shallots (about 3 or 4)*
¼ *teaspoon thyme leaves, chopped into a powder*
1 *large bay leaf, crumbled and chopped into a powder (the thyme and bay leaf can be pulverized in an electric coffee mill)*
2½ *teaspoons salt*
1½ *teaspoons freshly ground black pepper*
1 *tablespoon good cognac*
3 *tablespoons dry white wine*
1 *tablespoon truffle juice (optional)*
½ *teaspoon sodium nitrate (optional) (see note, technique 181)*

Bone out a fresh pheasant following the directions for *poulet en saucisse*, technique 152, but remove all the bones. You do not have to worry about keeping the skin in one piece. You should have about 18 ounces of meat. Put aside the two fillets from the breast. Cut each breast into two strips and add to the fillets. You should have ¾ pound clean meat left. Finely chop the remaining meat in a food processor. Reserve the bones, skin, neck and gizzard for the stock.

Put aside the lard strips, the caul fat, the pieces of breast, the livers and the truffle. Mix all the other ingredients thoroughly. Place the reserved ingredients on top. Cover with plastic wrap and refrigerate for about 4 days.

THE STOCK

Place the bones, skin, neck and gizzard in a kettle with cold water. Add some salt, peppercorns, celery leaves, thyme and 1 carrot. Bring to a boil and cook for 2 hours. Strain. You should have approximately 5 cups of liquid. If not, adjust to 5 cups by adding water. Let cool and remove the fat from the surface.

THE ASPIC

Mix 1 cup of green of leek, celery and parsley (see techniques 18 and 21) with 2 envelopes of plain gelatin and 3 egg whites. Add the cold stock. Bring to a boil, stirring once in a while to prevent scorching. As soon as it boils, reduce the heat to a simmer and let simmer 5 minutes. Remove from heat, let stand for 15 minutes, and strain through a sieve lined with wet paper towels. You should have 4 cups of aspic.

THE DOUGH

2½ cups flour
¾ stick (6 tablespoons) butter
2 tablespoons vegetable shortening
½ teaspoon salt
2 egg yolks mixed with 4 tablespoons cold water

Make a dough using the ingredients listed above. (You can replace the butter and shortening with lard.) Knead the dough twice (*fraisage*). The dough should be made one day ahead and kept refrigerated.

FINAL ASSEMBLY

1. The mold used in this technique has hinges and comes without a bottom. You could cook the pâté free form or choose another mold.

2. Roll the dough between ⅛ and ¼ inch thick. Cut it to the center and overlap the edges to make a "jacket." This makes the mold easier to line. Line the mold with the dough, pressing it into the corners so the dough will adhere well.

3. A piece of caul fat *(crépine)*—the lacy and fatty membrane which encases the stomach of the pig—is used to line the dough. Lard leaves can be used in its place.

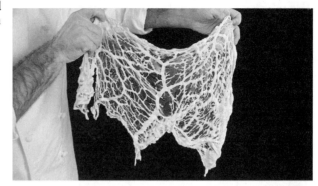

4. Line the dough with the caul fat. Place some of the forcemeat in the bottom of the mold.

5. Arrange half the lard strips, half the breast meat and the livers in the middle. The livers could also be wrapped in caul fat before being placed in the pâté as pictured here. Cover the livers with the truffle pieces.

6. Cover with more forcemeat, then more lard and meat strips and finally with the remaining forcemeat.

7. Bring the caul fat back onto the meat.

8. Bring the dough back onto the pâté and dampen with water.

9. Roll a piece of dough and place on top of the pâté. Press the side so that it sticks to the wet dough.

10. Trim around the edges.

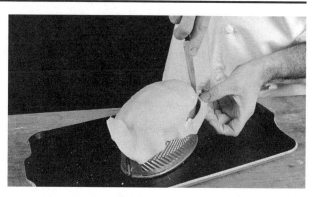

11. Roll more dough and cut shapes with a cookie cutter and a knife.

12. Wet the dough on the pâté and start building the pieces of dough as if you were laying a roof with tiles.

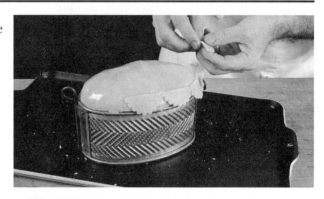

13. Overlap slightly, wetting the dough between each layer. When you finish, make a hole through the top of the dough so that the steam can escape during baking.

14. Cut lozenges of dough and mark with a knife to simulate the markings of the leaves.

15. Fold and position them around the hole, leaving the opening free.

16. Place a rolled piece of foil through the hole and into the meat. This will act as a chimney for the steam. Brush the pâté with egg wash (1 egg, beaten). Let the pâté "rest" for a few hours, then bake in a 330-degree preheated oven for 2 hours (the internal temperature should read about 150 degrees when done).

17. Remove from the oven and, when cool enough to handle, remove the mold by opening the hinges. Cool overnight.

18. Melt the aspic and cool in ice water until syrupy. Pour into the opening. If a "leak" develops through the crust, seal the hole with soft butter. Keep pouring aspic until all the holes inside the pâté are filled. The aspic should stay at the level of the opening without going down. Let set.

19. Brush the outsides of the pâté with syrupy aspic.

20. When slicing, use a serrated knife, holding the crust with the tips of your fingers. See finished pheasant pâté in crust, page 392a.

192. Stuffed Pig's Feet *(Pieds de Porc Farcis)*

YIELD: 6 servings

ORDINARY PIG'S FEET can be a delicacy whether you stuff them or not. They are excellent just simply boiled and served with a mustardy vinaigrette. They can be used to make aspic because they are very gelatinous in texture. They enhance the flavor and texture of tripe and cold jellied dishes, such as *Daube de Boeuf*. For our recipe the feet or "trotters" are first soaked in brine for six days. This improves the taste as well as the color. However, it is not absolutely necessary. If you omit the brine be sure to increase the salt in cooking and expect them to be grayish in color rather than pink. Use the front feet because although they are shorter, they are meatier. Prepare a brine as explained in technique 193.

Cooking

6 pig's feet (about 12 ounces each)
¼ cup white wine vinegar

Stuffing

1 tablespoon butter
½ cup finely chopped onions
2 cloves garlic, peeled and finely chopped
2 cups (loose) mushrooms, finely chopped
Dash of thyme leaves

½ teaspoon salt
¼ teaspoon pepper

To finish the feet

2 cups fresh bread crumbs
¾ stick (3 ounces) sweet butter, melted
2 tablespoons strong Dijon-style mustard

1. Soak the feet in the brine for 6 days, in a cool place, with a plate on top to keep them immersed in the brine. After 6 days wash in cold water and soak for 30 minutes in clear cold water. Place in a saucepan in one layer with the vinegar and cover with cold water. Cover and bring to a temperature of approximately 170 degrees. Poach at that temperature for about 3 hours. The water should not boil or the meat will come off the bones. If the feet have not been soaked in brine previous to cooking, add 2 teaspoons of salt to the cooking liquid.

2. Let the feet cool in the stock. When lukewarm, remove from the cooking liquid and pick all the bones off. Be careful to remove all the small bones in the hoof. Try to keep the meat together in a piece as best you can.

3. Sauté the onions in butter on medium heat for about 1 minute. Add the garlic, mushrooms and thyme. Cook until most of the liquid released from the mushrooms has evaporated (3 to 4 minutes). Allow the stuffing to cool. Then stuff the feet when they are still at room temperature. If they are allowed to cool off completely, they will harden and will be less easy to work with. Form little packages.

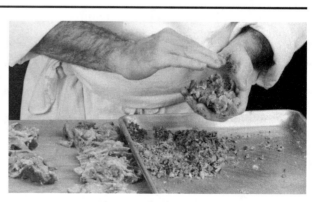

4. Place the stuffed feet, stuffing down, on a tray, one next to another, and place another tray on top with a weight. Refrigerate overnight. The "packages" will harden considerably when cold.

5. Trim each foot into a nice rectangular shape.

6. Brush the feet with the French mustard, covering the top and sides. The stuffed side should be underneath and the skin side on top.

7. Mix the bread crumb and melted butter and pat firmly onto each package to coat. Up to this point the feet can be done ahead and kept covered in the refrigerator for new for a few days. To finish them, heat on a tray in a preheated 400-degree oven for about 12 minutes or or until hot inside. Finish browning under the broiler for a few minutes. Serve immediately with more French mustard and French bread with boiled or mashed potatoes or fried potatoes. See finished stuffed pig's feet, page 529.

193. Rolled Headcheese (Hure de Porc)

YIELD: 16 to 18 servings

HEADCHEESE is jellied meat and rind of the pig's head. There are different ways of making headcheese. The meat is sometimes cut into 1- to 2-inch pieces, cooked with stock and seasonings and the whole mixture placed into molds and allowed to cool and harden in the refrigerator. Then, the "loaf" is cut into slices and served with a vinaigrette. In this recipe, however, the meat and rind are rolled into a large headcheese sausage. It is a bit more work this way but the headcheese is meatier with less aspic. Curing the meat in a brine before cooking (although it is not imperative) makes it tastier and gives it a nicer color. If it is not cured in brine, the meat will be more grayish than pink. The brine can be used for ham or other pieces of pork, spare ribs (*petit salé*), shoulder, feet, loin, etc.

1 *whole pork head with bone, weighing approximately 12 pounds (Be sure the head is perfectly cleaned of hair.)*

1 *teaspoon thyme leaves*
4 *bay leaves crushed*
½ *teaspoon allspice*
½ *teaspoon coriander*
½ *teaspoon cloves*

Brine

6 *quarts water*
4 *cups kosher-type salt (1¼ pounds)*
1½ *cups brown sugar (about 10 ounces)*
1 *tablespoon sodium nitrate, optional*
(see Note, technique 181)

First cooking

1 *small leek, cleaned and chopped fine, white only ½ cup*
4 to 6 *shallots, peeled, chopped fine (¼ cup)*
¼ *cup chopped parsley*
½ *cup dry white wine*

Second cooking

1 *teaspoon freshly ground black pepper*
½ *teaspoon salt*
2 *cups dry white wine*
3 *cups well-seasoned chicken or beef stock, or a mixture of both*

1. To prepare the brine, crush the spices with a rolling pin or the bottom of a heavy saucepan. Place the water, salt, sugar and saltpeter in a large non-aluminum kettle and bring to a boil. Add the thyme, bay leaves, allspice, coriander and cloves, cover and remove from the heat. Let cool covered before using.

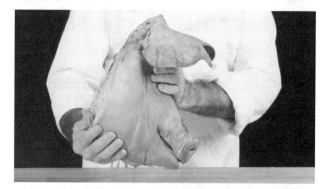

2. Split the skull into halves using a saw or a large cleaver. Remove the brains which can be poached, and fried in black butter or used with scrambled eggs. Do not cut through the skin under the chin.

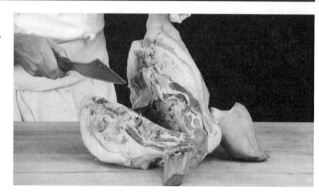

3. Bone the head all around the central bone. Do not worry if some meat is left on the bone because the meat can be removed easily after cooking. You should have approximately 6½ pounds of meat, rind and fat plus the remaining bones.

4. Place the meat and bones in the brine solution with a weight on top to keep the meat immersed. Keep in brine for 6 days in a cold place or refrigerate if possible. Wash bones and meat well under cold running water. Cover the meat and bones with cold water (salt is not necessary because the meat has been cured in brine) in a huge kettle and bring to a boil. Keep the meat submerged in the cooking liquid by placing a plate or lid and a weight on top. Simmer slowly for 1½ hours.

5. Let cool for ½ hour and remove the meat and bones to a tray. The headcheese should not cook too long because it will crumble and lose elasticity; it tastes better if it is a bit chewy. When the meat is cold enough to handle, start to pick the meat off the bones and discard the bones. Remove as much fat as you can from between the layers of meat and skin. There will be large chunks of fat which must be removed and either discarded or kept to make *rillettes* (technique 186) or used in stews or to sauté potatoes or other vegetables.

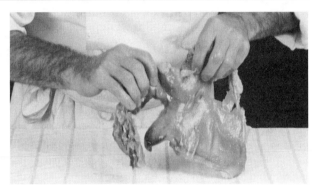

6. Spread out the largest pieces of skin on a towel—outside skin down.

7. Place the ½ cup of wine, shallots, parsley and leek in a small saucepan. Simmer 4 to 5 minutes until the vegetables are wilted and most of the wine has evaporated. Cover the skin with the mixture and sprinkle black pepper and salt to taste on top of the meat.

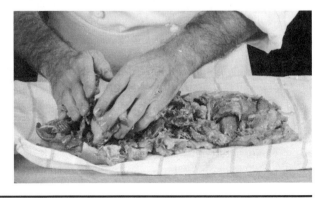

8. Place the remaining pieces of meat on top of the shallot mixture and roll in the towel to form a large sausage with as much skin as possible on the outside. If you do not have a large fish poacher or *pâté* mold to accommodate the headcheese, make two smaller sausages instead of one large one. Smaller headcheese are easier to handle and serve.

9. Tie the ends and center of the head-cheese with sturdy cotton kitchen twine.

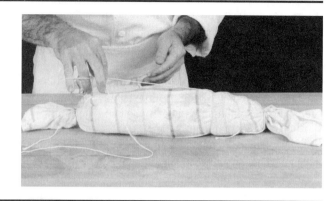

10. Place the sausage in a fish poacher or a large *pâté* mold and cover with white wine, the stock, salt and pepper.

11. To make sure the meat is immersed, weight it down with something heavy. Bring to a boil on top of the stove and simmer very gently for approximately 15 minutes. Allow to cool with the weight in place.

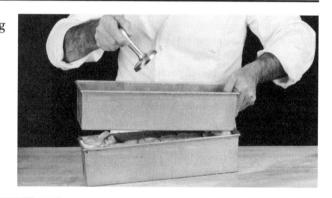

12. Cool overnight, then unmold and unwrap the towel. Keep the stock for later use. (It can be frozen or used to make aspic.) Cut the headcheese into thin slices and serve with sour pickles, French mustard, a dry white wine or light red wine and crunchy bread. Excellent as a snack or as a first course, for a country-type dinner. See finished rolled headcheese, page 529.

194. Black Pudding *(Boudins)*

YIELD: 20 *boudins*

T HE BLACK PUDDING or *boudin* is a very common country dish in France. Each region has its own variation, each one pretending to be the one and only original recipe. Some use apples, some leeks, some spinach, some chestnuts, etc. Regardless of the seasoning used, the *boudin* is bound with blood and enriched with pork fat.

The recipe given below is classic and simple. Pork blood gives the best result but it is hard to find in the United States. Calf's blood or beef blood is a good substitute. The blood can be ordered from your butcher and will very likely come frozen, although, of course, it is better fresh. It is usually packed in half-gallon containers which will make approximately 40 *boudins*. The casing used for the *boudins* can be hog casing, approximately 1 to 1½ inches in diameter, or a small beef middle casing, as used in our recipe, which is also approximately 1½ to 2 inches in diameter. Casings usually come packed in salt. When served, the natural casing is usually discarded although some people like to eat it. (For more information about casings see page 470). Serve one *boudin* as a first course and two as a main course

---

8 *to* 10 *feet hog or beef middle casings*
1 *quart pork or beef blood*
1½ *pounds* panne, *the pork fat around the kidney*
1¼ *pounds onions, peeled and chopped (about 2½ cups)*
4 *leeks, peeled, white and light green parts only, sliced very thin (1½ cups)*
1½ *cups heavy cream*
1¼ *teaspoons salt*
½ *teaspoon freshly ground white pepper*
¼ *teaspoon thyme*

---

1. The *panne* or pork suet is white, very waxy and surrounds the kidneys and lines the tenderloin. It is the best fat for *boudins*, *pâtés* and salamis. Grind the fat in a meat grinder or food processor. (If chopped in the food processor, it should first be cut into 1-inch chunks.) Place one-third of the fat in a large saucepan and melt for about 10 minutes on medium to high heat. Add the onions and leeks and cook for another 5 minutes on medium heat.

2. Add the remaining fat and cook for another 10 minutes. Let cool for atleast 15 minutes or until lukewarm and stir the blood, cream and seasonings. Run the dry casings under water. Place the opening of the casing over the end of the faucet and let tepid water run through. Let the casing soak in lukewarm water for about 10 minutes, then squeeze to get rid of the water and place on a large cookie sheet.

3. Tie one end with kitchen string and fit the other end over as large a funnel as will fit. Ladle the mixture into the casing.

4. When filled, tie the other end of the casing with kitchen string. Leave a few inches of casing empty before the knot. The bit of extra space is for expansion during cooking and to accommodate the amount of casing taken in when you divide the *boudins* into individual portions.

5. Divide the filled casing into 5-inch lengths. You can simply twist the casing (reversing the twist for each different sausage) in order to separate the portions.

6. Or you can tie off the portions with pieces of kitchen string.

7. Place the *boudins* in a large saucepan into a coil. Use a wide saucepan that can hold the *boudins* in one layer. Add hot tap water to at least 1 inch above the meat. Place over high heat and bring the water to approximately 170 to 180 degrees. Do not boil or the *boudins* will burst.

8. Poach at the same temperature for 20 minutes. Prick the *boudins* with a needle to check the cooking. It is cooked when the liquid coming out of the casing is clear and only a few drops come out and stop.

9. When cooked, lift the *boudins* from the poaching liquid and let cool on a cookie sheet. When cold, separate into serving portions.

10. The *boudins* can be covered and stored in the refrigerator. It is at this stage that they can be bought in a *charcuterie* in France. At serving time, place in a skillet on medium heat. No fat is necessary. Cook for about 2 minutes on each side. Reduce to low heat, cover and let cook slowly for 10 minutes. Serve with freshly made mashed potatoes and/or sautéed apples on the side. This lovely country-style main course can be served for lunch as well as for dinner. See finished black pudding, page 529.

195. Tripe with Wine and Calvados

(Tripes à la Mode de Caen)

YIELD: Serves 8 to 10 servings

Tripe usually refers to the stomach of ox or beef, although in France certain parts of the intestine are considered to be tripe as well. The tripe (the honeycomb or *estomac* or *panse* in France) usually is thicker and fattier on one side and this side is what is used for the *gras-double,* a specialty of Lyonnaise cooking. The *pieds paquets* is a specialty of Marseille, made from lamb tripe mixed with the *feuillet* (part of the huge intestine), formed into little packages and cooked slowly for a long time. There are many different recipes for tripe and the one given here is the classic version cooked in Normandy and finished with Calvados. Beef feet are usually added to give a more gelatinous consistency to the dish. The tripe should be cooked slowly for a long time—the longer the better.

Tripe

10 *pounds beef tripe (honeycomb)*
2 *beef or calf feet, 1½ to 2 pounds each*
3 *carrots, peeled (about ½ pound)*
2 *large onions, peeled and cut into halves*
1 *large leek or 2 to 3 smaller ones, cleaned*
2 to 3 *stalks of celery*
3 *bay leaves*
1 *teaspoon thyme*
1½ *tablespoons salt*
1½ *teaspoons ground black pepper*

2 *quarts light, good chicken or beef stock or a mixture of both*
1 *quart dry white wine*

To finish the dish

Calvados
1¼ *cups flour*
½ *cup lukewarm water*
1 *egg, beaten, for glaze*

1. The tripe will come cleaned and already blanched. If you are unable to obtain it fresh, defrost it slowly under refrigeration.

2. Split the beef feet into halves. Cut the meat all around the central bone and in the middle of the hoof. It is not necessary to cut through the bone.

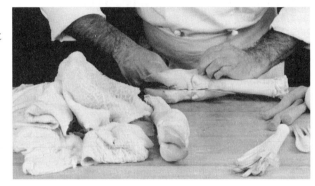

3. Arrange the feet and all the seasonings in a large kettle. Place the tripe on top and add the stock and wine. Cover and bring to a boil. Lower the heat and simmer very slowly for at least 4 hours. Set aside to cool.

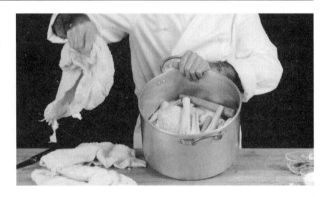

4. When cool enough to handle, lift the tripe, feet and vegetables from the liquid. Reduce the liquid on high heat to 2 quarts. Meanwhile, bone out the feet and cut the meat into 1-inch pieces. Discard the bones. Cut the tripe into 2-inch pieces and chop all the vegetables coarsely. Combine with the reduced stock. You should have just enough liquid to cover the tripe.

5. Bring to a boil. Taste for seasoning. You may have to add salt and pepper depending on the strength of the stock. It should be well seasoned.

6. At this point, the tripe could be divided into containers and frozen. When ready to use, defrost under refrigeration for 48 hours, and simmer gently another 2 hours. Serve with a sprinkling of Calvados (apple-jack brandy), approximately ½ teaspoon per person. The tripe is customarily served in bowls with boiled potatoes.

7. For a fancier way of serving tripe, place in earthenware crocks, seal the lid with dough so no steam escapes and bake in the oven. Make a dough by mixing the flour with water and kneading for 1 minute. Roll pieces of dough into 1-inch-thick strips, wet with water and place around the lid. Press to flatten the dough to make sure it adheres well. Brush with the egg wash, and place on a cookie sheet in a preheated 325-degree oven for 2 hours. Serve as is from the oven. At the table, break the dough and lift the cover in front of your guests. Tripe is customarily served as a main course with boiled potatoes. You will notice that after the first cooking—after the 4 hours, at the point when the tripe can either be frozen or placed in terrines in the oven—there is still a lot of liquid and the seasoning is not strong. Keep in mind that it has another 2 hours of cooking and the liquid will reduce and the taste will become more concentrated. See the finished tripe with wine and Calvados, page 529.

196. Rabbit with Prunes *(Lapin aux Pruneaux)*

YIELD: 6 to 8 servings

Rabbit is plump, tender, high in protein, low in fat—and is now available ready to cook in most good supermarkets. The wild rabbit and hare have a much stronger taste as well as darker meat than the domesticated rabbit. The former is excellent for pâtés, but for stews most people prefer the latter with its white, lean and tender meat. A rabbit is tender at about 2 ½ to 3 months old. A good size is approximately 5 pounds, which is how much the one pictured below weighed, eviscerated but with the head and skin on and liver and kidneys inside. There are countless recipes for rabbit—roasted, boiled, with prunes and onions and a slightly acidic sauce. Though we show you how to skin a rabbit, your butcher will do it for you if you prefer.

Stew

1 *rabbit, about 5 pounds, eviscerated but with*
 skin and head on (3½ pounds headless and skinless)
½ *teaspoon freshly ground black pepper*
½ *stick (2 ounces) sweet butter*
2 *tablespoons flour*
1½ *cups dry white wine*
2½ *cups chicken stock*
3 *garlic cloves, peeled and crushed*
Liver and kidneys of the rabbit
½ *cup dry white wine*

30 *small, white pearl onions the size of a large*
 olive, peeled (about ¾ pound)

Sauce

¼ *cup good red or white wine vinegar*
3 *tablespoons sugar*
⅓ *cup water*
2 *cups large prunes, pitted*

1. Make an incision with a knife through the skin in the middle of the rabbit's back.

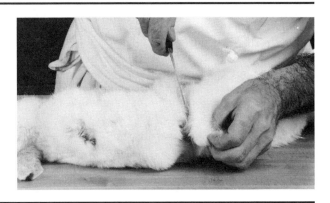

2. Place both hands in the incision and pull on each side to separate the skin from the flesh. You need strength but the skin should come off easily.

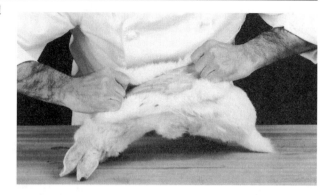

3. As you pull the skin off and expose the meat, you will notice that it is almost completely free of fat.

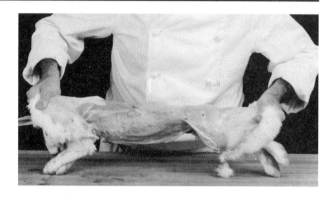

4. Pull off the skin toward the tail to expose the back legs. Cut at the tail, then break the foot bone with the back of a large knife, and cut through.

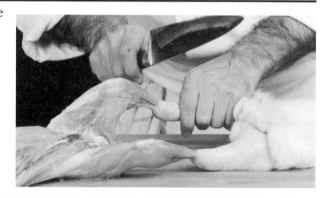

5. Proceed in the same manner with the front legs. Pull the skin toward the head and cut at the neck. (In France the head is often used in stock or stew. Although the fur can be kept and processed for use as clothing, it is rarely done.)

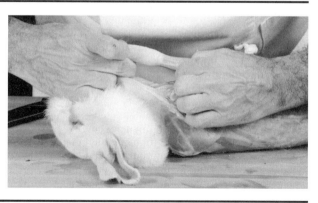

6. When the rabbit is clean, place on its back and cut through the pelvic bone.

7. Stretch the pelvic bone open to expose a piece of the intestines which runs in between the bone.

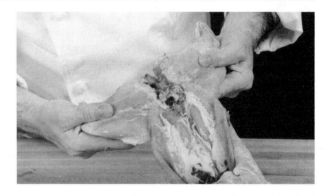

8. Pull and cut out the intestine and discard.

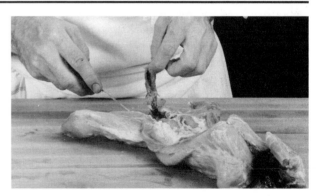

9. Separate the two back legs, then the flanks which run along the saddle or the back part of the rabbit.

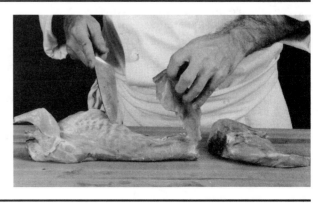

10. Sever the two front legs from the shoulder by sliding your knife along the shoulder blade. Cut the back loin into 3 pieces cut across the ribs, then the rack into 3 pieces. Then cut each of the back legs in half.

11. You now have the rabbit cut up into 12 to 14 pieces. The liver and the kidneys are kept aside. You should have approximately 3½ pounds of meat. Sprinkle the meat with salt and pepper. Melt the butter in a very large saucepan and brown the pieces all around on medium heat for 10 minutes. Sprinkle with the flour, stir well and cook for another 1 or 2 minutes. Deglaze with 1½ cups of white wine and the chicken stock. Cover and cook on low heat for 20 minutes. Place garlic, liver, kidneys and ½ cup white wine in a food processor and purée. Add this purée to the rabbit and stir well. Cover and simmer another 15 minutes then add the onions. Keep cooking on medium heat for 15 more minutes. Meanwhile, prepare the vinegar mixture that finishes the sauce.

12. In a saucepan, combine the vinegar and sugar and cook 4 to 5 minutes, until it caramelizes. Add the water to liquefy the caramel (be careful as it may splash). When the caramel is melted, add to the rabbit with the prunes. Cover and simmer slowly for another 10 minutes. Taste for seasonings and add salt and peper if needed. Serve with fresh mashed potatoes, a purée of celery root, the *pommes savonnettes* (technique 133) or other fried potatoes.

Pork spread, parsleyed ham

Cured, raw country ham

Chicken liver custards, goose liver pâté in aspic

Tripe with wine and Calvados, rolled headcheese, black pudding, stuffed pig's feet, chittlering sausages

Carving

197. Carving Gravlax (Découpage du gavlax)

AFTER THE FILLETS have been cured, technique 87, they are ready to be served. They should be used within a few days or they may turn sour. Keep them refrigerated until ready to carve as it is much easier to carve when the fish is very cold.

1. Unwrap the fillets. Place the fillet flat on the table and, holding it stable with the flat side of a fork, start carving long, paper-thin slices. Cut on a slant.

2. This requires some practice.

3. Try to cut slices as thin as you possibly can. Spread and arrange about 3 to 4 slices to a plate.

4. Sprinkle 1 teaspoon drained capers on top of each portion.

5. Sprinkle 1 teaspoon of the finest virgin walnut or olive oil and ½ teaspoon good red wine vinegar on each portion. Serve with buttered toast or black bread.

198. Carving Poached Salmon
(Découpage du Saumon Poché)

1. Poach and decorate the salmon, technique 88. The salmon should be cold and well "set" to carve easily. Using a thin sharp blade and holding the fish with the flat side of a fork, cut down to the central bone and across to the center line. Prepare a cold plate with lettuce leaves and some of the garnishes.

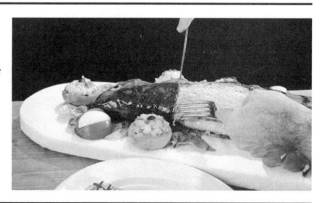

2. Cut across in the same manner, approximately 3½ to 4 inches below the first cut.

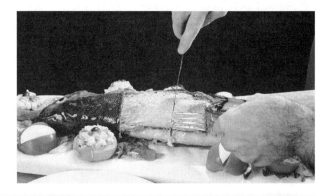

3. Cutting down the center line, loosen and lift a neat little "block" of salmon in one piece. Place on the lettuce.

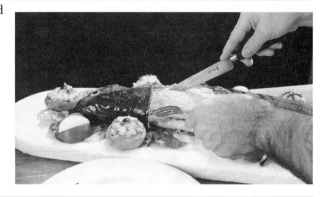

4. A more elegant method is to carve the block into ⅜-inch slices and arrange them overlapping on the lettuce.

5. Repeat with another "chunk," pushing off the decoration as you carve and removing the bones, if any.

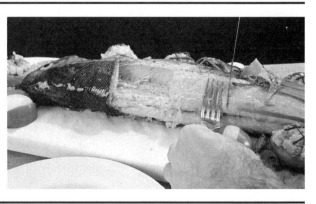

6. This procedure can be used only for a fish like salmon which has a tight, very compact flesh. For fish like striped bass, pike or large trout, serve the whole portion in one piece.

199. Carving Roast Chicken
(Découpage du Poulet Roti)

1. There is nothing as simple and as delicious as a well-cooked roast chicken. Unfortunately, to get it properly done in a restaurant is as rare as it is simple. Truss the chicken, technique 143. Season the chicken with salt and pepper inside the cavity and outside. Melt 3 tablespoons butter in a large skillet and roll the chicken all around in the melted butter. Place on its side and bake in a 400-degree preheated oven for 15 minutes. Turn on the other side and bake another 15 minutes. Place on its back and baste well with drippings.

2. Bake for another 30 to 35 minutes, basting every 5 minutes. To baste, incline the saucepan on one side and scrape out the juices and drippings. Pour over the chicken. This will give moisture to the meat and crustiness to the skin. Five minutes before removing from the oven, pour ⅓ cup water into the pan to melt the solidified juices and make a natural gravy.

3. Remove the string. Place the chicken on its side. Insert a fork in the leg and pull lightly while cutting the skin all around.

4. Pull the leg up and separate from the body. It should come off easily. If you have difficulty, cut the sinews at the joint as you pull.

5. Holding the chicken with the fork, cut through the shoulder joint.

6. Cut along and all the way down to the bone of the breast.

7. Pull the wing and breast off, keeping the chicken from moving by holding the body with the flat side of the knife.

8. Turn the chicken on the other side and lift up the other leg.

9. Cut the shoulder at the joint.

10. Continue cutting down along the breastbone.

11. Then lift up the wing and breast piece.

12. The only piece left is the central portion of the breast, the sternum *(bréchet)*. Sever at the joint to separate from the backbone.

13. You now have the backbone plus five pieces of chicken.

14. Place the pieces back on the bone in their original position.

15. Chicken carved and reconstituted. Serve with natural gravy.

200. Carving Turkey *(Découpage de la Dinde)*

1. Truss the turkey, technique 143. Rub with salt, pepper and ½ stick soft butter. Place in a roasting pan and bake in a 330-degree preheated oven. A 10-pound turkey will take 2¼ hours. Baste every 20 minutes after the first hour. Thirty minutes before the baking time is over, add 1 cup hot water to the pan. Place the turkey on a large serving platter. Insert a kitchen fork into the leg. Cut the skin all around the leg.

2. Pull off the leg, holding the turkey steady with the knife.

3. Place the leg on a plate and separate the thigh from the drumstick at the joint.

4. Slice the thigh around the bone.

5. Slice the drumstick, arranging the dark meat on a hot plate.

6. With a long, thin knife, cut the breast straight down into very thin slices.

7. Hold the turkey with the fork while cutting.

8. Arrange the slices in order on a hot plate.

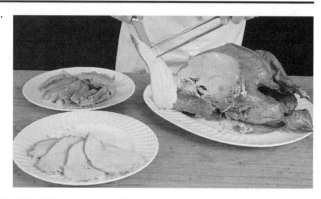

9. Separate the wing at the joint.

10. Dark and white meat from one side of the turkey. Repeat on the other side and serve with the natural gravy.

201. Carving Saddle of Lamb

(Découpage de la Selle d'Agneau)

1. Trim and tie the saddle, technique 159. Sprinkle the saddle with salt and pepper. Melt 2 tablespoons butter in a saucepan and brown the saddle all around on medium to high heat (about 7 to 8 minutes).

2. With the skirts tucked underneath, remove the strings. For a *selle d'agneau provençale,* mix together: 2 tablespoons melted butter, 1 tablespoon chopped shallots, 1 teaspoon chopped garlic, ¼ cup chopped parsley and ½ cup fresh bread crumbs.

3. Gently pack and press the bread mixture onto the surface of the saddle. Place in a 425-degree preheated oven and bake for approximately 20 minutes, depending on the size of the saddle. It should be served pink. Let the meat "rest" at least 10 minutes in a lukewarm oven before carving. Serve with the drippings.

4. Cut off the pieces of skirt tucked under the saddle.

5. Slice on an angle into small pieces if you decide to serve it to your guests. (These pieces are not usually served in restaurants.)

6. There are two different ways to carve the saddle. First method: Holding your knife flat, cut along the flat T-bone which is between the loin and the tenderloin.

7. Slice the loin vertically into very thin slices.

8. Arrange slices on a warm plate as you carve.

9. Keep carving until you reach the backbone. Repeat on the other side, or try the second method.

10. Second method: I do not find this method as desirable as the first because it yields fewer slices, and the crusty herb mixture on top is only on the first slice. Nonetheless it is carved this way in many well-respected establishments. Cut alongside the backbone straight down to the flat T-bone.

11. Holding your knife flat, slice the loin into wide, thin slices.

12. Keep slicing until the flat T-bone is clean of meat. Arrange the slices on plates as you go along.

13. Turn the saddle upside down. Slice the tenderloin off in one piece.

14. Follow the bone as closely as you possibly can so that you get most of the meat off.

15. Remove the other tenderloin. Slice into smaller pieces so that each guest gets a small bit of the tenderloin. The T-bone should be "cleaned" on both sides. (The day after, pick off the bone and eat cold with a garlicky salad.)

16. Carved saddle. The plate in front shows two slices, one from each method. Be sure to have very hot plates and to carve the meat as swiftly as you possibly can because lamb cools off very fast. Serve with the drippings and a creamy potato such as *gratin dauphinois* (potato slices in garlic and cream sauce).

202. Carving Rack of Lamb
(Découpage du Carré d'Agneau)

1. After you have trimmed the rack of lamb, technique 162, sprinkle it with salt and pepper. Melt 2 tablespoons of butter in a skillet and brown the meat all around on medium to high heat (about 5 to 6 minutes). Place in a 425-degree preheated oven for about 10 minutes (depending on size). Let the rack "rest" 5 to 10 minutes before carving. (For *provençale*, see steps 2 and 3 in technique 201.) Holding the meat with the flat side of a fork, cut chops by slicing between ribs. For thinner slices cut one chop with the rib and one between the ribs.

2. Another method of carving is similar to the method used for the saddle in the preceding technique. Holding the rack up with a fork, cut down along the bones but do not separate the meat from the ribs.

3. Holding your knife flat, carve very thin, wide slices from the loin. When serving lamb, the plates should be extra hot, and the carving should be done quickly because the meat cools off very fast. Coat the slices with the natural juices and serve with a puree of carrot, technique 106, and/or a puree of celeriac.

203. Carving Rib Roast *(Découpage de la Côte de Boeuf)*

1. Trim, tie and cook the roast, technique 170. The meat should be rare. Remove the large piece of fat tied on top of the roast. Place the roast under the broiler for 5 to 6 minutes to lightly brown the top. Let the roast "rest" for 20 minutes before carving.

2. "Sit" the roast on its larger side. Using a sharp paring knife, cut straight down a few inches, following the ribs. This cut will give a nice clean edge to the slices of meat.

3. Holding the roast in place with the flat side of a fork, carve holding your knife flat.

4. Cut thin slices and

5. arrange several pieces per person on a warm plate. Serve with the natural gravy.

204. Carving Large Fillet or Tenderloin Steak (Découpage du Chateaubriand)

THE CHATEAUBRIAND is the largest cut from the fillet (see technique 174). It should be broiled or sautéed rare. Let it "rest" 5 minutes before carving.

Carve on a slant with a thin, sharp knife. Arrange slices on a warm plate, pour some drippings over the top and serve immediately.

205. Carving Flank Steak *(Découpage de la bavette)*

FLANK STEAK makes an excellent lunch. It is not too expensive and it cooks very fast. Sprinkle a 2¼- to 2½-pound trimmed flank steak (see technique 175) with salt and pepper. Place under the broiler for about 7 to 8 minutes on each side. Let the meat "rest" 5 minutes before carving.

1. Holding the meat with the flat side of a fork,

2. cut thin slices on a slant. The thinner the slices the more tender the meat will be. It is important that the meat is cut against the grain or it will be stringy and tough. Arrange the thin slices on a platter. Serve immediately with its natural juice.

"To be a great chef you first have to be a technician—great cooking favors prepared hands."

Photo: Tom Hopkins

"In addition to being tasty and well presented, the dishes of a professional chef have to be prepared quickly and in quantity, tasks that are impossible to achieve without knowledge of the proper techniques."

—Jacques Pépin

Breads

Pullman bread, country bread, baguettes, straight crescents, Provence-style pizza, "head of wheat" bread, chocolate rolls, shrimp bread, small milk breads

206. Country Bread *(Pain de Ménage)*

YIELD: 2 to 3 round loaves and 4 to 5 baguettes, about 1 pound each

VERY SIMPLE RECIPES are often the most deceptive because they are the hardest to make well. What is wine? Simply fermented grape juices. What is salami? Seasoned ground meat dried in a casing. What is French bread? Water, flour and yeast. Yet these ultra-simple recipes demand years of practice to achieve perfection. Once a recipe becomes complicated, the list of ingredients expands and the recipe becomes easier to adjust, change and control. But try to improve a hard-boiled egg! In addition to years of knowledge, professional bakers have the right flour, special equipment, temperature control, humidity control, and especially the brick-lined oven which gives enormous amounts of heat as well as forced steam which gives the texture and the crust of the French bread. We have a friend, a professional *boulanger,* who makes bread at home once in a while with results that are never as good as the bread he makes at his shop.

There are a few things to keep in mind when making bread. Use a hard wheat flour, high in gluten, which is the protein part of the flour and gives you the elasticity needed for the bread to develop (unbleached all-purpose flour is satisfactory). Keep in mind that the thick, crisp crust is usually caused both by forced steam and dough made only with water. Bread made with milk and with fat will have a soft crust. If a bread collapses, it is likely that it was not kneaded enough or that there was too much water in the dough. The smaller the amount of yeast used, the longer the rising time, and the larger the air bubbles in the bread. Some bakers add ascorbic acid (vitamin C) to the dough to make the air bubbles hold better and the bread stronger. Sugar, as well as a warm temperature helps the enzymes (the yeast) to develop better and faster. If the water or temperature is cold, the bread rises very slowly. Under a certain temperature, the enzymes won't develop any more. Salt is often added at the end of a recipe because it tends to prevent the development of the yeast. Fresh yeast usually comes in .6-ounce packages, and dry yeast comes in 7-gram (¼-ounce) packages. They can be used interchangeably. A *levain* or a dough starter can also be added to the dough to start the fermentation; this gives the dough a slightly nutty, sour taste. It is usually supplemented with yeast. The starter can be made by taking a piece of finished dough and keeping it in a jar with water. Refrigerated, it will keep there for a week to ten days. Through all the bread-making techniques that follow, we will use all-purpose, unbleached flour. To measure out the flour, scoop a cup directly from the flour bag. This produces a fairly tightly packed cup and 3 generous cups will amount to 1 pound of flour. The moisture in the flour varies from season to season. Humidity will be absorbed by the flour in the summer and water should be decreased in the recipe. Vice versa in winter. The following recipe makes a basic dough used to make large country breads as well as thin *baguettes* or small breads.

9 cups all-purpose, unbleached flour (about 3
  pounds)
3 envelopes yeast or 3 fresh yeast cakes (.6 ounce
  each)
3½ cups water at about 80 degrees
1 tablespoon salt

1. Mix the yeast and water together, and place two-thirds of the flour, about 6 cups, in the bowl of an electric mixer.

2. After 2 or 3 minutes, stir the water and yeast mixture again. Wait another 5 minutes until the water starts to bubble on top. Add the yeast mixture to the flour and using the dough hook, beat on medium for about 5 minutes. Add the salt and keep mixing for a few seconds.

3. Notice that the dough at this point is still quite soft. All the flour cannot be added to the mixture at first because the machine is not strong enough and would stop. However, working two-thirds of the flour with the water for 5 minutes allows us to still let the machine do the hardest part of the work. Add 2 more cups of the flour and keep beating on low speed for 1 minute.

4. Place the dough on the table and knead by hand with the rest of the flour. More or less flour will be needed, depending on weather, humidity, etc. Reserve at least ½ cup flour for the end. Work the dough by folding it with the palms of your hands.

5. Keep folding and pushing down to get some air in the dough and develop the gluten which gives the dough elasticity.

6. Keep pressing the dough and folding it for at least 7 to 8 minutes. Sprinkle it with flour if it is sticky and absorbent. The dough should be satiny and resilient.

7. To know if the dough has been sufficiently kneaded, place your hand flat on top and leave it on the dough for 5 seconds. Then, remove your hand; the dough should only stick slightly to your palm and spring back like rubber. It should be soft and shiny, already forming some small bubbles on top.

8. Sprinkle the dough with flour and place it in a large bowl to allow for expansion. Place the bowl in a plastic bag to prevent a skin from forming on the top and to retain moisture. Allow to raise for 2 hours in an 80- to 85-degree area. The dough will more than double in volume.

9. To make a starter, take a piece of dough and place it in a jar. Fill the jar with cold water and place in the refrigerator. When making dough, add the whole mixture to the flour at the beginning. Reduce your yeast by one-third and reduce the water so the dough won't be too soft.

10. After 2 hours, check the dough by plunging two fingers into it. If the depression made by your fingers remains, the dough has risen enough.

11. Knead the dough for a few seconds to knock down the air bubbles. You can now let the dough raise a second time or knead it for 1 to 2 minutes and divide it in whatever shapes you wish (see technique 207). See finished country bread, baguettes and "head of wheat" bread, page 552.

207. Baking Country Bread and Baguettes *(Pain de Campagne et Baguettes)*

1. To simulate as closely as possible a baker's oven lined with fire bricks, arrange clay tiles or fire bricks on a large cookie sheet which fits your oven. You may have to cut the tiles to fit the cookie sheet. Place the tile-covered tray in a preheated 425- to 450-degree oven. Place a can of water in the oven to generate steam.

2. Use the country bread dough (technique 206). Let the dough rise once or twice. If the dough has risen twice the bread will be a bit lighter, with larger air bubbles inside. Knead the dough on the table for 1 to 2 minutes to make it tighter and push out all the air bubbles.

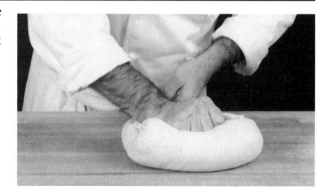

3. Using a dough scraper or a knife, cut the dough into the size you desire. If you want *baguettes,* cut long strips so you just have to pull them a bit, without having to do much more shaping after they've been cut. Each *baguette* should weigh approximately ¾ to 1 pound.

4. To mold the *baguette* use a flat piece of wood and a kitchen towel with wood sticks in between. This technique is similar to what is done in a professional kitchen, where long canvas is folded continuously and all the *baguettes* arranged in the pleats of the canvas.

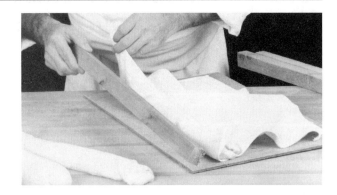

5. Once the *baguettes* are molded in the kitchen towel, let them raise in an 80-degree humid place (if possible) for about 1 hour. The dough can also be placed into special gutter-like bread molds.

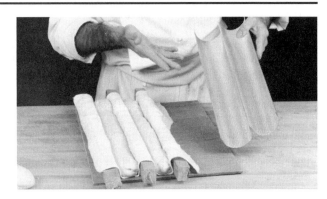

6. Let the *baguettes* raise until they have approximately doubled in volume (about an hour in a warm area). Wash the dough with a beaten egg or sprinkle with flour. Then mark with a knife and bake.

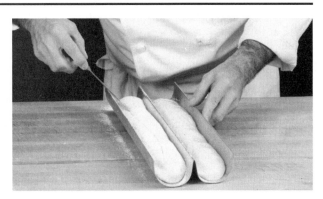

7. For the baguettes which have been molded with the towel, sprinkle a board with semolina, farina or any coarse-grain flour, then invert the baguette right on top of the coated surface. The bottom of the dough, which is the softer part, is now on top. Sprinkle the top with flour or wash with the egg wash.

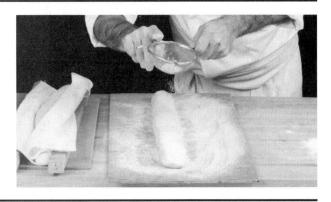

8. Then make long diagonal slashes along the top of the loaf with a razor blade. Note how the end of one slash and the beginning of the next correspond. They are on the same plane. Make approximately 5 slashes in each loaf.

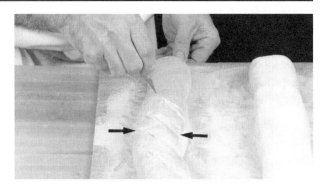

9. It requires practice to cut with a razor blade and the dough cakes and sticks. You may find it easier to use a long thin knife. Hold it on an angle and slide it gently on top of the dough until it cuts through.

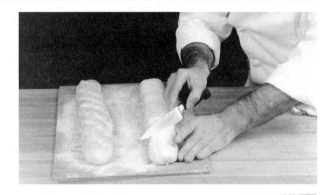

10. Slide the bread in one stroke onto the preheated tiles. It should be done directly in the oven but as it is difficult to photograph, we did it on the table. Sprinkle about ¼ cup water in the oven and close the door immediately. It creates steam along with the can of water already in the oven. Bake 30 minutes for the *baguettes* until nicely brown and hard. The bread should sound hollow when tapped.

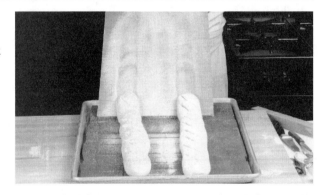

11. The metal-molded *baguettes* should be removed from the mold and cooled on a rack. Knock the *baguettes* with the handle of a knife. A hollow sound is an indication that they are well cooked. This *baguette* had only one long slit on top.

12. This bread was brushed with egg wash, slit across with the razor and cooked on the quarry tiles.

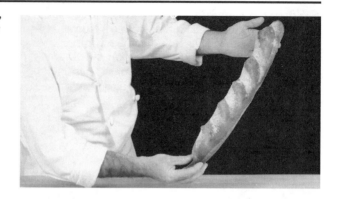

13. The *baguette* on the left was washed with the egg wash and cut diagonally with the knife. The one on the right was sprinkled with flour and cut in a crisscross pattern. Both were cooked on the tiles.

14. This large country bread was made with 1¾ pounds of dough and had risen 1½ hours. It was sprinkled with flour, cut in a crisscross pattern with a knife, cooked in a preheated 425-degree oven for 50 to 60 minutes and cooled on a rack. See finished country bread and baguettes, page 552.

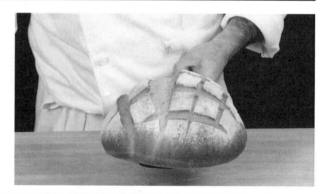

208. Milk Bread *(Petits Pains au Lait)*

YIELD: About 2 dozen 2½-ounce rolls

DOUGH MADE WITH MILK and butter will have a more tender crust and a slightly more delicate inside than the regular country bread. This type of dough is used to make individual "rolls" usually served for breakfast. The dough is started in the machine and finished by hand although it can be made entirely by hand.

2⅓ cups milk at about 90 degrees
2 packages dry yeast or 2 packages fresh yeast
6 cups all-purpose, unbleached flour
2 teaspoons salt
1 teaspoon sugar
½ stick (2 ounces) sweet butter, softened

1. Mix the milk, yeast and sugar together and let the mixture "work" for 20 minutes at room temperature. Meanwhile, place 4 cups of flour in the bowl of the mixer. Add the butter and salt. After about 10 minutes, stir the milk and yeast mixture. Let it rest another 10 minutes, then combine with the flour. Beat on medium speed for about 5 minutes.

2. Add another cup of flour to the bowl and mix to incorporate the flour. The dough should come out of the bowl soft but rubbery.

3. Place the dough on a board and work in more flour by hand, depending on the humidity and temperature. You may need all the flour or even a few tablespoons more or a few tablespoons less.

4. Knead for about 5 minutes, until the dough doesn't stick to your fingers. (It will be slightly softer and stickier than the country bread dough in technique 206).

5. Place the dough in a buttered bowl, turning the dough around so it is buttered on top. Cover with a towel and let raise in an 80-degree place for 1 hour.

6. To approximate the type of heat in a baker's oven, line a cookie sheet with quarry tiles and place them in the lower shelf of the oven preheated to 425 degrees. Set a tray of water between the lower shelf and the oven floor to generate humidity and steam. Cut the dough in about 2½-ounce pieces and roll in a ball with the palm of your hand, pushing out the air bubbles. Shape the rolls into rounds, ovals or any shape you fancy.

7. For the *épi* ("head of wheat"), shape about 1 pound of the dough into a long loaf about 2 inches in diameter. Butter a tray lightly, place the dough on top and cut with a pair of scissors. Divide the dough into wedges to simulate a blade of wheat. Alternate from one side of the dough to the other, without cutting completely through. Pull out each "wheat" so it forms a pointed head. Let the breads and *épi* raise for 45 minutes to 1 hour at room temperature. Brush with egg wash and place in a preheated 425-degree oven for 25 minutes for

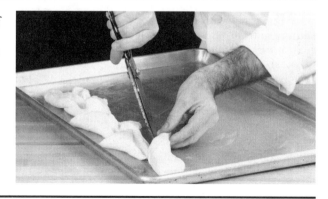

the small breads and 30 minutes for the *épi*.
Every so often check that there's water in
the oven, throwing in some water to produce steam during the first 10 to 15
minutes of cooking. See "head of wheat"
bread and small milk breads, page 552.

209. Pullman Bread *(Pain de Mie)*

YIELD: 1 16-inch loaf (4 inches wide by 4 inches high)

THE PULLMAN BREAD is often hollowed out and filled up with little sandwiches to serve at a buffet. Whereas sandwiches are usually trimmed on
four sides, and the trimmings used for bread crumbs, in this technique, the
whole loaf is trimmed of its crust and the crust becomes a receptacle. After
the party it can be transformed into bread crumbs. The dough for the pullman bread is softer than for the *petits pains au lait*.

6 cups all-purpose unbleached flour (2 pounds)
2 cups milk
1 cup hot water
1½ envelopes dry yeast
1 tablespoon sugar
1 tablespoon salt
1½ sticks (6 ounces) sweet butter, softened

1. Mix the water and milk (the temperature
should be about 95 degrees). Mix in the
sugar and yeast and stir until dissolved.
Place 5 cups of the flour into the bowl of an
electric mixer and add the yeast mixture.
Using the dough hook, place on medium
speed for 5 to 6 minutes. Then add the rest
of the flour, the salt and the butter. Mix
again on low speed for 2 minutes. The
dough will be sticky when you pull it off the
hook, but it will come of clean and spring
back as though it were rubber.

2. Butter a large bowl and place the dough in it. Turn the dough in the bowl to coat the top with a film of butter. Place the bowl in a large plastic bag and set it in an 80-degree oven or a warm area for 2 hours. The dough, when pushed in with your fingers, should hold the indentation, which is an indication that it has risen enough. Knock the dough down by kneading it a few seconds in the bowl.

3. Place in a buttered 16- by 4- by 4-inch mold or two smaller molds. Be sure to butter the mold well. The dough should come about one-third of the way up the mold. Let it raise again for 1 to 1½ hours, depending on the humidity, until the dough comes about three-quarters of the way up the mold. Brush with the egg wash (one whole egg, beaten).

4. A pullman bread mold has a special lid that slides in; or you can improvise a cover for the mold. Butter a cookie sheet, place on top of the bread and place a rock on top to hold it down. Place in a preheated 425-degree oven for 20 minutes, then remove the cookie sheet or the cover. By then the dough is set and will not rise further. Bake for another 40 minutes until the bread sounds hollow when tapped. If the top browns too much, top with a piece of aluminum foil to prevent further browning. Unmold the bread and cool on a rack.

5. Pictured here is the round country bread, crisscross cut on top (technique 207), and the long, cooked pullman bread. If the pullman bread is baked without a cover, it will be rounded on top.

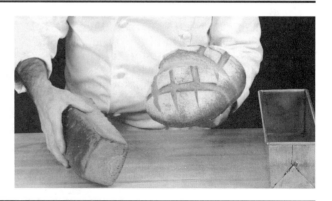

6. After cooling, cut off the top of the bread to form a lid. Using a small pointed knife, cut all around the bread, about ¼ inch from the edge, to loosen the inside. It is now holding only from the bottom.

7. Place the bread on its side. Insert the knife into the bread about ¼ inch from the bottom crust and pivot the blade back and forth to loosen a section of the bottom.

8. The object is to loosen the bottom of the bread without cutting the bottom crust off. Make a few incisions along the base of the loaf, jiggling the knife back and forth at each point of entry to eventually loosen the whole inside.

9. Remove the inside, which should come out easily. Notice that the bottom crust is attached to the sides, except for a few holes along the edge where the knife was inserted.

10. Slice the bread into ¼- to ⅜-inch slices. You should have approximately 40 slices. Make different varieties: sliced chicken with fresh herbs and mayonnaise; prosciutto with butter; anchovies fillets and butter; boiled ham and mustard; etc. Avoid fillings that could bleed on other sandwiches. Pack the sandwiches together, cover with the lid and place on the buffet table. The bread container can be dried and used as a basket. See finished pullman bread, page 552.

210. Provence-Style Pizza *(Pissaladière)*

The *pissaladière* is a French pizza that's usually made from a bread dough rolled very thin and covered with onions, garlic, anchovies, olives and olive oil. Other ingredients such as tomatoes, green peppers, tuna and cheese are used to vary the filling.

Dough for one large *pissaladière*

1 pound all-purpose flour (3 generous cups)
1¼ cups water, at about 80 to 90 degrees
2 ¼-ounce packages dry yeast or 2.6-ounce packages fresh yeast
2 tablespoons olive oil
1 teaspoon salt

Filling

3 tablespoons good olive oil
8 cups sliced onions, loosely packed
4 to 5 cloves garlic, peeled, crushed and chopped (1 tablespoon)
½ teaspoon salt
3 2-ounce cans anchovies in oil
Generous dozen Spanish or Greek oil-cured black olives

1. Mix the water and yeast and let rest at room temperature for ten minutes. Meanwhile, place two cups of flour in the bowl of an electric mixer. Add the salt and 2 tablespoons of olive oil and beat on medium speed with a dough hook for about 3 minutes. Then add the remaining flour. Mix to incorporate the the flour, then turn the dough out on a board and knead by hand for about 2 minutes until the dough is smooth and satiny. Oil a bowl, place the dough in it and turn over to coat with the oil all around. Cover with a towel and let

raise for 1 hour at room temperature, at about 75 to 80 degrees. The dough should double in volume. Check by making indentations with your fingers. If the holes remain, the dough has raised enough.

2. Make the filling. Heat the oil in a saucepan and add the onions. Cook on medium to high heat for about 10 minutes, until the onions are cooked and lightly brown. Add the garlic and salt. (It is a small amount of salt because the anchovies are salty.) Add the pepper. Spread the dough out by hand on the table or directly on the cookie sheet.

3. Oil a 16- by 12-inch cookie sheet or 2 round pans. Spread out the dough with your hands to enlarge and line the pans. The dough should be about ¼ inch thick all around.

4. Arrange the cooked onions on the dough and the anchovies in a crisscross pattern on top. Remove the pits from the olives, cut them in half, and position one in each anchovy diamond. Sprinkle the "pizza" with 1 tablespoon of olive oil and bake for 30 minutes in a preheated 425-degree oven.

5. Allow it to cool in the pan for at least 10 to 15 minutes. Brush again with olive oil before serving. It should be served at room temperature. See finished Provence-style pizza, page 552.

211. Crescent Rolls *(Croissants)*

YIELD: Approximately 16 small croissants

C ROISSANTS are the essence of the French breakfast. They are never eaten at other meals. The large twisted croissants bought in *cafés* in the morning are often made with a mixture of shortening and butter. The small straight croissants are usually made with only butter. For *pain au chocolat,* or chocolate rolls, strips of chocolate are rolled up in rectangular pieces (about 3 x 5 inches) of croissant dough and baked at the same temperature and for the same amount of time as the straight and crescent-shaped rolls. Croissant dough requires skill to make. It has some of the qualities of puff paste as well as of brioche. It acquires flakiness through the rolling and folding technique of puff paste, but it is also a yeast dough, which needs proofing before cooking. We made our croissants with all purpose flour (which is high-gluten, hard-wheat, elastic flour), because we found that using pastry flour (a soft wheat flour with less gluten) did not make much difference. Small croissants are about $1^{1}/_{4}$ to $1^{1}/_{2}$ ounces each; large croissants are about 3 ounces each. See technique 269 for puff paste before starting the croissant dough.

1 *pound all-purpose, unbleached flour (a good 3 cups tightly packed)*
2 *tablespoons extra flour to mix with the butter*
3 *sticks (12 ounces) sweet butter, softened*
1 *generous cup milk, at approximately 90 to 100 degrees*
1 *¼-ounce package dry yeast or a .6-ounce package fresh yeast*
1 *tablespoon sugar*
1½ *teaspoons salt*

1. Place the yeast, sugar and milk in a bowl. Mix well and let it work for about 5 to 10 minutes at room temperature. Meanwhile, place 2½ sticks (10 ounces) of the butter in the bowl of an electric mixer with the 2 tablespoons of flour and mix well with the flat beater for about 5 to 10 seconds, until you have a creamy, homogenized mixture.

2. Place the flour with the remaining 2 ounces of butter, salt and yeast-milk mixture in the bowl of an electric mixer and mix on low speed using the flat beater for about 10 seconds, until it forms a ball. Shape the dough into a rectangle.

3. Place on a floured board and roll the dough into a rectangle 20 inches long by 12 inches wide. Use extra flour to help in the rolling. With the palm of your hand or a spatula, spread the butter mixture from step 1 over two-thirds of the dough.

4. Leave about 1 inch along the edges of the dough unbuttered.

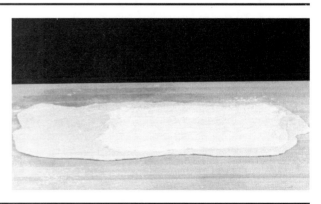

5. Lift the unbuttered third and fold on the buttered part.

6. Fold the remaining third over and press all around the edges.

7. Place the dough in a plastic bag and refrigerate for 2 hours or longer. The object is to get the dough and the butter well set and to the same temperature so it rolls out uniformly. On a floured board roll the dough into a 24- by 12-inch rectangle and give it a double turn (see technique 269). Roll the dough once again into a 24- by 12-inch rectangle and give it another double turn. Refrigerate the dough for 1 to 2 hours so it relaxes and becomes workable again (without refrigeration the dough becomes too elastic to roll). Then roll the dough into a 24- by 12-inch rectangle once again and give it a third double turn. Refrigerate for another 2 hours, at which point the dough can be cut into croissants or left refrigerated overnight.

8. If you refrigerate the dough overnight, it will still proof somehow despite the low temperature in the refrigerator. Flatten it with the palm of your hand. We reserved approximately one-quarter of the dough to make *petits pains au chocolat* in technique 269. Roll the remainder of the dough in a rectangle approximately 12 inches wide by 25 inches long. It should be quite thin.

9. Cut the rectangle in half lengthwise to make 2 strips, approximately 6 inches wide by 25 inches long. Cut into triangles about 5 inches at the base. Each triangle will weigh about 1¼ to 1½ ounces. If the dough gets rubbery at any time, just let it rest again in the refrigerator. Remember that cold temperature and time are allies.

10. Take each triangle and roll it to enlarge it both in width and length.

11. With the rolling pin, crush the point of the croissant so it sticks to the table. Starting at the base of the triangle, use both hands to roll the dough, spreading it as you roll to extend the croissant.

12. Wet the apex of the triangle with water. Keep rolling the dough on itself until you reach the apex which will stick.

13. Line a cookie sheet with parchment paper and arrange the croissants, bent into a crescent shape or straight, on top. Be sure that the point of the croissant is on top, curving inward toward the tray. Let proof in a moist 80- to 90-degree oven with a pilot light, or in a warm, humid place. In very dry weather, the dough tends to dry out and form a crust on top which prevents proofing. Make sure that the croissants proof in a humid area. If proofed in an oven, place a pot of warm water close by to create humidity. The croissants should proof a good hour.

14. Brush with a glaze (made of 1 egg plus 1 egg yolk beaten together) about 15 minutes before you put them in the oven, then brush once again just before you put them in. Bake in a preheated 425-degree oven for 15 to 18 minutes, until well browned and crisp. Let cool on the tray for at least 20 minutes before serving. See finished straight, crescent-shaped and chocolate-filled rolls, page 552.

212. Brie in Brioche Dough *(Brie en Brioche)*

YIELD: 12 to 14 servings

THE BRIE in brioche makes a nice presentation to be served at the end of a dinner. Serve the cheese in slices with its own brioche. In the photographs that follow, the decorations were made with regular pie dough. It stands out because it doesn't brown as much as the brioche dough during baking. Of course the decorations can be made with strips of brioche dough. You need a ripe, 2-pound brie and the brioche dough described in technique 213.

1. Spread out a piece of the brioche dough with your hands or roll it with a pin to about ½ to ¾ inch larger than the brie all around and about ¼ inch thick. Place on a cookie sheet lined with parchment paper. Place the brie on top. Fold the edges of the dough back onto the brie.

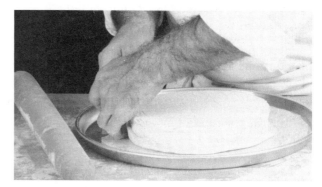

2. Roll out another piece of dough ¼ inch thick and 1 to 2 inches larger than the brie all around. Brush with egg wash (1 egg plus 1 egg yolk, beaten).

3. Cover the brie, egg-washed side down, and press the dough on the sides so it sticks to the bottom layer. Trim it all around.

4. Brush the dough with egg wash and decorate with little strips of pie dough, puff paste or brioche dough. Decorate to your fancy with strips to imitate flowers with borders, etc. Brush the decorations with the egg wash and let brie proof for about 20 minutes at room temperature.

5. Bake in a preheated 350-degree oven for 25 to 30 minutes until golden brown. Let the brie rest at room temperature for a couple of hours, otherwise the cheese will be too runny inside. If done several hours ahead, and the brioche is cold, place in a preheated 400-degree oven for 5 to 6 minutes, just to warm up the brioche without heating the cheese. Cut into slices and serve.

213. Brioche Dough *(Brioche Dough)*

BRIOCHES ARE THE SMALL, moist and buttery cakes eaten for breakfast throughout France. In parts of the country, like Lyon, this yeast-risen dough is used to encase sausage, goose liver, game and other pâtés. The brioche dough is not as difficult to make as *pâte feuilletée*. It is easiest to use a large mixer rather than beating by hand, but both methods give excellent results. The dough should be very satiny and elastic. A *brioche mousseline*, which is especially good, is a brioche dough loaded with butter. This recipe will make from 18 to 20 small brioches.

½ teaspoon sugar
¼ cup lukewarm water
1 (¼-ounce) package dry yeast, or ½ cake fresh yeast
2¼ cups all-purpose flour
4 large eggs
2 sticks (½ pound) sweet butter, at room temperature and cut into ½-inch pieces
½ teaspoon salt

In a bowl, mix the sugar, water and yeast until smooth. Set the mixture aside and let it "work" for 5 minutes (the yeast will make it foam or bubble). Place the remaining ingredients in the bowl of an electric mixer. Using the flat beater, start mixing on low, adding the yeast mixture slowly. When all the ingredients hold together, scrape the sides and bottom picking up any loose pieces. Place on medium speed and beat for 5 minutes. Scrape the sides and bottom twice more during the process so the ingredients are well blended. The dough should be elastic, velvety and hold into a lump around the beater. It should separate easily from the beater if pulled.

1. If you are making the dough by hand instead of by machine, make a well in the flour, add the mixture, eggs, butter and salt, and mix until it comes together. Work it for at least 10 minutes. Grab the dough on both sides,

2. lift it from the table and

3. flip it over, slapping it on the table. Repeat for 8 to 10 minutes.

4. It should come up in one lump from an unfloured table. Place the dough in a bowl, set in a draftless, lukewarm place, cover with a towel and let rise until it has doubled in bulk (about 1½ to 2 hours).

5. Break the dough down by pushing and lifting with your fingers. If you are not going to use the dough immediately, wrap it in a towel and plastic wrap and place it in the refrigerator (the cool meat drawer) to prevent the dough from developing too much. It can be made a day ahead.

6. To make small brioches, generously butter individual brioche molds. Divide the dough into balls the size of a golf ball (about 2½ to 3 ounces) and roll on the table in a circular motion to give body to the brioche.

7. With the side of your hand, "saw" a small piece of the brioche in a back and forward motion.

8. This forms a small lump which should remain attached to the body of the brioche.

9. Lift the brioche by the "head" and place in the buttered mold.

10. Push the head down into the brioche.

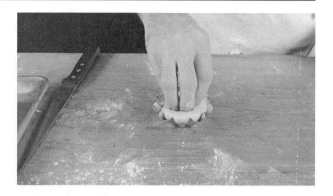

11. Brush with an egg wash (1 whole egg, beaten).

12. A large brioche (*brioche parisienne*) is done similarly, but slits are cut all around to give texture to the finished brioche.

13. Let the brioches rise in a warm place for 1½ to 2 hours.

14. Bake the small brioches in a 400-degree preheated oven for approximately 25 minutes, and the large ones for approximately 45 minutes. They should be golden. Keep in a plastic bag to avoid drying out.

Photo: Tom Hopkins

"Knowledge of the basics is so rewarding, in that it allows you to try out new ideas, to remedy potentially catastrophic miscalculations, and to tackle any kind of recipe because you will comprehend the mechanics behind it." —Jacques Pépin

Pastry and Dessert

214. English Custard Cream *(Crème Anglaise)*

CRÈME ANGLAISE is a basic and essential cream. It is served with innumerable desserts, flavored in different ways. With the addition of sweet butter, it can become a fine butter cream *(crème au beurre);* and with the addition of whipped cream and chocolate it can become a chocolate mousse; frozen it becomes ice cream. It is the base of such desserts as *bavarois,* charlotte and the like. The recipe below will yield 1 quart of *crème anglaise*.

3 *cups milk*
8 *egg yolks*
1 *cup sugar*
1 *teaspoon pure vanilla extract*
½ *cup cold milk or cream*

1. Bring the 3 cups milk to a boil. Set aside. Place the yolks, sugar and vanilla in a bowl and beat with a wire whisk for 3 to 4 minutes until it forms a "ribbon." The mixture should be pale yellow in color, and when lifted with the whisk, it should fall back into the bowl like a ribbon folded on itself. When the ribbon is "stretched," it should not break.

2. Combine the hot milk and the yolk mixture in a saucepan. Cook for a few minutes on medium heat, stirring with a wooden spatula, until the mixture coats the spatula. Test by sliding your finger across the cream; the mark should remain for a few seconds. Do not over cook or the eggs will scramble. As soon as it reaches the right consistency, add the cold milk. Strain through a fine sieve into a cold bowl. Cool, stirring once and a while. Refrigerate until ready to serve.

215. Vanilla Pastry Cream *(Crème Pâtissière)*

CRÈME PÂTISSIÈRE is a versatile and important basic cream. It can be used as a filling for éclairs, cream puffs, cakes and napoléons, or as a base for sweet soufflés. It can be made richer by replacing some of the milk with heavy cream. It can be varied with the addition of whipped cream, or flavored with chocolate, coffee, liqueurs and the like. With the addition of fresh sweet butter, it becomes a "lean" butter cream *(crème au beurre)*.

2 *cups milk*
6 *egg yolks*
⅔ *cup sugar*
1 *teaspoon pure vanilla extract*
½ *cup flour*

Bring the milk to a boil. Set aside. Place the yolks, sugar and vanilla in a bowl and work with a wire whisk until it forms a "ribbon" (see step 1 in the preceding technique); this should take 3 to 4 minutes. Add the flour and mix well.

1. Add half of the hot milk to the yolk mixture and mix well.

2. Pour the yolk mixture into the remaining milk, mixing as you go along.

3. Bring to a boil on medium heat, stirring constantly with the whisk. The sauce will thicken as soon as it reaches the boiling point. Reduce heat and cook for 2 to 3 minutes, stirring constantly to avoid scorching.

216. Praline Cream *(Crème Pralinée)*

CRÈME PRALINÉE is *crème pâtissière* with the addition of a powdered almond and sugar mixture. It is used as a filler for desserts like *Paris-Brest*, technique 267.

1. To make the *nougatine* (the cooked almond and sugar mixture), place 1 cup confectioners' sugar and ½ cup almonds in a heavy saucepan. Stir with a wooden spoon. Place on medium heat and cook, stirring constantly, until the sugar starts to melt. Since there is no liquid in the mixture, it will take a few minutes. However, as soon as it melts, it will turn rapidly into caramel. This method produces a very hard and tight caramel.

2. As soon as it turns into caramel, pour the mixture onto an oiled marble or an oiled tray. When cold, break into pieces and blend into powder in a food processor or blender.

3. Fold the mixture into the *crème pâtissière*, technique 60.

217. Snow Eggs with Custard Sauce
(Oeufs à la Neige)

1. To make tender floating islands, the egg whites should be poached in water that doesn't exceed a temperature of 170 degrees. Beat 6 egg whites with a dash of salt in the electric mixer or by hand. When the egg whites are firm, add ¾ cup sugar and continue beating for 30 seconds. Stop the beating and fold in another ¼ cup sugar (see technique 219, step 1).

2. Using an ice-cream scoop, dish the whites out. Round the top of the scoop with your finger to get an "egg" as round as possible.

3. Drop the eggs into the hot (170 degrees) water.

4. Poach for 2 minutes on one side, then turn the eggs on the other side and poach for another 2 minutes; then lift the eggs onto a paper-lined tray. Prepare a *crème anglaise*, technique 214, let it cool and place in the bottom of a oval or round dish. Arrange the cold eggs on top of the cream.

5. Mix ¼ cup sugar with ¼ cup corn syrup. Cook until it turns into caramel. Let cool for a few minutes so the mixture thickens. Using a fork, drip the hot caramel over the eggs. The threads should be scattered all over the eggs. Do not refrigerate but keep in a cool place until serving time. Serve cool. See finished dish, below.

This recipe serve 8 to 10.

Chocolate meringue nut cake, snow eggs with custard sauce

218. Floating Island *(Ile Flottante)*

YIELD: 8 to 10 servings

THE FLOATING ISLAND is a type of cold soufflé cooked for a short time in a *bain-marie* at a low temperature, unmolded and served with a sauce. The mixture is the same as for *oeufs à la neige* (pages 586-587). Butter and sugar heavily a 1-quart charlotte mold. Set aside until ready to use.

Soufflé mixture

5 *egg whites*
½ *cup sugar*
⅓ *cup slivered almonds, roasted, plus extra for decoration*
½ *teaspoon vanilla extract*

Coffee cream

1 *cup milk*
½ *cup coffee extract (these are the first drops from a drip coffee maker) or*
1 *tablespoon instant coffee and boiling water to make ½ cup*
4 *egg yolks*
⅓ *cup sugar*
1 *cup heavy cream*

---

1. Beat the egg whites with a whisk until stiff but not dry and grainy and add the sugar. Keep beating for another 15 to 20 seconds. Fold in the almonds and vanilla extract.

2. Pour the mixture into the mold. It should fill the mold. Smooth the top with a spatula, butter a piece of parchment paper and cover the top of the mold. Place in a saucepan with tepid water around. The water should reach one-half to three-quarters of the way up the mold. Place in a preheated 325-degree oven for 15 minutes. The mixture will only rise slightly higher than the rim of the mold. Allow to cool at room temperature. It will deflate to the height of the mold.

3. To make the sauce, bring the milk and coffee to a boil. Meanwhile, work the egg yolks and sugar with the whisk until they form a ribbon, about 1 minute. Add the egg yolk mixture to the milk and place back on the stove. Cook, stirring until it reaches about 170 degrees (see step 3, technique 255). Place the cream in a bowl. As soon as the custard reaches the right temperature, strain it at once through a sieve into the cream and stir. This will cool the custard and prevent it from curdling. Unmold the floating island.

4. Blot up any liquid that leaks out so it won't thin the sauce down. Put some of the mocha cream around and serve the rest on the side. Decorate with little pieces of slivered almonds. See finished floating island, page 789.

219. Meringue

THIS BASIC EGG WHITE and sugar mixture is employed in different ways to produce innumerable desserts. It can be dried and called meringue; it can be poached and called *oeufs à la neige,* technique 217; it can be piped into a shell and called *vacherin;* it can be mixed with nuts and called a *dacquoise;* it can be used to make cookies like ladyfingers and as a base for an *omelette soufflée.* I begin here with the simple dried meringue "cookies" and proceed in the next few techniques through the more elaborate meringue confections.

1. For the whites of 6 large eggs, use 1½ cups superfine sugar. Whip the whites by hand or machine, adding a small dash of salt or a few drops of lemon juice before you start to whip. Whip on medium to high speed. When the whites are holding a nice shape, gradually add 1 cup of the sugar and keep beating for 1 minute. The mixture should be stiff and shiny. Fold in the remaining ½ cup sugar, technique 60. Folding in a part of the sugar at the end makes for a tender meringue.

2. Coat a cookie sheet with butter and flour, technique 61. Fill up a pastry bag, technique 62, and pipe out plain and fluted meringues. Lift the tip of the bag in a quick, swift motion to avoid a long tail (see technique 224, step 4).

3. Dip your fingers in cold water and push the tails down. Bake for 1¾ hours in a 180- to 190-degree preheated oven. (In restaurants, the meringues are often dried in a plate warmer at about 135 degrees for 24 hours.) They should be well dried. Though some people insist that meringues should be absolutely white, I fail to see the reason and do not mind if they become slightly beige during baking. Stored dry in a covered container, meringues will keep for months.

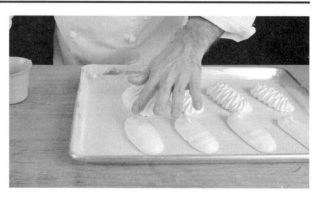

4. Meringues can be served on top of ice cream, with chestnut puree, puree of fruits, or plain whipped cream. Place some whipped cream on the flat side of one fluted meringue and

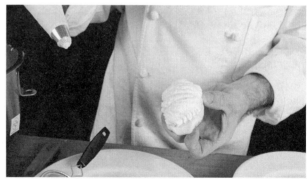

5. place another meringue against the cream. Place the double meringue on its side and decorate the top with more whipped cream.

6. Add grated chocolate.

7. To dress up plain meringues sprinkle with bitter cocoa and place two together with whipped cream in between.

8. Decorate the top with whipped cream and sliced almonds. See finished meringues with whipped cream and chocolate, page 598.

220. Meringue Mushrooms
(Champignons en Meringue)

THESE LITTLE MUSHROOMS made out of meringue are very decorative. They are occasionally served by themselves as finger food for cocktail parties or buffets. Most often they are used to decorate large cakes such as a *bûche de Noël*. Make the basic meringue mixture following the instructions in the preceding technique. Coat a cookie sheet with butter and flour, technique 61.

1. Fill up a pastry bag, technique 62, with the meringue, using a small plain tube. Squeeze some rounded small meringues and some pointed ones to be used for the "stems" of the "mushrooms." Make them pointed by pulling the meringue mixture up after some of it has been squeezed out of the bag.

2. Flatten the "tails" of the "caps" using a little cold water on your fingers. Bake in a 180- to 190-degree preheated oven for 75 minutes. Let cool for 15 minutes. (The small *vacherin* pictured in the background are described in the next technique.)

3. Holding the cap of the mushroom in one hand, dig a small opening on the flat side with the point of a knife.

4. Using a paper cornet, technique 66, fill the opening with meringue mixture and

5. stick a stem into place. Bake in a 180- to 190-degree preheated oven for 45 minutes.

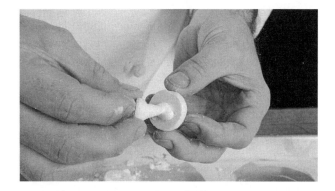

6. You should have perfect little mushrooms.

7. You can sprinkle them with bitter cocoa before using them for decoration. See finished meringue mushrooms, page 614a.

221. Small Meringue Shells *(Petit Vacherin)*

PETIT VACHERIN are the small shells made of meringue that are customarily filled with ice cream, chestnut purée, flavored whipped cream and the like. Make the basic meringue mixture following the instructions in technique 219. Coat a cookie sheet with butter and flour, technique 61.

1. Fit a pastry bag with a fluted tube and fill with the meringue mixture, technique 41. Form small *vacherin* by squeezing out the bottom and piping a circle on the outside to make a "nest."

2. Bake in a 180- to 190-degree preheated oven for 1¾ hours and let cool. Fill with a scoop of ice cream and cover with a peach half. Coat with melba or raspberry sauce.

3. Decorate the top with sliced almonds and whipped cream. Serve immediately. See small meringue shell melba, page 598.

222. Large Meringue Shells *(Vacherin)*

A LARGE VACHERIN makes an impressive dessert for a party. It is not as complicated as it seems, and most of the work can be done ahead of time with little last-minute preparation. Prepare the basic meringue mixture, technique 219. You need 1½ times the amount given which means you'll be working with 9 egg whites instead of 6.

1. Coat several large cookie sheets with butter and flour, technique 61, and make outlines with a flan ring or any round object about 10 to 11 inches in diameter.

2. Place some meringue mixture in a pastry bag fitted with a plain tube, technique 62. Fill in one of the outlines to make a solid base.

3. Make plain rings on the other trays,

4. or double rings if you want to go a bit faster. You will need 6 single rings or 3 double ones. Bake the base and rings in a 180- to 190-degree preheated oven for 1¾ hours. Let cool in the oven for 15 minutes. Keep in a dry place.

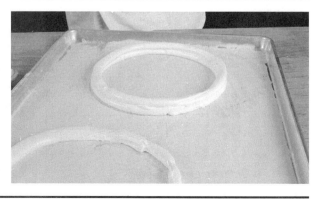

5. Using a paper cornet, technique 66, place dots of meringue mixture on the baked base.

6. Place a baked ring on top and keep building the vacherin with rings 'cemented" with the meringue mixture.

7. Continue until all the rings have been used.

8. Using a metal spatula, coat the outside of the rings with meringue, filling up holes and making it smooth all around.

9. Decorate the top and bottom with a border of meringue.

10. Make strips, or any other motif which suits your fancy, all around the *vacherin*.

11. Embed small pieces of candied violets in the meringue. Return to a 180- to 190-degree preheated oven and bake for 1 hour. Cool in a dry place.

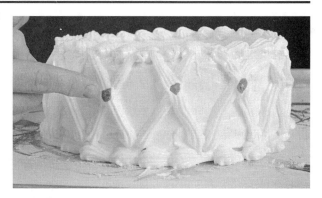

12. At serving time, fill the *vacherin* with slightly softened ice cream. Arrange strained peach or apricot halves on top of the ice cream and cover the fruit with a thick melba or rasberry sauce. Decorate with whipped cream and candied violets. See finished large meringue shell melba, page 598.

Clockwise from the right: large meringue shell melba, small meringue shell melba, small meringues with whipped cream and chocolate

223. Chocolate Meringue Nut Cake

(Dacquoise au Chocolat)

T
HE DACQUOISE mixture is akin to meringue but it is made with the addition of nuts and cornstarch, and it is cooked at a much higher temperature than a meringue. The cake is comprised of two flat disks filled with a chocolate butter cream and a rum-flavored whipped cream. The disks should be dry and brittle like a meringue.

¾ *cup sugar*
1¼ *cups nuts (half almond, half filbert), browned in the oven and ground*
1 *tablespoon cornstarch*
6 *egg whites*
Dash of salt
Chocolate butter cream (technique 228)
1½ *cups heavy cream*
2 *tablespoons confectioners' sugar*
1 *tablespoon dark rum*

1. Coat two cookie sheets with butter and flour, technique 61. Mark the coating with 10-inch rings (see technique 222, step 1).

2. Mix together the sugar, nuts and cornstarch. Whip the whites by machine or hand adding a small dash of salt before you begin. Beat until firm. Fold in the sugar and nut mixture, technique 60. Work fast to keep the whites from becoming grainy.

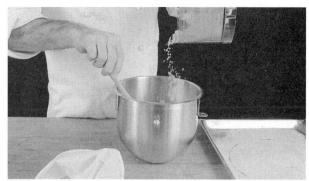

3. Fill a pastry bag fitted with a plain tube, technique 62, with the meringue mixture. Pipe a ring on each tray, following the outline of the 10-inch ring.

4. Divide the remaining meringue mixture between the two rings.

5. Spread evenly with a spatula.

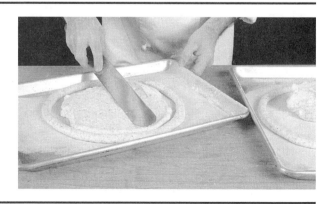

6. The disks should be the same thickness all over. Bake in a 350-degree preheated oven for 20 to 25 minutes, or until nicely browned.

7. Let the disks set for a few minutes, then slide off the tray to a wire rack.

8. After a half hour or so, the meringue should be dry and brittle.

9. Trim the edges to have perfect wheels. Save the trimmings.

10. Make a chocolate butter cream, technique 228. Place one wheel on a serving platter and, using a pastry bag fitted with a fluted tube, pipe a border all around the wheel.

11. Place a small amount of the butter cream in the middle of the wheel and sprinkle with the trimmings of the cake.

12. Combine the cream, confectioners' sugar and rum. Whip until firm. Arrange the cream in the middle of the wheel.

13. Place the other wheel, smooth side up, on top.

14. Sprinkle with confectioners' sugar, coating the entire top.

15. Decorate the edges and the middle with the chocolate butter cream.

16. Cake ready to be served. Place in the refrigerator and serve cold, a small wedge per person. Use a serrated knife to cut the cake. See finished chocolate meringue nut cake, page 587.

This recipe serves 8 to 10.

224. Ladyfingers *(Biscuits à la Cuillère)*

IN FRANCE, ladyfingers are traditionally served as a cookie with champagne. They are also used to line molds, such as for a charlotte, technique 285, or in an *omelette soufflée*, technique 225. The following recipe will make 20 to 25 ladyfingers. The raw ingredients should be at room temperature.

3 large eggs
½ cup superfine sugar
½ teaspoon pure vanilla extract
⅔ cup all-purpose flour
Confectioners' sugar

1. Separate eggs, technique 25, and beat the egg whites by machine or by hand. When beating egg whites, be sure the bowl is clean and that there is no egg yolk mixed with the white. If you are not using a copper bowl, a dash of salt or cream of tartar or a few drops of lemon juice can be added to the whites to help the whipping process.

2. When the whites are firm, add the superfine sugar and continue beating for about 1 minute. Using a spatula, fold the vanilla, then the egg yolks into the meringue, technique 60.

3. Sieve the flour on top of the mixture, folding it in as you go along.

4. Coat two cookie sheets with butter and flour, technique 61. Fit a pastry bag with a plain tube, and fill with the mixture, technique 62. Pipe the ladyfingers onto the sheets. They should be approximately 4 inches long by 1 inch wide. Lift up the tip of the bag in a swift stroke against the end of the ladyfinger to avoid a long tail.

5. To make tear-shaped cookies, squeeze some mixture out of the bag; then, stop squeezing the bag and "pull" the mixture to a pointed tail.

6. Sprinkle the ladyfingers heavily with confectioners' sugar. They should be sprinkled twice. Let them absorb the sugar for 5 minutes between sprinklings.

7. Turn the filled sheet upside down and give it a little bang with a knife to make the excess sugar fall on the table. This operation should be done rapidly and swiftly. If the mixture is the right consistency, the ladyfingers will not change shape at all. Bake in a 325-degree preheated oven for 12 to 15 minutes. Let cool for 15 minutes. They should slide easily from the sheet. The color should be pale beige. To avoid drying, stick one against the other and store in a covered container

225. Soufflé Omelet (Omelette Soufflée)

T HE OMELETTE SOUFFLÉE is closer to a soufflé than an omelet. It is lighter than a regular soufflé because it is not made with a starch base (a *béchamel* or *crème pâtissière*). It can be put together quickly and easily but it cannot be prepared in advance as regular soufflés can. It will also deflate faster than a regular soufflé. To bake an *omelette soufflée*, you need an ovenproof platter—silver, stainless steel or porcelain—at least 16 × 12 inches. The same mixture can be used in a baked Alaska (*omelette surprise* in French). It is much finer than the boiled frosting normally used. This recipe will serve 10.

8 *egg whites*
1 *cup superfine sugar*
6 *egg yolks*
8 *to* 10 *ladyfingers, technique 224, or the same amount of* génoise, *technique 226*
⅓ *cup Grand Marnier, cognac or kirsch*
1 *tablespoon confectioners' sugar*

Coat the platter generously with butter and sugar, technique 61. Beat the egg whites until they hold a soft peak. Reduce the speed and add the sugar in a steady stream. Return to high speed for 1 minute. Beat the yolks lightly with a fork and fold into the whites, technique 60.

1. Spread about one-fourth of the mixture in the center of the platter.

2. Arrange the ladyfingers or sponge cake on top and moisten with the liqueur or brandy.

3. Cover with more mixture.

4. Smooth with a spatula.

5. Be sure that the ladyfingers are equally covered all over.

6. Fit a pastry bag with a fluted tube and fill with the remaining mixture, technique 62. Pipe out a decorative border around the edge.

7. Decorate the top and sides to your fancy.

8. Sprinkle with confectioners' sugar and bake in a 425-degree preheated oven for 10 to 12 minutes, or until well glazed.

9. Baked *omelette soufflée.* You may sprinkle it with more confectioners' sugar when it comes out of the oven. Serve immediately.

226. Basic Sponge Cake (Génoise)

THE GÉNOISE—a basic sponge cake—is the base of countless cakes. It is also used for *croûtes aux fruits,* petits fours glacés and to line molds. The batter can be made with an electric mixer, as shown in the photographs that illustrate this technique, as well as by hand. The recipe makes two 8-inch cakes. The flour is sifted into the batter rather than folded in, because if poorly incorporated the cake will be grayish and heavy and will have lumps. The melted butter, added at the end, is very heavy and brings the mixture down. To correct this problem, "overwork" the batter slightly. If the butter is omitted or reduced (many cooks use none or only a tiny amount of butter), the mixture should not be whipped more than 5 to 6 minutes. If it is beaten too much, the cake will run over and go up and down like a soufflé, and the result will be a flat and crumbly cake.

6 *large eggs, at room temperature*
¾ *cup sugar*
½ *teaspoon pure vanilla extract*
1 *cup flour (use all-purpose, or* ⅔ *cup all-*
   purpose and ⅓ *cup cake flour)*
¾ *stick (6 tablespoons) sweet butter, melted*

1. Butter and flour two 8- by 1½-inch cake pans, technique 61. Place the eggs, sugar and vanilla in the bowl of the electric mixer. Mix well to combine the ingredients and stir over boiling water, or the burner, for about 30 seconds, so that the mixture is barely lukewarm. Place on medium to high speed and beat for 10 minutes. The mixture should make a thick ribbon. It should be pale yellow, and it should have at least tripled in volume.

2. Using a wide spatula, fold the mixture with one hand, technique 60, and sift in the flour with the other.

3. Add the butter, using the same procedure.

4. Fill the prepared cake pans about three-fourths full. Place pans on a cookie sheet and bake in a 350-degree preheated oven for 22 to 25 minutes.

5. Remove from the oven and, after 5 minutes, turn

6. upside down on racks.

7. The bottom and sides should be pale golden in color. The cakes should be flat (no sagging) and soft and springy to the touch. When cool, place the cakes in plastic bags to keep them from drying. They will keep for a few days without refrigeration.

227. Rolled Cake *(Biscuit Roulé)*

THIS BATTER IS FOR CAKES such as jelly rolls and the like. It is essentially the same as the *génoise* described in the preceding technique with the addition of an egg yolk. The egg yolk makes the cake moist and easier to roll. (*Biscuit roulé* is used to make *bûche de Noël, technique 228.*)

3 *large eggs, at room temperature*
1 *egg yolk*
½ *cup sugar*
¼ *teaspoon pure vanilla extract*
½ *cup all-purpose flour*
¼ *stick (2 tablespoons) butter, melted*

Place the eggs, egg yolk, sugar and vanilla in a mixing bowl and let the mixture get lukewarm by placing the bowl over boiling water for a few seconds. Remove from the heat and beat on medium to high speed for 5 to 6 minutes. Add the flour, then butter (see steps 2 and 3 in the preceding technique).

1. Butter lightly, in 2 or 3 spots, a 16-×-12-inch cookie sheet and line with a piece of parchment or wax paper. (The butter anchors the paper to the tray.) Butter and flour the paper, technique 61. Spread the mixture evenly in the tray and bake in a 330-degree preheated oven for 11 to 13 minutes.

2. Let the cake set for 5 minutes. Place a piece of wax paper on the table and turn the cake upside down on top of it. Remove the paper which covered the bottom of the cake and loosely place it back on the cake.

3. Let the cake cool to barely lukewarm; then, roll between the two sheets of paper.

4. Fold both ends to enclose the cake and keep refrigerated or in a plastic bag until you are ready to use.

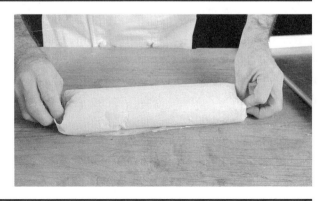

228. Christmas Yule Log *(Bûche de Noël)*

Yᴇᴀʀs ᴀɢᴏ ɪɴ Fʀᴀɴᴄᴇ, it was custom to keep a log burning throughout the Christmas supper. This log was the inspiration for the *bûche de Noël*, the traditional French Christmas holiday cake.

Biscuit roulé, *technique 227*
3 *tablespoons lukewarm water*
1 *tablespoon dark rum*
1 *teaspoon sugar*
1 *cup* crème pâtissière, *technique 215*
1 *cup heavy cream*

Make the *biscuit roulé* and set aside until ready to use. Mix the lukewarm water, rum and sugar together to make a syrup. Set aside. Whip the cream until stiff and combine with the *crème pâtissière*. Set aside. Make the chocolate butter cream.

CHOCOLATE BUTTER CREAM

3 *ounces chocolate (1 semisweet, 2 bitter)*
⅓ *cup sugar*
¼ *cup water*
3 *egg yolks*
2 *sticks (½ pound) sweet butter, softened*
2 *to 3 drops green food coloring*

Melt the chocolate in a small bowl (see Note, technique 247). Mix the sugar and water in a saucepan. Bring to a boil, and boil for 2 minutes over medium heat.

    Meanwhile, place the egg yolks in the bowl of an electric mixer. Pour the sugar syrup on top of the yolks, mixing at medium speed. Put on high speed and keep beating for 5 minutes until the mixture is thick and pale yellow. Add the butter bit by bit, mixing at medium to low speed until the cream is smooth. Take 1 tablespoon of the butter cream, mix in 2 or 3 drops of green food coloring and set aside. Take 2 tablespoons of the butter cream and set aside. Now, add the melted chocolate to the remaining butter cream and beat until smooth. Set aside.

1. Unroll the *biscuit roulé*. Remove the wax paper on top. Sprinkle with rum syrup. Spread the *crème pâtissière* mixture on top.

2. Roll the cake up, removing the bottom sheet of wax paper as you go along. Place on a serving board or a platter.

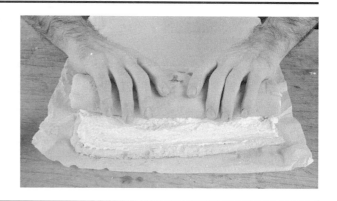

3. Trim one end of the cake.

4. With the trimmings, form a little stump on top of the log.

5. With a spatula, spread the chocolate butter cream all over the log. Spread the reserved white butter cream over both ends and on top of the stump.

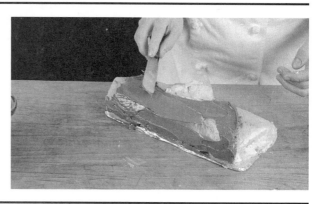

6. Pull the tines of a fork down the full length of the roll to simulate bark.

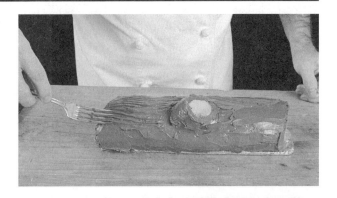

7. You can use a bit of the chocolate cream to decorate the cut stump and the ends of the cake to imitate the veins in the wood. Use a paper cornet, technique 66.

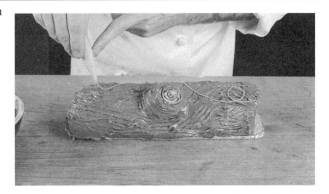

8. Place the reserved green butter cream in another paper cornet. Cut a straight end and make a thin, long strip to simulate an ivy vine.

9. Cut the tip of the same cornet on both sides (see technique 66, steps 12 and 13) and pipe small leaves along the vine. Refrigerate until serving time, then decorate with meringue mushrooms, technique 220. See finished Christmas Yule log, page 614a.

Christmas Yule log, tarte Tatin

Multilayered mocha cake, Kirsch flavored cake

614a

229. Christmas Log With Chocolate Bark *(Bûche de Noël au Chocolat)*

YIELD: 8 to 10 servings

T HE CHRISTMAS OR YULE LOG is usually made with a butter cream and a *génoise* batter. This version is made with a soufflé-like batter, rolled, filled with a coffee cream and covered with a light *ganache*. Read the introduction to technique 290 for more information about beating egg whites.

Cake

½ cup sugar
⅓ cup strong coffee
6 large eggs, separated
6 ounces bittersweet chocolate, melted

Filling

1 tablespoon freeze-dried coffee
3 tablespoons boiling water
1 envelope unflavored gelatin
2 cups heavy cream
2 tablespoons sugar

Ganache

3 ounces bittersweet chocolate, melted
½ cup heavy cream
1 teaspoon dark rum
1 tablespoon unsweetened cocoa powder to sprinkle on top

Chocolate bark (technique 230)

1. To make the cake batter, bring the sugar and coffee to a boil and boil gently for 1½ to 2 minutes. Place the yolks in the bowl of an electric mixer and add the sugar syrup to it. Beat on high speed for 5 to 6 minutes. It should about triple in volume and become very fluffy and light. Add the bittersweet chocolate. Beat the egg whites until firm, and, using a whisk, stir half the whites into the chocolate mixture. Fold in the remaining whites, using a large rubber spatula. Work fast or the whites will break down and become grainy.

2. Cut a piece of parchment or wax paper large enough to line a 12- by 16-inch cake pan. Spread butter on the cookie sheet so the paper will stick to the pan. Then butter and flour the paper.

3. Pour mixture on top of the paper, trying not to work it too much so it won't deflate. Spread to about ½ inch thick. Bake in a preheated 375-degree oven for about 15 minutes. Cool at room temperature.

4. Place a piece of parchment paper on the table and invert the cake on it.

5. Remove the paper from the back of the cake, then place it back loosely. Roll the cake between the two sheets of paper. Refrigerate until ready to use. It will keep for a few days.

6. Prepare the filling. Combine the instant coffee with the boiling water and sprinkle the gelatin on top. Mix the cream and sugar together and whip until the cream holds a peak but is still soft. When the gelatin has been absorbed by the water (about 1 minute), mix in until smooth. Quickly pour the gelatin mixture into the whipped cream and whisk fast until well combined. The cream will harden almost immediately.

7. The cream stiffened and holding a peak well.

8. Unroll the cake and remove the top layer of paper. Spread with a ½-inch layer of cream.

9. Use the bottom paper to help roll the cake. Don't press down on the cake too much or the cream will seep out. Continue rolling.

10. When the cake is rolled, the seam should be underneath.

11. Make the *ganache*. Combine the cream with the melted chocolate and the rum and beat the mixture with a whisk until it holds a peak, about ½ minute. Do not overbeat or the mixture will get too hard and grainy.

12. Spread the *ganache* ¹/₁₆ inch thick all around the yule and, using large spatulas or the bottom of a removable-bottom cake pan, lift up the yule and place it on a board covered with a towel or on a platter.

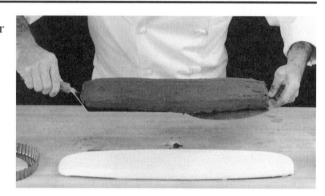

13. Sprinkle the top with the cocoa powder.

14. Place the bark around the cake. If the chocolate is too stiff to fold, warm with your hands to soften. Then remove the paper.

15. Place another length of bark on the other side, folding the ends so the cake is wrapped all around. Cut more bark into pieces and decorate to look like a log. Refrigerate until ready to serve. See finished Christmas log with chocolate bark, page 772.

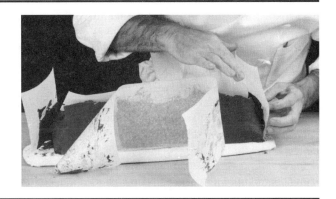

230. Chocolate Bark *(Écorce en Chocolat)*

WHEN YOU BUY chocolate to make leaves, bark, curls or any other decoration, get the best available. Good-quality chocolate is usually higher in butter fat content (cocoa butter), which makes it more elastic and therefore easier to work with and help it remain shiny. We use a bittersweet chocolate for all the chocolate techniques. Sweeter chocolate can be used if you prefer.

1. Melt approximately 1 pound of chocolate in a double boiler, or place it in a gas oven with the pilot light on and leave it overnight so it melts very slowly. Be careful when melting chocolate not to heat it too much or it will lose its shine. Be careful when melting chocolate on direct heat because it scorches easily. Lay out a length of parchment paper and pour the chocolate on it in two long lines.

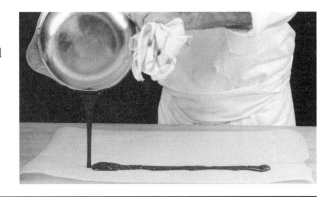

2. Spread out the chocolate with a spatula. If you are decorating a Christmas log (technique 228), make the strips about $1/16$ inch thick. One edge of the chocolate strip should be pegged with curves and dents to imitate broken tree bark. Let set and harden in a cool place or refrigerate.

3. Lift the chocolate from the paper by sliding a spatula underneath or transfer directly onto the yule log while still attached to the paper and then remove the paper. Remember that if the strips are not wide or long enough, or if the shape is not attractive enough, the chocolate can always be re-melted and used again. The strips can be prepared ahead and kept refrigerated.

231. Multilayered Mocha Cake (Gâteau Moka)

To make this six-layer mocha cake, bake 2 *génoises*, technique 226, a few hours in advance or the day before so the cake is set and will not crumble when sliced. In addition to the cake, you need melted apricot jam, a rum syrup and a coffee-flavored butter cream.

APRICOT JAM

Empty a 10-ounce jar apricot jam into a heavy saucepan. Melt slowly over low heat to avoid scorching. When liquefied, strain through a metal sieve and reserve.

RUM SYRUP

1 *cup strong coffee, lukewarm*
3 *tablespoons sugar*
2 *tablespoons dark rum*

Mix together and reserve.

COFFEE BUTTER CREAM

½ *cup sugar*
½ *cup very strong espresso coffee*
3 *egg yolks*
2 *sticks (½ pound) sweet butter, softened*

Combine the sugar and coffee in a saucepan, bring to a boil and boil for 2½ to 3 minutes. Set aside. Place the yolks in the bowl of an electric mixer. Beat at medium speed, adding the sugar syrup slowly. Then beat on high speed until the mixture is the consistency of light mayonnaise (this should take about 5 to 6 minutes). Return to medium speed and add the softened butter, piece by piece, until the whole mixture is smooth and homogenous.

1. Cut a piece of cardboard the exact size or slightly larger than the cake so that it will come level with the cream topping. Using a long-bladed serrated knife, cut each *génoise* into three horizontal slices, rotating the cake as you cut through it.

2. Keep one hand flat on the cake and hold your knife perfectly flat so the slices are the same thickness throughout. This requires some practice.

3. Rearrange the slices in order as you cut.

4. Place one layer, crusty side down, on the cardboard (it must be a top or bottom layer) and moisten with some rum syrup.

5. Spread a ¼-inch layer of butter cream all over with a thin, flexible metal spatula.

6. Place another layer on top.

7. Moisten it with more rum syrup and spread about 3 tablespoons of melted apricot jam on top.

8. Continue with a layer of syrup-moistened cake topped with butter cream.

9. Alternate fillings, finishing with a layer of butter cream. Smooth the top as flat as you can.

10. Holding the cake flat on one hand, ice all around. Turn the cake on your hand against the direction of the spatula.

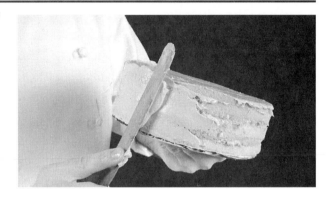

11. Smear some cream on one side. Starting at the top of the cake, go down and forward with the spatula in a smooth, direct motion. The butter cream should not be too cold.

12. Let the cake cool for at least 1 hour in the refrigerator. Using the serrated edge, hold the knife on an angle and slide left to right in a swivel motion to decorate the top.

13. Place some reserved cream in a pastry bag fitted with a plain tube, technique 62, and decorate the top to your fancy.

14. With a fluted tube, make a border all around.

15. Place some melted chocolate in a paper cornet, technique 66, and "draw" on top of the cream.

16. Holding the cake in one hand, take a handful of cake or cookie crumbs and coat around the bottom of the cake (about 1½ inches high), turning the cake as you go along. Refrigerate until ready to serve. Do not cut your wedges too fat. See finished mocha cake, page 614a.

232. Kirsch-Flavored Cake (Gâteau au Kirsch)

P REPARE ONE *génoise* (half the recipe in technique 226) and cut it into three layers (see steps 1–3 in the preceding technique). Make a syrup with cup strong coffee, 1 tablespoon sugar and 1 tablespoon kirsch of the best possible quality. You will need ½ cup of cake crumbs. (Grind stale cake, roasted almonds or butter cookies if you don't have cake trimmings on hand.)

KIRSCH BUTTER CREAM

½ cup sugar
¼ cup water
3 egg yolks
2 sticks (½ pound) sweet butter, softened
3 tablespoons kirsch

Combine the sugar and water in a saucepan, bring to a boil and boil for 2 minutes. Set aside. Place the yolks in the bowl of an electric mixer. Beat at medium speed, adding the sugar syrup slowly. Then beat on high speed until the mixture is pale yellow and the consistency of a light mayonnaise (this should take about 5 to 6 minutes). Return to medium speed and add the softened butter, piece by piece, adding the kirsch a little at a time in between the pieces of butter. Set aside until ready to use.

1. Place a cake layer, crust side down, on a round piece of cardboard covered with foil. Sprinkle with the kirsch syrup. Spread some of the butter cream on top. Repeat with the next two layers.

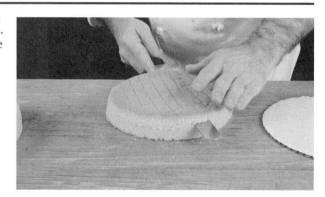

2. Holding the cake in one hand, press the crumbs all around the cake.

3. Arrange chocolate cigarettes, technique 247, on top, the longest ones in the middle of the cake.

4. Trim the chocolate all around.

5. Lay strips of wax paper on top of the cake and sprinkle with confectioners' sugar.

6. Remove the wax paper carefully. See finished kirsch-flavored cake, page 614a.

233. Fresh Fruit Cake *(Croûte de Fruits)*

YIELD: 8 servings

THIS EASY DESSERT is very simple to assemble. A base of *génoise* (sponge cake) or pound cake is covered with about a cup of *crème patissière*, topped with fruits and glazed with an appropriate glaze.

1 *slice sponge cake about ¾ inch thick and 8 inches in diameter*
¾ *cup* crème *patissière (technique 215)*
Ripe fruits
½ *cup apricot preserves, strained through a food mill and flavored with 2 teaspoons kirsch, rum or Cognac*
½ *cup* génoise *crumbs (made from trimmings in a blender or food processor)*

1. Cut a piece of cardboard the size of your *génoise* and place the *génoise* on top. Cover the top and the sides of the sponge cake with the *crème patissière*.

2. Peel and cut the fruits into wedges. Arrange on top. In this case we used fresh peaches, grapes and cherries. Use any combination of fruits that are attractive in color.

3. Hold the cake in one hand and press the crumbs all around the cake with the other. Using a brush or a spoon, glaze the top with the apricot glaze. If you have the ingredients, this dessert takes just a few minutes to assemble. Do not assemble more than 1 hour before serving because the *génoise* will get soggy. See finished fresh fruit cake, page 641.

234. Chocolate Cake (Gâteau au Chocolat)

This recipe makes two 3-layer chocolate cakes. Each cake uses a *génoise* as the base and is filled with *ganache soufflé*, topped with *ganache* and decorated with *glace royale*.

The *ganache* is a delicate, glossy chocolate icing that is made from quality chocolate and heavy cream brought to a boil. The mixture is poured on the cake while still slightly tepid. If the *ganache* is allowed to cool, it will become too thick and won't run down the sides of the cake properly. If it is too hot, it will melt the filling and won't stick to the cake.

The *ganache soufflé*—the filling for the cake—is simply a *ganache* that has been cooled and then worked with a whisk. It lightens in color, gains in volume and becomes fluffy due to the addition of air.

The *glace royale* is a simple sugar and egg white icing that is piped onto the chocolate icing in a decorative motif. I have used a motif for each cake.

Begin by baking 2 *génoises* (the whole recipe in technique 226). If you want the cakes themselves to be chocolate, you can substitute ⅓ cup bitter cocoa for ⅓ cup of the flour in the basic recipe. Make cardboard bases for the cakes and cut each cake into 3 layers (see technique 231, steps 1–3).

Whipped Chocolate Filling (Ganache Soufflé)

1 *cup heavy cream*
8 *ounces (squares) chocolate (4 ounces bitter, 4 ounces semisweet)*
1 *tablespoon dark rum*

Combine the cream and chocolate in a saucepan. Place on low to medium heat and bring to a boil, stirring to melt the chocolate and avoid scorching. As soon as it boils, cool, mixing once in a while, until it starts to thicken and set. When cool, place in the bowl of an electric mixer. Add the rum and beat on high speed for 4 to 5 minutes. It will lighten in color and approximately double in volume. Use immediately; it will quickly become hard and unspreadable.

Chocolate Icing *(Ganache)*

12 *ounces (squares) good chocolate (6 ounces*
  bitter, 6 ounces semisweet)
1½ *cups heavy cream*
2 *to 3 tablespoons water (optional)*

Melt the chocolate in the cream, stirring with a wooden spoon. Bring to a boil. Set aside. Let cool to barely lukewarm. If too thick or too oily, add 1 to 2 tablespoons water.

Royal Icing *(Glace Royale)*

½ *cup confectioners' sugar*
⅓ *of 1 egg white*
3 *to 4 drops lemon juice*

Combine the sugar, egg white (do not use more than ⅓ of 1 egg white) and lemon juice in a bowl. Work the mixture with a wooden spatula for about 2 minutes until it is nice and creamy and thick enough to form a ribbon.

1. Place one layer, crusty side down, on each cardboard base and spread the surfaces with some *ganache soufflé,* using a thin, flexible metal spatula. Place the next layer on, add more *ganache soufflé,* and then the last layer. Smooth out the coating on top, leaving a little lip of cream all around.

2. Holding the cake in one hand, use your spatula to smooth out the sides. Go in a down-forward motion, getting rid of the lip as you go along (follow technique 231, steps 10 and 11). Refrigerate the cakes for at least 1 to 2 hours. They should be cold and well-set. While the cakes are cooling prepare the *ganache* and the *glace royale.*

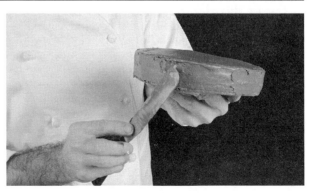

3. You will have at least one-third too much chocolate icing for both cakes, but you need a great amount to coat the cake correctly. The leftover can be kept for at least one month in the refrigerator. Don't be skimpy; pour half of the chocolate icing on top of one cake.

4. Spread rapidly with a long metal spatula.

5. Make sure all the sides are coated and the layer is about ¼ inch on top and around. If you take too long, the chocolate will cool off and become very thick.

6. Lift up the wire rack and tap it gently on the table to help smooth the sides and the excess chocolate at the bottom. Run your fingers or a spatula under the cake rack to smooth out the droppings of chocolate.

7. The cakes should be decorated with the *glace royale* while the chocolate on top of the cake is still slightly soft. It should not be too set and too hard. Place some icing in a paper cornet, technique 66. Cut the tip and, for the first cake, pipe out lines about 1 inch apart.

8. Turn the cake and run a long, thin-bladed knife through the lines. The knife should just barely touch the chocolate. Pull toward you so the white lines are "dragged" through the chocolate.

9. Cleaning the blade of the knife with a wet rag after each stroke, repeat about every 1½ inches.

10. Turn the cake around and drag the knife between each stroke in the same manner, but pulling the icing in the opposite direction. This design is called *décor Mexicain*. Refrigerate to have it cold before serving.

11. Using the paper cornet and the *glace royale*, decorate the second cake by drawing a coil. It requires practice to draw it uniformly.

12. Keep going without pausing to avoid breaking the line. You need a steady hand.

13. Using your knife, draw 8 equidistant lines from the center to the outside of the cake.

14. Repeat between each line but this time dragging the knife from the outside to the center. Refrigerate before serving.

235. Yeast Cake Babas and Savarin

(Savarin et Babas)

YIELD: 1 savarin and 12 babas

THE BABAS AND THE SAVARIN are made with the same dough, but raisins are usually added to the baba dough. Both cakes are usually made ahead and kept in a tin box unrefrigerated or packed in plastic bags and refrigerated or frozen. Before serving, the cakes are soaked in a rum syrup and glazed with preserves. In addition they can be coated with a sugar frosting as we did here. Babas are generally served plain while the savarin is usually filled with whipped cream (below) or with fruit salad.

Dough

1¼ *pounds all-purpose, unbleached flour*
1 *cup milk, at about 90 to 100 degrees*
1¼-*ounce envelope dry yeast or one .6-ounce package fresh yeast*
2 *teaspoons sugar*
1½ *sticks (6 ounces) sweet butter, softened*
6 *large eggs*
1½ *teaspoons salt*
1 2-*ounce package raisins*

Syrup for savarin and babas

3 *cups sugar*
4 *cups lukewarm water*
1 *tablespoon pure vanilla extract*
3 *tablespoons dark rum*
½ *cup strained apricot preserves*

Frosting

1 *cup powdered sugar*
2 *tablespoons light corn syrup*
About ½ *teaspoon lemon juice*
4 *drops red food coloring*
1½ *tablespoons water*

Filling

2 *cups heavy cream*
2 *tablespoons sugar*
A *few candied violets*

1. Mix the milk, yeast and sugar together and allow to work for about 5 minutes in a warm place, about 80 degrees. Place the flour, salt and 3 eggs in the bowl of an electric mixer and add the milk mixture. Beat with the flat beater beater on low seed until smooth. Add 2 more eggs and work 1 minute on medium speed. Finally add the last egg and work another 2 to 3 minutes on medium speed. Then add the butter piece by piece, still beating for 1 minute on the same speed. Cover the bowl loosely with a towel and let proof in a warm place, about

80 degrees, for 25 minutes. The dough should have almost doubled in volume. Knock down. Place some of the dough in a buttered savarin mold. Add the raisins to the remaining dough and divide between the buttered baba molds. The dough should come no higher than one-third of the way up the molds. Cover loosely with a towel and let proof for 35 to 45 minutes in a warm place until it reaches almost the top of the mold. Do not overproof or the cakes will expand too much and will be dry and crumbly after cooking. Brush the babas and savarin with an egg wash (1 egg, plus 1 egg yolk, beaten), and bake in a preheated 400-degree oven for about 35 minutes or until well browned and cooked inside. The savarin may take 5 to 8 minutes more than the babas, depending on its thickness.

2. When the savarin and babas are cooked, remove from the oven and let set about 10 minutes, then remove from the molds and place on a wire rack to cool. At this point they can be refrigerated, frozen or packed in tins and stored for future use.

3. Stir the sugar with the water and vanilla to dissolve. Place the babas and/or savarin into a deep pan and pour the syrup on top. Let the cakes absorb the syrup for about 30 minutes. Turn them from time to time. Allow the cakes to absorb as much syrup as they can.

4. When well impregnated, drain the cakes on a rack for 15 to 20 minutes. Reserve the extra syrup for other uses. Brush the savarin and babas with the dark rum. By brushing the rum on the cakes instead of putting it in the syrup, you get a stronger rum taste.

5. Strain the apricot preserves and brush the tops and sides of the cakes with it. Decorate with slivered almonds with crystallized violets in the center to simulate flowers. Serve the babas as is.

6. Mix all the frosting ingredients with a whisk and spoon over the top of the savarin. Place on a serving platter. Combine the cream and sugar and whip until firm. Place two-thirds of the cream in the cavity of the savarin and the remaining cream in a pastry bag fitted with a fluted top. Decorate the top with the cream and top with the candied violets. Serve at once. See finished savarin and rum babas, page 789.

236. Proust's Small Coffee Cakes
(Madeleine de Commercy)

YIELD: About 18 madeleines

HERE ARE THE FAMOUS SMALL CAKES so dear to Proust in *A la Recherche du Temps Perdu*. They originated in the small town of Commercy. The madeleines can be made in a special tray or in small individual brioche molds.

1 *stick (4 ounces) sweet butter, softened*
½ *cup sugar*
½ *teaspoon baking powder*
½ *teaspoon pure vanilla extract*
½ *teaspoon grated orange rind*
2 *eggs*
1 *cup all-purpose flour*

1. Place the butter and sugar in the bowl of a electric mixer and work on medium to fast speed until light and fluffy, about 1 minute. Add the baking powder, vanilla, orange rind and 1 egg. Beat on low speed for about 1 minute, until

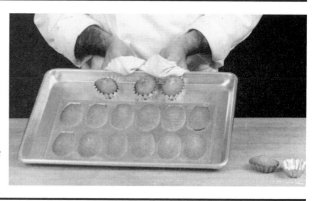

smooth and light. Add the other egg and mix another minute at the same speed. Finally, stir in the flour with a whisk until the mixture is smooth. Do not overwhisk. Butter a madeleine tray well and place 1½ tablespoons of the soft cake dough in each mold. Hit the tray on the table to flatten the dough in the molds or push it down with the tips of your fingers. Bake in a preheated 400-degree oven for about 20 minutes.

2. Let the madeleines rest or set 10 minutes before unmolding. Unmold, cool on a wire rack and, when cold, place in a plastic bag or a tin box to prevent drying. Use as needed. They are the ideal coffee cake but are also served as garnish for ice cream, or with berries and whipped cream as a type of shortcake.

237. Linzer Torte *(Tarte à la Confiture)*

T HE LINZER TORTE is a specialty of Austria. The dough, extremely rich and delicate, is easier to spread than roll. The torte is easy to make and is well suited to buffets or whenever desserts have to hold for a few hours.

YIELD: 8 servings

Linzer dough

1¾ *cups flour*
1 *cup ground almonds*
⅓ *cup granulated sugar*
2 *sticks (8 ounces) sweet butter, softened*
3 *egg yolks*
¼ *teaspoon powdered cinnamon*
½ *teaspoon pure vanilla extract*
¼ *teaspoon mace powder*

Jam filling

1 *12-ounce jar quality raspberry preserves*
1 *tablespoon raspberry brandy*
Powdered sugar

1. Combine the flour and ground almonds on a work table and make a well. In the center, place the butter cut in pieces, and the remaining ingredients. Start mixing with your fingertips.

2. Gather the ingredients together. With the palm of your hand, smear the dough away from you, a piece at a time, in the technique called *fraisage*. Gather the dough and repeat once more.

3. The dough will be very soft. Use a dough scraper to place it on a piece of wax paper.

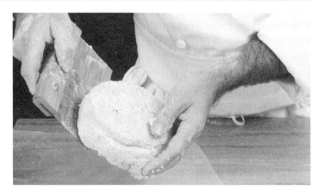

4. Set a 10- to 12-inch flan ring on a cookie sheet. Place about three-quarters of the dough in the bottom of the ring and spread it out, using a piece of parchment or wax paper to help spread. It should be about ¼ inch thick all over the bottom.

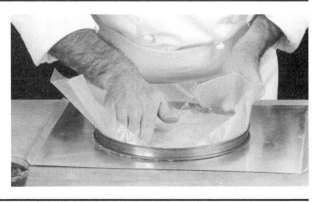

5. Roll some dough into strips and press inside to form the edges.

6. Use the wax paper again to thin the sides to about ¼ inch thick. Trim the excess dough.

7. Strain the raspberry preserves and combine with the raspberry brandy. Spread the mixture on the bottom of the dough.

8. Roll leftover dough into thin cylinders. Flatten the cylinders into strips and arrange on top of the jam lattice fashion—about four strips in each direction.

9. Fold the edges of the torte in toward the torte, on top of the jam and strips. Flatten gently with your fingertips.

10. Bake in a preheated 375-degree oven for 35 minutes until nicely browned and crisp. Let rest at least 10 minutes, then remove the ring. Sprinkle with powdered sugar and clean the crumbs of dough around the bottom edge.

11.Slide the linzer torte onto a serving platter. Be careful as it is delicate and brittle. Serve in wedges at room temperature.

238. Strawberry Strip *(Bande aux Fraises)*

YIELD: 8 to 10 servings

T HE DOUGH for the fruit strip can be cooked a day ahead but the custard (if any), as well as the fruits, should not be placed on the dough more than 30 minutes before serving or the dough will get soggy. The bottom of the cooked shell can be smeared with a *crème patissiére* then covered with the fruits and finally glazed, which should not take more than 10 minutes. Our version is done without the *crème patissiére*.

1 pound puff paste (see technique 269)
2½ baskets fresh strawberries or raspberries
2 tablespoons powdered sugar
¾ cup glaze made with raspberry preserve or
  warm currant jelly, strained, mixed
  with 1 tablespoon raspberry brandy,
  kirsch or Cognac

1. Roll the dough into a rectangle approximately 15 inches long by 10 inches wide and not more than ⅛ inch thick. Line a large cookie sheet with parchment paper.

2. Roll the dough on the rolling pin and unroll on the parchment paper. Trim the edges of the dough to make them straight. The dough should be about 9 inches wide after trimming. Brush the long edges with water then fold each in toward itself.

3. Remove a small strip from the outside edges so that instead of being folded the border is two layers.

4. Brush the borders and the dough between with an egg wash made of 1 egg plus 1 egg yolk, beaten together. Prick the center of the dough with a fork to prevent it from puffing too much and score the border with the point of a knife to form a design. Place in the freezer for 10 to 15 minutes or in the refrigerator for 1 hour so the dough sets before cooking. Then bake in a preheated 375-degree oven for 25 minutes. If the center puffs too much while cooking, push it down with a towel. The dough should be browned and well cooked.

5. Clean the berries and set two-thirds of the nicest aside. Arrange the remaining fruit on the bottom of the baked, cooled strip, sprinkle with powdered sugar and press down to crush them slightly so they release a little of their juice. Arrange the nicer berries on top and, using a brush or a teaspoon, glaze with the glaze (cold strained raspberry preserves or warm red currant jelly). Serve as soon as possible. See finished dessert, below.

Fresh fruit cake, strawberry strip, small fruit tarts

239. English Trifle *(Trifle Anglais)*

YIELD: 8 to 10 servings

THE ENGLISH TRIFLE, like the preceding dessert, is simple to assemble. Unlike technique 238, it can be done a few hours ahead because in this case the cake should get soft. It is a colorful, festive and delicious dessert. It can be made with sponge or pound cake, with or without fruits, with pastry cream or only whipped cream. Keep refrigerated until ready to serve.

2 génoises *(8 to 10 ounces each)* or 1 *large pound cake*

Pastry Cream

2 *cups milk*
¼ *cup granulated sugar*
½ *teaspoon pure vanilla extract*
4 *egg yolks*
2 *tablespoons flour*

Filling

½ *cup quality raspberry jam*
¼ *cup good, dry Sherry*
1½ *cups heavy cream*
2 *tablespoons granulated sugar*

Fruits

½ *cup sugar*
1½ *cups water*
Rind of ½ lemon
2 *pears*

1. Bring the milk to a boil. Place the sugar, egg yolks and vanilla in a bowl and work with a whisk until the mixture is pale yellow and thick, about a minute. Mix in the flour; then pour in the boiling milk. Mix well. Place the whole mixture back in the saucepan and bring to a boil, stirring with a whisk. Let it boil for a few seconds, then transfer to a clean bowl, cover with plastic wrap and allow to cool. Strain the jam through a fine strainer. Cut the *génoises* into 3 layers each and spread one with the raspberry jam. Cut into 6 triangles.

2. To poach the pears, boil the sugar, water and lemon rind for 2 minutes. Peel the pears and cut each one into 6 wedges. Drop in the boiling syrup and simmer for 2 to 3 minutes. Let it cool in syrup and drain. Line the bottom of a glass or crystal bowl with the triangles, jam side down.

3. Place a layer of plain *génoise* in the middle of the bowl and sprinkle with 1 tablespoon of Sherry. Pour the cooled custard on top. Break slices of *génoise* into pieces and embed in the custard to cover. Sprinkle with 2 tablespoons of Sherry.

4. Combine the cream with the granulated sugar and 1 tablespoon of the Sherry and beat until firm. Place a generous cup of the whipped cream into a pastry bag fitted with a tube, and spread the rest on top of the custard and *génoise* cake.

5. Spread the whipped cream with a spatula so that the top is smooth. Spread another layer of *génoise* cake with the jam, cut into triangles. Place on top of the whipped cream.

6. Arrange the wedges of pear between the triangles of coated *génoise* cake.

7. Decorate the edges and the center with the whipped cream.

8. The jam-coated *génoise* cake shows through the bowl as well as being visible on top. Refrigerate until serving time. Serve with a spoon. See finished English trifle, page 815.

240. Poached Peaches with Raspberry Sauce (*Pêches Pochés à la Purée de Framboises*)

YIELD: 8 servings

POACHED FRUITS are easy to make, light and elegant and particularly well suited as a finale to an elaborate meal. Make them in the summer when peaches are ripe and tasty. If you cannot find good peaches, you can substitute pears, apricots or even apples.

Poaching

8 *ripe peaches (about 2¾ pounds), at room temperature*
2 *cups sugar*
6 *cups water*
Juice and skin of 1 lemon

Sauce

1 *cup fresh raspberries*
1 *package (10 ounces) frozen raspberries*
½ *cup good raspberry preserves*
1 *tablespoon raspberry brandy, Cognac or kirsch*

To finish the dish

1 *pound cake cut into 8 ½-inch slices, each slice cut into a disk with a cookie cutter (use the trimmings to make a pudding)*
1 *branch fresh mint, cut into sprigs, one for each peach*

1. To make the sauce, bring all the ingredients except the brandy to a boil and simmer for 2 to 3 minutes. Strain through a fine strainer or a food mill, cover with plastic wrap and let cool. When cool, stir in the brandy. Mix the sugar, water and lemon juice in a saucepan, bring to a boil and boil for 5 minutes. Add the peaches. Place a piece of paper towel on top of the peaches and push them down into the syrup so the paper towel gets wet with the syrup. If the peaches are in contact with air, they will discolor. Cover with a lid and simmer for 3 to 5 minutes. Let the peaches cool in the syrup. When the peaches are cold, remove from the syrup and peel the skin off. (Reserve the syrup to poach other fruit.) Spread approximately 2 tablespoons of raspberry sauce in each individual plate and place a disk of pound cake in the center. Place a peach on the cake and decorate with a sprig of fresh mint. For an alternate method, coat the peaches with the raspberry sauce, then arrange on the pound cake and decorate with the mint.

See finished poached peaches with raspberry sauce, page 666.

241. Poached Oranges with Candied Rind *(Oranges Pochées Pelures Confites)*

YIELD: 6 servings

CANDIED ORANGE RIND is useful to enhance desserts. Candied peels of lemon and grapefruit can be done in the same manner. They are excellent served with ice cream, poached fruit or ice-cold soufflés. The candied rind of oranges is good dipped in melted chocolate. Dip half of the rind in chocolate and leave the other half plain to have a contrast of colors and taste.

6 *large seedless oranges*
1 *cup sugar*
4 *cups water*
2 *tablespoons Grand Marnier*
¾ *cup extra sugar to coat the rinds*

1. Peel the oranges with a vegetable peeler, removing only the uppermost orange part of the skin (the zest) which is where you have the essential oils and most of the taste. Cover the peels with cold water, bring to a boil and boil for about 30 seconds. Drain, rinse under cold water, cover again with cold water, bring to a boil and boil for about 3 minutes. Drain and rinse under cold water. Set aside.

2. Using a sharp paring knife, remove the white skin of the orange, moving your blade in a jigsaw pattern. Make sure the orange is completely "nude."

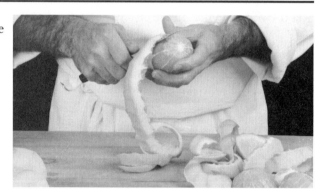

3. Return the peels to the pan, add sugar and water and bring to a boil. Simmer for 10 minutes. Place the oranges in the liquid, cover, bring to a boil and simmer for 10 minutes. Using a slotted spoon remove the oranges and set aside. Place the syrup and the rinds back on medium heat and allow to boil slowly for 40 minutes. There should be almost no liquid left.

4. Spread out the extra sugar on a piece of parchment paper and, using a slotted spoon, lift the peels from the syrup and place on the sugar. Toss and separate the rinds in the sugar until each piece is well coated. Because the rinds are still hot, they should separate easily. Allow the rinds to cool until crisp. When cold, arrange them on a platter or store in a jar. Pour whatever syrup is left over the oranges. When the oranges are cold, sprinkle with the Grand Marnier.

5. Refrigerated, the rinds will keep for months. To serve with the poached oranges, place each orange in an individual glass bowl or in a wineglass, divide the syrup among the oranges and, just before serving, sprinkle the top with candied orange rinds. If the rinds are positioned too early, they will get wet and the sugar coating will dissolve. See finished poached oranges and candied orange rinds, page 735.

242. Glazed Strawberries *(Glaçage des Fraises)*

W HEN STRAWBERRIES are in season, fresh and abundant, they always make welcomed desserts, either plain with brown sugar and sour cream, or simply topped with a dusting of sugar. For a buffet or elegant dinner they are glazed and passed to the guests at the end of the meal. Here are three different ways of glazing strawberries. One is a currant jelly glaze, the other an egg white and sugar coating, and the third one—the most sophisticated and delicate—is a cooked sugar syrup.

Currant jelly glaze

1 *dozen medium-size strawberries, preferably with the stems*
1 *jar (12 ounces) currant jelly*

Frosted strawberries

1 *dozen medium-size strawberries, preferably with the stems*
1 *egg white, lightly beaten with a fork*
1½ *cups granulated sugar*

Sugar-syrup glaze

1 *dozen medium-size strawberries, preferably with the stems*
1 *cup sugar*
¼ *cup water*
½ *teaspoon cream of tartar diluted with 1 teaspoon water*

1. Currant-glazed strawberries. Place the currant jelly in a saucepan on the stove and bring to a boil. Mix with a spoon until smooth. If the mixture is not smooth it will have to be strained. Holding the cold strawberry by the stem, dip in the mixture, twist to coat and allow excess jam to fall off. Place on a plate refrigerate. The coating will harding as it cools. At serving time transfer to a clean plate.

2. Frosted strawberries. Beat the egg white lightly with a fork until slightly foamy and loose. Brush the strawberries lightly with the egg white, then roll them in sugar until well cooled. Sprinkle sugar on a plate and place the strawberries on top. Let dry and set in the refrigerator for at least 30 minutes before serving. The coating will get hard. Transfer to a serving dish and serve.

3. Sugar-syrup-glazed strawberries. Place the sugar and water in a heavy saucepan and stir just enough to wet the sugar. Bring to a boil but do not stir the mixture or the sugar may crystallize. Boil for 4 to 5 minutes, then add the cream of tartar. Boil for another minute at which point it should be at the hard-crack stage (about 310 degrees), which is the stage before it turns into caramel. Dip a teaspoon in the mixture, lift it and dip in cold water right away. If the mixture sets hard on the spoon, it is at the hard-crack stage. Incline the pan so the syrup gathers in one corner. Dip the strawberries one by one in the hot sugar syrup. Twist the berry and rub gently against the sides of the saucepan so the excess syrup drips off. The coating should be thin. Place on an oiled metal tray until hard. The hot syrup will begin to cook the berry and the berry will release juices, which, in about ½ hour, will start melting the sugar coating. The berries should be eaten just before the sugar coating starts to melt as at that moment the coating is the thinnest.

Glazed Strawberries

243. Candied Pineapple *(Ananas Confit)*

C̲ANDIED PINEAPPLE is served with sherbert, or cut into small pieces to decorate a soufflé. Canned pineapple packed in pure pineapple juice gives perfectly fine results.

8 slices pineapple
About ⅔ cup pure pineapple juice
1 cup sugar
1 cup water

1. Place the pineapple juice, sugar and water in a flat, large saucepan and bring to a boil.

2. Add the pineapple slices. They should lie flat on the bottom of the pan without overlapping too much. Boil on medium heat for 45 minutes to 1 hour until the juices have almost caramelized and the pineapple slices are almost transparent.

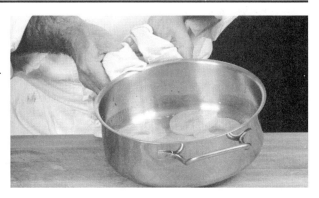

3. Place the pineapple slices in a dish with the syrup. Let macerate in the syrup for 4 to 5 hours, turning the slices every hour.

4. Place on a rack and allow to dry at room temperature for 48 hours. Then pack the slices in containers and keep in the refrigerator until needed.

244. St. Valentine Custard Cake

("Gâteau" de Semoule St. Valentin)

T HIS UNUSUAL CREATION is not a cake in the traditional sense of the word but rather a molded custard served with poached fruit. It is made with farina, though rice or semolina could be used instead. Serve with any fruit in season—pear, peach, apricot or apple—or serve plain, without fruit, like a rice pudding.

8 medium-sized pears (William, Comice or
* Bartlett)*
1 stick vanilla
Peel of 1 lemon and 1 orange
1½ cups sugar
Grated rind of 1 orange, technique 49
5 egg yolks
1 teaspoon vanilla extract
1½ envelopes unflavored gelatin
2 cups milk
¼ cup farina
2 cups heavy cream

3 tablespoons confectioners' sugar
Almond or peanut oil to coat mold
1 (10-ounce) jar apricot jam
Food coloring
1 ounce chocolate (½ ounce bitter, ½ ounce
* semisweet)*
2 tablespoons lukewarm water
Pear brandy

1. Peel the pears, leaving the stem attached, and place in a large casserole. Add the vanilla stick, lemon and orange peel, 1 cup sugar and enough cold water to cover the pears. Bring to a boil. Place a piece of paper towel over the casserole, so that the tops of the pears are kept moist and do not discolor. Cover and simmer slowly for 5 minutes if the pears are well-ripened, and up to 35 minutes if they are green and hard. They should be tender to the point of a knife. Let cool slowly in the liquid overnight.

2. Remove the paper.

3. Drain the pears on paper towels.

4. Mix together the grated orange rind, egg yolks, the remaining ½ cup sugar, the vanilla extract and gelatin. Whisk until the mixture forms a ribbon.

5. Bring the milk to a boil and add the farina. Boil, stirring, for 2 minutes.

6. Add the egg yolk mixture and bring to a boil again. Remove from the heat, transfer to a clean bowl and cool, stirring occasionally to avoid a skin forming on top.

7. Mix the heavy cream with the confectioners' sugar. Whip to a soft peak. Do not overwhip or the custard will taste of butter, rather than of sweet cream.

8. When the farina mixture reaches room temperature, fold in the whipped cream, technique 60.

9. Rub a 6-cup mold very lightly with almond or peanut oil. Pour the mixture in, cover with plastic wrap and refrigerate overnight.

10. Run a knife around the *"gâteau."*

11. Invert on a large platter and cover for a few seconds with a towel wrung in hot water to help the unmolding.

12. Unmold.

13. If the sides or top are a little rough or coarse from the unmolding, smooth out with a spatula or knife.

14. Place 1 tablespoon of the apricot jam in each of 3 cups. Add a couple of drops of red, green and yellow food coloring to have three different colored jams. If you object to food coloring, you may use mint jelly (for green), currant jelly (for red) and apple jelly (for yellow). Prepare 4 small paper cornets, technique 66.

15. Melt the chocolate in a small bowl (see Note, technique 247). Add 1½ teaspoons luke-warm water and mix. It will curdle; add more water (up to 2 tablespoons) a little at a time, and stir well until the mixture is smooth and shiny. Fill a paper cornet with chocolate and cut the tip off. Draw letter, flowers, leaves and the like according to your fancy.

16. Fill the 3 cornets with the different colored jams, and squeeze inside the chocolate outlines.

17. Place the pears around and coat with lukewarm apricot glaze (see technique 260, step 11) diluted with pear brandy. Serve with extra apricot glaze.

245. Flamed Bananas *(Bananes Flambées)*

FLAMED BANANAS are an inexpensive and delicious dessert.

1. For 6 servings, trim the ends of 6 large ripe (not over ripe) bananas. With the point of a paring knife, make an incision down one side of each banana.

2. Place in a roasting pan or on a cookie sheet and bake in a 400-degree preheated oven for 15 minutes.

3. The skin will turn black and the bananas will become soft to the touch. Keep at room temperature until serving time.

4. At serving time, melt 1 stick (¼ pound) sweet butter and add ⅓ cup sugar, the juice of 1½ limes, the juice of 1 lemon and ¼ cup water. Cook on high heat for about 5 minutes, or until it turns to a nice caramel color. "Unwrap" the bananas into the sauce.

5. Using a spoon and fork, turn the bananas in the sauce. Add ⅓ cup of good dark rum, shake the pan and ignite.

6. Baste the bananas with the sauce until the flames subside.

7. Serve on warm plates, 1 banana per person with sauce.

246. Crêpes Suzettes

THOUGH CRÊPES ARE BEST when they are fresh out of the pan, they can be refrigerated (stacked and covered) and kept for a few days. The basic crêpe can be used both for desserts and entrées. The best-known dessert crêpe is the crêpe suzette, flavored with orange and flamed at serving time with Cognac and orange liqueur. You will need a large handsome skillet and a powerful gas or electric burner. This recipe makes 2 dozen crêpes.

THE BATTER

1½ cups all-purpose flour
3 large eggs
1 teaspoon sugar
¾ teaspoon salt
1½ cups milk
⅔ stick sweet butter, melted
½ cup cold water

THE SAUCE

2 sticks (½ pound) sweet butter, softened
8 tablespoons sugar
Grated rind of 2 oranges or 4 tangerines, technique 49
Juice of 1 orange or 2 tangerines
Cognac and Grand Marnier

1. To make the batter, place the flour, eggs, sugar, salt and half of the milk in a bowl. Whisk until the mixture is smooth. By adding just enough liquid to work the dough into a thick batter, you eliminate the possibility of lumps. Add the remaining ingredients and stir well. The consistency should be that of a light syrup.

2. Use a small cast-iron crêpe pan, or a nonstick pan, 5 to 6 inches in diameter. Heat your skillet on a medium to high flame. Do not grease the skillet. The melted butter in the batter will suffice to prevent the crêpes from sticking. (The first few may stick until the pan "gets into the mood.") Hold the pan slightly tilted and pour about 3 tablespoons of batter on the high side.

3. Quickly tilt the pan so that the batter has a chance to coat the whole bottom before hardening. Shake the pan to force the batter all over. The thinner the coating, the better the crêpes.

4. Another method is to pour a lot of batter in the hot skillet so that it fills the bottom and

5. then pour the excess batter back into the bowl. This also gives a thin crêpe, but

6. the "lip" has to be trimmed off for each crêpe.

7. Cook the crêpes on medium heat for approximately 50 seconds. Then bang the skillet a few times on a potholder or a folded towel to release the crêpe.

8. Flip the crêpe over or turn it with a spatula and cook approximately 30 seconds on the other side. You will notice that the side which was browned first is nicer than the other. When stacking them, place the nicer side underneath so that it shows on the outside after the crêpe is folded.

9. To make the sauce, place the butter, sugar, grated rind and juice in a food processor and process until smooth. Transfer to a bowl.

10. At serving time, melt 4 to 6 tablespoons of the sauce in the skillet (about 1 tablespoon per crêpe).

11. When sizzling hot, place 4 to 6 crêpes flat in the sauce. Using a fork and a spoon, turn the crêpes in the sauce. When coated, fold each one into fourths (the nice side showing) and arrange in the skillet as you go along.

12. Pour 1½ to 2 tablespoons of both cognac and Grand Marnier on top of the crêpes.

13. Ignite with a match and, keeping your head back, stir the crêpes in the flaming sauce.

14. Serve the crêpes on warm plates, 2 or 3 per person, with some sauce. Repeat to make all the crêpes in several batches. Add more cognac and Grand Marnier to each batch.

247. Chocolate Cigarettes *(Cigarettes en Chocolat)*

CHOCOLATE IS TRICKY to work with. Bitter chocolate curdles easily when combined with another ingredient; sweet chocolate (or semisweet) is often to light and too sweet. I usually use baking chocolate in 1-ounce squares and mix half bitter and half semisweet. The proportions may be varied to suit your own taste.

Take your time when you melt chocolate. Chocolate burns easily, stiffening and becoming granular and bitter when burned. The best method is to place the chocolate in a glass or stainless-steel container and leave it overnight in a regular oven with the pilot light on. Stir to get it smooth. You may also place the container of chocolate in a pot of boiling water. The water should be as high as the chocolate. Cover and let melt for 10 to 15 minutes. Then stir until smooth.

Chocolate cigarettes, as well as chocolate strips and flowers, are often used in decoration. They require a bit of practice to make, but the ingredients can be reused as many times as necessary until the technique is perfected.

1. You need to work on a flat, hard surface such as marble, stainless steel or glass. Pour 6 ounces of melted chocolate on the marble surface.

2. Spread with a long, narrow spatula, going back and forth until the top of the chocolate becomes cloudy. It should be thin, but not too thin, at least ⅛ inch thick.

3. Take a large, strong knife. Holding it on an angle, start cutting into the chocolate, applying pressure down and forward on the blade of the knife. The pressure is strong enough to bend the blade slightly.

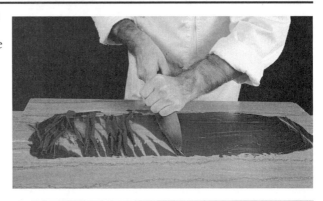

4. The chocolate rolls on itself as you move the knife down. The consistency is very important. Chocolate which is too soft will gather in a mush; chocolate which is too hard will flake and crumble under the blade. Scrape it from the marble, melt it again and try until it works. Practice makes perfect.

248. Angle Hair *(Cheveux d' Ange)*

Angel hair is very decorative and though making it is a messy business, it can turn an ordinary dessert into a glorious affair. It is akin to the spun sugar cotton candy is made from. Although it can be made with sugar and water, we use corn syrup instead of the water because it prevents the sugar from crystallizing during and after cooking, making it more "flexible" and easier to use.

1. Combine 1 cup sugar and ¾ cup corn syrup in a saucepan. Mix well and place on medium heat. Do not stir the mixture anymore. After it boils, cook 12 to 14 minutes on medium to low heat until the sugar turns into a very light ivory color (about 318 degrees on a candy thermometer). If there is any crystallized sugar on the sides of the pan, cover the saucepan for 30 seconds to 1 minute during the cooking. The steam produced will melt the sugar crystals.

2. Remove the sugar from the heat and grate approximately 2 teaspoons pure beeswax candle into the saucepan (optional). The pieces will melt right away and mix with the sugar. Angel hair has a tendency to stick together, especially during hot summer days. The wax will coat the sugar threads, making them "dry," smooth and easier to store and use. The pure beeswax is from the honeycomb and is a natural, edible product.

3. Let the syrup cool off a few minutes. You may place the saucepan in a bowl of cold water to accelerate the process. Using 2 forks side by side, lift some of the syrup. It should be thick.

4. Cover the floor with newspaper. Place a wooden spatula on the table so it extends over the edge of the table. Dip both forks into the syrup and wave it over the spatula, high enough and broad enough so that the threads are long, thin and have time to solidify in the air. You may have to use a stepstool to get higher.

5. Slide it away from the wooden spatula and use or store in a tightly covered container.

249. Swan in Melon *(Cygne en Melon)*

A MELON like the honeydew, with its smooth and large graceful round shape, lends itself to carving. Here it gets transformed into a swan, then hollowed into an elegant serving receptacle for ice cream, sherbets, fruit salad, or whatever. Use the flesh to make a sherbet or cut into small pieces, sprinkle with sugar and serve for dessert.

1. Use a pen or the point of a knife to draw the outline of the swan on the melon. Draw the head so it looks like a question mark. With a sharp, small knife, cut along the outlined head and on both sides to form the wings. Cut the back of the swan in between the wings to accentuate their shape. When the whole outline is carved, remove the seeds with a spoon.

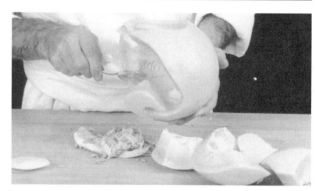

2. Cut inside about ¼ inch in from the rind to separate the flesh from the shell.

3. This is the swan seen from the back. Keep removing melon from the inside to make the shell thinner and more elegant looking. The shell shouldn't be much more than ⅜ inch thick.

4. Cut little dents in both wings to imitate the feathers. Cover with plastic wrap and keep refrigerated. At serving time, drain of any juices and fill. See finished swan on the following page.

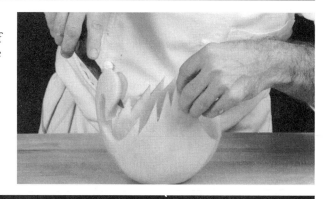

250. Fruit Salad *(Salade de Fruits)*

YIELD: 6 to 8 servings

ENHANCED WITH ALCOHOL and sugar, this fruit salad is always served as a dessert. the mixture of preserves, lemon juice and sugar preserves the color of the fruits. Taste improves if the fruit sits an hour in the syrup before serving. Keep an eye for colors. Remember that bananas, pears, apples and pineapple have about the same color after peeling. Use dark grapes, plums, cherries and also some dried fruit, such as figs, apricots or prunes, sliced thin and sprinkled in the salad. The fruit salad is beautiful presented in the swan melon described in the previous technique.

Juice of 1 large lemon (⅓ cup)
3 tablespoons strained apricot preserves
2 tablespoons quality kirsch or pear brandy
¼ cup sugar
4 small ripe plums, cut into wedges
2 ripe peaches, cut into wedges
1 ripe apple, peeled and cut into slices
1 ripe pear, peeled and cut into slices
1 ripe banana, peeled and sliced
Small bunch of white grapes, cleaned
    (about 1 cup)

Small bunch of dark grapes, cleaned
    (about 1 cup)

Vary the fruits according to availability.

1. Mix the lemon juice, apricot preserves, kirsch and sugar in a stainless steel or glass bowl until well combined.

2. Cut the fruits (bananas, peaches, etc.) directly into the bowl. If the peaches, plums and grapes are ripe, they don't need peeling. The apples and pears are usually peeled. Mix all the fruits in the marinade and let sit at least 1 hour before serving. Arrange in the swan. See finished dish, below.

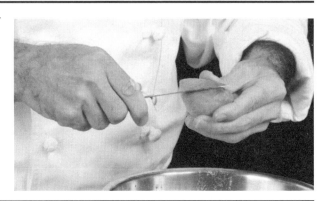

Poached peaches with raspberry sauce

Fruit salad in melon

251. Strawberry Sherbet *(Sorbet aux Fraises)*

YIELD: 6 servings

THERE ARE lots of different types of "iced desserts"—ices, *sorbet, spum, marquise, granité*. All are conventionally made from fruits or fruit juices or wines although different cooks may interpret them differently. In this and the next few techniques we'll keep to *sorbets* and *granités* (frozen sweetened purée of fruits) and ice cream made with egg yolks, milk and cream. Fruit sherbets or *sorbets* have a truer taste when made only with water, sugar and a fruit purée. With the addition of cream the fruit tends to lose its identity. Fruits like apples and bananas don't make good sherbet. Very juicy fruits like lemon or pineapple, or berries such as black currants, raspberries or strawberries, make the best sherbets. Commercial sherbets are made with ice-cream machines. We prefer to use the machine for regular ice cream only, because it tends to emulsify the mixture too much. Beating air into a mixture of milk, cream and eggs makes it light and smooth. However, in *sorbets* too much air changes the color and taste of the fruit. It makes it too light and too foamy and changes the texture, as well as diluting the fruit taste. The less distinctive the taste of the fruit, the less it should be emulsified. Melon *sorbet* for example is ruined if it's done in an ice cream machine. The color changes too much and the taste of the melon practically disappears.

1½ pounds fresh strawberries or raspberries, ripe, hulled
¾ cup sugar (or more or less depending on the sweetness and ripeness of the fruit)
Juice of ½ large lemon (¼ cup)
2 tablespoons corn syrup
Raspberry sauce (see technique 290)

1. Place all the ingredients in a food processor and process for about 1 minute. Strain if you object to seeds. Place the mixture in a stainless steel bowl in the freezer for 2 hours. Stir it once in a while.

2. When the mixture is partially frozen and grainy, place it back in the food processor for 1 minute to emulsify. It will liquefy and get softer, whiter and much smoother. Place back in a bowl, cover with plastic wrap and freeze to harden (for a few hours) before serving. At this point, the mixture is usually spooned with an ice cream scoop and served with the raspberry sauce.

3. To make individual bombes: line small containers with plastic wrap, fill with the sherbert and freeze. When the mixture is hard, hollow the center with a spoon, place a piece of plastic wrap into the cavity and keep it in the freezer until needed.

4. Before serving time, fill the center of the mold with fresh berries, top with a plate and invert. See finished strawberry bombe and strawberry sherbert with raspberries, below. Serve with raspberry sauce around.

Praline ice cream, horns, cigars and ice cream shells, strawberry sherbert with raspberries, strawberry bombe

252. Melon Sherbet *(Sorbet au Melon)*

YIELD: 6 servings

For best results, choose melons that are very ripe and of the utmost quality.

2 *ripe cantaloupe melons (about 3 pounds each), peeled*
and seeded
⅓ *cup sugar (or more or less depending on*
sweetness and ripeness of fruit)
⅓ *cup fresh lime juice*
2 *tablespoons honey*

1. Cut one melon in small chunks and place in the food processor just long enough to liquefy. Add the sugar, lime juice and honey. Place in a bowl and freeze for about 2 hours. Stir the mixture every half hour. When the mixture is frozen and grainy, place back in the food processor and whip for about 10 seconds to smooth and emulsify it a bit. Cover with plastic wrap and return to the freezer for a few hours to harden.

2. Serve with fresh melon. Cut a second melon into wedges and cut the skin off. Using a vegetable peeler, slice into very thin slices.

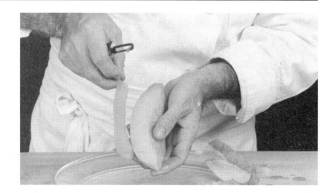

3. Arrange the slices in a round on individual plate. Make more slices and keep on the side.

4. At serving time, place a scoop of melon sherbert in the center of the plate and wrap melon slices around. Cut the rind into thin triangles and arrange around the sherbert. Serve right away. See finished melon sherbert, below.

Candied pineapple, grapefruit ice, jam toasts, melon sherbert, pineapple sherbert

253. Pineapple Sherbet *(Sorbet d'Ananas)*

YIELD: 6 to 8 servings

THE DELIGHTFUL AROMA of a ripe pineapple is unmistakable. You can recognize that the fruit is ripe if the center leaves can be pulled out easily. The following recipe calls for one pineapple. However, if you want to use an empty pineapple as a container, plan on using two pineapples to have enough sherbert to fill to the top.

1 large ripe pineapple (about 3 ½ pounds)
*⅓ cup sugar (or more or less depending on
    sweetness and ripeness of the fruit)*
Juice of 1 large lime or lemon (about ¼ cup)

1. Using a long, sharp knife, cut straight
down, about ¼ inch in from the skin. Cut
all around several times until the inside
flesh is loose.

2. Insert the point of your knife straight
through the pineapple about ½ inch from
the bottom.

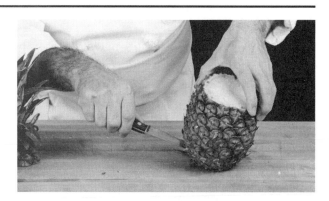

3. Move the blade from left to right without
making the opening wider so the blade inside severs the pineapple flesh without
cutting through the skin.

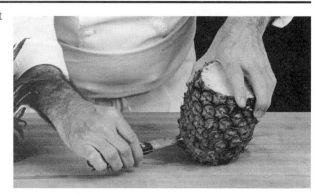

4. Use a kitchen fork and twist left to right
to loosen the inside. Pull out in one piece.

5. Cut the flesh from around the core and discard the tough core.

6. Cut the flesh in chunks (you should have about 1¾ pounds of flesh) and, using a spoon, scrape out all the pulp left in the shell. Freeze the shell.

7. Do not freeze the top which will be used as a decoration.

8. Place the pineapple chunks in the food processor and blend for about 30 seconds. Mix in the sugar and lime juice and place the mixture in the freezer for 2 hours, mixing every hour so the mixtures freezes evenly into a grainy mush.

9. When frozen, place back in the food processor and emulsify for about 1 minute. The mixture will become slightly runny, whiter and smoother. Return to the bowl or place in containers or in the pineapple shell. Cover with plastic wrap and freeze for a few hours to harden before using. See finished pineapple sherbert, page 670.

254. Grapefruit Ice *(Granité de Pamplemousse)*

YIELD: 6 to 8 servings

THE *granité* is a rough unemulsified *sorbet*. The mixture is condensed, tight, grainy and not too sweet. *Granités* are usually served between courses in the middle of an elaborate meal to clear the palate and excite the appetite for the course to come.

4 *medium grapefruit (about 3 ¼ pounds altogether, or ¾ pound each)*
¾ *cup sugar*
2 *tablespoons vodka*

1. Using a vegetable peeler, remove the top layer of the skin (the "zest") without getting any of the white underneath. Cover the skins with cold water, bring to a boil and boil for 5 minutes. Drain and wash under cold water. Set aside.

2. Cut the blanched skins coarsely and place in a food processor until finely chopped. Set aside.

3. Cut the fruit in half and press the juice into a bowl. (You should have about 2 to 2 ½ cups) Strain the juice to eliminate the seeds. Combine the juice with the chopped skin.

4. Use a spoon to scrape the pulp out of the shells. Do not remove any membranes or white skin. Add the sugar and Vodka and stir well. Freeze for 4 to 5 hours, mixing every 45 minutes. The addition of alcohol slows the freezing process. The mixture should be grainy and coarse, but frozen. Pack in plastic containers until ready to use. Serve in glasses with a swirl of grapefruit skin on top or a sprig of mint. *Granité* is always served in a glass. See finished grapefruit ice, page 670.

255. Praline Ice Cream *(Glace au Pralin)*

YIELD: 10 servings

ICE CREAM made with egg yolks and cream is usually called French ice cream and the mixture is close to a basic *crème anglaise* (custard cream).

The addition of coffee to the basic ice-cream mixture makes it mocha ice cream, the addition of chocolate makes it chocolate ice cream, and so on. In this technique the custard is flavored with *pralin*. An ice-cream maker is needed for this ice cream. It emulsifies the mixture, making it light, smooth and voluminous.

Pralin

¾ cup sugar
3 tablespoons water
½ cup oven-browned hazelnuts with skins
½ cup oven-browned almonds with skins
1½ teaspoons almond or peanut oil

Ice cream mixture

8 egg yolks
1 cup granulated sugar
1 teaspoon vanilla extract
3 cups milk
1 cup heavy cream

To freeze

Crushed ice
Salt

1. The *pralin* is a *nougatine* (caramelized sugar and nuts) ground to a paste. The cold mixture is usually crushed and reduced to a paste by machine, in the process of which some of the essential oils from the almond are extracted. A food processor doesn't achieve the exact effect but produces a good enough fascimile. Place the nuts on a tray and roast in a preheated 350-degree oven until golden brown. Place the sugar in a heavy saucepan and mix in the water. Stir this just once then place on the stove. Cook until it turns into a nice golden caramel color, about 5 minutes. Add the nuts and shake to mix well. Oil a cookie sheet lightly and pour the mixture on top. Let cool until hard and brittle. Break in a mortar into large crumbs. Reserve a quarter of the crumbs to use as a garnish.

2. Place the remainder of the *nougatine* in the food processor and powder for 1 minute. It should begin to look crumbly and soft. Add the oil and blend for another 2 to 3 minutes, stopping the machine every 20 or 30 seconds until it looks pasty and slightly wet. Set aside. At this point the *pralin* can be placed in a jar in the refrigerator and kept for months, using it to flavor ice cream, custards or butter creams.

3. Place the milk in a heavy saucepan and bring to a boil. Meanwhile, combine the egg yolks, sugar and vanilla in a bowl and work with a whisk for 2 to 3 minutes, until the mixture is light, smooth, pale colored and has reached the ribbon stage. Add to the milk and place back on medium heat. Cook, stirring constantly with a wooden spoon, for about 2 minutes until the mixture thickens slightly. Be careful not to overcook the sauce (the temperature should be about 170 degrees) or it will scramble. Place the cream in a clean bowl and, as soon as the custard is ready, strain through a fine sieve directly into the cream and mix well. The cream, being cold, brings down the temperature of the mixture and eliminates any further danger of the eggs scrambling. Whisk in the *pralin* paste. Let cool to room temperature.

4. Pour the cream into the central container of the ice-cream machine and secure the beater and motor following the manufacturer's instructions.

5. Because of its sugar and fat, the cream mixture has to be brought lower than 32 degrees in order to freeze. A mixture of salt and water (this brine—like sea water—can withstand temperatures lower than freezing before it hardens) is used to lower the temperature until it's cold enough to freeze the viscous mixture. Place a layer of crushed ice all around the container of cream and cover with about ½ cup of salt. Place another layer of ice on top and sprinkle another ½ cup of salt. Turn the machine on and run for 15 to 25 minutes, adding more ice and salt as the mixture melts. Do not plug the hole on the side of the bucket. If there's too much brine in the ice-cream maker, it will leak out through the hole rather than seep in to the container of ice cream. Most electric machines stop automatically when the ice cream is ready.

6. Lift out the central container taking care that the salted ice doesn't drip into the ice cream.

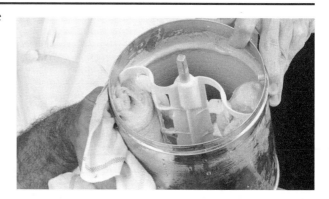

7. Pack the ice cream into containers, cover tightly and freeze until ready to use. Serve in lacy ice-cream shells (technique 288), with crumbled *nougatine* on top. See finished praline ice cream, page 668.

256. Pie Dough and Pie Shell
(Pâte Brisée et Croûte)

T HE PIE DOUGH, *pâte brisée,* is certainly the most useful all-purpose dough in French cooking. Though the dough is easier to make with a combination of butter and shortening, an all-butter dough is finer. However, for quiche, *tourte* (meat pies) and the like, the difference is difficult to detect. The reasons are that the quiche is served hot or lukewarm, and the filling (bacon, mushrooms, onions and the like) has a strong taste of its own. The difference would be quite apparent in a shell for a raspberry tart because it is served cold and the filling is very delicate.

When working with dough, remember that the more you knead and the more water you use, the more elasticity and shrinkage you get. The less water and the more fat you use, the more crumbly and lax the dough will be. At one end of the spectrum you have the bread dough (flour and water) which is elastic, springy and unrollable. At the other end of the spectrum, the cookie dough (mainly flour and fat) is soft, crumbly and hard to roll. The pie dough is in the middle and will lean toward one side or the other, depending on your ingredients and method. This recipe makes enough dough for one 9-inch pie.

2 *cups all-purpose flour*
1½ *sticks (6 ounces) sweet butter, very cold and*
 cut into ¼-inch cubes
¼ *teaspoon salt*
½ *teaspoon sugar*
⅓ *cup cold water (approximately)*

1. Place the flour, butter, salt and sugar in a large bowl. Mix the ingredients enough so that all the butter pieces are coated with flour.

2. Add water and start kneading the ingredients to gather the dough into a ball. Do not worry if there are little pieces of plain butter here and there. This will give flakiness to the dough, making it slightly similar to a puff paste. The dough should be malleable and usable right away. If overworked, it will become elastic, in which case you should let it "rest" in the refrigerator for 1 hour before using.

3. Place on a floured board and roll uniformly, turning the dough a quarter of a turn as you are rolling so that it forms a nice "wheel." Be sure the board is well floured underneath. The dough should be approximately ⅛ inch thick, although many cooks like it thicker.

4. Roll the dough back

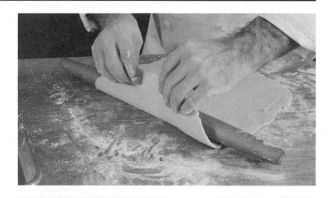

5. on the rolling pin.

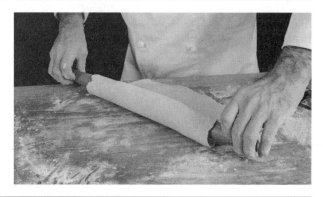

6. Lift up and

7. unroll on a flan ring or other mold.

8. With the tips of your fingers, push in the corners so that the dough does not get stretched, which would cause it to shrink during the baking.

9. Squeeze a lip all around the inside of the flan ring, working the dough between your thumb and forefinger.

10. Use a knife, or roll your pin on top of the ring to trim the excess dough.

11. Remove. (The excess dough can be stored in the refrigerator for a few days, or frozen.)

12. Re-form the edge between your thumb and forefinger.

13. Mark the edges with a dough crimper or the tines of a fork, or by squeezing it between your fingers.

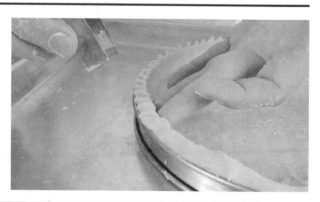

14. Shell, ready to be used. If your recipe calls for a precooked shell, line the shell with wax paper and weight it down with beans or the like (see steps 4 and 5 in the next technique) to prevent the dough from shrinking during the first 15 minutes of baking.

257. Sweet Pie Dough and Pastry Shell *(Pâte Sucrée et Croûte)*

T HE SWEET PIE DOUGH, *pâte sucrée,* is quite different from the *pâte brisée* described in the preceding technique. The texture is not flaky or tender, but rather is close to that of a cookie dough. The dough is not at all elastic or springy. It rolls easily but is a little difficult to pick up. It makes an excellent shell for runny ingredients because it does not get soggy as easily as regular pie dough. This recipe makes enough dough for two 9-inch pies.

3 *cups all-purpose flour*
2½ *sticks (10 ounces) sweet butter, softened and
        cut into pieces*
½ *cup sugar*
¼ *teaspoon salt*
1 *egg, beaten lightly with a fork*
1 *egg yolk*

1. Place the flour in the middle of the working table. Make a well in the center and add the remaining ingredients. Gather the dough, with a pastry scraper or your fingers, into a compact mass.

2. Place the dough close to you and, with the heel of your hand, take a mass about the size of a golf ball and "smear" it about 10 inches forward. Keep your fingers pointed upwards. Repeat, smearing more and more of the dough forward, until it has all been processed. Gather the dough into a ball and repeat the operation once more. The two smearings (*fraisage* in French) help homogenize the ingredients, making a well-blended dough.

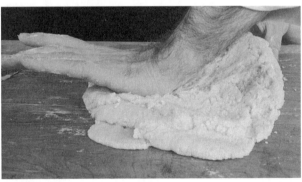

3. Roll the dough and fit it into a mold as described in steps 3–13 of the preceding technique. You can use a flan ring or a tart mold with a removable bottom, as pictured here.

4. Cut a round disk of wax paper (see technique 63, step 1) and fringe the edge with a pair of scissors.

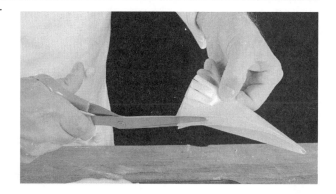

5. Line up the dough with the paper. Fill the shell with dry beans, rice, pebbles or any heavy, dry ingredient, to hold the dough in place during the baking.

6. Place on a cookie sheet and bake in a 400-degree preheated oven for approximately 45 minutes. Remove the paper and beans and keep for later use.

7. Brush the inside of the shell with an egg wash (1 whole egg, beaten). Return to the 400-degree oven for 5 to 8 minutes.

8. Remove from mold. The egg coating forms a waterproof layer and prevents the dough from getting soggy when filled with cream or juicy fruits. The same technique is used with *pâte brisée* on those occasions when you precook a shell for quiche or custard.

9. The dough should always be well cooked and crunchy (better overcooked than underdone). If, by a stroke of bad luck, the dough burns underneath, turn upside down when cool, and rub with a grater to remove the blackened part.

258. Upside-Down Pastry Shell
(Croûte en Pâte à l' Envers)

PASTRY SHELLS are often baked upside down. The gravity pulls the dough down, and the weight on top keeps the dough in shape, avoiding any shrinkage during baking.

1. Roll the dough to a ⅛-inch thickness (see technique 256, steps 3–7).

2. Place directly on top of an upside-down pie plate.

3. Fit another pie plate on top of the dough.

4. Turn the plates right side up and trim the dough.

5. Place upside down on a cookie sheet and bake in a 400-degree preheated oven for approximately 35 minutes, or until well browned.

6. Remove the shell and use, according to your recipe.

259. Scalloped Pastry Shells *(Coquille en Pâte)*

Little individual pastry shells can be used as a first course (stuffed with eggs or avocado), as a main course (stuffed with fish, lobster, chicken livers and the like) or as dessert (with berries and whipped cream). Use *pâte brisée*, technique 256, for salted dishes, or *pâte sucrée*, technique 257, for desserts.

1. Roll the dough about ⅛ inch thick. Butter the outside of the shells. Slide the shell under the dough.

2. Press the dough on the buttered side of the shell. Trim by pushing the dough on the edges with your fingers.

3. Holding the lined shell in one hand, push the dough slightly around the edge of the shell to anchor it. This prevents too much shrinkage during baking. Brush the dough with an egg wash (1 whole egg, beaten), place on a cookie sheet and bake in a 400-degree preheated oven for 25 to 30 minutes, or until nicely browned.

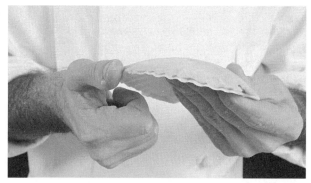

4. Pick the pastry off of the shell (it should slide easily) and garnish to your liking.

260. Apple Tart *(Tarte aux Pommes)*

OPEN-FACED TARTS are as distinctly French as apple pie is American. The dough can be arranged in a flan ring as shown below, or in a removable bottom mold or in a regular pie plate. It can also be cooked free form on a cookie sheet with the edges rolled to hold in the filling. I like the dough rolled very thin and the shell well-cooked. Any apple can be used, keeping in mind that some are more tart than others, and some hold their shape better than others while cooking (see technique 261).

1. Make your pie dough, technique 256, and fit it into a 9-inch ring or mold. Trim both the stem and flower ends of 4 to 5 good-sized apples. Holding a paring knife by the blade, use only the point of the knife and your thumb as a pivot to cut the stem off. (This technique can also be used for pears, tomatoes and the like.)

2. Using a vegetable peeler or a sharp paring knife, peel the apples. Cut into halves through the stem and remove the seeds with the point of the knife, using the method described in step 1.

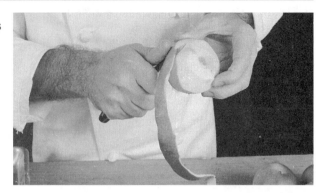

3. Cut into about ¼-inch slices. Chop the end slices coarsely, reserving the uniform center slices.

4. Arrange the chopped apples on the bottom of the pie shell.

5. Fan out the center slices as you would a deck of cards and

6. arrange on top of the chopped apples. (You may arrange the slices one by one if you feel it is easier.)

7. Arrange apple slices in the center of shell

8. to simulate the petals of a rose.

9. Sprinkle 3 tablespoons sugar on top and 2 tablespoons sweet butter, cut into pieces.

10. Bake in a 400-degree preheated oven for approximately 75 minutes. It should be well browned and the crust golden. Remove the flan ring. The pie shrinks slightly during baking making the ring easy to remove.

11. Using a large metal spatula, remove the pie from the cookie sheet and glaze (optional) with an apricot or apple jam. (Strain apricot jam through a fine sieve and dilute slightly with calvados, cognac, kirsch or even water, if you object to alcohol.) Serve at room temperature; refrigeration is not recommended.

This recipe serves 8 to 10.

261. Tarte Tatin

THE UPSIDE-DOWN OPEN TART, first made by the old "demoiselles Tatin," has become a classic of the French repertoire. There are many interpretations of it which are quite simple and satisfactory. The one below is a little more involved, but the result is quite distinctive.

Prepare half of the recipe for *pâte brisée,* technique 256, Trim, peel and slice 8 apples (see steps 1–3 in the preceding technique). Use firm apples that will hold their shape during cooking—Calville, Rennet, Granny Smith or the all-purpose green or Golden Delicious. You should have 6 cups of sliced apples. For a 10-inch pie plate, place ⅓ cup sugar and ¼ cup water in a saucepan, bring to a boil and keep boiling until it turns a nice caramel color.

1. Pour the caramel into the pie plate.

2. Tilt it so that the whole bottom and half of the sides are coated. Do this quickly before the caramel cools off and hardens.

3. Grate the rind of 1 lemon, technique 49, Use only the yellow part of the skin. You should have about 1 teaspoon of grated rind.

4. Place ½ stick (4 tablespoons) sweet butter in a large saucepan and melt until foaming. Add the apples, ⅓ cup sugar and the lemon rind. Sauté for 5 to 6 minutes, being careful not to break the slices too much. Pour onto a large cookie sheet to cool.

5. When cool enough to handle, start arranging the nicest slices from the middle of the pie plate out. Overlap the slices so the rounded sides are hidden. The nicest side shows after unmolding when the bottom of the pie plate becomes the top.

6. Continue to arrange in layers until the whole bottom and part of the sides are covered.

7. Fill the cavity with the remaining apples.

8. Unroll the dough on top of the apples.

9. Trim the dough so that it comes to the edge of the apples, brush the dough with an egg wash (1 whole egg, beaten) and prick with a fork or a knife.

10. Bake on a cookie sheet in a 400-degree preheated oven for 45 minutes, or until the dough is nicely browned. Run a knife all around to loosen the crust. Let the pie set for 5 minutes.

11. Place a platter on top of the pie plate and

12. turn upside down.

13. The pie plate should come off easily. If some slices stick to the bottom, pick them up and arrange them in the design. If the pie is taken out of the oven and turned upside down immediately, it may collapse during unmolding. However, if left to set too long, the caramel will harden and half of the bottom will stick. If this happens, heat the pie plate for a few seconds directly on the gas burner before unmolding.

14. You may brush the top with an apricot glaze (see step 11 in the preceding technique), and decorate with sliced almonds. Eat barely cool; do not refrigerate. See finished tarte tatin, page 614a.

This recipe serves 8 to 10.

262. Galette of Apple *(Galette de Pommes)*

YIELD: About 10 servings

THE GALETTE OF APPLE, thin and crunchy, done free form, is real country-looking and perfect to take along on picnics or to serve on a buffet. Whether you use puff paste or *pâte brisée,* it is important that the dough be very thin and the layer of apples very thin. The galette should be well browned and very crisp. The apricot glaze is not always used in country cooking, but it makes the tart taste and look beautiful.

Pâte brisée

2 *cups flour*
1½ *stick (6 ounces) sweet butter, cut in ¼-inch
    pieces and kept very cold*
¼ *teaspoon salt*
½ *teaspoon sugar*
⅓ *cup water, very cold*

Apple filling

6 *to 8 large apples, Pippin, Golden Delicious,
Greening, etc.*
⅓ *stick (1⅓ ounces) sweet butter, cut into small
    pieces*
⅓ *cup sugar*

Apricot glaze

½ *cup quality apricot preserves, strained, com
    bined with 1 tablespoon kirsch,
    Calvados or Cognac*

1. Combine all the dough ingredients together and work just long enough for it to hold together. You should still see pieces of butter spotted throughout the dough. Refrigerate for a good hour. Sprinkle the board with flour and roll out the dough as thin as possible. It should not be more than ⅛ inch thick. Roll the dough onto the rolling pin.

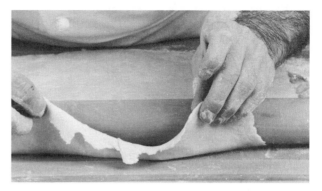

2. Unroll onto a 16- by 12-inch cookie sheet.

3. Peel the apples, cut them into halves and remove the central core. Cut each half into slices about ¼ inch thick. Arrange the slices in diagonal rows, overlapping to simulate the tiles of a roof. Leave approximately a 1½-inch border of dough arround the apples.

4. Fold the border back onto the apples. Patch holes, if any, or the juices will run and burn on the tray during cooking. Dot with pieces of butter and dust with the sugar. Dust some sugar on the border where it will crystallize while cooking and form a crunchy cookie-like edge. Bake in a preheated 400-degree oven for 75 minutes. It needs this long cooking time to be really crunchy. The dough is better if it's slightly too dark than too light.

5. Let the galette rest for a few minutes, then spoon the apricot glaze on top. Spread gently so as not to disturb the pattern.

6. After 15 or 20 minutes cut into large slices. Eat at room temperature or slightly warm, but never cold straight from the refrigerator.

263. Galette of Lemon *(Galette au Citron)*

YIELD: 2 galettes serving about 12

THE GALETTE is an open-faced tart, very thin and crunchy, usually made in a round shape and cut into large, pizza-type slices. Although it is usually a country dessert, it can become very elegant with the addition of a sauce. The lemon galette is made with a *pâte sucrée* (sweet dough) and the apple galette (technique 262), with a *pâte brisée* (pie dough). It is a good dessert for a large party. It's easy to make and serve, and keeps quite well for hours.

Pâte sucrée
3 cups all-purpose flour
2½ sticks (10 ounces) sweet butter, softened
½ cup granulated sugar
¼ teaspoon salt
1 egg, plus 1 egg yolk, beaten

Sauce
3 egg yolks
½ cup powdered sugar
3 tablespoons Grand Marnier
2 cups sour cream

Lemon filling
10 egg yolks
1 tablespoon, plus 1 teaspoon, cornstarch
¾ cup granulated sugar
Grated rind of 2 lemons (approximately 1 tablespoon)
Juice of 3 lemons (approximately ⅔ cup)
1 lemon, peeled and cut into very thin slices

1. To make the dough, combine the ingredients in a bowl and work until it holds together. Place on the table. Crush or smear the mixture with the palm of your hand a few times until the mixture is well blended (see technique 271). Divide into two pieces. Roll the first piece into a 14-inch round, about ¼ inch thick. Roll the dough on your rolling pin and unroll onto a cookie sheet.

It is a delicate dough to roll as it tends to break. Remembering that the *pâte sucrée* cannot be rolled as thin as a *pâte brisée* or a puff paste or it will burn. Trim the edge of the dough and fold it back onto itself all around.

2. Fold the dough over once again to make a border approximately ½ inch high. Press the border with your fingers to bring it to a point on top. The base will be wide and the top pointed like a triangle (see arrow). This keeps the border from collapsing during cooking.

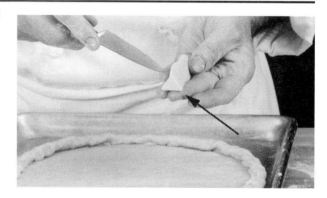

3. Use your fingers to pinch and press a decorative border all around.

4. Roll the rest of the dough and trim it into a rectangular or square shape. Make the border.

5. Place both "shells" in a preheated 400-degree oven for 12 to 15 minutes to pre-cook lightly. They will be baked again later with their fillings. (For a different dessert, cook the shells entirely, which will take about 25 minutes, and fill with a *crème patissière*, top with fresh berries such as strawberries, raspberries, or slices of bananas and glaze with a fruit jam that complements the fruit used.) If there are any holes in the crust, patch with a bit of extra dough or water mixed with flour.

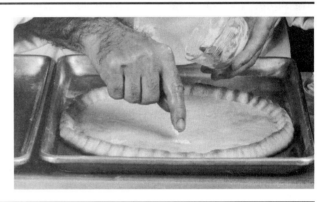

6. The lemon galette batter is liquid and if there are any holes it will seep through during cooking. To prepare the lemon filling, mix the yolks and sugar together and whip with a whisk for 2 to 3 minutes, until it reaches the ribbon stage. Add the cornstarch and lemon rind, mix well, then add the lemon juice. Divide the mixture onto the two pre-cooked shells.

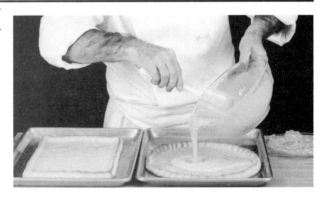

7. Arrange the slices of lemon on top and immediately place in a preheated 375-degree oven. The oven rack and the cookie sheet must be very flat or the batter will run on one side or spill over. Bake for 18 to 20 minutes.

8. As the dough cooks, the batter will pleat and pull around the slices of lemon and form a design by itself. Let cool and cut into wedges. For the sauce, mix the 3 egg yolks and sugar together and work with a whisk for 1 to 2 minutes. Stir in the Grand Marnier and sour cream. Serve 2 tablespoons next to each slice.

264. Cream Puff Dough *(Pâte à Choux)*

ALONG WITH the *pâte brisée,* technique 256, and *feuilletage,* technique 269, *pâte à choux* is one of the mother doughs of French pastry making. It is used to make countless desserts such as éclairs and *choux, gâteau St.-Honoré* and *Paris-Brest* as well as such dishes as *pommes dauphine* and even quenelles. It is always made with what is called a *panade*—a combination of water, butter and flour—to which eggs are added.

1 *cup water*
½ *stick (4 tablespoons) sweet butter*
¼ *teaspoon salt*
1 *cup all-purpose flour*
4 *large eggs*

1. Place the water, butter (cut into pieces) and salt in a heavy saucepan. Bring to a boil. When the butter is completely melted, remove from the heat and add the flour all at once. Mix rapidly with a wooden spatula.

2. Place the mixture on top of a low flame and "dry" for 1 to 2 minutes, mixing with the wooden spatula. The dough should be soft and should not stick to your fingers when pinched. This mixture is called the *panade.*

3. Transfer the *panade* to a clean bowl. You will notice that the bottom of the pan is covered with a thin crust (an indication that the dough has been sufficiently dried). The eggs are mixed into the *panade* in the bowl because if they were added in the pan, the white crust at the bottom would break into dried little pieces that would stick in the dough.

4. Let the dough cool for at least 5 minutes. Add the eggs one at a time, beating carefully after each addition so that the mixture is smooth before the next egg is added.

5. The dough should be smooth, shiny, and as thick and as heavy as mayonnaise. This makes enough dough for 14 to 16 *choux* or éclairs which are described in the following technique.

265. Cream Puffs *(Choux et Eclairs)*

THE ONLY DIFFERENCE BETWEEN a *choux* and an éclair is that the former is round and the latter is long. Both can be filled with flavored whipped cream, *crème pâtissière,* ice cream, jam and the like. The smallest *choux* are known as *profiteroles* and are often filled with vanilla ice cream and served with a lukewarm chocolate sauce. (The *ganache* used for the icing in the *gâteau au chocolat,* technique 234, can be diluted with water and used as a chocolate sauce.)

1. Prepare the *pâte à choux* following the recipe in the preceding technique. Fill a pastry bag with the dough and coat a large cookie sheet with butter and flour, techniques 62 and 61, Squeeze out puffs about the size of a golf ball or elongated éclairs.

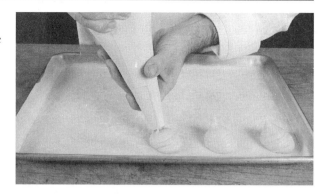

2. Brush the tops with an egg wash (1 whole egg, beaten), pushing down the "tails." The *choux* can also be formed by dropping spoonfuls of dough on the cookie sheet.

3. Drag the tines of a fork to make a design on top of the éclairs. Let the *choux* and éclairs dry for at least 20 minutes before cooking. (The egg wash gives a shiny glaze, providing it is allowed to dry for a while before baking.)

4. Bake in a 375-degrees preheated oven for 35 minutes, or until well puffed and golden. Shut off the heat, open the oven door halfway (to get rid of any steam) and let the puffs cool slowly and dry for 30 minutes. *Pâte à choux* will soften and collapse if cooled to fast. Cut into haves to fill or, if you want to, keep them whole. (See technique 268, steps 4 and 5.) See finished cream puffs, page 710.

266. Cream Puff Swans (Cygnes en Pâte à Choux)

1. Prepare the *pâte à choux* following the recipe in technique 264, Fill a pastry bag with the dough and coat a large cookie sheet with butter and flour, techniques 62 and 61. Squeeze large teardrops of dough onto the cookie sheet (see technique 224, step 5).

2. Make a paper cornet, technique 66, fill with dough and squeeze out small "question marks." Make a pointed "beak" by "pulling" the cornet up.

3. Brush with an egg wash (1 whole egg, beaten). Bake in a 375-degree preheated oven for 10 to 12 minutes. Remove the small question marks and return the cream puffs to the oven for another 25 minutes, a total baking time for the cream puffs of 35 to 40 minutes. Shut off the heat and open the oven door halfway, allowing the steam to escape. Let cool and dry for 30 minutes.

4. Holding the *choux* on the side, slice off the top on a diagonal with a sharp, long-bladed knife.

5. Cut the lid into halves.

6. Fill the *choux* with sweetened whipped cream.

7. Place both pieces of the lid back on the cream to simulate wings.

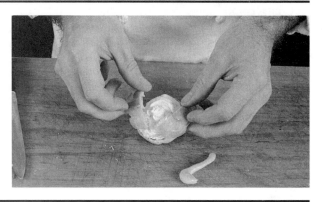

8. Stick the "neck" into the cream between the point of the wings.

9. Sprinkle with confectioners' sugar.

Variation: Place 1 tablespoon of raspberry jam in the bottom of the opened swan. Top with a small scoop of vanilla ice cream and decorate with whipped cream. Place the wings and the necks into place. Just before serving, pour diluted raspberry jam or raspberry sauce into a large platter. Arrange the swans so they are "swimming" in the sauce. Surround with angel hair, technique 248. See finished cream puff swans, page 710.

267. Cream Puff Ring *(Paris-Brest)*

THE PARIS-BREST is made from a ring of *pâte à choux* that is baked and filled with praline cream and whipped cream, then topped with sliced almonds and confectioners' sugar. The cake serves 16.

1. Coat a cookie sheet with butter and flour, technique 61, Using a flan ring, or any circular mold, mark an outline about 10 inches in diameter.

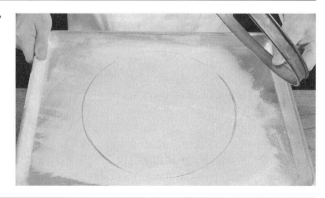

2. Prepare the *pâte à choux,* technique 264, Fit a pastry bag with the dough, technique 62, Squeeze out a ring of *pâte à choux* about 1 inch wide, following the outline.

3. Squeeze another ring inside or outside the first, depending on how large you want the cake to be.

4. Squeeze 1 ring on top of the others.

5. Brush with an egg wash (1 whole egg, beaten).

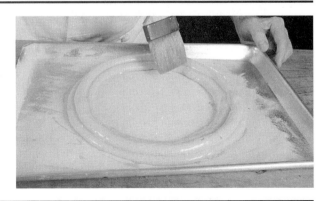

6. Sprinkle 1 tablespoon sliced almonds on top.

7. Let the cake dry for about 20 minutes. Bake in a 400-degree preheated oven for 45 minutes. Shut off the heat, open the oven door halfway to let the steam escape and leave the cake in the oven for 1 hour so it cools and dries. Using a long-bladed knife, cut a lid off the cake.

8. Fill the bottom part with *crème pralinée,* technique 216.

9. Then decorate with slightly sweetened whipped cream.

10. Place the lid back on top.

11. Sprinkle with confectioners' sugar. Keep in a cool, not too cold, dry place. Cut into small wedges with a serrated knife. See finished cream puff cake, page 710.

268. Cream Puff Cake *(Gâteau St.-Honoré)*

THIS CLASSIC FRENCH CAKE was named for the patron saint of bakers. It is made from *pâte brisée* (or *pâte sucrée*) base that is topped with cream-filled choux coated with caramel. I use larger choux then are normally used (a personal preference) and instead of the classic St.-Honoré cream, which is made from hot *créme pâtissiére* mixed with beaten egg whites, I use a *créme pâtissiére* combined with whipped cream.

Make the *crème pâtissière,* technique 215, adding 1 envelope unflavored gelatin to the sugar in the recipe. When the cream is cool, fold in 2½ cups unsweetened heavy cream, whipped firm, technique 60.

Make half the recipe for *pâte brisée,* technique 256, and a batch of *pâte à choux,* technique 264. Bake 10 *choux* and reserve the remaining mixture for use in step 2.

1. Roll the *pâte brisée* dough ⅛-inch thick and place on a cookie sheet. Using a flan ring, or another round object about 10 inches in diameter, trim the dough into a wheel.

2. Fit a pastry bag with a tube with a small opening and fill with the remaining *pâte à choux*, technique 62. Squeeze 3 small rings around the edge of the *pâte brisée*.

3. Prick the center with a fork and bake in a 400-degree preheated oven for 30 minutes. It should be well baked and nicely browned.

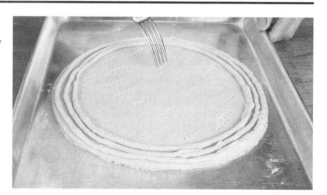

4. Using the tip of a knife, make a hole in the bottom of each *choux*.

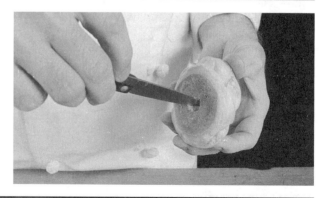

5. Fill a pastry bag with the *crème pâtissière* and fill each *choux* by inserting the tube through the opening at the bottom and squeezing the cream inside.

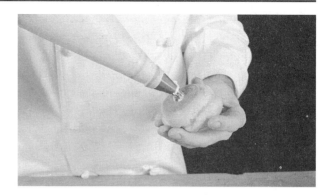

6. Make a caramel using 1 cup sugar mixed with ¾ cup corn syrup. Let the caramel cool off for at least 5 minutes so it thickens. Place the saucepan containing the caramel in a pot of hot water to keep it at the right consistency. Holding the filled *choux* by the bottom, dip the top into the caramel. Be careful not to burn your fingers. Lift up and

7. let the excess drip on the cream puff border. Quickly set the *choux,* glazed side up, on the drips of caramel so that the *choux* is anchored on the border.

8. Repeat all around, arranging the *choux* in an orderly fashion, fastening them with the caramel drips.

9. Scoop some of the remaining *crème pâtissière* into the middle. Place some in a pastry bag with a fluted tube and decorate the top. Place the last puff in the middle of the cake. See finished cream puff cake, below. You may decorate with angel hair, technique 248. Place in a cool, not cold, dry place until serving time.

This cake serves 10 to 12.

Clockwise from top: apple charlotte, cream puff cake, cream puffs, cream puff swans, cream puff ring

269. Classic Puff Paste *(Feuilletage Classique)*

PUFF PASTE, or *feuilletage*, is the hardest dough to make, and it has its pitfalls even for professionals. The dough will be easier to make and will rise fantastically if you use shortening, which melt at a higher temperature than butter. However. nothing can replace the taste or the fragrance of butter. The difference is evident, even though some restaurants are naïve enough to believe they are fooling their customers.

Puff paste is made with flour and butter in equal proportions. The flour is bound is bound with a liquid, usually water, into an elastic and shiny dough (*détrempe*). The butter is encased in the dough, and both elements are rolled together. By folding, rolling and folding the dough, a multilayered effect is achieved, with layers of elastic dough and layers of butter. The butter melts during cooking and develops steam which tries to escape, "pushing" the layers up into the "thousand-leaf" effect. American all-purpose flour is high in gluten (the protein part of the flour that makes the dough elastic). You can use about one-fifth cake flour with the regular all-purpose flour to "tone down" the resilience of the dough, or you may use pastry flour which is more akin to the French flour.

The butter and the basic dough should be the same temperature and consistency. If the butter is too cold, it will break and crumble and push through the dough during the rolling. If it is too soft, it will be "squished" and will run between the layers. Beware of hot and humid days; the ingredients are limp and have a tendency to blend together.

Puff paste tends to darken and become quite elastic when stored in the refrigerator. However, well wrapped, it freezes beautifully. You cannot make a recipe for less than 1 pound of flour, or it will not be uniform. It is preferable to weigh the flour because it is not accurate with cup measurement. Three cups of tightly packed flour equals 1 pound. On the other hand, 1 pound of sifted flour may fill up 4 cups.

Cream can be used instead of water in the basic dough, making an extremely light, tender and delicate pastry. Use the best sweet butter available.

2 pounds sweet butter
2 pounds flour (see above) and 1 cup for rolling
2 cups water or 2½ cups heavy cream
2 teaspoons salt

1. Place the butter on the work table, flatten with the roller and sprinkle ¾ cup flour from the preweighed 2 pounds. Using a pastry scraper and your hands, work the mixture together until well mixed and smooth.

2. Form a square "cake" with the mixture and refrigerate.

3. Place the flour in the mixing bowl (if you use an electric mixer) or on the table. Make a well in the center and add the water (or cream) and the salt. Mix carefully into a homogenous and shiny dough. Do not overwork.

4. Make a crisscross cut on top of the dough and roll or spread out with your hands the four sections of the dough, making a large four-leafed clover.

5. Place the butter on top of the dough.

6. Bring the edges back on top of the butter.

7. Seal the leaves to enclose the butter tightly inside.

8. Roll the dough into a thick rectangle. Roll gently, without pressing down too much.

9. Place in the refrigerator for a good 30 minutes. This will give the dough and butter a chance to get to the same temperature, insuring uniform rolling.

10. Roll the dough gently into a long rectangle, about ⅜ inch thick. Roll the dough enough to thin it and spread it out but do not roll it back and forth relentlessly or you will make the dough too resilient. Roll from the center out. Be careful in this first rolling as the dough is at its most delicate and can easily open letting butter squish through. Fold the dough back on itself to a point about two-thirds up the rectangle.

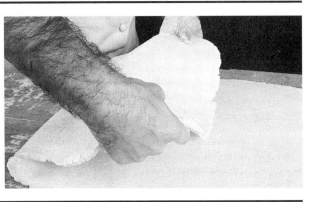

11. Roll the folded part lightly to equalize it.

12. Holding your rolling pin at the edge of the folded dough, strike the single layer with the pin to make a depression in the dough. This will make a "hinge."

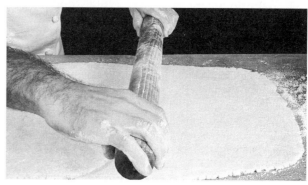

13. Fold the single layer back onto the dough. You now have a three-layered package. This is known as one "turn." Place on a large cookie sheet, cover with a towel and refrigerate for 15 to 20 minutes.

14. Place the folded dough, narrow (open) side facing you, on the floured board. Roll the dough uniformly, pushing and rolling at the same time. Remember that excess rolling will make the dough contract and develop too much elasticity.

15. During the rolling, it is important that the board is properly floured so that the dough can slide and spread uniformly. If the dough sticks at any point, pushing with the roller will smear and break the layers, making the butter bleed during cooking.

16. Be sure to dust the dry flour off the dough before folding. Dry flour "imprisoned" between layers will result in a dry and tough pastry. If the dough is not too elastic, you may give two turns consecutively. Otherwise, let the dough "rest" for 15 to 20 minutes before the next turn.

17. Imprint the number of turns into the dough with your fingertips so that you don't forget. The classic puff paste gets six turns. However, if the dough becomes too elastic and hard to work, stop after five turns. Cover and refrigerate before using. When you need a piece of the dough, cut the dough "widthwise." Whatever trimmings you have left, gather in a ball and refrigerate or freeze. The trimmings, called *roqnures*, are quite adequate for tarts, *fleurons*, sausage or pâte in crust and the like.

270. Fast Puff Paste *(Feuilletage Rapide)*

When in a hurry, you can always prepare a fast puff paste in one hour at the most, and use it right away. It is quite satisfactory in the most instances, except for large vol-au-vent (patty shells). Te dough does not develop quite as uniformly and is not as flaky as the classic dough described in the previous technique, but the differences are small and apparent only when the doughs are compared side by side. The dough can be made with regular all-purpose flour, as well as with instant flour.

4 sticks (1 pound) sweet butter, very cold
1 pound flour (all-purpose or instant)
        plus ¾ cup for rolling
1 teaspoon salt
1 cup cold water

1. Dice the cold butter into ⅜-inch cubes. Arrange a well in the flour and place the butter and salt in the center.

2. Using a pastry scraper, "cut" the butter into the flour.

3. Add the water and combine all ingredients into a mass rapidly. Do not knead the dough.

4. At this point, the dough will look very lumpy (the butter is still in pieces), but it should hold together. Flour the working table generously. (This dough requires more flour during the rolling than a conventional dough.) Roll the dough into a ⅜-inch-thick rectangle.

5. Brush the flour from the surface and fold one end in to the center of the rectangle.

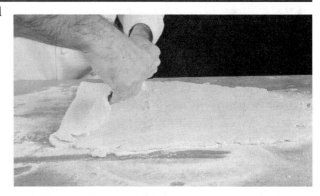

6. Fold the other end in. Both ends should meet in the center. Brush again to remove excess flour.

7. Fold the dough in half.

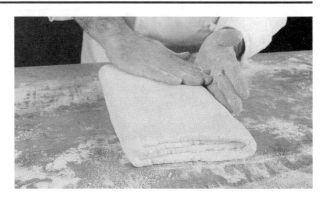

8. You now have one double turn that gives you 4 layers of dough. Give two more double turns—a total of 3 altogether. This is the equivalent of 4 to 5 single turns and is enough for a fast puff paste. If the dough does not become too elastic, the 3 turns can be given consecutively. Handle and store as you would classic puff paste.

271. Egg Yolk Puff Paste (Feuilletage à Pâté)

There are several different types of puff paste. In this recipe we have added egg yolk which makes the dough stronger and particularly well suited pâtes and other situations where it has to withstand pressure from the steam building inside. (for a lighter version, omit the egg yolk and increase the butter to 14 ounces.) Work very fast with ice-cold ingredients and equipment so the mixture will not have time to get to elastic. before the dough is finished. Place the flour in the freezer for a few hours so it gets extremely cold. Cut the butter into tiny ¼-inch dice. (Cut the sticks of butter in half lengthwise, then cut each half into halves, lengthwise, and then dice the strips.) Spread the butter pieces on a plate and place in the refrigerator. Owning a piece of marble also makes it easier. If it is winter, place the marble outside to cool or cool it in a refrigerator or freezer or by placing a tray full of ice cubes on top of it. If the ingredients and marble are cold, the dough doesn't stick and almost no flour is needed in the rolling. The dough can be made in not much more than 10 minutes.

1 *pound flour (3 cups tightly packed)*
3 *sticks (12 ounces) sweet butter*
2 *egg yolks mixed with 1 cup cold water*
1 *teaspoon of salt*

1. Combine the egg yolks with the water and place in the refrigerator for a few hours, or in the freezer until very cold. Refrigerate the butter and flour, too.

2. Stir all the ingredients in a bowl fast, so it barely holds together.

3. Place the dough on the cold marble. Gather and press it together until it holds a shape.

4. Flatten the dough with the palms of your hands by pushing and pressing it down so it extends to about 1 inch in thickness.

5. As you spread the dough, you will see pieces of butter distributed throughout. Use the dough scraper to lift the dough if it sticks. Keep rolling, using as little flour as possible, into a rectangle about 15 inches long and 10 inches wide. Fold the dough like a letter into thirds. This is a single turn.

6. Working as fast as you can, roll the dough into a rectangle about 18 inches long by 10 inches wide and ½ inch thick. Fold so the edges join in the center.

7. Press to flatten and then fold in half. This is called a double turn (four layers). Moving as fast as you can, roll the dough out again into a rectangle about 18 inches by 10 inches. Fold again into a double turn. Turn the dough and roll again, this time into a longer and wider rectangle about ¼ inch thick. Fold again into a double turn. A lot of physical strength is needed in the rolling. Use a rolling pin at least as big as the one in the picture. A large ball bearing or *tutove* pin will make the rolling easier and faster.

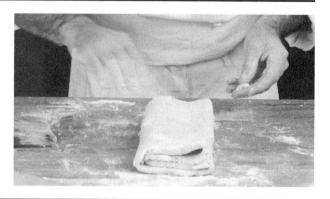

8. At this point the dough will be too elastic to use. After refrigeration, the dough can also be cut and frozen.

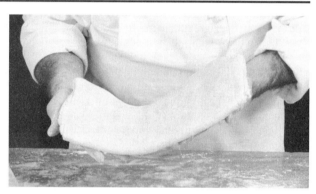

To recap the process: The mixture was first crudely spread by hand and folded into thirds. Then, rolled and folded into a double turn. Then rolled and folded double again, then finally rolled and folded double once more. The 3 double rolls or turns are equivalent to 5 single turns. If the mixture gets too sticky and the ingredients tend to blend together, give it one less turn. If the dough becomes too elastic to be worked, do not fight it. Refrigerate for 30 minutes. Remember that cold, as well as time, is your best ally.

272. Large Patty Shell *(Vol-au-Vent à l'Ancienne)*

V OL-AU-VENT ARE CUSTOMARILY FILLED with sweetbreads, chicken, quenelles and mushrooms, lobster meat and the like, usually bound with a sauce. They are one of the most delicate pastries to make and must be made with perfect classic puff paste dough. The shell should be cut from the middle of the dough because the middle develops more uniformly than the edges. Begin by making the classic puff paste dough, technique 269. One pound of flour will make enough dough for 2 vol-au-vent. A filled vol-au-vent serves 8.

1. Roll the dough ⅜ inch thick. Using a round object as a guide (in this case, a cake pan), cut two disks 8 inches in diameter. Be sure to cut the dough with a sharp knife. If the dough is cut with a dull blade, the layers will squish together and will not rise properly.

2. Using a smaller round object, cut a disk from one of the wheels to make a ring. The ring should be at least 1¼ inches wide. Reserve the center of the ring for half puff paste *(demi-feuilletage)*.

3. Place the solid wheel on a cookie sheet lined with parchment paper. Brush the surface with an egg wash (1 whole egg, beaten).

4. Place the ring of dough carefully on top and press all around so that it adheres well to the bottom layer. The dough is now ¾-inch thick at the edge.

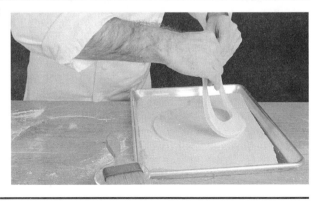

5. Brush the ring with the egg wash. It is important that the wash does not run down the sides of the shell. If this happens, the layers will be "glued" together by the wash and will have difficulty rising.

6. Using the dull side of the blade, mark the edge all around.

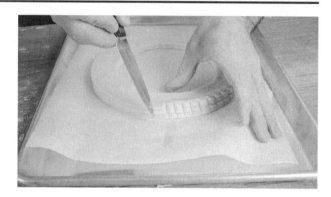

7. Cut about 1/8-inch deep into the bottom layer following the curve of the ring to create the "lid." Carve a trellis in the center of the lid. Cool the vol-au-vent for 1 hour. Bake in a 425-degree oven for 40 to 45 minutes. If, after 10 minutes the shell is rising unevenly, cut the high side at the lid incision to let steam escape and allow the other side to level off. When baked, cut off and remove the lid. discard some of the mushy dough from the inside, fill, cover the lid and serve. See finished large patty shell, old style, page 732.

273. Large Patty Shell *(Vol-au-Vent à la Moderne)*

T HIS IS AN EASIER and more dramatic way of making a large patty shell, and it doesn't require a dough as perfect as the one just described. Fast puff paste as well as puff paste trimmings (half puff paste or *demi-feuilletage*) are adequate, and it can also be done with a *pâte brisée*, although it is not as spectacular as when made with puff paste. Make the puff paste, either the classic or the fast, technique 269 or 270.

1. Roll the dough approximately ³/₁₆ inch thick. Using a round object as a guide, cut out an 8-inch circle. Place the circle on a wet, or parchment-lined cookie sheet. Place a ball of aluminum foil, about 3½ inches in diameter, in the middle of the circle. Brush the dough all around the ball with water.

2. Roll another sheet of puff paste and place on top of the foil. Push all around to have the top layer adhere well to the bottom. Be sure that the dough is stretched uniformly around the foil ball.

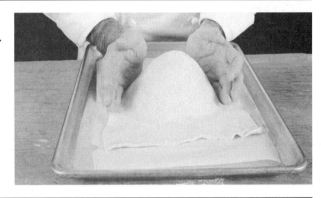

3. Trim the top layer of dough so it is even with the bottom. You can do this freehand or use an 8-inch flan ring as a guide. Cut with a sharp knife.

4. Brush the dough with an egg wash (1 whole egg, beaten). Do not let the wash run on the edges. Cut out little triangles from the edges.

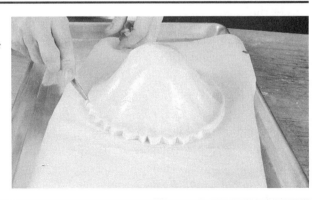

5. Cut long, thin strips of dough and decorate the shell to your fancy.

6. Cut lozenges from the dough to simulate leaves and finish decorating the shell. Brush again with egg wash.

7. Make a hole at the top to let the steam escape during baking. Let the shell "relax" in a cool place for 1 hour. Bake in a 425-degree preheated oven for 30 to 35 minutes.

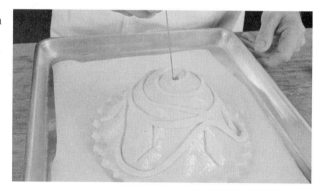

8. Let the shell cool for 10 to 15 minutes and cut the "lid" off, following the outline of the decoration.

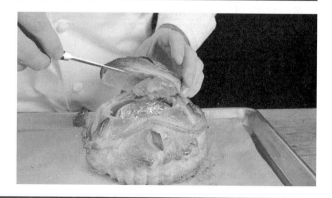

9. Being careful not to damage the shell, slide your thumb and index finger on both sides of the aluminum foil and squeeze to reduce the size of the ball.

10. Pull the foil out. The shell is now ready to be garnished. See finished large patty shell, new style, page 732.

274. Individual Patty Shells *(Bouchées)*

MAKE THE CLASSIC PUFF PASTE DOUGH, technique 269. For individual patty shells, as well as for *fleurons,* cheese straws and other puff paste garnishes described in the following technique, it is preferable to roll the dough in long sheets (about ³⁄₁₆ inch thick) the day before, allowing it to "relax" overnight in the refrigerator. This prevents the dough from shrinking when it is cut.

1. Cut rounds about 3 inches in diameter with a plain or fluted edge cutter. Be sure that the cutter is sharp. If the edge is dull, the layers will get squeezed together and will not rise properly.

2. Using a smaller cutter, cut a piece from the center of half of the rounds. The outside rings are used to form the walls of the patty shells. They should be ½ inch wide.

3. Rub your finger underneath the cutting edge of the cutter to be sure that the outside ring of the dough is "free."

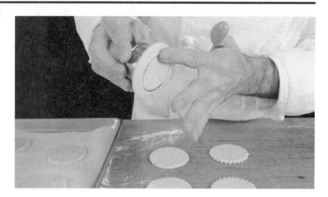

4. Place the rounds on a cookie sheet lined with parchment paper. Brush the top with an egg wash (1 whole egg, beaten). Position the ring (still attached to the cutter) over the round and push it into place. Remove the cutter. Reserve the piece of dough inside the cutter for tart or pie shells.

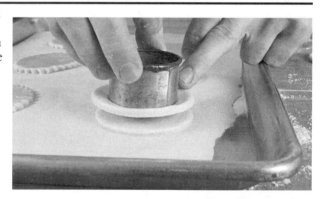

5. Brush the ring with egg wash. Do not let it run down the sides.

6. To prevent the shells from falling over while baking, place a wire rack on top. The shells should rise five to six times their original thickness. Hence, the wire rack should not be more than 2 inches high at the most. If the shells rise crookedly, the high side will be stopped when it touches the rack, and the other side will equalize itself. Bake in a 425-degree preheated oven for 20 to 25 minutes. Lift the lid and fill to your liking. Place the lid back on top of the food before serving. See finished individual patty shells, page 732.

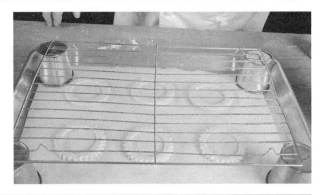

275. Puff Paste Cheese Straws and Crescents *(Paillettes, Diablotins, Fleurons)*

PAILLETTES AND DIABLOTINS are cheese straws; the first are flat strips and the other twisted. You can serve them with consommé for a very elegant first course, or with cheese or drinks. *Fleurons* (crescents) are classically used to decorate whole fish or fish fillets served with a sauce and glazed, such as sole *Bercy.* Both can be made with classic puff paste, fast puff paste or the trimmings of either *(demi-feuilletage),* techniques 269 and 270.

1. For the cheese straws, roll the dough ⅛ inch thick. If you have the time, it is preferable to roll it out the day before and let it "relax" in the refrigerator overnight. This will reduce shrinkage and irregular puffing. Brush the surface of the dough with an egg wash (1 whole egg, beaten). Mix together ⅔ cup freshly grated Parmesan cheese and ¼ cup good paprika. Sprinkle the mixture on top and rub so that the whole surface is covered.

2. Turn the dough upside down and coat the other side with the mixture.

3. Both sides of the dough are now covered with the cheese and paprika mixture. Fold in half.

4. Cut strips about ⅜ inch wide.

5. Unfold strips. To make twisted cheese straws, place one hand at each end of the strip. In a swift movement, roll the strip forward with one hand and, at the same time, roll backward with the other. The strip will be twisted into a corkscrew-like spiral.

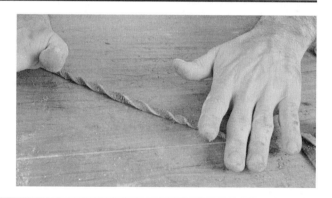

6. Place the strips, whether they are twisted or flat, on a wet or parchment-lined cookie sheet. To prevent the strips from shrinking during baking, smear the ends onto the cookie sheet so they stick and hold the dough stretched.

7. Bake in a 425-degree preheated oven for 7 to 8 minutes, or until nicely browned and crisp. Trim the ends off and cut into 4-inch sticks.

8. To make *fleurons,* roll the dough about ³/₁₆ inch thick and brush with an egg wash. Cut the half-moon crescents with a cookie cutter. Move forward and cut only with the front half of the cookie cutter. Let the *fleurons* "relax" for 20 minutes at least, then bake in a 425-degree preheated oven for 9 to 10 minutes. See finished twisted and flat cheese straws and puff paste crescents, page 732.

276. Anchovy Sticks *(Allumettes aux Anchois)*

ANCHOVIES WRAPPED IN PUFF PASTE make attractive finger food for buffets or to serve as an hors d'oeuvre with drinks. They are customarily shaped into sticks (Method 1), but can also be made to look like little fish (Method 2). Make the puff paste, either the classic or fast, techniques 269 and 270, or use leftover trimmings of either (*rognures*). It is preferable to roll the dough the day before, allowing it to "relax" overnight in the refrigerator before using.

METHOD 1

1. Roll the dough into 4-inch-wide strips, about ⅛ inch thick. Brush with an egg wash (1 whole egg, beaten).

2. Arrange anchovy fillets (preserved in olive oil) about 2 inches apart on a sheet of dough. Sprinkle the anchovies with chopped hard-boiled egg and chopped parsley. Place another layer of dough on top.

3. Press the side of your hand between each anchovy so that the top layer of dough adheres well to the bottom.

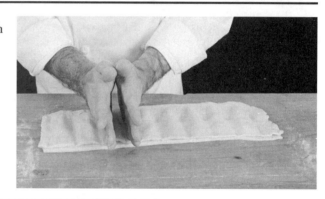

4. Brush again with egg wash and cut into individual pieces.

5. Decorate the top of each piece with the point of a knife. Let "relax" for at least 1 hour before baking. Bake in a 425-degree preheated oven for 20 to 25 minutes.

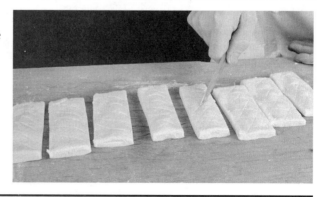

METHOD 2

1. Roll and cut the dough into 2½-inch-wide strips. Brush with an egg wash. Place two rows of anchovies side by side, slightly staggered. Cover with a top layer of dough and press so the layers adhere. Brush again with egg wash.

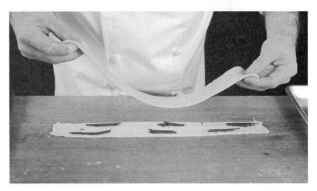

2. Separate the rows of anchovies, cutting in a sinuous pattern to simulate the shape of a fish. Separate into individual pieces.

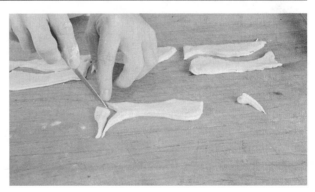

3. Trim the "tail" of the fish.

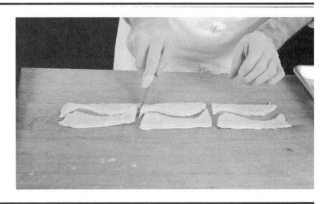

4. With the point of a knife, "draw" the scales, gills and eyes of a fish. Let the dough "relax" for a good hour.

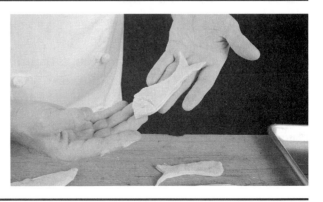

5. Bake in a 425-degree preheated oven for 22 to 25 minutes.

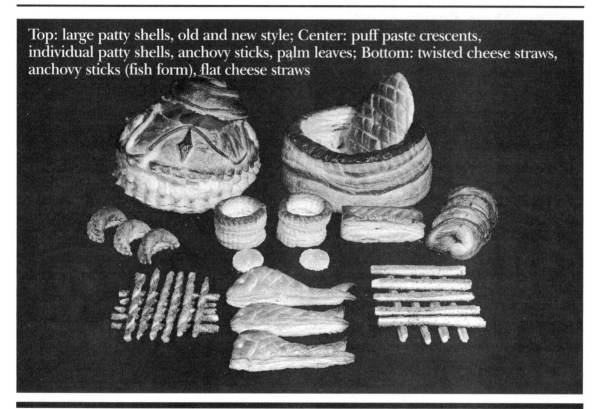

Top: large patty shells, old and new style; Center: puff paste crescents, individual patty shells, anchovy sticks, palm leaves; Bottom: twisted cheese straws, anchovy sticks (fish form), flat cheese straws

277. Puff Paste Almond Cake *(Pithiviers)*

THE PITHIVIERS is usually served as a coffee cake. Although it is a specialty of the town of Pithiviers in the south of France, it has become a classic made in most good pastry shops. Make puff paste following technique 271. You will need about 1½ pounds of puff paste.

Almond cream mixture

¾ cup finely ground almonds or almond powder
2 tablespoons sweet butter, melted

½ cup granulated sugar
2 tablespoons dark rum
3 egg yolks
2 tablespoons heavy cream

1. Roll the puff paste to ¼ inch thick. Unroll on a cookie sheet or a pizza plate lined with parchment paper. Using a flan ring as a mark, cut a circle about 10 inches in diameter. Combine the almond cream ingredients together and spread in the center of the puff paste, being careful to leave about 1 inch uncovered all around.

2. Brush the uncovered edge with an egg wash (1 egg, plus 1 egg yolk, beaten). Roll another circle of puff paste, cut it with the flan ring and place on top of the almond cream mixture.

3. Press the edges together so the two layers adhere. Invert a cake pan on top of the dough to help press it down and act as a guide to mark a scalloped edge.

4. Brush the top of the cake with the egg wash, make a hole in the center with the point of a knife and, using the point, mark a spiral from the edges toward the center hole, cutting into the dough about ¹/₁₆ inch deep. Place the cake in the refrigerator for 2 hours or in the freezer for 1 hour, then bake in a preheated 400-degree oven for ½ hour. Cover loosely with foil, reduce the temperature to 375 degrees and bake for another 20 minutes.

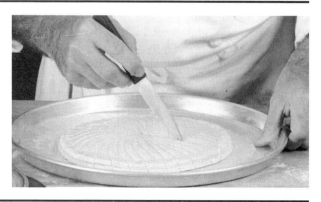

5. Remove the aluminum foil and generously sprinkle the top with powdered sugar. Return the cake to the oven for 5 to 10 minutes until the sugar melts and forms a beautiful glaze on top. If the sugar doesn't melt fast enough, place under the broiler for 1 minute. If the sugar melts in one place first, cover the melted spot with aluminum foil to prevent further cooking and place the pithiviers under the broiler so the remaining sugar melts evenly on top.

278. Pears in Caramel on Puff Paste

(Feuilleté de Poires au Caramel)

YIELD: 6 servings

ROLLED PIECES of sugared puff paste, cut into ovals and baked, are called *carolines*. They are large puff-paste cookies and can be served with fruit, or whipped cream, or with poached pears and a caramel cream sauce as we do below.

1 *pound puff paste (half of the recipe technique 269)*
1 *cup sugar*
3 *medium-sized pears, ripe, peeled and cut in halves*
½ *cup sugar*
¼ *cup water*
1 *cup heavy cream*

1. Spread 1 cup of the sugar on the table. Using the sugar as if it were flour to prevent the dough from sticking, roll the dough approximately ¼ inch thick. Sprinkle with sugar and fold into thirds like a letter. Roll out the dough again into a rectangle about ⅜ inch thick. Using a large oval cookie cutter (about 5½ inches long by 3 inches wide), cut 6 *carolines*. Place them on a cookie sheet lined with parchment paper and set in the refrigerator for 1 hour or in the freezer for 30 minutes.

2. Bake in a preheated 400-degree oven for 25 minutes until nice and brown. Remove from the paper as soon as possible or the sugar which has melted around the dough will harden and make the paper stick. Let cool on a wire rack.

3. Peel the pears, cut them in half and core. Mix the $1/2$ cup of sugar and water together in a large saucepan and place on high heat. Cook until it turns into a caramel, then add the pears, cover, and cook on low heat about 5 minutes, depending on the ripeness of the fruit. Do not let the pears fall apart. When tender to the point of a knife, add the cream, bring to a boil and simmer for about 3 minutes, uncovered. Cool until cool. Remove the pears from the caramel, slice each half and arrange on top of a caroline. Pour some of the sauce on top and around the puff paste and serve immediately. See finished dessert, below.

Poached oranges, puff paste of pears, candied orange rinds.

279. Small Fruit Tarts *(Tartelettes de Fruits)*

SMALL FRUIT TARTS are an ideal summer dessert. The shells are precooked, filled with a purée of fruit or *crème patissière,* topped with fruit and glazed. For raspberries, strawberries or blueberries, use a glaze of currant jelly or raspberry preserves. If a jelly is used, heat to liquefy, and brush on while still warm. Any preserve which is not jelled need only be sieved and flavored with alcohol. For fruits such as banana, pear, pineapple, oranges, etc., use an apricot or peach preserve, strained and seasoned with a bit of Kirschwasser or Cognac. Use the *crème patissière* in technique 215.

1. Roll out the pâte sucrée (see technique 257) to ¼ inch thick. It should not be too thin. If too thin, *pâte sucrée* tends to burn. Line up your tartelette molds. (They line up better if they are all the same shape and size—unlike ours.) Roll the dough back onto the rolling pin and unroll on top of the molds.

2. Take a lump of dough, dip it in flour so it doesn't stick, and use it to push and stretch the dough into each mold.

3. Trim the dough by rolling the pin on top of the molds. The weight of the pin will cut through the dough. Finish by pressing with your fingers.

4. Place another mold on top of the dough and press it down, to keep the dough from puffing during baking. Alternatively line with wax paper and weight with rice or beans. Bake in a preheated 375-degree oven for 5 to 8 minutes. Remove the upper molds and return to the oven for 10 more minutes or until lightly brown. *(Note:* The molds can also be inverted and the dough cooked on the outside.)

5. Fill with about 2 tablespoons *crème patissière* per shell, then arrange the fruits on top. Glaze with the appropriate preserve and serve as soon as possible. See finished small fruit tarts, page 641.

280. Fruit Tart Strips *(Bandes pour Tartes aux Fruits)*

THIS RECTANGULAR FRUIT TART is excellent for large gatherings because it is easy to serve. You just carve across at the end of each piece of fruit. The tart is made from a base of dough bordered with strips. The dough is baked, spread with a layer of *crème pâtissière* and then topped with poached fruit. The pastry can be made from fast puff paste or puff paste trimmings (*demi-feuilletage*), technique 270. Sometimes the base is made from *pâte brisée* or *pâte sucrée* and only the border is puff paste.

1. Roll the dough ¼ inch thick. Cut in a strip the length of your cookie sheet and about 5 inches wide. Cut two strips about ½ inch wide for the border. Wet about 1 inch on each side of the base and position the strips in place, pressing to make sure they adhere.

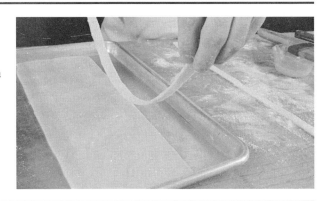

2. Using the dull side of the blade, decorate the edges of the tart with a knife. Brush the border with an egg wash (1 whole egg, beaten).

3. Prick the center with a fork (you don't want the dough to develop too much in the center). Let the dough "relax" for at least 30 minutes. Bake in a 425-degree preheated oven for 20 minutes. It should be well browned. In the photograph on the right, *pâte sucrée* has been used for the base. It is the hardest of the doughs, the most compact and will resist becoming soggy the longest.

4. Place a ¼- to ½-inch layer of *crème pâtissière,* technique 215, on the bottom and arrange poached apricot or peach halves on top. (Be sure the fruits are well drained to prevent the cream from thinning down.) You may use any kind of berries also.

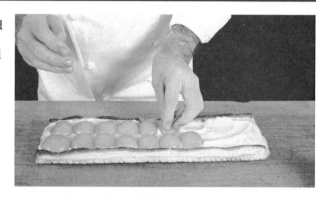

5. Brush the fruits with an apricot glaze (see technique 260, step 11), and sprinkle confectioners' sugar on the border.

281. Square Fruit Tart *(Tarte Carrée)*

MAKE SOME PUFF PASTE, either classic or fast, techniques 269 and 270, or use leftover puff paste (*rognures*). If you can spare the time, roll the dough the day before and let it "relax" in the refrigerator overnight to avoid shrinkage and irregular puffing.

1. Roll the dough ⅛ inch thick. Let it "relax" for at least 1 hour.

2. Fold the dough in half diagonally and trim it to have a folded square. You now have a right-angle triangle.

3. Cut a border on both square sides of the triangle, about ¾ inch wide.

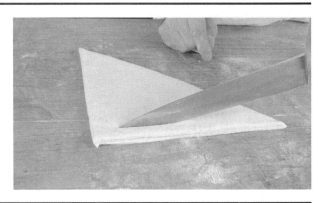

4. Be sure that the borders are still attached in the right-angle corner.

5. Unfold the dough and wet the edges with water.

6. Bring half the border over and place on the wet edge of the dough.

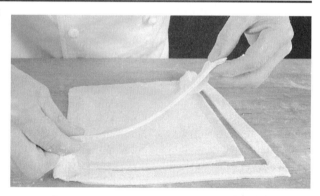

7. Then bring over the other half. Press to make the border adhere.

8. Trim the corners where the dough overlaps.

9. Prick the center with a fork. Bake in a 425-degree preheated oven for 20 to 25 minutes. If the dough still develops in the center during baking, just press it down with a fork.

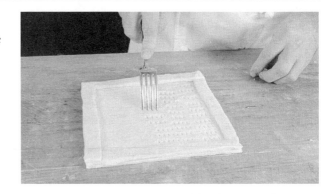

10. Make a caramel with ½ cup sugar and ¼ cup water and pour inside the shell, covering the whole bottom with a thin layer. The caramel gives crunchiness to the tart and keeps the cream from making the dough soggy.

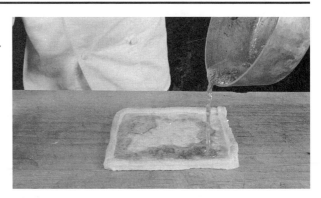

11. Cover with *crème pâtissière,* technique 215.

12. Fill with orange sections, technique 47, banana slices, berries or the like. Glaze the top with an apricot, raspberry or strawberry glaze (see technique 260, step 11).

282. Palm Cookies *(Palmiers)*

1. Prepare the puff paste, technique 269, or 270. Sprinkle the board and dough generously with sugar. Roll the dough in the sugar instead of flour. Roll to about ⅛ inch thick.

2. Do not brush the surface sugar off. Fold both ends of the dough so that they meet in the middle.

3. Roll the pin lightly on top to make it flat.

4. Fold again so that the ends meet again in the middle. Roll lightly with the pin.

5. Fold both sides together to make a simple loaf. Let the dough "relax" in the refrigerator for at least 1 hour.

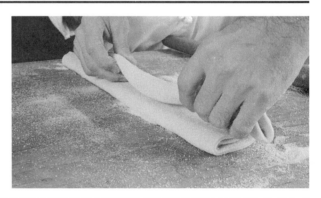

6. Slice into cookies about ⅜ inch thick.

7. Arrange the cookies flat on a cookie sheet. Turn the edges outward slightly to give them a nicer shape. Bake in a 425-degree preheated oven for approximately 25 minutes. After 15 to 20 minutes, turn the cookies on the other side so that both sides are uniformly glazed with the sugar. See finished palmiers, page 732.

283. Glazed Puff Paste *(Allumettes Glacées)*

YIELD: 12

THE *allumettes glacées* are often served with ice cream or plain as a coffee cake.

About 1 pound puff paste (technique 296, on your own)

Glaze

1 *cup powdered sugar*
1 *egg white*
3 *tablespoons cornstarch*

1. Roll the puff paste into a rectangle about 14 inches long by 6 inches wide and ¼ inch thick. Combine the sugar and egg white in a bowl and work for about 2 minutes until creamy. Add the cornstarch and work for another minute. Pour on top of the puff paste right away. If the glaze is kept it should be covered with a wet towel or a crust will rapidly form on top.

2. Use a spatula to spread the mixture as evenly as you can on top of the puff paste. Refrigerate for at least 2 to 3 hours so the icing stiffens and forms a crust.

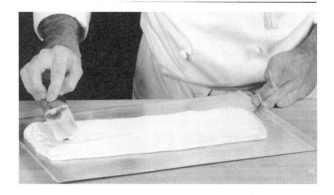

3. Trim the outside of the puff paste and cut into strips about 1½ inches wide.

4. Bake in a preheated 375-degree oven for 30 minutes. The icing should be beige in color, shiny and brittle. Let cool before using. See finished small glazed puff paste, page 815.

284. Apple Charlotte *(Charlotte de Pommes)*

THERE ARE TWO KINDS of desserts called charlotte. The first and the oldest is the hot or lukewarm apple charlotte created by an unsung chef during the reign of George III and named in honor of his Queen. The other charlotte, made with cream and lined with ladyfingers or *génoise* cake, is served cold and was created by Carême. The apple charlotte is the subject of this technique, and the cream-filled charlotte is described in the next.

8 *to* 10 *apples, depending on size*
¾ stick (6 tablespoons) sweet butter
Grated rind of 1 lemon
Juice of 1 lemon
2 to 3 tablespoons sugar (depending on sweetness
of apples)
3 tablespoons apricot jam
10 to 12 slices firm white bread

Pare and core the apples and cut into ¼-inch slices. Use a variety of apples. Pick apples that will hold their shape during cooking (Calville, Rennet, Granny Smith or the all-purpose green or Golden Delicious). Melt 4 tablespoons butter in a large skillet. Add the apple slices and sauté until all the juices are released and they start to boil. Add the lemon rind, juice and sugar. Cook on medium heat until all of the liquid has evaporated. Take off the heat and stir in the apricot jam. It is important that the apple mixture be thick and tight; otherwise, the charlotte will collapse when it is unmolded. Set aside. Butter a 1-quart charlotte mold generously with the remaining 2 tablespoons butter.

1. Cut 4 of the bread slices in half diagonally and trim into triangles.

2. Arrange the triangles tightly together in the bottom of the mold.

3. Trim the crusts off the remaining bread slices and cut into halves lengthwise. Arrange overlapping around the side of the mold.

4. Fill the prepared mold with the apple mixture.

5. Pack it as much as you can in the center because the charlotte sinks as it cools. Cover with a round piece of wax paper. Bake in a 400-degree preheated oven for approximately 35 minutes.

6. Remove from oven. Press down with a spoon to pack the apple mixture tightly. Trim the pieces of bread which are exposed above the apple mixture and place on top. Cover with wax paper and return to the oven for 15 to 20 minutes. Let cool until lukewarm.

7. Run a knife around the charlotte.

8. Place a platter on top of the charlotte, then turn upside down.

9. Remove the mold. Serve with an apricot sauce. See finished apple charlotte, page 710.

This charlotte serves 8 to 10.

APRICOT SAUCE

1 *cup thick apricot jam*
1 *tablespoon sugar*
3 *tablespoons water*
3 *tablespoons Armagnac, cognac or kirsch*

Place jam, sugar and water in a saucepan. Bring to a boil and boil for 2 to 3 minutes. Strain through a fine sieve. Cool, stirring occasionally. When lukewarm, add the alcohol. Pour half the mixture on top of the charlotte. Serve lukewarm with the remaining sauce on the side.

285. Chocolate Charlotte *(Charlotte au Chocolat)*

Ladyfingers
4 *egg yolks*
½ *cup confectioners' sugar*
1 *tablespoon dark rum plus ¼ cup dark rum or*
  cognac
8 *ounces chocolate (4 ounces sweet, 4 ounces*
  bitter)
2 *sticks (½ pound) sweet butter, softened*
1 *tablespoon warm water (optional)*

8 *egg whites*
Whipped cream
Candied violets
Crème anglaise, *technique 214 (optional)*

1. Prepare both long and tear-shaped lady-fingers, technique 224. Trim the tear-shaped ones slightly.

2. Place a round piece of wax paper in the bottom of a 1-quart charlotte mold. Arrange the tear-shaped ladyfingers upside down in a petal effect on the bottom of the mold.

3. Place a fringed strip of wax paper around the inside of the mold. Trim one end of the long ladyfingers and the sides so that they are slightly narrower on one end. Arrange the "fingers," cut end down, with the rounded side touching the wax-paper-lined mold.

4. Be sure they fit tightly, one against the other.

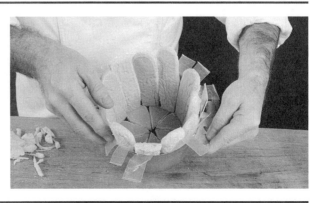

5. Combine the egg yolks, sugar and 1 tablespoon rum in a bowl. Beat with a whisk for 4 to 5 minutes until nice and fluffy. Melt the chocolate (see technique 247). Combine the chocolate and softened butter and whip for 1 minute. Combine with the egg yolk mixture. If it curdles, add 1 tablespoon warm water and whisk until it smooths out. Keep the mixture lukewarm.

6. Whip the egg whites until stiff. Whisk about one-third of the whites with the chocolate mixture. Fold in remaining whites, technique 60. The mixture will lose volume. Try to go as fast as you can to prevent the whites from getting too grainy.

7. Fill the mold alternating the chocolate mixture with a layer of ladyfinger trimmings sprinkled with rum or cognac until all ingredients have been used. End with the chocolate mixture.

8. With a pair of scissors, trim the lady-fingers at the level of the filling and place on the chocolate to cover. Cover and refrigerate for at least 2 hours.

9. Unmold and remove the wax paper. Decorate with whipped cream and candied violets, and serve with *crème anglaise*. See finished chocolate charlotte, page 754.

This charlotte serves 8 to 10.

286. Bavarian Royal Cake *(Charlotte Royale)*

T HIS IS A SOMEWHAT UNCONVENTIONAL charlotte. It is made with a *gènoise*-type biscuit colored with different jams and filled with kirsch-flavored fruits and custard. The cake, technique 227, should be made first and be ready to receive the filling.

1. Combine ⅓ cup mixed candied fruits with ¼ cup good kirsch and set aside. This mixture will keep almost indefinitely in the refrigerator. In fact, it is better if it is made a few days ahead. Prepare the *biscuit roulé* and let it cool for 30 minutes, covered. Do not roll. Cut into halves. (Leave the bottom sheet of wax paper in place.)

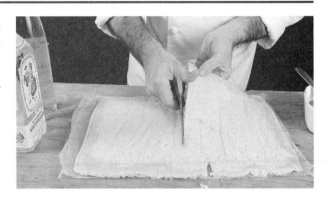

2. Place 1½ (10-ounce) jars good apricot jam into a saucepan. Add 2 tablespoons water and bring to a boil. Boil for 1 minute until the mixture is loose. Strain through a fine sieve into a bowl. Cover with plastic wrap. When cold, add 2 tablespoons good kirsch. The mixture should be thick but spreadable. Spread on one half of the *biscuit*.

3. Take ½ pint fresh raspberries, or 1 (10-ounce) package frozen raspberries, and combine with 1 (10-ounce) jar good raspberry preserves. Blend in a food processor or blender, place in a saucepan, bring to a boil and reduce by half. Strain the mixture through a fine sieve into a bowl. Cover with plastic wrap. When cold, add 2 tablespoons good raspberry liqueur like *framboise blanche*. Spread the raspberry mixture on the other half of the *biscuit*.

4. Cut each piece into halves. A pair of scissors is easier to use than a knife. Cut right through the paper.

5. Place a piece of wax paper on top of one of the coated pieces. Turn the coated cake, jam side down, on your hand and peel the back paper. Place the piece, uncoated side down, on top of a piece coated with the other flavored jam. Repeat, stacking the 4 pieces, alternating layers of raspberry and apricot jam. Remove the paper as you go along. The bottom and top layers are uncoated.

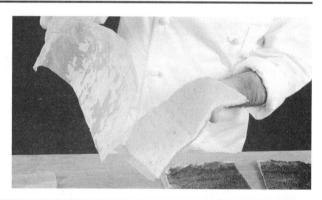

6. Cut the stacked layers into ½-inch slices. Trim one end of the slices into a point. Line a 5- to 6-cup bowl with the strips so they meet in the center.

7. Place smaller "wedges" snugly between the first strips.

8. Make the filling (recipe below) and place one-third of the filling in the bottom of the lined bowl. Sprinkle with one-third of the kirsch and fruit mixture. Cover with more filling and then more fruit mixture.

9. Cover the filling with leftover pieces of cake. Place a piece of wax paper or plastic wrap on the top and refrigerate for at least 3 to 4 hours before unmolding. Decorate with whipped cream, or serve plain or with a *crème anglaise*. See finished Bavarian royal cake, page 754.

This finished charlotte serves 12.

THE FILLING

1 *cup milk*
2 *egg yolks*
⅓ *cup sugar*
1 *envelope unflavored gelatin mixed with the sugar*
½ *teaspoon vanilla*
1 *large ice cube*

Prepare a *crème anglaise* using the above ingredients and following the steps in technique 214. Use the ice cube instead of cold milk to stop the cooking. Stir once in a while until room temperature. Do not let the mixture set. Meanwhile, whip 1½ cups heavy cream not too stiff. If the cream is over-whipped, the dessert will taste "buttery," instead of tasting of sweet cream. Fold the whipped cream into the *crème anglaise*. If the custard is too "set," whip it with a whisk for a few seconds to smooth it.

English custard cream, Bavarian royal cake, chocolate charlotte

287. Cat's Tongue Shells
(Cassolettes en Langue de Chat)

YIELD: About 12 shells

CAT'S TONGUES are thin narrow cookies (about 3 inches long by 1 inch wide), which are customarily served with ice cream, fruit salads or custards. In this technique we use the same cat's tongue dough and shape it into shells to fill with ice cream, *sorbet*, fruits and the like. The shells can be formed in small tulip-shaped brioche molds or on the outside of a cup or small ramekin or bowl.

½ stick (2 ounces) sweet butter, softened
½ cup sugar
2 egg whites
¼ teaspoon vanilla extract
½ cup flour

1. Cream the butter and sugar together with a whisk for 1 minute. Add the egg whites and vanilla, mix a few seconds and finally fold in the flour with a rubber spatula. Take a piece of thin cardboard and cut out a disk about 6 inches in diameter.

2. Line a cookie sheet with parchment paper. Unless you have large professional cookie trays, you can only make two shells at a time. Lay the cardboard flat on top of the parchment paper. Place a heaping tablespoon of dough in the center and spread it thinly using a metal spatula. Keep the spatula flat, almost parallel to the table. The dough should be evenly spread (about $1/16$ inch thick). If the dough is not spread uniformly the thinner part will burn during cooking.

3. Remove the cardboard and use it to make another disk next to the first one. You will have two thin pancakes on the parchment paper. Set in a preheated 350-degree oven and bake for 6 to 7 minutes.

4. Remove from the oven and slide a spatula underneath to lift the shell off the paper. Shape while still hot because if it is allowed to cool the cookie will become brittle and will break during shaping.

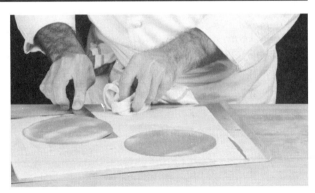

5. Push it into a mold, making it conform to the shape of the mold.

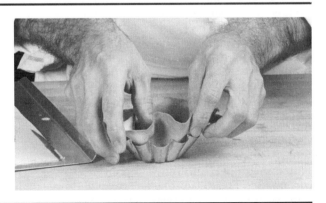

6. An alternate method is to place it on the outside of a plain cup and press it so it takes the shape of the cup. Notice that the dough will pleat in one or two places. The inside can be brushed with melted chocolate, then filled with whipped cream or a custard, or it can be used in one of the ways described in the introduction to this technique. See finished ice cream shells, page 668.

288. Lacy Ice Cream Shells *(Caissettes Dentelles)*

THE DOUGH for the lacy ice cream shells doesn't need to be spread out like the cat's tongue dough in the previous technique. It spreads by itself during baking and forms little holes exactly like a lace. It is a brittle, delicate cookie and should be cooked on parchment paper to prevent sticking. If the cookie still sticks, butter and flour the parchment paper. The dough can be prepared a day ahead and refrigerated until ready to use.

1 *cup finely ground blanched whole almonds*
¾ *cup granulated sugar*
¾ *stick (3 ounces) soft sweet butter*
4 *teaspoons flour*
2 *tablespoons milk*

1. For this cookie to work perfectly, the quantities have to be exact and the directions followed exactly. Combine all the ingredients in a smooth paste. If the dough has been refrigerated, soften with a spoon or wooden spatula before dividing it into cookies. Cut parchment paper into 6-inch squares. You should be able to fit 4 squares on a large cookie sheet. Place 1 large tablespoon of the dough in the center of each square. Wet your finger with cold water and flatten the dough into rounds about 3 inches wide.

2. Bake in a preheated 350-degree oven for 12 to 13 minutes. The cookies should brown nicely and should have spread to about 6 inches in diameter.

3. Let the cookies set for about 1 minute. If you try to mold them right away they will fall apart. Lift each cookie on its own piece of paper and place upside down on a small pyrex or glass bowl. The bowls should be about 3 inches in diameter. Remove the paper before you start molding the cookie or the paper will get caught in the pleats and will be hard to remove. Press the cookie down so it takes the shape of the cup. Work fast because the cookies become brittle as they cool. Remove from the mold when hardened.

4. The cookie can also be molded around a metal cornet or horn. Place the horn on top of the cookie and roll the cookie around it.

5. The cookie can also be rolled around the handle of a wooden spatula or a wooden stick into a large cigar shape.

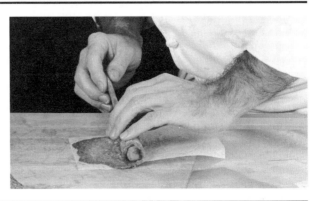

6. The "horn of plenty" and the cigar can be served plain or filled with sweetened whipped cream or berries as a dessert.

7. For a variation, brush the inside of the cookie with melted chocolate. Then, fill with ice cream, whipped cream or fruit. The cookies will keep well in a tinned box in a dry place.

8. Shape the dough to your fancy. If the mold is small the cookie spreads out and looks more like a flower. See finished horns, "cigars" and ice cream shells, page 668.

289. Jam Toasts *(Croûtes de Confiture)*

YIELD: 2 dozen

J AM TOASTS are easy to make and very decorative. They are ideally served with fruit sherberts, although they are good served with whipped cream or custard. The shape and color can be varied at will. Ours are made with apricot and raspberry jams. Use a dense buttery pound cake.

1 pound cake, day old and preferably homemade
About ¾ cup quality apricot jam
About ¾ cup quality raspberry jam

1. Strain the apricot jam through a fine strainer, food mill or sieve and repeat with the raspberry jam. Cut the pound cake into ½-inch-thick slices.

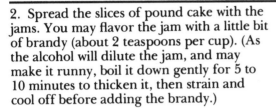

2. Spread the slices of pound cake with the jams. You may flavor the jam with a little bit of brandy (about 2 teaspoons per cup). (As the alcohol will dilute the jam, and may make it runny, boil it down gently for 5 to 10 minutes to thicken it, then strain and cool off before adding the brandy.)

3. Cut into triangles.

4. Also cut into rectangles, lozenges, squares or rounds with a cookie cutter. Keep refrigerated. Arrange on a nice platter when when ready to serve. See finished jam toasts, page 670.

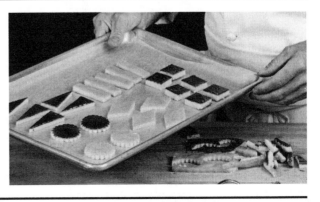

290. Raspberry Soufflé *(Soufflé aux Framboises)*

YIELD: 6 to 8 servings

EVEN FOR THE PROFESSIONAL, making a soufflé always involves an element of suspense. A soufflé is usually made of a base into which egg whites are folded. As the soufflé bakes, the air beaten into the egg whites, in the form of little bubbles, swells and pushes the soufflé up. Hot expands and cold deflates. Therefore a soufflé folds if allowed to cool.

Soufflés are served as first courses, main courses or desserts—for brunch, as well as lunch, dinner or supper. Although regularly made in a special soufflé mold, they can be made in any oven-proof container. Soufflés are also served unmolded or lukewarm and rolled. The ice-cold soufflé is a made-up soufflé—an unbaked mousse mixture shaped in the form of a soufflé.

There are two basic types of soufflés. The most common is made with a cream sauce base *(béchamel)* flavored with spinach, cheese, etc., into which egg yolks and beaten egg whites are added. The second type uses a purée of the main ingredient as a base, to which egg yolks and the beaten egg whites are added. It can be a purée of cauliflower or mushrooms, or fish or, in our case, raspberries. The flourless soufflé cooks faster and is lighter in texture.

Most soufflés can be prepared ahead, placed in a mold and kept refrigerated for a couple of hours before cooking. Our lobster soufflé (technique 83. cannot be assembled ahead because the top layer would liquefy into the hot lobster sauce. Remember that the smaller the soufflé, the easier and better it works. Large soufflés are harder to make and an 8- to 10-cup soufflé is about the maximum. It is important that large soufflés be cooked in the center of the oven so there's equal heat all around. The highest, best-textured soufflés are the ones cooked in a *bain-marie,* like the caramel soufflé (technique 291). However, other soufflés made this way won't get brown around because, being cooked in a bath of water, the outside is not exposed to enough heat to brown it. In the caramel soufflé, the caramel melts during cooking and colors the outside.

Remember that the equipment used to beat the whites must be immaculately clean. The egg whites should be at room temperature and there should be no egg yolk in them. If not, the egg whites will not expand to the right volume during beating. Beat the whites in an unlined copper bowl cleaned with vinegar and salt for the most volume. (Or add a dash of salt or lemon juice or cream of tartar for the same effect.) Do not beat the whites in aluminum or they will discolor. Have the base ready before you beat the whites. When you start beating do not stop. If you stop, the whites become grainy. As soon as they are ready, combine with the base as fast as possible. At that point the mixture can be placed in the mold and kept for a while. The base should be lukewarm when the whites are added. If too cold the mixture won't combine well and will be grainy; if too hot, the whites cook before baking and the soufflé won't raise properly. If the base is too light, the soufflé will run; if too thick, the soufflé will split. Whisk about a third of the egg whites into the base mixture to lighten it, then fold the rest of the whites in with a spatula. If all the whites are beaten into the base instead of being folded in, the mixture will lose volume and become too dense. The size of the mold is important and the mixture should fill it to the rim. A half-full soufflé mold will not look right after baking even if the mixture has risen properly. The soufflé should go from the oven directly to the table, so seat your guests in advance.

Be sure when separating the eggs that all the white is removed from the shell. If a bit is left it will amount to a whole egg white for every five or six eggs. If the eggs are small add one or two egg whites. It is better to have too much egg white than not enough

For the recipe that follows you will need a 5- to 6-cup soufflé mold. Butter the mold, coat with sugar and set aside.

Sauce

1 *cup fresh raspberries*
1 *10-ounce package frozen raspberries, defrosted*
²/₃ *cup raspberry preserves*
1 *tablespoon raspberry brandy, kirsch or Cognac*

Strain combined sauce ingredients through a fine strainer or food mill.

Soufflé

2 *cups very ripe raspberries*
6 *egg whites*
³/₄ *cups of sugar*
Pinch of salt

1. Place the egg whites and a pinch of salt in the bowl of an electric mixer and beat on medium to high speed until they form a peak. Add sugar gradually while continuing to beat. keep beating on high speed for about 30 seconds. With a fork, crush ¹/₂ cup of raspberries coarsely and

Raspberry soufflé

fold along with the whole ones into the egg whites. Fill the mold with the soufflé mixture. Smooth the top with a metal spatula and make ridges with the spatula to decorate. place the soufflé on a cookie sheet in a preheated oven for 20 minutes. Remove from the oven and sprinkle powdered sugar on top. Serve immediately with raspberry sauce. If, after 10 to 15 minutes of cooking, the soufflé appears to be browning too fast, place a loose piece of aluminum over it and continue to bake.

291. Lemon and Caramel Soufflé
(Soufflé au Citron et Caramel)

YIELD: 8 servings

T HE LEMON AND CARAMEL SOUFFLÉ is cooked in a double boiler and this gives it a particularly good texture. The soufflé can be served sprinkled with powdered sugar, hot out of the oven, or, as in the case below, allowed to cool, unmolded and served in wedges with a caramel sauce, a whipped cream or a custard. When it cools it deflates and becomes denser like a pudding. For this recipe you will need a 1½- to 2-quart soufflé mold.

Caramel	Soufflé mixture
1 *cup sugar*	1½ *cups milk*
¼ *cup water*	4 *egg yolks*
	⅓ *cup sugar*
	1 *teaspoon vanilla extract*
	2 *teaspoons lemon rind*
	2 *tablespoons cornstarch*
	7 *egg whites*

1. Combine the water and sugar in a saucepan and cook over medium to high heat until it turns a light caramel in color, about 6 minutes. Immediately pour most of the caramel into a soufflé mold.

2. Tip the mold back and forth so the caramel coats the bottom and sides of the mold. Use a brush (not nylon) to spread it around the sides and edges well. Work as quickly as possible because the caramel hardens fast.

3. Bring the milk to a boil. Combine the yolks and sugar and work together for 1 minute with a whisk until they form a ribbon. Mix in the vanilla, lemon rind and cornstarch. Add the milk to the mixture. Return the whole mixture to the pot and bring to a boil, stirring with a whisk. When it reaches a strong boil, pour into a large stainless steel bowl. Beat the egg whites until stiff. Add one-third of the whites to the cream mixture and stir. Fold in the remaining whites. Work fast. Pour into the mold and place in a deep saucepan.

4. Place tepid water around the mold and bake in a preheated 350-degree oven for 1 hour. If the scoufflé is brown enough on top after 35 to 40 minutes, place a piece of aluminum foil on top to prevent further browning.

5. The soufflé can be sprinkled with powdered sugar and served hot with or without a sauce.

6. For our "pudding," allow the soufflé to deflate and cool at room temperature. Note that the soufflé won't go lower than the rim of the bowl. Cool the pudding for a few hours or overnight in the refrigerator. To unmold, run a knife around the edge to loosen the caramel stuck to the rim.

7. Invert on a platter. If you have time, refrigerate with the mold on top. The soufflé will unmold itself slowly. Cut the pudding into slices and serve with whipped cream, a caramel sauce or a light sabayon.

292. Chocolate Soufflé with Rum Sauce *(Soufflé au Chocolat Sauce au Rhum)*

YIELD: 6 to 8 servings

THIS SOUFFLÉ is better without flour, because the chocolate has enough body to hold the egg whites. More than any other soufflé, the chocolate soufflé should not be overcooked but slightly wet in the center. Serve hot right out of the oven with the sauce or let it cool, unmold and serve in wedges like a cake with or without a sauce.

Rum sauce

1½ cups milk
2 teaspoons cornstarch
1 teaspoon pure vanilla extract
3 egg yolks (reserve the whites for the soufflé)
¼ cup sugar
2 tablespoons good dark rum

Place the milk, cornstarch and vanilla in a saucepan. Mix with the whisk and bring to a boil. Meanwhile, combine the egg yolks and sugar in a bowl and whisk for 1 to 2 minutes until the mixture is light, fluffy and pale yellow. Pour the boiling milk all at once directly on top of the yolks whisking to combine well. The hot milk will cook the egg yolks. Cover with plastic wrap and let cool. When cold, add the rum.

Soufflé

4 *large eggs at room temperature, separated, plus
the 3 egg whites leftover from the sauce*
4 *ounces bittersweet chocolate (or 3 ounces sweet
and 1 bitter)*
½ *cup milk*
3 *tablespoons sugar*

1. Butter and sugar a 6-cup soufflé mold and refrigerate until ready to use. Place the chocolate in a saucepan with the milk and melt on top of the stove. Stir until it comes to a simmer. Remove from the heat and whisk the yolks in. Beat the 7 egg whites until they reach a soft peak and add the sugar. Keep beating for about 1 minute until very stiff.

2. Whisk about one-third of the mixture into the chocolate. Pour the chocolate mixture back onto the beaten egg whites.

3. Carefully fold the chocolate mixture into the egg whites, then pour into the soufflé mold. It should reach the rim of the mold. At this point, the soufflé can be kept for a good hour, refrigerated or at room temperature.

4. Place on a cookie sheet in a preheated 375-degree oven and cook for 18 to 20 minutes. The soufflé should be moist in the center. Sprinkle with powdered sugar and serve immediately with the rum sauce around.

5. You can leave the soufflé to deflate and cool overnight and then unmold it, cut into wedges and serve with sweetened whipped cream or with the rum sauce. It will have the consistency of a very light cake.

293. Chocolate and Vanilla Soufflé
(Soufflé Panaché)

YIELD: 6 to 8 servings

IN THIS TECHNIQUE two soufflé mixtures are cooked together in the same mold. The contrast of color and different tastes make it unusual and attractive. Serve it with a *crème anglaise* or the rum sauce from technique 292, or just plain.

Chocolate base

2½ ounces bittersweet chocolate
⅓ cup milk
2 egg yolks

Vanilla base

¾ cup milk
2 egg yolks
¼ cup sugar
½ teaspoon vanilla extract
1 tablespoon flour

For both mixtures

7 egg whites
3 tablespoons sugar

1. Butter and sugar a 2-quart soufflé mold and cut a piece of wax paper as wide as the bowl to act as a divider. Set aside until ready to use. The base mixtures are made separately but the egg whites for both mixtures are beaten together. Melt the chocolate in a saucepan with the ⅓ cup milk and when hot and smooth, whisk in the egg yolks and pour the mixture into a large bowl. You will notice that when the yolks are combined with the milk it thickens the mixture. For the vanilla base, bring the ¾ cup milk to a boil. Meanwhile mix the egg yolks and sugar and beat about 1 minute with a whisk. Stir in the vanilla extract and the flour until smooth. Pour the boiling milk into the yolk mixture, stirring constantly. Place the whole mixture back on the stove and bring to a boil, stirring with a whisk. Pour the mixture into a large bowl.

2. Beat the egg whites until they hold a peak, then add the 3 tablespoons of sugar and keep beating for ½ minute until the mixture is stiff. Place about a cup of the egg white mixture into the chocolate mixture and stir with the whisk. Do the same thing with the vanilla mixture. Then divide the remaining whites into each of the soufflés and fold it in with different spatulas. Work fast. Holding the wax paper in the center of the mold, spoon in the soufflés alternating each soufflé from one side to the other, so the paper is held in place.

3. Keep filling both sides until the mold is full. Then gently pull the paper divider out.

4. Place the soufflé on a cookie sheet and bake in the center of a preheated 375-degree oven for about 25 minutes. Sprinkle powdered sugar on top and serve immediately. If the top browns too quickly, cover with a piece of aluminum foil.

5. Sometimes the soufflé cracks during cooking. To prevent splitting, a "collar" of parchment or wax paper can be placed around. The paper should be wide enough to touch the cookie sheet and rise to about 2 inches above the mold. Butter and sugar or flour the paper to keep the soufflé mixture from sticking to it. Secure with a piece of kitchen string. Remove before serving.

294. Chocolate Truffle Cake
(Gâteau au Chocolat Albert)

YIELD: 10 to 12 servings

THIS CAKE is made from layers of chocolate *génoise*, a cream *ganache* and a dense, buttery layer of cookie dough in between. It can be shaped round, square or rectangular. Its taste is even better when it is 1 day old. It freezes well provided it is properly wrapped.

Chocolate *génoise*

3 extra large eggs, or 4 smaller ones
½ cup sugar
½ cup flour
1 tablespoon unsweetened cocoa powder
2 tablespoons unsalted butter, melted

Chocolate cookie dough

3 cups all-purpose flour
3 sticks (12 ounces) sweet butter, softened
2 ounces bittersweet chocolate
⅓ cup hot water

Ganache cream

12 ounces bittersweet chocolate
1½ cups heavy cream
1 tablespoon dark rum
½ stick (2 ounces) sweet butter, softened

Syrup

2 tablespoons sugar
2 tablespoons hot water
2 tablespoons dark rum

1. For the chocolate *génoise*, place the eggs and sugar in the bowl of an electric mixer and mix well. Place the bowl in a pan of warm water for about 1 minute, mixing until the mixture is barely tepid. Whip on high speed for 8 to 10 minutes. (The mixture whips better when the eggs are slightly warm.) Combine the flour and the cocoa and sift over the beaten egg mixture, folding it in with a spatula as you sift. Then fold in the melted butter gently. Do not overfold.

2. Cook the *génoise* in cake pans or flan rings or a mold shaped the way you want the cake to be. Our rectangular flan mold is 20 inches by 4 inches wide. Butter and flour the cookie sheet and the mold. Place the mold on top of the cookie sheet. Pour the batter inside and level with a spatula. Bake in a preheated 350-degree oven for about 18 minutes.

3. Let cool for ½ hour before unmolding. Run a knife around the edges of the mold and remove the flan ring. When cool, wrap the *génoise* in a plastic bag. It can be kept this way for a few days. When ready to be used, cut the *génoise* in half. Each half should be about ½ inch thick.

4. The *génoise* should be smooth and soft in the center without being wet or crumbly. (A dry *génoise* is a product of overbeating; a wet, tight one indicates underbeating or undercooking.)

5. For the cookie dough, combine the chocolate and hot water and stir until melted. Place the flour in the bowl of a mixer and add the butter in pieces. Mix for about 10 seconds, add the chocolate mixture and mix for another 15 seconds. The mixture should be like a paste. Spread the dough with a spatula on a large cookie sheet. It should be at least as long as the rectangular mold.

6. Place a piece of parchment paper on top of the dough and spread the dough out with your hands. It should be twice as wide as the rectangular mold and no more than ¼ inch thick. It should be equally thick all over. If thinner in one place, it will burn. Remove the parchment and cook in a preheated 425-degree oven for 20 minutes.

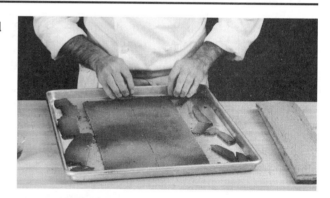

7. Let the biscuit cool for 5 to 6 minutes, then cut it into 2 strips, using the flan mold as a guide.

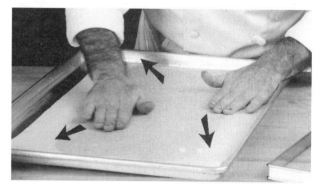

8. Use a large spatula and the bottoms from a removable-bottom cake pan to lift the strip which is fragile and may easily break. Place it on a platter, a piece of wood or a piece of cardboard cut to the exact size of the cake.

9. For the *ganache,* combine the cream and chocolate in a heavy saucepan. Bring to a boil, stirring. Remove from the heat and let cool until thick, but not too hard. Place in a bowl and add the softened butter and the rum. Beat with a whisk for 1 to 2 minutes, which will expand the volume and whiten the cream. The cream should not be overbeaten or it will absorb too much air and become grainy and hard to spread. If this happens, remelt slightly and stir gently until soft enough to use. Spread a thin layer of *ganache* on top of the biscuit.

10. Prepare the syrup by mixing the water, sugar and dark rum together. Place one layer of *génoise* cut side up on the *ganache* and moisten it all over with the rum syrup, using a brush. Cover with another layer of *ganache,* about ¼ inch thick, then with the other cookie strip, and again *ganache* and finally the last of the *génoise,* smooth side up. Moisten again with the rum syrup, then cover the top and the sides with the remaining *ganache* cream (about ⅛ inch thick all around).

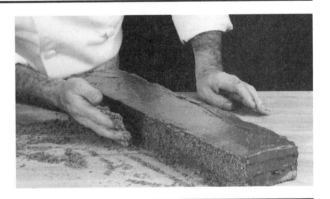

11. Place the cookie trimmings in a food processor and crumble into fine crumbs. (The crumbs may also be mixed with powdered almonds.) Pat the crumbs all around the cake. Then place the rest of the crumbs on top. Scrape the top of the cake gently with a spatula to remove the excess crumbs. and make the top flat.

12. Cut pieces of wax paper and arrange on top of the cake. Sprinkle powdered sugar on top to make a design. In our case, we put two strips on each side and two at the end. Refrigerate until serving time. If the cake is to be kept several days, wrap well in plastic wrap to prevent it from picking up refrigerator odors. See chocolate truffle cake, following page and page 815.

Chocolate leaves, christmas log with chocolate bark, chocolate truffle cake, chocolate box with truffles

295. Chocolate Leaves *(Feuilles en Chocolat)*

T HE BEST and easiest way to make chocolate leaves is to coat real leaves with the chocolate. Natural leaves come in all shapes and sizes and make beautiful designs. Use dark chocolate, milk chocolate (which has a lighter color) or white chocolate.

1. Select your leaves. Try to pick leaves all the same size. Decide whether you are going to coat the top or the underside of the leaves. The design on the underside is usually in more relief and will give more texture to the chocolate. Melt the chocolate in the oven or over hot water.

2. Dip a side of the leaf in the chocolate, making sure that it is coated all over.

3. Place the leaves, chocolate side up, flat on a piece of parchment or wax paper, chocolate showing.

4. White chocolate is usually thicker. It is not runny enough to coat by dipping. Instead, use a spatula or a knife to spread it well. Place the coated leaves flat on the paper.

5. When the chocolate is almost set but still soft, place in a curved pan to mold. If the chocolate is still too soft it will run toward the center of the leaves; if it is too hard it will break when bent. Set the mold in the refrigerator until the leaves are set.

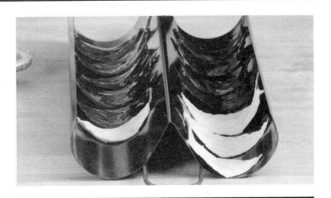

6. Pull the leaf from the chocolate. It should come off easily.

7. A white chocolate leaf. Arrange all your leaves on a platter or use to decorate a cake or a cold soufflé. See finished chocolate leaves, page 772.

296. Chocolate Box *(Boîte en Chocolat)*

YIELD:1 9-inch box

A ROUND CHOCOLATE BOX is very festive and decorative. Filled with chocolate truffles, it makes an ideal presentation for Christmas or Easter holidays. Melt about 1½ pounds of chocolate in the oven or in a double broiler.

1. To make the bottom and the lid, pour some chocolate on two pieces of parchment paper.

2. Spread it out with a spatula to about ⅛ inch thick. The disks should be at least 9 inches in diameter. Let set to harden either in the refrigerator or in a cool place.

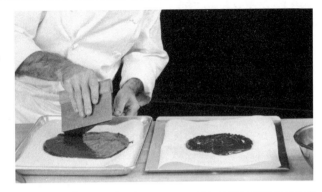

3. Meanwhile, cut a long strip of waxed paper and pour a line of chocolate on it. This will be the sides of the box. Be sure that the strip is long enough to go around the disk. Let set in the refrigerator.

4. When the chocolate disks have set—they should be hard enough not to run but not too brittle—set a 9-inch flan ring on top and trim into a neat circle.

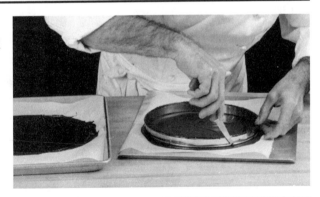

5. Remove the trimming. Remember that if anything goes wrong, the chocolate can be remelted and the process started again.

6. The disk should lift easily from the paper.

7. Trim the strip on both sides to have a clean length about 1 inch wide for the side of the box.

8. Lift the strip with the paper and fold it around the disk so it encases the whole bottom. If the strip is too long, trim so the ends abut.

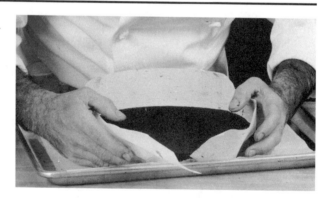

9. Remove the wax paper and, using a paper cone, squeeze a bit of melted chocolate inside, at the joint.

10. With the tip of your finger smooth out the melted chocolate. When it hardens it will secure the sides to the bottom.

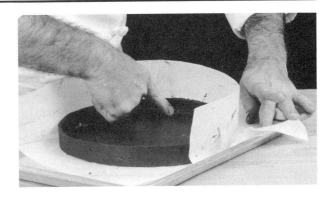

11. Use the second disk for the cover. Etch a design free hand with a nail or the point of a knife.

12. Fill a paper cone with melted chocolate and pipe a line on the design.

13. Place a chocolate rose or carnation in the center (technique 297) with a bit of melted chocolate under it to secure it to the lid. See finished chocolate box, page 772.

297. Chocolate Flower *(Fleur en Chocolat)*

PROFESSIONAL CHOCOLATE WORK is an art which requires special equipment. However, if you have a large chunk of chocolate to carve from and a vegetable peeler, you can make curls and flowers. Buy a piece of chocolate thick enough to be held and worked with. It should be quality chocolate that's high in butter content, which makes it more malleable. Most important is the temperature of the chocolate. Keep overnight in a place no warmer than 90 degrees; not hot enough for the chocolate to melt but hard enough so it can withstand a knife or peeler, yet soft enough so it can be molded into shapes.

1. When you work with chocolate, work fast and be sure to have dry hands. Using a vegetable peeler, cut strips of chocolate. Use each strip right away before it hardens.

2. To make a rose, roll a strip so it is pointed on top. This will be the heart of the rose. (For more information on rose making, see technique 307.)

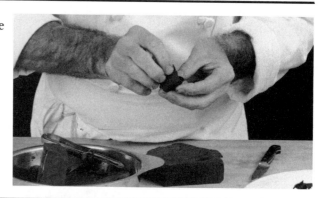

3. Peel another strip and wrap it around the center. Curl the edge outward. Continue cutting strips to make more petals. Wrap them around the rose which will get larger and larger. Curl the edges outward.

4. Five or 6 strips should make a big enough rose. Work fast so the chocolate doesn't melt in your hands.

5. Make other roses of varying sizes and degrees of openness. When the roses are done, place them on a plate with the nicest part showing and let them cool in the refrigerator until hard and brittle. The chocolate will be dull rather than shiny. See finished chocolate rose, page 772.

6. To make a carnation, use the point of a knife and scrape the top of the chocolate over and over to build up a long wrinkled strip of chocolate on the end of the blade. Then roll the strip into a curl around the point of the knife. (This technique is similar to the one used to make butter decorations, technique 34.)

7. Make a second and a third curl smaller than the previous one and combine to make a large flower.

8. To make chocolate rolls, peel a strip with the vegetable peeler. Sometimes the chocolate will curl by itself.

9. If it does not curl, roll gently into a curl with the tip of your fingers.

298. Chocolate Truffles *(Truffes en Chocolat)*

YIELD: 3 to 4 dozen truffles

CHOCOLATE is sometimes tricky to use and is always very sensitive to heat. It can scorch, curdle, change color and go from the brightest to the very dull, depending on the amount of heat. It contains cocoa butter, which, like other fats, is not easily incorporated into liquids. Sweet chocolate is easier to work with. Because of its milk and sugar content it absorbs liquid more readily than unsweetened chocolate, which is pure fat and cocoa powder.

These chocolate truffles are conventionally served to guests around the Christmas holidays in France. They are called truffles because of their similarity in shape and color to the expensive truffle found in the southwest of France.

Make the basic truffle recipe, then divide it and flavor each portion differently. We used three flavors and coated each differently so as to recognize one flavor from another. The basic recipe will yield three to four dozen truffles. However, they can be made smaller since they are very rich.

Basic mixture

¾ *pound (12 ounces) bittersweet chocolate*
4 egg yolks
⅔ *stick (2⅔ ounces) sweet butter, softened*

First flavor

1 tablespoon rum
1 tablespoon coffee extract
  (These are the first drops from a drip
  coffee maker.)

Second flavor

½ *cup praline (see technique 255)*
2 tablespoons Cognac

Third flavor

Rind of 1 orange (about 1½ teaspoons)
1½ tablespoons Grand Marnier

1. Melt the chocolate in a double boiler or in an oven until the chocolate is lukewarm. Add the egg yolks and stir with a whisk for a few seconds. It will probably tighten and lose its shine.

2. Add the butter in pieces and whisk well. The mixture may become smooth or it may remain somewhat separated. Do not worry about it. Divide the basic mixture into three small bowls.

3. In one bowl add the coffee and rum, in the second the *pralin* and Cognac, and in the third the Grand Marnier and orange rind. Work each flavor in with a whisk. At this point the mixture should become smooth. If it doesn't, add 1 teaspoon of hot water to each bowl and whisk until it does. Keep adding water a few drops at a time until smooth. It should not require more than 1 tablespoon of water at most. Cover each bowl with plastic wrap and refrigerate for a few hours.

4. With a spoon, divide the mixture into little balls the size of extra-large olives or smaller.

5. Roll in the palm of your hand to smooth. Keep each flavor separate and refrigerated until very cold.

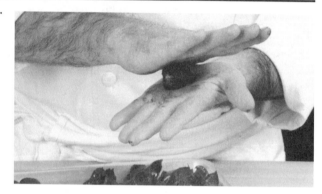

6. For the first coating, melt chocolate. Secure a toothpick in each ball (we used the Grand Marnier-flavored balls) and dip each one into melted chocolate. As you lift the ball out, roll it slightly on the side of the bowl to eliminate the excess.

7. Secure the toothpicks in a piece of foam rubber or styrofoam so the chocolate drips along the toothpick. If the balls are placed on a plate they will flatten on one side and the chocolate will accumulate at the base. Let set until very hard.

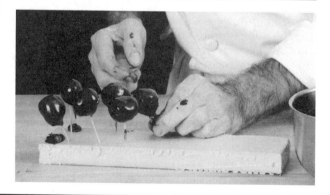

8. Roll the rum and coffee-flavored balls in unsweetened cocoa powder. Shake the pan so the balls roll around and get coated.

9. Use a vegetable peeler to grate some chocolate on top of the third batch of truffles.

10. Or roll balls in slivered almonds and chocolate shavings for another effect.

11. The three types of chocolate truffles.

12. Slice off the excess chocolate that accumulated around the toothpick, then remove the toothpick. Arrange the different flavored truffles in a chocolate box (technique 296). Truffles will keep in the refrigerator for a couple of weeks. See finished chocolate box with truffles, page 772.

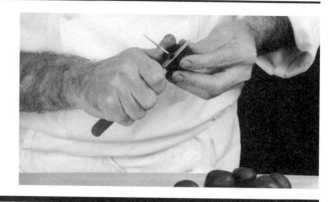

299. How to Peel and Glaze Chestnuts *(Épluchage et Marrons Confits)*

WHEN BUYING chestnuts, select carefully, checking for small holes which indicate that the chestnut is wormy. Choose them plump and shiny. Fresh chestnuts are delicious just plain roasted in the oven, over charcoal or in the fireplace. However, after roasting and peeling they can be braised and served whole or boiled and puréed. Although dehydrated chestnuts are readily available, they do not compare to fresh ones. Before braising chestnuts with a roast pork or turkey, both the outer shell and inside skin have to be removed.

For a purée, usually served with a red wine venison stew or other game, cover the peeled chestnuts with water (or water and chicken stock), add a dash of salt and a rib of celery and simmer, covered, for about 40 to 45 minutes until tender. Then purée through the fine blade of a food mill and finish with butter, salt, pepper and a bit of heavy cream.

For a dessert purée, such as the celebrated Mont-Blanc (a concoction of meringue, whipped cream and purée of chestnuts), peel the chestnuts, then cook in milk with a dash of sugar and vanilla. Purée in the food mill and sweeten with a sugar syrup.

For a stuffing, peel the chestnuts, cook in water for about 30 minutes, then mix with the other stuffing ingredients. If the chestnuts are not cooked in water first, they will be tough in the stuffing.

Regardless of how they are served, the chestnuts must be peeled first.

To glaze chestnuts

12 *cups water*
2 *cups sugar*
1 *teaspoon vanilla extract*
1 *pound chestnuts*
1 *tablespoon rum or Cognac*

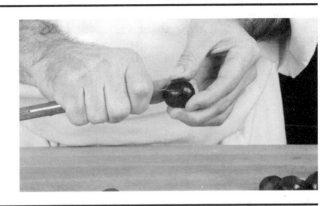

1. Make a slice against the grain on both sides of the chestnuts. Be careful to slice only the outer and inside skins without going into the flesh.

2. Place on a cookie sheet and roast approximately 15 to 20 minutes in a preheated 400-degree oven. Press the chestnuts to crack them open.

3. The chestnut should come out in one piece. Put the ones that don't peel easily back into the oven for a few minutes. Don't roast too many at one time unless you have helpers to peel them with you while they are hot. As they cool, they become hard to peel.

4. Pieces of glazed chestnuts are mixed with ice cream, Bavarian cream or whipped cream and served as dessert. Whole, they are served as bonbons or dipped into caramel (technique 301). To glaze the chestnuts, place the water, sugar and vanilla in a large shallow saucepan, bring to a boil and boil for 1 minute. Add the chestnuts.

5. Bring the water to a bare simmer and cook gently, covered, for about 3 hours at a 180-degree temperature. Uncover and cook slowly for another hour, or until a heavy syrup has formed and all the chestnuts are coated with it.

6. Probably half of the chestnuts will be broken. Fortunately, most recipes call for pieces of candied chestnuts. Let the chestnuts cool then place in a jar. Add 1 tablespoon of rum or Cognac to the syrup. Cover with the syrup. Keep refrigerated and use when needed.

300. Almond Chestnuts (Marrons en Pâté d'Amandes)

YIELD: About 8 to 10 "chestnuts"

THE ALMOND "CHESTNUTS" are the perfect decoration for the chocolate chestnut cake (technique 302). They could also be arranged as a centerpiece or presented in the chocolate box (technique 296). They are not chestnuts but little balls of almond paste dipped in chocolate to look like unpeeled chestnut.

About ¾ pound almond paste
½ pound bittersweet chocolate, melted
2 to 3 drops green coloring for leaves
About 2 to 3 tablespoons powdered sugar
About ½ teaspoon egg white for the icing

1. Work the almond paste until it is smooth. Divide into little balls the size of an olive and roll in the palm of your hand, making them slightly flat on one side to imitate a chestnut.

2. Pierce each ball with a skewer or, as pictured here, a piece of metal hanger. Incline the pan of melted chocolate on one side and dip the almond ball in. Coat about three-quarters of it.

3. As you lift each ball from the chocolate, the excess chocolate will drip into a point at the end of each one, making it look even more like a chestnut. Let the "chestnuts" dry over a bread pan so they harden without changing shape.

4. Mix the remaining almond paste with green food coloring. While the chestnuts harden, make leaves and shells with the green almond paste. Press pieces down with a spatula to flatten and shape into the form of leaves. (See Almond Paste Flowers, technique 307.) Use powdered sugar to prevent the paste from sticking. Use a fork to make indentations in the "leaves." Mold little shells around your thumb.

5. Mix the powdered sugar with egg white and, with a wooden spoon, work for about 1 minute into a smooth, thick, shiny icing. Place in a paper cone. Decorate the shells with dots of icing squeezed from the paper cone.

301. Caramel Glazed Chestnuts
(Marrons Glacés au Caramel)

T HE "CHESTNUTS" in technique 300 are made from almond paste dipped ir chocolate. In this technique we use actual pieces of chestnuts although little balls of almond paste could be substituted. Instead of glazing the chestnuts with chocolate, we dip them into a chocolate-flavored caramel. The caramel drips in a long thread which hardens into a very decorative ornament for a cake or for a buffet centerpiece.

12 *of the best candied chestnuts (technique 299)*
1 *cup sugar*
1 *tablespoon unsweetened cocoa powder*
¾ *cup water*

1. Mix the sugar, cocoa powder and water in a sturdy saucepan and bring to a boil. Cook into it turns into a caramel, for about 12 to 15 minutes. The temperature should be at about 320 degrees. Check the temperature by dipping the point of a knife or fork into the caramel and then into cold water. The caramel should harden immediately. The mixture will be dark in color because of the cocoa powder, and you won't see, as you usually do with caramel, when it changes color and is ready. Let the caramel cool for a few minutes until it thickens. Impale the chestnuts on skewers and when the caramel stops bubbling and is thick, dip each chestnut in the mixture.

2. Let the chestnuts hang from the side of a pan until they are hard. To free the skewer, use a pair of scissors to cut and crack away the caramel around the skewer. The caramel chestnuts can now be used for decoration. See finished caramel chestnuts on following page.

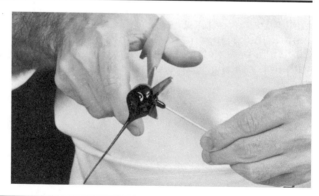

Savarin, floating island, chestnut and chocolate cake, caramel chestnuts, rum babas

302. Chestnut Chocolate Cake *(Turinois)*

YIELD: 18 to 20 servings

THIS IS A RICH CAKE, made with melted chocolate, purée of chestnuts and butter. It should be served very cold, cut in thin slices, plain or with a chocolate sauce or a *crème Anglaise*. Leave plain or decorate with powdered sugar and glazed or almond chestnuts (techniques 300 and 301). If you decorate the top with powdered sugar do it at the last moment because the sugar will dissolve within 20 to 25 minutes because of the moistness of the cake.

2 *pounds peeled chestnuts (about 2¾ pounds un-*
    peeled)
2 *sticks (8 ounces) sweet butter*
¾ *cup sugar*
1 *pound bittersweet chocolate, melted*
2 *tablespoons dark rum*
½ *cup pieces of candied chestnuts, optional (tech-*
    nique 299)

1. Place peeled chestnuts in a kettle and cover with water. Bring to a boil and simmer gently for 40 to 45 minutes until tender. The 2 pounds of chestnuts will absorb moisture during cooking which will bring their weight up to about 3 pounds when cooked. Drain the chestnuts (most will have broken) and pass through the fine blade of a food mill while still hot.

2. Mix the butter and sugar together and work with a whisk until smooth. Add the chocolate, the purée of chestnuts and the dark rum and mix well until the mixture is smooth. Then add the pieces of candied chestnuts (optional).

3. Line a loaf pan with a large strip of parchment paper. Place the mixture in the mold.

4. Refrigerate for at least 3 to 4 hours before unmolding. Run a knife all around the cake, unmold, then remove the paper.

5. To decorate, make a rectangular stencil with a piece of wax paper and place on top of the cake. Sprinkle powdered sugar over the stencil, then remove.

6. Decorate the top with almond or candied chestnuts. Serve plain or with a custard sauce flavored with rum (see recipe in technique 292). See finished Chestnut chocolate cake, page 789.

303. Cream Puff Cake *(Croquembouche)*

T HE *croquembouche* is a cream puff cake usually served at weddings in France. The puffs are sometimes built around a bottle or arranged in a special conical mold made for *croquembouche*. We built ours in the bowl of an electric mixer. If the cake has to be transported somewhere, it should be transported in the mold. For a big party, instead of building an extra large *croquembouche* which is delicate and difficult to move, make a small *croquembouche* and arrange the leftover puffs around. Avoid making it on a humid summer day because the caramel will stick and melt and the cake may collapse, especially because the stuffed puffs are heavy. The *choux*, which should be fairly small, can be cooked ahead and so can the cream. This recipe yields about 80 small cream puffs.

Puff dough

1½ cups milk
1 stick (4 ounces) sweet butter
1 teaspoon salt
1½ cups all-purpose flour
6 large eggs

Crème patissière (cream filling)

2 cups milk
8 egg yolks
1 tablespoon vanilla extract
¾ cup sugar
½ envelope unflavored gelatin
⅔ cup flour
¾ cup heavy cream
½ stick (2 ounces) sweet butter, at room temperature

Caramel glaze

2 cups sugar
½ cup water
¼ teaspoon cream of tartar diluted in 1
    tablespoon water

When ready to assemble the *croquembouche*, make a second batch of caramel.

1. To make the cream puff dough, place the milk, butter and salt in a heavy saucepan and bring to a boil. As soon as it boils, add the flour in one stroke and mix rapidly with a wooden spatula. Keep cooking the mixture (*panade*) on low heat for about 1 minute to dry it out. Place the mixture in a clean bowl and stir about 1 minute to cool it off slightly. Add 2 eggs and mix well until blended. (You will notice that the mixture will stay loose for a while and suddenly tighten. When tight add the other eggs. Repeat the process each time you add eggs.) Add another egg and mix until smooth. The eggs are added to the *panade* in 4 additions. At the third addition the mixture should be worked a little more to give it the proper texture. The mixture can also be made in an electric mixer. Very lightly butter and flour 2 or 3 cookie sheets. (If the sheets are coated too thickly the puffs will not stick.) Using a pastry bag fitted with a plain tube with a ¼-inch opening, form the *choux*.

2. To form the *choux* hold the pastry bag straight down and squeeze without moving your hand. Then stop squeezing and lift up the bag in a sudden short upswing. The puffs will have small tails. Wet a towel and press the tail down to make the *choux* rounder. Place in a preheated 400-degree oven and bake for 30 to 35 minutes until the puffs are well browned and dry.

3. Keep the door of the oven slightly ajar during the last 10 minutes of baking so the *choux* dry out and don't collapse. If the weather is humid, let cool in the turned off oven with the door ajar. For the *crème patissière,* place the milk in a heavy saucepan and bring to a boil. Combine the yolks, vanilla, sugar and gelatin in a bowl and work with a whisk until pale yellow and foamy, about 1 to 2 minutes. Stir in the flour. Pour the boiling milk on top of the egg mixture and mix carefully. Then place the mixture back in a saucepan and bring to a boil stirring constantly with the whisk until it boils and thickens. Let boil for 15 to 20 seconds, then stir in the cream. Pour into a bowl. Cover with plastic wrap and refrigerate until it reaches room temperature. Then add the softened butter with a whisk, piece by piece, and let cool.

4. Fit a pastry bag with a small fluted or starred tube and fill with the cream. Twist the flat bottom of the puff on the tube to make a hole and squeeze the cream inside. If the tube is plain it will not pierce the puff. In which case, make a hole with the point of a knife in each puff before filling.

5. Make the first batch of caramel by mixing together the sugar and water, stirring just enough to moisten the sugar. Place on heat and bring to a boil. After 3 minutes, add the cream of tartar dissolved in the water. Cook until it turns into a light caramel, about 10 minutes. Remove from the heat (it will continue to cook and darken for a few minutes). If it darkens too much, place the saucepan in lukewarm water to stop the cooking. If it gets too thick, remelt it on top of the stove. Holding the *choux* by the bottom, dip the top into the hot caramel.

6. Slide the top of the *choux* against the side of the pan to remove the excess caramel. Glaze all the *choux* on top. Then make the second batch of caramel to build the *croquembouche*.

7. This time the caramel should be light in color. As soon as the sugar mixture gets slightly blond, remove from heat. Use any type of metal mold you have but be sure to oil the inside. Begin by making a crown or ring for the top of the cake. Dip a side of a *chou* into the caramel, then stick it to another *chou*. Repeat to form a crown, about 6 to 7 *choux* around.

8. Place that crown in your oiled mold so the caramelized top of the *choux* touch the metal. Then start building up the sides of the mold. Try to stack the *choux* tightly, with the least space possible between each. Dip each *chou* in the caramel and fit it into the space.

9. Keep building. When you get to the top try to make it the same height on all sides. Remember that the *croquembouche* will be turned upside down. If too high on one side or the other, cut a *chou* in half to even out. It can go one or two layers above the side of the bowl. If any of the *choux* are not holding properly, dab some caramel in between with the point of a knife.

10. Unmold the *croquembouche* by turning it upside down on a platter. If some caramel leaked between the puffs, it may stick to the bowl. If so, pass the bowl quickly over a flame a few times to melt the caramel.

11. If you had to heat the bowl to unmold the *croquembouche,* there will be some strands of caramel sticking out. Remove with a pair of scissors. The *croquembouche* can now be decorated with *nougatine* and almond flowers (techniques 306 and 307). At serving time, lift the flowers off the cake, and starting at the top and working down, break off the choux with two spoons, one or two at a time. See finished cream puff cake, page 795a.

Cream puff cake with nougatine and almond flowers, glazed stuffed fruit, caramel cage

304. Sugar-Coated Stuffed Fruits
(Fruits Déguisés)

THE *fruits déguisés* are dried fruits stuffed with almond paste and coated with a hot sugar syrup. They are passed around to guests after a formal dinner. The dried fruit, unlike the glazed strawberries (technique 242). can be prepared ahead because they don't release juices that would melt the sugar coating. Use dates, dried apricots, prunes and figs and color the almond paste with food coloring.

For the glazed fruits, the sugar should be cooked to the hard-crack 308). to 310 degree) stage. When you make a caramel, as for the *croquembouche* in the preceding technique, the sugar may crystallize (the mixture hardens into large opaque lumps) but it is not too important because crystallized sugar will eventually melt and turn into caramel if exposed to further cooking. However, when the sugar has to be cooked to the hard-crack stage, whether for glazing fruits or to make flowers (technique 308), crystallization can be a problem. To prevent crystallization, make sure that the pan is very clean. The sugar should be moistened with water but not stirred afterwards. The addition of cream of tartar, lemon juice or even vinegar will prevent, up to a point, crystallization of the sugar. When little crystals show around the edges just above the cooking liquid, they should be melted with a wet brush. However if the sugar still crystallizes it cannot be used to glaze fruits. To salvage it, make a caramel sauce: Keep cooking until the pieces melt and turn into caramel. Then, add water (about one-third of the caramel amount) a bit at a time to melt the caramel. Let cool and use as needed.

12 *each of dried dates, prunes, figs and apricots*
About 1 pound almond paste, divided into dif-
ferently colored batches

Coating

2 *cups sugar*
½ *cup water*
¼ *teaspoon cream of tartar mixed with 1 tea-*
spoon water

1. Slice open the dates in the middle. Take a little piece of almond paste and roll it in your hand to make it oval.

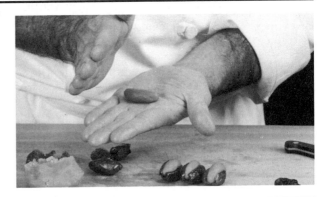

2. Place in the opening of the date then press both sides to make it fit snugly. Cut apricots in half and press almond paste between both pieces.

3. Make little almond paste balls and place in the center of each prune. Press with your finger to flatten and make it fit nicely. Cut the figs in half. Put a piece of almond paste on the bottom half and use the top half as a hat.

4. Mark a crisscross pattern on the round almond paste shapes and stripes on the oval shapes. Make eyes and noses on the little "Santa Clauses." Stick each stuffed fruit with a toothpick.

5. Place the sugar in a clean stainless steel or copper saucepan. Moisten with the water and shake the pan lightly so all the sugar gets "wet." Do not stir anymore. Boil the sugar and water for about 1 minute and add the cream of tartar diluted with water. With a wet brush, clean around the saucepan while cooking to melt the crystallized sugar—if any. (Another method is to cover the boiling sugar with a lid for 1 minute. The steam will melt the crystals.) The sugar must be cooked to the hard-crack stage (approximately 300-310 degrees).

6. Incline the pan and dip the whole fruit in the syrup. Lift and brush gently against the side of the pan to remove the extra syrup. Place on a lightly oiled cookie sheet until set and hard. Then twist the toothpicks back and forth to loosen and remove. If the fruits get sticky in very humid weather, put in front of a fan to dry out. See finished glazed stuffed fruit, page 795a.

305. Caramel Cage (Cage en Caramel)

THESE EXCEPTIONALLY DECORATIVE caramel cages can be placed atop desserts such as *oeufs à la neige,* poached fruit, different coupes, ice cream, and whipped cream-filled shells. The cages can be made in different shapes.

1. Make the caramel from technique 303, Cream Puff Cake. When the caramel is ready, let it cool off a bit until it is thick enough to form long threads. If it hardens too much, it can be remelted. Use Pyrex or stainless steel bowls. Oil the outside of the bowl, then, using a teaspoon filled with caramel, drape long threads on the top and sides of the bowl.

2. The threads should be long enough to weave back and forth from one side of the bowl to the other. If the threads are too short, the cage will break when unmolded.

3. A large stainless steel bowl can be used to make a cage large enough to cover a cake or mousse.

4. Let the cage cool off. Then pry gently on one side, then the other. It should come off easily.

5. Different types of cages can be used with different desserts. Some cages are tightly woven; others are more airy. See finished caramel cages, page 795a.

306. Almond Brittle (Nougatine)

A *nougatine* is a mixture of caramel and sliced almonds. The mixture is cooled, rolled and cut into different shapes used to decorate cakes or made into *barquettes* (shells) to fill with fruits, whipped cream or custards. The *nougatine* is also crushed into a powder and used to flavor ice cream or custard. When crushed long enough with special equipment, it becomes a *pralin* paste (technique 255). In this technique we go one step further and shape and glaze the *nougatine* with sugar icing to make a very finished and elegant decoration for a *croquembouche*.

Nougatine (enough to decorate a large cake)

2 *cups sliced almonds (with or without skin)*
3 *cups granulated sugar*
½ *teaspoon lemon juice*

Royal icing

½ *cup powdered sugar*
2 *teaspoons egg white*
2 *to 3 drops lemon juice*

1. Spread the sliced almonds on a cookie sheet and brown in a hot oven or under the broiler for about 2 minutes. Keep lukewarm. For the caramel you will need a heavy saucepan and a spatula. They should be very clean. The caramel is made without water which makes it very hard and dry. Place half of the sugar in the saucepan and place over medium to high heat. Nothing will happen for 2 to 3 minutes, then it should start melting around the edges.

2. Stir the melted sugar around the edges into the dry sugar in the center, and continue cooking, stirring occasionally, until all the sugar has liquefied.

3. Add the lemon juice and stir in another ¾ cup of sugar, stirring until smooth. Then stir in the last ¾ cup of sugar. Cook until it melts and turns into a light caramel. During the cooking the sugar may crystallize. Keep cooking and stirring, the mixture will eventually turn into caramel.

4. Stir the browned lukewarm almonds into the caramel with a wooden spatula.

5. Pour the mixture onto an oiled slab of marble. The heat of the caramel will damage most other surfaces. It will even buckle stainless steel.

6. Use a spatula coated with oil to spread the *nougatine* on the marble and turn it upside down.

7. After about 1 minute the *nougatine* should be workable. Roll it with an oiled metal rolling pin. (A piece of cast-iron piping, 1½ inches in diameter, works perfectly.) Roll while it's still hot. Work as fast as possible because once the *nougatine* cools off it gets hard and can't be rolled any longer.

8. Using a sturdy knife and the rolling pin as a hammer, cut the *nougatine* into 2 or 3 pieces.

9. Place the pieces on an oiled cookie sheet in a preheated 225-degree oven to soften a bit. Take one piece out at a time and place on the marble.

10. Roll each piece as thin as possible (about ¼ inch thick) and cut into shapes before it becomes too brittle. In this case we cut triangles.

11. Place the triangles on the rolling pin to shape them. If too hard, soften in the oven for a few minutes. Let the triangles harden on the roller. You can also make *barquettes* or plain flat shapes.

12. To make the base of the decoration, place a piece of rolled, soft *nougatine* on a small inverted cake pan and press around with your fingers as fast as you can until it takes on the shape of the pan. Trim around using the knife and the metal roller. Work as fast as you can.

13. Place the *nougatine* base on top of the *croquembouche*. Pass the base of the triangles over a flame for a few seconds to soften. Then hold it in place on the base until it sets. Repeat with the other triangles.

14. Decorate the *nougatine* with the royal icing *(glace royale)*. To make the icing, work the sugar and egg white with a wooden spatula for 1 minute. Add the lemon juice and work a few seconds more. Place in a paper cone (for instructions to make paper cones, see page 66), and outline on the edges of the nougatine. Finish decorating the cake with almond paste flowers in the center (technique 307). See finished cream puff cake, page 795a.

307. Almond Paste Flowers
(Fleurs en Pâte d'Amandes)

ALMOND PASTE is used to flavor cream or ice cream, to coat a cake, to stuff dried fruits or, as in this technique, to make little objects like animals, vegetables or flowers. Although almond paste can be made from scratch, the commercial product on the market is quite good and easy to use. Keep it in a plastic bag or a well-sealed container since it dries very fast. If it gets too dry, work it with a tiny bit of egg white until it gets smooth and malleable. If the paste is too soft, work it with powdered sugar to harden to the right consistency. Sometimes the almond paste turns oily, in which case add both sugar and egg white and work to the right consistency. Use powdered sugar instead of flour to roll out the almond paste. The flowers are soft as they are being shaped but after a while they dry out and harden. They can be kept for a few days on a cake and a few weeks in a closed tin box.

1. If the almond paste is too soft, mix with powdered sugar to make it harder. If slightly dry, add a dash of egg white and work until smooth and soft.

2. Divide the paste and work a few drops of red, yellow and green food coloring into each batch. (The green is kept for the stems and leaves. Make flowers with the other colors or with plain white paste.)

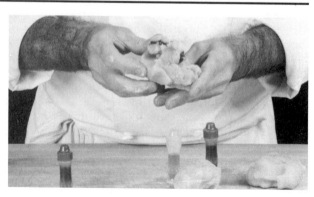

3. To make a rose, shape a piece of paste into a cone. This will be the heart of the rose.

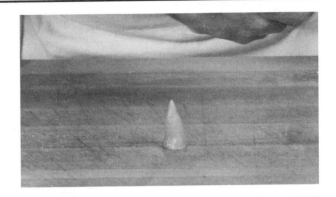

4. Flatten a piece of almond paste with the tip of your finger or a metal spatula, to make it very thin on one edge.

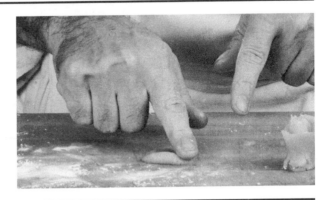

5. Lift the flat piece with a spatula and roll it around the center cone.

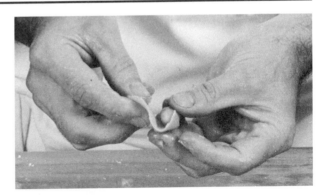

6. Roll another piece flat and place around the flower bud. Continue the process, adding more petals. Turn the petal edge outward.

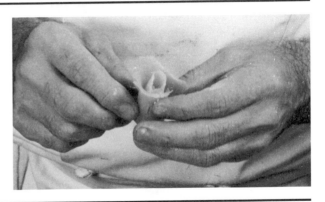

7. To make a carnation, use pink almond paste. Roll in a long cylinder about ¼ inch thick and flatten with a spatula, pressing forward so that one edge of the strip is ultra thin. Use powdered sugar to prevent sticking.

8. Using a fork, make ridges on the thin side if the strip. The tines of the fork must go through the almond paste.

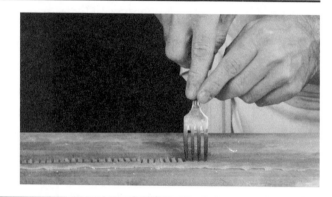

9. Slide a flexible metal spatula under the strip to loosen it.

10. Fold the strip left to right on top of itself into wave-like pleats.

11. Roll the end of the strip around the flower to encase.

12. Press the bottom together gently between your fingers.

13. Squeeze and the carnation will open to form a beautiful flower. Make small and large carnations. Let rest and dry out for at least 1 hour.

14. To make stems for the flowers, roll out a strip of green almond paste and, with the point of a knife, cut little indentations on each side to simulate thorns, nodes, etc.

15. Form lozenge- or triangle-shaped leaves and use your knife to sketch veins in the leaves. Fold in different shapes and let dry. Decorate the cake with the flowers, leaves and stem. See finished cream puff cake, page 795a.

308. Sugar Flower *(Fleur en Sucre)*

THE CENTERPIECES at culinary expositions are often intricate figures or flowers made of pulled or blown sugar. These are the work of specialists who practice for years to become proficient at it. Hot sugar burns fingers, is hard to pull and demands exact temperature in the cooking to be workable. (See the discussion on crystallization of sugar, technique 304). Long wide ribbons and large baskets are particularly hard to make well. Flowers are more manageable. One of the simplest flowers to make is the rose. Work with small batches of melted sugar rather than a large amount which will harden fast and be difficult to handle. To keep the sugar workable, place on a mesh sieve under an infra-red lamp or on a tray in a 180-degree oven. Make sure all your equipment is spotless. You will need a slab of marble oiled lightly with vegetable oil. Sugar flowers will get sticky and melt in humid weather. Do not refrigerate. Keep in a tin box with pieces of limestone to absorb humidity.

1 generous cup granulated sugar (½ pound)
¼ cup water
⅛ teaspoon cream of tartar mixed with 1 teaspoon water

1. Combine the sugar and water in a clean, heavy saucepan. Shake the pan to wet the sugar. If you have to stir the mixture, do it quickly or the stirring will make the sugar crystallize. Place on heat, bring to a boil and skim off any scum which comes to the top. Brush the inside of the saucepan to melt the crystallized sugar (see technique 304). After 2 to 3 minutes, add the cream of tartar. Keep cooking until it reaches the hard-crack stage (about 310 degrees). The higher the temperature, the harder the sugar will be to work with.

2. Pour the melted sugar on the oiled marble and add a few drops of coloring. You may divide it into two batches and color each differently.

3. Let the sugar cool a bit, then lift each side with an oiled spatula and fold onto itself.

4. Keep lifting and folding the sugar onto itself until it is solid enough to hold.

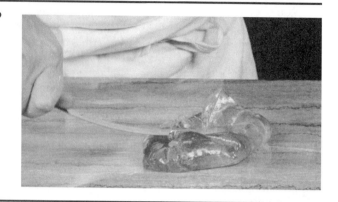

5. Oil your hands, grab the sugar and start pulling it. It is hot and you have to work fast. Note that the sugar is still transparent and clear.

6. Keep pulling and folding for about 1½ minutes. Note that the sugar becomes shiny and opaque.

7. When the sugar is very shiny and glossy it is ready to be shaped, however it will be too hard. Place an oiled tray in a 180-degree oven for a few minutes to soften a bit.

8. Remove from the oven and pinch the top of the sugar lump with both thumbs and forefingers and pull it apart to open out and spread the sugar into a thin "veil." Grab the center of the veil and pull out.

9. Twist and break into a very thin petal. The petal will have the imprint of your thumb.

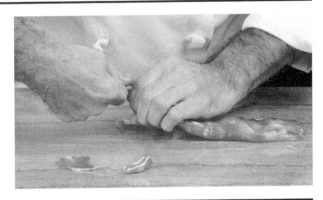

10. Roll the petal into a cone to simulate the bud or heart of a rose (see step 3, technique 307).

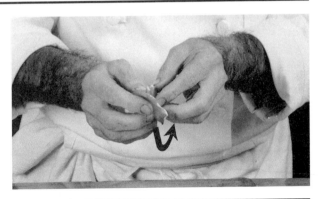

11. Pull out a second petal and roll it tightly around the center of the rose. Continue pulling out petals and placing them around the rose to enlarge it. Fold the edges outward. Work as fast as you can. When the sugar becomes too hard, let it soften slightly in the oven or under the infra-red lamp.

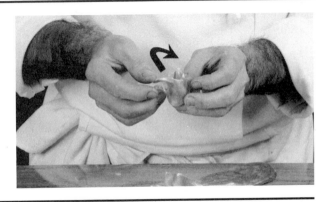

12. When the rose is completed, set in a small glass so it keeps its shape while hardening. The ribbon is made from loops glued together into a bow. Each loop is made by pulling a strip of sugar, folding it in half, side by side, then pulling and folding again (side by side). Each time the ribbon will get wider and wider. It should be about 1 1/2 to 2 inches wide. Cut sections and fold them on themselves to make loops.

13. Pull strips and fold to imitate leaves.

14. Pull thin long strips from the sugar.

15. Roll into tendrils to simulate vines and stems of flowers.

16. To make a bow, pass the ends of the loops over a flame to melt, then glue the loops together. Use the flowers, bows and leaves to decorate a cake. See finished sugar flowers, page 815.

309. Cake Glazed with Fondant
(Gâteau Fondant)

Cakes, especially wedding cakes, are beautiful glazed with a shiny *fondant* (sugar icing). To make a cake, layer a *génoise* with a butter cream or *ganache*, then cover with a layer of almond paste so the top is absolutely smooth for the *fondant*.

1 8- *to 10-inch diameter cake about 3 inches high*
About 1 pound almond paste

Fast *fondant*

3 cups powdered sugar
¼ cup hot water
1 tablespoon light corn syrup

1. Place the cake on a cardboard round. Roll the almond paste to about ⅛ inch thick. Use powdered sugar instead of flour to help in the rolling.

2. Roll the almond paste back onto the rolling pin, lift it up and place it on the cake.

3. Press the paste all around the cake so it adheres well. Trim the base. If there are any cracks, patch closed. Brush the cake. It should be smooth all around and on top.

4. To make the fondant, mix all ingredients together well. Work it for about 1 minute with a whisk. The mixture should be glossy and smooth. Use right away or cover with a wet towel or else it will crust on top very rapidly.

5. Place the cake on a wire rack and pour the fondant on top.

6. Spread with a spatula so the fondant runs all around. Work as fast as possible.

7. Lift the cake and bang the wire rack on the table a few times to encourage excess to drip off.

8. Lift the cake and run your fingers around the bottom edge to make it smooth. The cake can now be refrigerated or served, plain or with the sugar flowers described in the previous technique. See finished cake, below.

Fondant cake with sugar flowers, chocolate truffle cake, English trifle, small glazed puff paste

Conversion Tables

WEIGHT

American	British	Metric
1 ounce	1 ounce	28.4 grams
1 pound	1 pound	454 grams

VOLUME

American	British	Metric
1 U.S. teaspoon	1 U.K. level teaspoon	5 milliliters
1 U.S. tablespoon (3 teaspoons)	1 U.K. level dessert spoon	15 milliliters
1 U.S. cup (16 tablespoons)	$^5/_6$ breakfast cup (8 fluid ounces)	236 milliliters (about ¼ liter)
1 U.S. quart (4 cups)	$^5/_6$ Imperial quart	1 scant liter
1 U.S. gallon (4 quarts)	$^5/_6$ Imperial gallon	3¾ liters

LENGTH

American	British	Metric
1 inch	1 inch	2½ centimeters (25 millimeters)
12 inches (1 foot)	12 inches (1 foot)	30 centimeters

Note: All conversions are approximate. They have been rounded off to the nearest convenient measure.

Oven Temperatures

Fahrenheit	Centigrade	British Regulo Setting	French Setting
212°F	100°C		1
225°F	107°C	¼	2
250°F	121°C	½	3
275°F	135°C	1	3
300°F	149°C	2	4
325°F	163°C	3	4
350°F	177°C	4	4
375°F	191°C	5	5
400°F	204°C	6	5
425°F	218°C	7	6
450°F	232°C	8	6
475°F	246°C	8	6
500°F	260°C	9	7
525°F	274°C	9	8
550°F	288°C	9	9

Selected Measurements

American (spoons and cups)	British (ounces and pounds)	Metric
BREAD CRUMBS		
1 cup	2 ounces	60 grams
BUTTER		
1 teaspoon	⅙ ounce	5 grams
1 tablespoon	½ ounce	15 grams
½ cup (1 stick)	4 ounces	115 grams
1 cup (2 sticks)	8 ounces	230 grams
2 cups (4 sticks)	1 pound	454 grams
CHEESE (*grated*)		
1 cup	3½ ounces	100 grams
FLOUR (*all-purpose, unsifted*)		
1 teaspoon	⅛ ounce	3 grams
1 tablespoon	⅓ ounce	9 grams
1 cup	4¼ ounces	120 grams
3⅔ cups	1 pound	454 grams
HERBS (*fresh, chopped*)		
1 tablespoon	½ ounce	15 grams
MEATS (*cooked and finely chopped*)		
1 cup	8 ounces	225 grams
NUTS (*chopped*)		
1 cup	5½ ounces	155 grams

ONIONS *(raw—chopped, sliced, or minced)*

1 tablespoon	⅓ ounce	9 grams
1 cup	5 ounces	140 grams

PEAS *(fresh)*

1 pound unshelled = 1 cup shelled	1 pound, unshelled	454 grams, unshelled

RICE *(raw)*

1 cup	7½ ounces	215 grams

SPINACH *(fresh, cooked)*

1¼ pounds, raw = 1 cup, cooked (squeezed dry, chopped)	1¼ pounds, raw	550 grams, raw

SUGAR *(regular granulated or superfine granulated)*

1 teaspoon	⅙ ounce	5 grams
1 tablespoon	½ ounce	15 grams
1 cup	6½ ounces	185 grams

confectioners' (powdered, unsifted)

1 teaspoon	⅛ ounce icing sugar	4 grams
1 tablespoon	⅓ ounce icing sugar	9 grams
1 cup	¾ ounces icing sugar	100 grams

TOMATOES *(fresh)*

¾–1 pound, whole = 1 cup, peeled and seeded	¾–1 pound, whole	340 grams

VEGETABLES *(raw—chopped fine, such as carrots and celery)*

1 cup	8 ounces	225 grams

A Note to the User: All conversions are approximate. The weights have been rounded off to the nearest useful measure for the purposes of the recipes in this volume. Weights and measures of specific ingredients may vary with altitude, humidity, variations in method of preparation, etc.

Index